WEBSTER'S ENGLISH/SPANISH DICTIONARY

This book was not published by the original publishers of the Webster's Dictionary, or by any of their successors.

a *prep.* at; to
a-ba-ce-ría *f.* grocery
a-ba-ce-ro *m.* grocer
á-ba-co *m.* abacus
a-bad *m.* abbot
a-ba-de-sa *f.* abbess
a-ba-di-a *f.* abbey
a-ba-jo *adv.* beneath; down; below; *prep.* down
a-ba-lan-zar *v.* to hurl
a-ban-de-ra-mien-to *m.* registration (nautical)
a-ban-de-rar *v.* to register
a-ban-do-na-do, -da *adj.* derelict; careless
a-ban-do-nar *v.* to desert; forsake; abandon; give up
a-ban-do-no *m.* abandonment; neglect
a-ba-ni-car *v.* to fan
a-ba-ni-co *m.* fan
a-ba-ra-jar *v.* to catch
a-ba-ra-tar *v.* to lower; become cheaper
a-bar-car *v.* to embrace; comprise; encompass
a-ba-ti-do, -da *adj.* downcast; dejected; despondently; glum
a-ba-ti-mien-to *m.* dejection
a-ba-tir(se) *v.* to knock down; depress; discourage
ab-di-var *v.* to abdicate
ab-do-men *m.* abdomen
ab-do-min-al *adj.* abdominal
a-be-dul *m.* birch
a-be-ja *f.* bee
a-be-jo-rro *m.* bumblebee
a-be-jón *m.* hornet
a-be-rra-cion *f.* aberration
a-bert-u-ra *f.* aperture; gap
a-be-to *m.* fir
a-bier-ta-mem-te *adv.* outright
a-bier-to, -ta *adj.* open; clear
a-bi-ga-rra-do, -da *adj.* many-colored; variegated; motley
a-bis-mal *adj.* abysmal
a-bis-mo *m.* abyss
ab-ju-rar *v.* to abjure
a-blan-dar(se) *v., n.* to soften; mollify

a-bla-tivo *m.* ablative
a-blu-ción *f.* ablution
ab-ne-ga-ción *f.* abnegation
ab-ne-gar *v.* to renounce; abnegate
a-bo-car *v.* to decant
a-bo-car-dar *v.* to ream
a-bo-chor-na-do, -da *adj.* suffocating
a-bo-chor-nar *v.* to blush; suffocate
a-bo-fe-tear *v.* to slap
a-bo-ga-cí-a *f.* bar; law; advocacy
a-bo-ga-do *m.* attorney; counsel; lawyer
a-bo-gar *v.* to plead; to advocate
a-bo-len-go *m.* ancestry
a-bo-li-ción *f.* abolition
a-bo-li-cio-nis-ta *m., f.* abolitionist
a-bo-lir *v.* to abolish
a-bo-lla-du-ra *f.* dent
a-bo-llar *v.* to emboss; dent
a-bo-mi-na-ble *adj.* abominable
a-bo-mi-na-ción *f.* abomination
a-bo-mi-nar *v.* to abominate; loathe
a-bo-nar *v.* to fertilize; give credit
a-bo-no *m.* manure; fertilizer; subscription; guarantee
a-bo-ri-gen *adj. m., pl.* aboriginal
a-bo-rre-cer *v.* to hate; abhor
a-bo-rre-ci-ble *adj.* detestable; abhorrent; loathsome; hateful
a-bo-ree-ci-mien-to *m.* hate; hatred; abhorrence; loathing
a-bor-tar *v.* to abort
a-bor-tivo, a *adj.* abortive
a-bor-to *m.* abortion
a-bo-to-nar *v.* to button up
a-bo-za-lar *v.* to muzzle
a-bra *f.* cove
a-bra-sion *f.* abrasion
a-bra-si-vo *adj.* abrasive

a-bra-za-de-ra f. clamp; brace

a-bra-zar(se) v. to hug; cuddle; embrace

a-bra-zo m. hug; embrace

a-bre-car-tas m. letter opener

a-bre-var v. to soak; water

a-bre-via-ción f. abbreviation

a-bre-viar v. to abridge; abbreviate; curtail; condense

a-bri-gar(se) v. to shelter; harbor; protect

a-bri-go m. shelter; coat; overcoat

a-bril m. April

a-bri-llan-tar v. to cut into parts; polish; brighten

a-brir(se) v. to open up; to spread out; open

a-bro-char v. to button up; fasten; buckle

a-bro-ga-ción f. abrogation

a-bro-gar v. abrogate; repeal

a-bru-ma-dor, a adj. crushing

a-bru-mar v. to overwhelm

a-brup-to, -ta adj. abrupt; steep; blunt

a-bru-ta-do, -da adj. bestial

abs-ce-so m. abscess

ab-so-lu-ción f. absolution

ab-so-lu-to, -ta adj. complete; absolute

ab-sol-ven-te adj. absolving

ab-sol-ver v. to acquit; clear; absolve

ab-sor-ben-cia f. absorbence

ab-sor-ben-te m. absorbent

ab-sor-ber v. to soak up; engross; absorb

ab-sor-ción f. absorption

ab-sor-to, -ta adj. absorbed; intent

abs-ten-cion f. abstention

abs-te-ner-se v. to abstain; refrain

abs-ti-nen-cia f. abstinence

abs-trac-to, -ta adj. abstract

abs-tra-er v. to abstract

abs-tru-so, -sa adj. abstruse

ab-sur-di-dad f. absurdity

ab-sur-do, -da adj. silly; preposterous; absurd

a-bue-la f. grandmother

a-bue-lo m. grandfather; grandparent

a-bun-da-mien-to m. abundance

a-bun-dan-cia f. abundance; amplitude

a-bun-dan-te adj. plentiful; abundant; ample

a-bun-dar v. to abound

a-bun-do-so adj. abundant

a-bu-rri-do adj. boring; bored

a-bu-rri-mien-to m. boredom

a-bu-rrir v. to bore

a-bu-sar v. to misuse; maltreat; abuse; impose

a-bu-si-vo, a adj. abusive

a-bu-so m. encroachment; abuse

ab-yec-ción f. abjectness

ab-yec-to, -ta adj. abject

a-cá adv. here

a-ca-ba-do, -da adj. end; conclusion

a-ca-bar v. to accomplish; end; fail

a-ca-de-mia f. academy

a-ca-dé-mi-co adj. academic

a-ca-li-zar v. to alkalize

a-cam-par v. to camp

a-ca-ri-ciar v. to pet; pat

a-ca-rrear v. to cart

a-ca-rreo m. cartage

ac-ce-der v. to accede

ac-ce-si-ble adj. accessible

ac-ce-so m. approach; access

ac-ce-so-rio, a m. accessory

ac-ci-den-ta-do, a adj. uneven; broken; eventful

ac-ci-den-te m. casualty; accident

ac-ción f. movement; action

a-ce-bo m. holly

a-ce-char v. to lurk; watch for

a-cei-te m. oil

a-cei-tu-na f. olive

a-ce-le-rar(se) v. to speed; accelerate

a-cen-to v. stress; emphasis; accent

a-cen-tuar(se) v. to emphasize; accent; stress

a-cep-tar v. adopt; accept; agree to something

a-cer-car(se) v. to bring near

a-ce-ro n.m. steel

a-cer-ti-jo m. riddle

a-cé-ti-co adj. acetic

a-ce-to-na f. acetone

á-ci-do m. acid

á-ci-do bo-ri-co m. boric acid

á-ci-do ci-tri-co m. citric acid

á-ci-do sul-fu-ri-co m. sulphuric acid

a-cla-ma-ción f. acclaim

a-cla-ra-ción f. clarification

a-cla-rar v. to clear; to clarify; to rinse

a-cli-ma-tar v. acclimate

ac-ne m. acne

a-co-bar-dar(se) v. to flinch; unnerve; cringe

a-co-gi-da f. welcome; shelter

a-col-char v. pad

a-có-li-to m. altar boy; acolyte

a-co-me-ter v. attempt; undertake; overcome; attack

a-co-mo-da-di-zo adj. easygoing

a-co-mo-da-dor m. usher f. usherette

a-co-mo-dar v. to suit; to accommodate; put up

a-com-pa-ñan-te m. escort mus. accompanist

a-com-pa-ñar v. to escort; attend; go with; accompany

a-con-di-cio-na-d or de ai-re m. air conditioner

a-con-se-jar(se) v. to take advice; advise; counsel

a-con-te-cer v. to chance; to happen

a-con-te-ci-mien-to m. occasion; event; occurrence; happening

a-cor-dar(se) v. to agree on; remember; agree

a-cor-de m. chord; in tune;

harmony; in accord

a-cor-deon m. accordion

a-cor-near v. to gore

a-co-rra-lar v. to round up; corral; intimidate; pen

a-cor-tar(se) v. to clip; shorten; lessen; obstruct

a-co-sar v. to harass; pursue; beset

a-cos-tar(se) v. to lie down; go to bed

a-cos-tum-brar(se) v. to be accustomed to; be used to; habituate

a-cre adj. acrid; sour

a-cre-cen-tar v. to advance; increase

a-cree-dor m. creditor

a-cri-mo-nia f. bitterness

a-cró-ba-ta n.m.f. acrobat

ac-ti-tud f. pose; position; attitude

ac-ti-var v. to activate

ac-ti-vi-dad f. movement; nimbleness; activity

ac-ti-vo, -va adj. alive; brisk; active; quick

ac-to m. event; act; function

ac-tor m. actor

ac-triz f. actress

ac-tual adj. instant; actual

ac-tual-men-te adv. at present; now; actually

ac-tuar v. perform; act; set in action

a-cua-rio m. aquarium

a-cu-á-til adj. aquatic

a-cu-chi-llar v. to slash; hack; knife

a-cue-duc-to m. aqueduct

a-cueo, a adj. watery

a-cuer-do m. remembrance; resolution; agreement; accord

a-cu-mu-lar v. to amass; stock-pile; accumulate; congest

a-cu-ña-cion f. coinage

a-cu-ñar v. to coin; mint

a-cu-sar v. to impeach; charge; indict; accuse

a-cús-ti-ca f. acoustics

a-chi-car v. diminish;

humble; bail

chis-pa-do, -da *adj.* tipsy

da-gio *m.* proverb; adage

da-lid *m.* commander

dap-ta-ble *adj.* adaptable; versatile

dap-ta-ción *f.* adaptation

dap-tar *v.* to fit; adapt; adapt oneself to; adjust

de-cua-do, -da *adj.* fit; suitable; adequate

de-fe-sio *n.* something gaudy; extravagance

de-ha-la *f.* tip; bonus

de-lan-ta-do, -da *adj.* fast; advanced

de-lan-tar(se) *v.* to further; proceed; overtake

de-lan-te *adv.* forwards; forward

de-lan-to *m.* progress; advance

del-ga-zar(se) *v.* to lose weight; taper; make thin; attenuate; slim down

de-mán *m.* attitude; gesture

de-más *adv.* besides; moreover; in addition

den-tro *adv.* inside; within

dep-to *m.* adept

de-re-zar *v.* adorn; garnish

de-re-zo *m.* finery; adornment; dressing

des-trar *v.* to train

deu-dar *v.* to debit; owe

d-he-ren-cia *f.* bond; adherence

d-he-ren-te *adj.* adherent; adhesive

d-he-rir(se) *v.* to cling; adhere; stick

d-he-sión *f.* adherence

d-he-si-vo, -va *adj.* ahesive

di-ción *f.* addition

di-cio-nal *adj.* more; extra; additional

dic-to, -ta *adj.* addicted

dies-trar(se) *v.* to exercise; train; practise

diós *m.* farewell; goodbye; good day

di-po-so, a *m.* fat; adipose

a-di-ta-men-to *m.* attachment; addition

a-di-ti-vo *m.* additive

a-di-vi-nar *v.* to foretell; to guess

ad-je-ti-vo *m.* adjective

ad-ju-di-ca-ción *m.* award; adjudgment

ad-ju-di-car(se) *v.* to allot; to award

ad-jun-tar *v.* to annex

ad-mi-nis-tra-ción *f.* administration; management

ad-mi-nis-tra-dor, -ra *m.* administrator; steward; manager

ad-mi-nis-trar *v.* to manage; dispense; administer

ad-mi-nis-tra-ti-vo, -va *adj.* administrative

ad-mi-ra-ble *adj.* fine; excellent; admirable

ad-mi-ra-ción *f.* admiration

ad-mi-rar(se) *v.* to wonder; admire; amaze

ad-mi-si-ble *adj.* acceptable; admissible

ad-mi-sión *f.* input; admission

ad-mi-tir *v.* to acknowledge; permit; admit

a-do-be *m.* adobe

a-do-les-cen-cia *f.* adolescence

a-dop-tar *v.* to embrace

a-dop-ti-vo, -va *adj.* adoptive

a-do-ra-ble *adj.* adorable

a-do-ra-ción *f.* adoration

a-do-rar *v.* to worship; adore

a-dor-me-cer(se) *v.* to fall asleep; drowse

a-dor-mi-de-ra *f.* poppy

a-dor-na-mien-to *m.* adornment

a-dor-nar *v.* to adorn; deck; ecorate; grace

a-dor-no *m.* adornment; ornament; array

ad-qui-rir *v.* to obtain; secure; acquire

a-dre-na-li-na *f.* adrenaline

ads-cri-bir *v.* assign; ascribe

a-dua-na *f.* customs

a-dua-ne-ro m. customs
a-du-cir v. to cite; adduce
a-du-ja-da adj. coiled
a-du-la-ción f. flattery; adulation
a-du-la-dor, a m. flatterer
a-du-lar v. to flatter; adulate
a-dul-te-ra-ción f. adulteration
a-dul-te-ra-dor, a m. adulterator
a-dul-te-rar v. to adulterate
a-dul-te-rio m. adultery
a-dul-to, -ta m. adult
a-dul-zar v. to make sweet
ad-ver-bi-al adj. adverbial
ad-ver-bio m. adverb
ad-ver-sa-rio m. opponent; adversary
ad-ver-si-dad f. adversity
ad-ver-so, -sa adj. averse; unfavorable; adverse
ad-ver-ti-do, -da adj. skillful; informed; intelligent; capable; sagacious
ad-ver-tir v. to notify; advise; caution; take notice of something; observe
ad-ya-cen-te adj. adjacent
ae-ra-ción f. aeration
aé-reo, -rea adj. aerial
ae-ro-di-na-mi-co adj. aerodynamic
ae-ro-náu-ti-ca, -co f. aeronautics
ae-ro-pla-no n. airplane; aeroplane
ae-ro-puer-to m. airport
a-fa-bi-li-dad f. affability
a-fa-ble adj. affable; genial; kind
a-fán m. anxiety; travail
a-fa-nar v. to urge; toil; strive
a-fa-no-so, -sa adj. anxious
a-fec-ción f. fondness; affection
a-fec-ta-ción f. pretense; affectation
a-fec-ta-do, -da adj. affected
a-fec-tar v. to affect
a-fec-to m. affection
a-fec-tuo-sa-men-te adv. fondly; affectionately

a-fec-tuo-so adj. affectionate
a-fei-ta-do, -da m. shave
a-fei-tar v. to shave
a-fei-te m. shave; cosmetic
a-fe-rrar(se) v. to grasp; furl
a-fian-zar v. to bail; clinch; quaranty
a-fi-ción f. liking; affection; inclination
a-fi-cio-na-do, -da m. fan; amateur; fancier
a-fi-jo, -ja m. affix
a-fi-lar(se) v. to sharpen
a-fi-liar(se) v. to join; affiliate; adopt
a-fín adj. related; contiguous; adjacent
a-fi-na-ción f. refining; tuning
a-fi-nar v. to refine; polish; complete; tune
a-fi-ni-dad f. affinity; relationship
a-fir-mar(se) v. to secure; assert; contend; affirm; make fast
a-fir-ma-ti-vo adj. affirmative
a-flic-ción f. anxiety; bereavement; afflication
a-fli-gi-do adj. stricken
a-fli-gir(se) v. to afflict
a-flo-jar(se) v. to loosen; slacken; weaken
a-flo-rar v. to emerge; sift
a-fluen-cia f. affluence; crowd; jam; fluency; abundance
a-fluen-te adj. affluent
a-fo-rar v. to appraise; guage; measure
a-fo-ris-mo m. aphorism; maxim
a-for-tu-na-do, -da adj. prosperous; lucky; fortunate
a-fren-ta f. to insult; affront
a-fren-tar(se) v. insult; affront; be affronted
a-fro-di-sia-co adj. aphrodisiac
a-fue-ra adv. outside; outkirts; suburbs
a-ga-char(se) v. to crouch; squat; bow down

a-ga-lla f. gill

a-ga-rrar(se) v. to grasp; seize; clutch; clinch

a-ga-rre m. gripping

a-ga-rro m. grip; lutch; grab

a-ga-rro-tar v. to compress; bind tightly

a-ga-sa-ja-dor adj. attentive

a-ga-sa-jar v. to entertain; fondle; welcoming

a-gen-cia f. bureau; agency

a-gen-ciar v. to obtain

a-gen-cio-so adj. industrious

a-gen-da f. diary; notebook

a-gen-te m. officer; agent

a-gil adj. nimble; agile; lithe; active; lithesome

a-gi-li-dad f. agility

a-gi-a-ción f. flurry; flutter; stir; excitement; agitation

a-gi-tar(se) v. to stir up; churn; flutter; shake

a-glo-me-ra-ción f. agglomeration

a-glo-me-ra-do adj. agglomerate

a-glo-me-rar v. agglomerate

a-glu-ti-na-ción f. agglutination

a-glu-ti-nan-te m. cement

a-glu-ti-nar v. to agglutinate

a-go-nia f. pain; agony

a-go-ni-oso adj. persistent

a-go-rar v. to foretell

a-gos-tar v. to consume

a-gos-to m. August; harvest

a-go-ta-mien-to m. exhaurstion; depletion

a-go-tar(se) v. to drain; give out; tire; exhaust

a-gra-cia-do, a adj. attractive

a-gra-ciar v. to award; grace

a-gra-da-ble adj. gracious; nice; pleasant; agreeable; delightful

a-gra-dar v. to please

a-gra-de-cer(se) v. to appreciate; acknowledge; thank

a-gra-de-ci-do, -da adj. thankful; grateful

a-gra-do m. liking; taste

a-gran-dar v. to grow bigger

a-gra-va-ción f. aggravation

a-gra-van-te adj. aggravating

a-gra-viar v. to harm; wrong

a-gra-vio m. offence; injury; grievance; harm

a-gra-vio-so adj. injurious; offensive; insulting

a-gre-dir v. to assault

a-gre-sión f. aggression

a-gre-si-vo adj. aggressive

a-gre-sor, a m. aggressor

a-griar v. to annoy; sour

a-gri-cul-tu-ra f. farming

a-grie-tar v. to split

a-gri-men-su-ra f. surveying

a-grio, a adj. acid; sour

a-gro m. farming

a-gro-nó-mi-co, -ca adj. agro-nomical

a-gru-pa-ción f. group

a-gru-par(se) v. to cluster; bunch; group

a-gua f. water

a-gua-ca-te m. avocado

a-gua-do, -da adj. diluted

a-gua-ma-ri-na f. aqua-marine

a-guan-tar(se) v. to support; endure; hold

a-guan-te m. endurance

a-guar-dar v. to await

a-gu-de-za f. acumen; keen-ness; sharpness; brightness

a-gu-di-zar v. to sharpen

a-gu-do, -da adj. sharp

a-güe-ro m. omen

a-gue-rri-do, a adj. seasoned

a-gui-la f. eagle

a-gu-ja f. needle

a-gu-je-ro m. hole

a-guo-so, -sa adj. watery

a-gu-zar v. to sharpen

a-hi adv. there

a-hi-ja-da f. goddaughter

a-hi-ja-do m. godson

a-hi-jar v. to adopt

a-hi-la-do adj. faint; soft

a-hi-lar v. to faint

a-hi-to, -ta adj. stuffed

a-ho-gar v. to oppress; drown; choke

a-ho-ra adv. now

a-hor-ca-jar(se) v. to straddle

a-hor-mar v. to fit

a-ho-rrar v. to spare

a-ho-rro m. savings

a-hue-va-do adj. egg-shaped

a-hu-ma-do, -da adj. smoky; cured; smoked

a-hu-mar v. to cure; smoke

ai-rar v. to annoy; anger

ai-re m. aspect; air

ai-re-a-do adj. aired out

ai-re-ar(se) v. to air; cool

ai-re-o m. ventilation

ais-la-do, -da adj. alone

ais-lar v. to seclude; isolate

a-ja-do, -da adj. withered

a-jar v. to mar; spoil

a-je-dre-cis-ta f., m. chess player

a-je-drez m. chess

a-jen-jo m. bitterness

a-je-no, -na adj. alien; strange; foreign

a-je-tre-o m. agitation

a-jo m. garlic

a-jo-bo m. burden

a-jus-tar v. to settle; adapt; adjust; fix; tighten

a-jus-te m. fitting; accommodation

a-jus-ti-cia-mien-to m. execution

a-jus-ti-car v. to execute

a-la f. wing

a-la-ban-za f. praise

a-la-bar v. to commend

a-la-bas-tro m. alabaster

a-la-crán m. scorpion

a-la-cri-dad f. eagerness

a-la-do, -da adj. winged

a-lam-bre m. wire

á-la-mo m. poplar

a-lar-de-o m. bragging

a-lar-gar(se) v. to rejoice; cheer; lengthen; extend

a-lar-ma f. alarm

a-lar-ma-dor, a adj. alarming

a-lar-mar v. to alarm

al-ba f. daybreak

al-ba-ri-co-que m. apricot

al-ber-ca f. tank

al-ber-gar v. to cherish

al-bi-no, -na adj. albino

al-bo-ro-ta-do, -da adj. rowdy; excited

al-bo-ro-tar v. to excite; incite

al-bo-ro-zo m. joy

al-ca-cho-fa f. artichoke

al-cal-de m. mayor

al-ca-li-no, a adj. alkaline

al-ca-loi-de m. alkaloid

al-can-for m. camphor

al-can-zar v. to attain; reach; pass; grasp

al-cau-cil m. artichoke

al-cá-zar m. castle

al-ce m. moose

al-co-ba f. bedroom

al-co-hol m. alcohol

al-co-hó-li-co adj. alcoholic

a-le-a-to-rio adj. uncertain

a-le-go-ría f. allergy

a-le-grar v. to happy; cheer; rejoice

a-le-gre adj. joyous; gay; glad

a-le-gre-men-te adv. gaily

a-le-grí-a f. gladness; gaiety

a-le-grón m. joy

a-le-ja-mien-to m. distance; withdrawal; estrangement

a-le-la-do adj. bewildered

a-len-ta-dor, ra adj. encouraging

a-len-tar v. to animate

a-ler-gia f. allergy

a-lér-gi-co, -ca adj. allergic

a-ler-tar v. to alert; warn

a-le-te-o m. flapping

al-fa-bé-ti-co adj. alphabetical

al-fa-be-to m. alphabet

al-fa-re-rí-a f. pottery

al-fi-le-rar v. to pin

al-fom-bra f. carpet

al-fom-brar v. to carpet

al-for-za f. pleat

al-ge-bra f. algebra

al-go pron. anything; something

al-go-dón m. cotton

al-guien pron. someone; anyone

al-gún adj. some

al-gu-no, a pron. anybody

al-ha-ja f. gem

al-ho-ce-ma f. lavender

a-lia-do, -da *m.* ally
a-lian-za *f.* alliance
a-li-bi *m.* alibi
a-lie-na-ble *adj.* alienable
a-lie-na-ción *f.* alienation
a-lie-nar *v.* to alienate
a-lien-to *m.* courage
a-li-ge-rar(se) *v.* to relieve
a-li-men-tar *v.* to feed
a-li-men-ti-cio *adj.* nutritious
a-li-men-to *m.* food
a-li-ne-a-ción *f.* alignment
a-li-ñar *v.* to tidy
a-li-ño *m.* tidiness
a-li-sar *v.* to smooth
a-lis-tar *v.* to list
a-li-viar *v.* to alleviate; allay
a-li-vio *m.* easing
al-ma *f.* spirit
al-má-ci-ga *f.* nursery
al-me-ja *f.* calm
al-men-dro, a *m.* almond tree
al-mi-dón *m.* starch
al-mi-do-nar *v.* to starch
al-miz-cle *m.* musk
al-mo-ha-da *f.* pillow
al-mor-zar *v.* to lunch
al-muer-zo *m.* lunch
a-lo-ca-do, -da *adj.* crazy
a-lo-cu-ción *f.* allocution
a-lo-jar(se) *v.* to house
a-lon-gar *v.* to stretch; to make longer
al-pi-no *adj.* alpine
al-qui-lar *v.* to hire; rent
al-qui-mia *f.* alchemy
al-qui-mis-ta *m.* alchemist
al-re-de-dor, ra *adv.* around *prep.* round
al-ta-men-te *adv.* extremely
al-tar *m.* altar
al-te-ra-ción *f.* alteration
al-ter-ca-ción *f.* altercation
al-ter-na-do *adj.* alternate
al-ter-nar *v.* rotate; alternate
al-ter-na-ti-va *f.* alternative
al-ti-me-trí-a *f.* altimetry
al-ti-tud *f.* altitude
al-to, -ta *adj.* upper; high
al-truis-ta *adj.* altruistic
al-tu-ra *f.* elevation; height
a-lu-ci-nar *v.* to hallucinate
a-lu-ci-na-to-rio *adj.* hallu-
cinatory
a-lu-dir *v.* to allude
a-lum-bra-do *m.* lightening
a-lu-mi-nio *m.* aluminum
a-lum-no, -na *m.* student; alumnus
a-lu-sión *f.* allusion
al-za-do *adj.* elevated
al-zar *v.* to hoist; lift up; raise
a-llá *adv.* there
a-lla-nar *v.* overcome; flatten
a-lle-ga-do, -da *adj.* related; close; near
a-llí *adv.* there
a-ma-bi-li-dad *f.* kindness
a-ma-ble *adj.* lovable; amiable; kindly
a-ma-do *adj.* beloved
a-ma-es-trar *v.* to train
a-ma-ne-cer *v.* to nurse
a-ma-ne-ci-da *f.* daybreak
a-man-ser *v.* to soothe; tame
a-ma-na-do *adj.* skillful; fixed
a-ma-ño *m.* skill
a-ma-po-la *f.* poppy
a-mar *v.* to love
a-mar-gar *v.* to make bitter
a-mar-gor *m.* bitterness
a-ma-ri-llo, a *m.* yellow
a-ma-rrar *v.* to fasten; tie
a-ma-teur *adj.* amateur
a-ma-tis-ta *f.* amethyst
am-bar *m.* amber
am-bi-ción *f.* ambition
am-bi-cio-so *adj.* ambitious
am-bien-ta-ción *f.* atmosphere
am-bi-güe-dad *f.* ambiguity
am-bi-guo *adj.* uncertain; ambiguous
am-bu-lan-cia *f.* ambulance
am-bu-lan-te *adj.* ambulatory
am-bu-lar *v.* amble
a-me-ba *f.* amoeba
a-me-na-za *f.* threat
a-me-na-zar *v.* to menace
a-me-ni-dad *f.* amenity
a-me-ri-ca-no *adj.* American
a-mi-ga *f.* girl friend
a-mi-gar *v.* to reconcile
a-míg-da-la *f.* tonsil
a-mi-go *m.* boy friend

a-mi-la-na-do adj. intimidated

a-mi-la-nar v. to discourage; intimidate; scare; frighten

a-mis-to-so, a adj. friendly

a-mo m. master; boss

a-mo-lar v. to sharpen

a-mol-dar v. to adjust; mold

a-mon-to-nar(se) v. to amass; hoard; huddle

amor m. lover

a-mo-ra-li-dad f. amorality

a-mo-ro-so, -sa adj. amorous; loving

am-pa-rar v. defend; protect

am-pliar v. expand; increase

am-pli-fi-ca-ción f. amplification

am-pli-fi-car v. to amplify

am-po-lle-ta f. hourglass

am-pu-ta-ción f. amputation

am-pu-tar v. to amputate

a-na-car-do m. cashew

a-na-de m. duck

a-na-gra-ma f. anagram

a-nal-ge-si-co adj. analgesic

a-na-lis-ta m. analyst

a-na-li-sis m. analysis

a-na-li-ti-co adj. analytical

a-na-li-zar v. to analyze

a-na-lo-gi-a f. analogy

a-na-na m. pineapple

a-na-quel m. shelf

a-na-ran-ja-do, a adj. orange

a-nar-quis-ta m., f. anarchist

a-na-to-mi-a f. anatomy

a-na-to-mi-co adj. anatomic

an-cia-no, -na adj. aged

an-cla f. anchor

an-cho adj. broad

an-cho-a f. anchovy

an-dar v. to go; ambulate

an-dra-jo-so, -sa adj. ragged

an-droi-de m. android

a-nec-do-ta f. anecdote

a-nec-do-tis-ta m. anecdotist

a-ne-gar v. to flood

a-ne-mi-co, -ca adj. anemic

a-nes-te-siar v. anesthetize

an-gel m. angel

an-ge-li-co, -ca adj. angelical

an-go-ra adj. angora

an-gui-la f. eel

an-gu-lo m. angle

an-gu-lo-so adj. angular

an-gu-rri f. greed

an-gus-tiar v. to anguish

an-he-lar v. to long for; yearn

a-ni-llo m. ring

a-ni-ma-ción f. animation

a-ni-ma-do, -da adj. lively; animate

a-ni-mal m. animal

a-ni-mar v. to become animated; enliven

a-ni-qui-lar v. to destroy; annihilate

a-ni-ver-sa-rio, -ria adj. anniversary

a-no-che adv. last night

a-no-ni-mo adj. anonymous

a-nor-mal adj. subnormal; abnormal

a-no-ta-ción f. note

a-no-tar v. to note

an-sar m. goose

an-sia f. yearning

an-siar v. to long for

an-sie-dad f. anxiety

an-te prep. before

an-te-bra-zo m. forearm

an-te-ce-der v. to anteced

an-te-de-cir v. to predict

an-te-pa-sa-do m. ancestor

an-te-rior adj. proir; anterior

an-tes de adv. before

an-ti-a-ci-do adj. antacid

an-ti-bio-ti-co m. antibiotic

an-ti-ci-pa-do adj. advanced

an-ti-ci-par v. advance

an-ti-cuer-po m. antibody

an-ti-do-to m. antidote

an-ti-guo adj. ancient; antique

an-ti-lo-pe m. antelope

an-ti-na-tu-ral adj. unnatural

an-ti-sep-ti-co m. antiseptic

an-ti-so-cial adj. antisocial

an-ti-to-xi-co adj. antitoxic

an-to-ni-mia f. antonymy

an-tro-poi-de adj. anthropoid

a-nual adj. annual

a-nua-rio m. annual

a-nu-blar v. to cloud

a-nu-lar v. to cancel

a-nun-cia-ción f. announcement

a-nun-cian-te *m.* advertiser

a-nun-ciar *v.* to announce

an-zue-lo *m.* fishhook

a-na-di-do *m.* addition

a-na-dir *v.* to add

a-ne-jo, -ja *adj.* old; mature

a-nil *adj., n.* indigo

a-ño *m.* year

a-pa-bu-llar *v.* to squash

a-pa-ci-ble *adj.* gentle

a-pa-ci-guar(se) *v.* appease

a-pa-dri-nar *v.* to support

a-pa-le-o *m.* thrashing

a-pa-nar *v.* to mend; to seize; grasp; repair

a-pa-ra-to *m.* apparatus

a-pa-ra-to-so *adj.* ostentatious

a-par-car *v.* to park

a-pa-ra-cer(se) *v.* to haunt; to come

a-pa-re-jar *v.* to prepare

a-pa-ren-te *adj.* seeming

a-pa-ri-ción *f.* appearance

a-par-ta-do *adj.* isolated

a-par-ta-men-to *m.* apartment

a-par-tar(se) *v.* to divide; to remove

a-par-te *adv.* aside; apart

a-pa-sio-nar *v.* to excite

a-pa-ti-a *f.* apathy

a-pá-ti-co, -ca *adj.* apathetic

a-pe-ar *v.* to chock; fell

a-pe-la-ble *adj.* appealable

a-pe-lar *v.* to appeal

a-pe-lli-dar *v.* to name; called

a-pe-lli-do *m.* name

a-pe-nar *v.* pained; to grieve

a-pen-di-ci-tis *m.* appendictis

a-pe-ro *m.* gear

a-pes-tar *v.* to annoy; infect

a-pe-ten-cia *f.* appetite

ape-ti-to *m.* appetite

a-pe-ti-to-so, a *adj.* delicious

a-pio *m.* celery

a-pla-car *v.* to placate

a-pla-nar *v.* to flatten; stun

a-plas-tar(se) *v.* to flatten

a-plau-dir *v.* to clap; applaud

a-plau-so *m.* clapping

a-pli-ca-ble *adj.* applicable

a-pli-ca-ción *f.* application

a-pli-car *v.* to apply

a-po-ca-do, -da *adj.* timid

a-po-de-rar(se) *v.* empower

a-po-do *m.* nickname

a-po-lí-ti-co *adj.* apolitical

a-po-rre-ar(se) *v.* to beat

a-por-tar *v.* to bring; arrive

a-po-sen-to *m.* lodging

a-po-si-ción *f.* apposition

a-pos-tol *m.* apostle

a-pos-tro-fo *m.* apostrophe

a-po-te-ca-rio *m.* apothecary

a-po-te-o-sis *f.* apothesis

a-po-yar(se) *v.* to rest on; to support

a-po-yo *m.* support

a-pre-cia-ción *f.* appreciation

a-pre-ciar *v.* to value; appreciate

a-pre-cio *m.* attention; appraisal

a-pre-hen-der *v.* to seize

a-pre-hen-sión *f.* comprehension; apprehension

a-pren-der *v.* to learn

a-pren-sión *f.* suspicion

a-pre-sar *v.* to seize

a-pre-su-rar *v.* to hurry

a-pre-tar *v.* to crowd; clutch

a-pro-ba-do, a *adj.* approved

a-pro-bar *v.* to pass

a-pro-pia-do *adj.* appropriate

a-pro-piar(se) *v.* appropriate

a-pro-vi-sio-nar *v.* provision

a-pro-xi-mar(se) *v.* to approximate

ap-ti-tud *f.* talent; aptitude

a-pues-to-t *f.* wager

a-pun-tar(se) *v.* to aim; point

a-pun-te *m.* notation; note

a-pu-rar(se) *v.* to worry

a-que-jar *v.* to distress

a-quel *adj.* that; those

a-quel *pron.* that one

a-qui-ado now; here; then

a-quie-tar *v.* to soothe; to calm down

a-ra *f.* altar

a-ra-na *f.* spider

ar-bi-trar *v.* unpire; arbitrate

ar-bi-tra-rio, a *adj.* arbitrary

ar-bi-tro, -tra *m.* arbitrator

ar-bol m. tree
ar-bo-re-to m. arboretum
ar-bus-to m. shrub
ar-ca-da f. arcade
ar-ca-is-ta f. archaist
ar-can-gel m. archangel
ar-ce m. maple tree
ar-co m. arch
ar-chi-du-que m. archduke
ar-chi-du-que-sa f. archduchess
ar-chi-var v. to file
ar-chi-vo m. archives
ar-der(se) v. to burn
ar-dien-te adj. ardent; burning
ar-di-lla f. squirrel
ar-dor m. heat
ar-duo adj. arduous
a-re-a f. area
a-re-no-so adj. sandy
a-ren-que m. herring
ar-gen-tar v. to silver-plate
ar-gen-ta-rio m.. silversmith
ar-go-lla f. ring
ar-guir v. to prove; argue
ar-gu-men-tar v. to argue
a-ri-do adj. dry
a-ris-co, -ca adj. wild; unfriendly; surly; churlish
a-ris-to-cra-cia f. aristocracy
a-ris-to-cra-ta f.,m. aristocrat
a-rit-me-ti-co adj. arithmetic
ar-le-quin m. harlequin
ar-ma f. weapon
ar-ma-do adj. armed
ar-mar v. to assemble; reinforce; arm; equip
ar-ma-rio, a m. buffet; closet
ar-mi-no m. ermine
ar-mis-ti-cio m. armistice
ar-mo-ni-a f. accord
ar-mo-ni-co m., adj. harmonicar
ar-mo-ni-zar v. to harmonize
a-ro m. hoop; ring
a-ro-ma m. fragrance
a-ro-mar v. to scent; perfume
a-ro-ma-ti-co adj. aromatic
a-ro-ma-ti-zar v. to perfume; scent
a-ro-mo-so adj. aromatic
ar-pis-ta m., f. harpist

ar-que-o-lo-gi-a f. archaeology
ar-qui-tec-to m., f. architect
ar-qui-tec-tu-ra f. architecture
a-rra-ci-ma-do adj. bunched
a-rran-car v. to seize; pull up; obtain; stem
a-rra-sar v. to clear; level
a-rras-trar(se) v. to pull; to crawl; to draw
a-rre-ar v. to harness; herd
a-rre-ba-ta-dor adj. exciting
a-rre-ba-to m. rage
a-rre-ci-fe m. reef
a-rre-gla-do adj. neat
a-rre-glar(se) v. order; settle
a-rre-glo m. understanding; arrangement
a-rre-me-dar v. to copy
a-rre-me-ter v. to attack
a-rren-dar v. to rent
a-rre-o m. drove; herd
a-rre-pen-tir-se v. to regret
a-rres-ta-do adj. arrested
a-rres-to m. arrest
a-rri-ba adv. above
a-rri-bar intr. to arrive
a-rri-bis-ta, -to adj. socialclimbing
a-rri-bo m. arrival
a-rrien-do m. renting
a-rries-ga-do, -da adj. hazardous; daring
a-rries-gar(se) v. to venture; jeopardize; risk
a-rri-mar v. to draw or bring near
a-rri-mo m. partition
a-rrin-co-na-do adj. distant
a-rrin-co-nar tr. to corner; to place in a corner
a-rris-ca-mien-to, -ta m. boldness; daring
a-rris-car v. to fold up; to turn up
a-rrit-mia f. lack of rhythm
a-rro-ba-mien-to m. rapture; ecstasy
a-rro-bar v. to enrapture
a-rro-di-llar(se) v. to kneel
a-rro-gan-te adj. proud; arrogant
a-rro-jar(se) v. to fling; emit;

throw

a-rro-jo, -ja *m.* boldness

a-rro-lla-dor, ra *adj.* overwhelming

a-rro-llar *v.* to carry or sweep away

a-rro-par *v.* to tuck in; to wrap with clothing

a-rro-rro *m.* lullaby

a-rro-yo *m.* brook; stream

a-rroz *m.* rice pudding

a-rro-zal *m.* rice paddy or rice field

a-rru-ga *f.* crease; fold; wrinkle line

a-rru-ga-do *adj.* wrinkled

a-rru-gar(se) *v.* to rumple; wrinkle

a-rrui-nar *v.* to destroy

a-rru-lla-dor *adj.* soothing

a-rru-llar *v.* to lull to sleep; to coo

a-rru-ma-co *m.* caress

a-rrum-bar *v.* to neglect; to put or cast aside

ar-se-nal *m.* storehouse; shipyard

ar-se-ni-co *m.* arsenic

ar-te *f.* craft; art

ar-te-fac-to *m.* appliance

ar-te-ria *f.* artery

ar-te-ro *adj.* sly; cunning

ar-te-sa-ni-a *f.* craftsmanship

ar-te-sa-no *m,f.* craftswoman or craftsman

ar-ti-cu-la-ción *f.* joint

ar-ti-cu-lar *v.* to articulate

ar-tis-ta *f., m.* artist

ar-ti-fi-cio, -cia *m.* item; article; thing

ar-ti-fi-cial *adj.* artificial

ar-tis-ti-co *adj.* artistic

ar-tri-tis *f.* arthritis

ar-zo-bis-po *m.* archbishop

as *m.* ace

a-sa-do *m.* roasted meat; barbecue

a-sa-dor *m.* grill

a-sa-la-ria-do, -da *adj.* salaried worker

a-sa-la-riar *v.* to set a salary for someone

a-sal-ta-dor, a *m.f.* assailant

a-sal-tar *v.* to attack

a-sal-to *m.* attack

a-sam-ble-a *f.* conference; meeting

a-sam-ble-is-ta *m.f.* assembly member

as-cen-den-cia *f.* ancestry

as-cen-den-te *adj.* ascending

as-cen-der *v.* to promote; ascend

as-cen-sión *f.* rise; ascension

as-cen-so *m.* ascent; promotion

as-cen-sor, a *m.* lift; elevator

as-cen-so-ris-ta *m., f.* one who operates an elevator

as-co *m.* disgust

a-se-ar *v.* to clean; to wash

a-se-char *v.* to trap

a-se-diar *v.* to bother; to pester

a-se-dio *m.* siege

a-se-gu-ra-do *adj.* insured

a-se-gu-rar(se) *v.* to fasten; assure; secure

a-se-me-jar(se) *v.* to resemble

a-sen-ta-de-ras *f.pl.* buttocks; behind

a-sen-ta-do *adj.* judicious

a-sen-tar *v.* to record

a-sen-ti-mien-to *m.* consent

a-se-o *m.* tidiness; neatness

a-se-qui-ble *adj.* understandable

a-ser-ción *f.* affirmation

a-se-rra-de-ro *m.* sawmill

a-se-rrar *v.* to saw

a-se-rrin *m.* sawdust

a-se-si-nar *v.* to murder

a-se-si-na-to *m.* murder; *pol* assassination

a-se-si-no *adj.* murderous *pol* assassin

a-se-sor, ra *adj.* advisory; advising

a-se-so-rar *v.* to advise

a-ses-tar *v.* to aim

a-se-ve-rar *v.* to assert

a·se·ve·ra·ti·vo *adj.*
affirmative; assertive

a·se·xua·do *adj.* asexual

as·fal·tar *tr.* to asphalt

as·fal·to *m.* asphalt

as·fi·xai *f.* suffocation

as·fi·xiar *v.* to asphyxiate

a·sí *adv.* so

a·sien·to *m.* seat

a·sig·nar *v.* allot; assign

a·sig·nar *v.* to appoint; to
assign

a·sig·na·cion *f.* course or
subject in school

a·si·lar *v.* to give shelter

a·si·lo *m.* asylum

a·si·mi·lar(se) *v.* assimilate

a·si·mis·mo *adj.* in a like
manner; likewise

a·sir(se) *tr.* grip; hold on to

a·sis·ten·cia *f.* attendance

a·sis·ten·cial *adj.* relier; as-
sisting

a·sis·tir *intr.* to accompnay;
to aid; to attend

as·ma *f.* asthma

as·ma·ti·co *adj. & m.f.*
asthmatic

as·na·da *f.* stupidity

a·so·cia·cion *f.* association

a·so·cia·do *adj.* associated

a·so·ciar(se) *v.* to associate
with

a·so·la·dor *adj.* ravaging

a·so·lar *v.* to scorch

a·so·le·a·mien·to *m.* sun-
stroke

a·so·le·ar *v.* to place in the
sun

a·so·mar *v.* to show; *intr.* to
appear

a·som·brar(se) *v.* to amaze;
to astonish

as·pi·rar *v.* to breathe; inhale

as·pi·ri·na *f.* aspirin

as·tro·lo·gia *f.* astrology

as·tro·no·mia *f.* astronomy

as·tu·ta *adj.* artful; sly;
canny; cunning

a·sun·to *m.* issue; concern

a·ta·car *v.* to assault; charge

a·ta·que *m.* attack

a·tar(se) *v.* to rope; tie; brace

a·ten·ción *f.* attention

a·ten·der *v.* to heed; attend

a·tes·ti·guar *v.* to testify

a·tie·sar(se) *v.* to tighten

at·le·ta *f., m.* athlete

at·lé·ti·co *a adj.* athletic

a·to·mi·co *adj.* atomic

a·to·mo *m.* atom

a·trac·ción *f.* attraction

a·trac·ti·vo *adj.* engaging

a·traer *v.* to engage; lure

a·tras *adv.* aback; back

a·tra·sa·do *adj.* backwards

a·tri·buir *v.* to ascribe

a·tro·ci·dad *f.* atrocity

a·tur·dir(se) *v.* to daze;
muddle; bewilder

au·di·ción *f.* audition

au·gus·to *adj.* August

au·men·tar(se) *v.* to augment; enhance

au·men·to *m.* raise; increase

aun *adv.* still

aun·que *conj.* although

au·sen·te *adj.* missing

au·ten·ti·ci·dad *f.* authen-
ticity

au·to·bus *m.* bus

a·to·gra·fo *m.* autograph

au·to·mo·vil *m.* car

au·to·ri·za·ción *f.* authoriza-
tion

a·van·zar(se) *v.* to advance

a·ve *f.* bird

a·ve·ni·da *f.* avenue

a·ven·tu·ra *f.* adventure

a·ver·sión *f.* aversion

a·via·ción *f.* aviation

a·vión *m.* plane; airplane

a·yú·da *f.* aid; help

a·yu·dar *v.* to assist; help

a·zo·rar *v.* to alarm

a·zo·rra·do *adj.* foxy

a·zo·ta·do *adj.* multicolored

a·so·tar *v.* to beat upon

a·zo·te *m.* spanking; whip

a·zu·car *m.* sugar

a·zu·ca·ra·do *adj.* sweet

a·zu·tre *m.* sulphur

a·zul *adj.* blue

a·zu·la·do *adj.* bluish

a·zu·lar *v.* color or dye blue

a·zu·le·jo *m.* glazed tile

ba-ba *f.* spittle
ba-bar-se *tr.* to dribble
ba-ba-za *f.* slime
ba-bear *v.* to drool
ba-bel *m.* confusion
ba-be-ro *m.* bib
ba-bie-ca *adj. m.f.* simple person
ba-bor *m.* port
ba-bo-se-ar *v.* to slobber
ba-ca-la-o *m.* cod
ba-ca-nal *a.* bacchanalian
ba-ci-lo *m.* bacillus
bac-te-ria *f.* bacterium
bac-te-rio-lo-gi-a *f.* bacteriology
bac-te-rio-lo-go, a *m.f.* bacteriologist
ba-che *m.* pothole
ba-da-jo *m.* bell clapper
ba-du-la-que *adj. & m.* follish person
ba-ga-je *m.* luggage
ba-ga-te-la *f.* trinket; trifle
ba-gre *m.* catfish
ba-hi-a *f.* bay
bai-la-dor *m.* dancer
bai-lar *v.* to dance
bai-la-ri-na *f.* ballerina
bai-le *m.* ball; dance
ba-ja *f.* drop
ba-jar(se) *v.* to fall; lower
ba-je-za *f.* lowliness
ba-jo, -ja *adv.* below; *adj.* low; short; small
ba-jon *m.* decline *mus* bassoonist
ba-la *f.* bale
ba-la-da *f.* ballad
ba-la-di *adj.* trivial
ba-la-dro *m.* shout
ba-la-dron *adj.* boasting
ba-la-dro-na-da *f.* boast
ba-la-dro-ne-ar *v.* to brag; to boast
ba-lan-cear(se) *v.* to teeter
ba-lan-ce-o *m.* rocking
ba-lan-za *f.* scale
ba-lar *v.* to bleat
bal-bu-ce-ar *v.* to babble
bal-con *m.* balcony
ba-li-do *m.* bleat
ba-lis-ti-ca *f.* ballistics

ba-lis-ti-co *adj.* ballistic
ba-lon-ces-to *m.* basketball
ba-lon-ma-no *m.* handball
ba-lon-vo-le-a *m.* volleyball
ba-lo-ta *f.* ballot
bal-sa *f.* balsa
bal-sa-mo *m.* balsam
ba-luar-te *m.* bastion
ba-lle-na *f.* whale
ba-lle-na-to *m.* whale calf
ba-lle-ne-ro, -ra *adj.* whaling
ba-lles-ta *f.* crossbow
ba-lles-te-ar *v.* to shoot with a crossbow
ba-lles-te-ria *f.* archery
bam-ba-le-ar *v.* to sway
bam-bo-le-om *m.* wobble
ba-llet *m.* ballet
bam-bu *m.* bamboo
ba-na-na *f.* bananna
ban-ca *f.* banking
ban-ca-rro-ta *f.* bankruptcy
ban-co *m.* bank; band; pew; bench
ban-da-da *f.* flock; group
ban-de-ra *f.* ensign; flag
ban-de-ja *f.* tray
ban-de-ro-la *f.* pennant
ban-di-do *m.* bandit
ban-do-le-ro *m.* bandit
ban-que-ta *f.* stool
ban-que-te *m.* feast
ban-que-tear *v.* to feast
ba-ñar(se) *v.* to bathe
ba-ño *m.* bathtub
ba-ra-jar *v.* to shuffle
ba-ra-to *adv.* cheaply; *adj.* inexpensive; cheap
bar-ba *f.* beard
bar-ba-coa *f.* barbecue
bar-ba-do *adj.* bearded
bar-ba-ri-dad *f.* outrage
bar-ba-ra *f.,* **-ro** *adj.* savage
bar-bear *v.* to shave
bar-be-ro *m.* barber
bar-be-lla *f.* chin
bar-bo-tar *v.* to mutter, mumble
bar-bo-te-o *m.* murmuring
bar-bu-do *adj.* heavily bearded
bar-bu-lla *f.* chatter; jabbering

bar-ca *f.* small boat
bar-ca-za *f.* launch
bar-co *m.* ship; boat
ba-ri-to-no *m.* baritone
bar-niz *m.* glaze; varnish; lacquer
bar-ni-zar *v.* varnish; lacquer
ba-ro-me-tro *m.* barometer
ba-ron *m.* baron
ba-ro-ne-sa *f.* baroness
ba-rra *f.* bar
ba-rra-ca *f.* booth
ba-rrer *v.* to sweep
ba-rre-ra *f.* barricade
ba-rri-ga *f.* belly
ba-rril *m.* barrel
ba-rrio *m.* neighborhood
ba-sal-to *m.* basalt
ba-sar *v.* to base
ba-se *f.* foundation
ba-si-co *adj.* basal
ba-si-li-ca *f.* basilica
bas-quet-bol *m.* basketball
bas-tan-te *adj.* sufficient
bas-tar *v.* to suffice
bas-tar-dear *v.* to debase
bas-to *adj.* rough
bas-ton *m.* baton; stick
ba-su-ra *f.* rubbish
ba-ta *f.* negligee
ba-ta-lla *f.* battle
ba-ta-llar *v.* to battle
ba-ta-llon *m.* battalion
ba-te-ria *f.* battery
ba-ti-do *m.* batter
ba-tir(se) *v.* to churn
ba-tu-ta *f.* baton
baul *m.* trunk
bau-tis-mo *m.* christening
bau-ti-zar *v.* to baptize
ba-ya *f.* berry
ba-yo *adj.* bay
ba-zar *m.* bazaar
ba-zu-ca *f.* bazooka
bea-ti-fi-car *v.* to beatify
bea-ti-fi-co *adj.* beatific
bea-ti-tud *f.* beatitude
be-be *m.* baby
be-ber *v.* to drink
be-bi-da *f.* beverage
be-ca *f.* scholarship
be-ce-rro *m.* calf
be-far *v.* to taunt

beige *m.* beige
beis-bol *m.* baseball
be-li-co-so, -sa *adj.* warlike
be-li-ge-ran-te *adj.* belligerent
be-lle-za *f.* beauty
be-llo *adj.* beautiful
be-mol *m.* flat
ben-de-cir *v.* to bless
ben-di-ción *f.* blessing
ben-di-to *adj.* holy
be-ne-fi-ciar(se) *v.* to benefit
be-ne-fi-cio-so *adj.* beneficial
be-ne-fi-co *adj.* charitable
be-ne-vo-lo *adj.* benevolent
ben-ga-la *f.* flare
be-nig-ni-dad *f.* kindness
be-nig-no *adj.* kind; mild
be-rrin-che *m.* tantrum
be-sar(se) *v.* to smooch
be-so, -sa *m.* kiss
bes-tia *f.* animal
bes-tial *adj.* bestial
Bi-blia *f.* Bible
bi-bli-co *adj.* Biblical
bi-blio-gra-fia *f.* bibliography
bi-blio-gra-fo, -fa *m.* bibliographer
bi-blio-te-ca *f.* library
bi-ceps *m.* biceps
bi-ci-cle-ta *f.* bicycle
bi-ci-clis-ta *m., f.* bicyclist
bi-cho *m.* bug
bien *m.* good
bien-ve-ni-da *f.* greeting
bi-fur-car-se *v.* to fork
bi-go-te *m.* mustache
bi-la-te-ral *adj.* bilateral
bi-lio-so *adj.* bilious
bi-lis *f.* bile
bi-llar *m.* billiards
bi-lle-te *m.* bill
bi-llon *m.* trillion
bi-na-rio *adj.* binary
bio-gra-fia *f.* biography
bio-gra-fi-co *adj.* biographic
bio-gra-fo *m.* biographer
bio-lo-gia *f.* biology
bio-lo-gi-co *adj.* biological
bio-lo-go *m.* biologist
biop-sia *f.* biopsy
bi-sa-bue-la *f.* **-lo** *m.* great-grandmother; -father

bi-se-car v. to bisect
bi-sec-cion f. bisection
bi-son-te m. bison
biz-guear v. to squint
blan-co adj. blank; white
blan-dir v. to flourish
blan-do adj. supple; soft
blan-quear v. to whiten
blas-fe-mar v. to swear
blas-fe-mia f. profanity
blin-da-do adj. armored
blo-que m. block
blo-quear v. to block
blu-sa f. blouse
bo-bo m. fool; ninny
bo-ca f. mouth
bo-ca-di-llo m. sandwich
bo-ca-do m. bite
bo-da f. marriage
bo-de-ga f. wine cellar
boi-co-teo m. boycott
bo-la f. fib; ball
bo-le-tin m. bulletin
bo-li-che m. bowling
bo-li-ta f. pellet
bol-sa f. bag; pouch
bol-si-llo m. pocket
bol-sis-ta m. stockbroker
bol-so m. handbag
bo-llo m. bump
bom-ba f. pump
bom-bar-de-ro m. bomber
bom-bear v. to pad; pump
bom-bi-lla f. bulb
bom-bon m. sweet
bon-dad f. kindness
bon-da-do-so, -sa adj. good
bo-ni-to, -ta adj. pretty
bo-quea-da f. gasp
bo-qui-lla f. nozzle
bor-de m. edge
bor-di-llo m. curb
bo-rra-cho m. drunkard
bo-rra-dor m. eraser
bos-que m. woods
bos-que-jar v. to outline
bo-ta f. wine bag
bo-ta-ni-ca f. botany
bo-te m. jackpot
bo-te-lla f. bottle
bo-ti-ca-rio m. druggist
bo-tin m. loot
bo-ton m. stud

bo-to-nes m. bellhop
bo-ve-da f. vault
bo-vi-no, -na adj. bovine
bo-xea-dor m. boxer
bo-xear v. to box
bo-ya f. buoy
bo-yan-te adj. buoyant
bo-zal m. muzzle
bra-man-te m. twine
bra-mar v. to bluster
bra-mi-do m. bellow
bra-vo, -va adj. brave
bra-za-do m. armful
bra-zo m. arm
bre-ve adj. short
bre-ve-dad f. conciseness
bri-bon adj. lazy
bri-llan-te adj. bright; shiny
bri-llar v. to glow; beam
bri-llo m. glow; shine
brin-car v. to jump; gambol
brio m. jauntiness
bri-sa f. breeze
bro-ca-do m. brocade
bro-che m. brooch
bro-mear(se) v. to joke
bro-mis-ta f. joker
bron-ce m. bronze
bron-cea-do m. suntan; bronze
bron-ce-ar v. to tan; to bronze
bron-co adj. coarse; rough
bron-quial adj. bronchial
bron-quio m. bronchial tube
bron-qui-tis f. bronchitis
bro-quel m. small sheild
bro-ta-du-ra f. budding; sprouting
bro-tar v. to bud
bru-je-ri-a f. witchcraft
bru-jo m. wizard
bru-ju-la f. compass
bru-mo-so adj. foggy; misty
bru-ni-du-ra f. polishing; burnishing
bru-nir v. to burnish; to polish
brus-co, -ca adj. sudden
bru-to m. beast; brute
bu-bon m. swelling or very large tumor
bu-ce-ar v. to swim under water

bu-cle *m.* curl; ringlet

bu-din *m.* pudding

bue-na-ven-tu-ra *f.* good luck; good fortune

bue-no, a *adj.* sound; good

buey *m.* ox

bu-fa-lo *m.* buffalo

bu-fan-da *f.* muffler; scarf

bu-fon *m.* clown; buffoon

bu-ho-ne-ro *m.* hawker; peddler

bui-tre *m.* vulture

bu-jia *f.* candle

bul-bo *m.* bulb

bu-le-var *m.* boulevard

bul-to *m.* mass; heft

bu-lla *f.* uproar; brawl; ctowd; mob

bu-lli-cio *m.* riot; racket; hubbub

bu-llir *v.* to boil

bu-me-ran-ang *m.* boomerrang

bu-nue-io *m.* fried dough

bu-que *m.* vessel; ship

bu-que *m.* bouquet

bur-bu-ja *f.* bubble

bur-de-os *adj.* deep red in color

bur-do *adj.* rough; coarse

bur-gue-si-a *f.* middle class

bu-ri-lar *v.* to engrave

bur-la *f.* taunt; joke

bur-lar(se) *v.* to gibe; joke

bur-les-co *adj.* burlesque

bu-ro-cra-ta *f.* bureaucrat

bu-rra *f.* stupid woman

bu-rro *m.* donkey; burro

bur-sa *f.* rubbish

bur-sa-til *adj.* stock market

bus-ca *f.* search

bus-ca-pie *m.* feeler

bus-car *v.* to look or search for

bus-ca-vi-das *m.f.* busybody

bus-que-da *f.* search

bus-to *m.* bust; chest

bu-ta-ca *f.* armchair

bu-ta-no *m.* butane

bu-ti-le-no *m.* butylene

bu-zo *m.* deep-sea diver

bu-zon *m.* mailbox

ca-bal *adj.* fair; precise

ca-ba-la *f. relig.* cabala

ca-bal-gar *v.* to ride on horseback

ca-bal-ga-ta *f.* cavalcade

ca-ba-lle-ria *f. milit.* cavalry

ca-ba-lle-ri-za *f.* stable

ca-ba-lle-ro *m.* gentleman

ca-ba-lle-te *m.* easel; sawhorse

ca-ba-lli-to, -ta *m.* pony, small horse

ca-ba-llo *m.* horse

ca-ba-llón *f.* ridge

ca-ba-na *f.* cabin

ca-ba-ret *m.* cabaret; night club

ca-be-ci-lla *m.* ringleader

ca-be-lle-ra *f.* head of hair

ca-be-llo *m.* hair

ca-ber *v.* to fit

ca-bes-tri-llo *m.* sling

ca-bes-tro *m.* halter

ca-be-za *f.* skull; head

ca-be-zón, o-na *adj.* bigheaded

ca-be-zo-ta *m.f. coll.* mule

ca-bil-dear *v.* to lobby

ca-bil-do *f.* town council

ca-ble *m.* cable

ca-ble-gra-fiar *v.* to cable

ca-ble-gra-ma *m.* cablegram

ca-ble-vi-sion *f.* cable television

ca-bo *m.* corporal; cape;

ca-bra *f.* goat

ca-brio *m.* rafter

ca-bri-to *m.* young goat, kid

ca-bro-na-da *f. coll.* dirty trick

ca-ca-hue-te *m.* peanut

ca-cao *m.* cocoa

ca-ca-re-ar *v.* to crow; cackle

ca-ca-tua *f.* cockatoo

ca-ce-ro-la *f.* casserole

ca-ci-que *m.* Indian chief

ca-ci-que-ar *intr. coll.* to order people around

ca-co *m.* burglar

cac-to *m.* cactus

ca-cha-lo-te *m.* sperm whale

ca-char *v.* to split; to chip

ca-cha-sa *f.* sluggish

ca-che-ar *v.* to frisk, to search

ca-che-mi-ra *f.* cashmere

ca-che-te-ar *v. Amer.* to slap; hit

ca-che-ti-na *f.* fist fight

ca-che-tu-do *adj.* plump or chubby-cheeks

ca-cho-rro m. puppy

ca-da *adj.* every; each

ca-dal-so *m.* platform

ca-da-ver m. body; corpse

ca-da-ve-ri-co *adj.* cadaverous

ca-de-na *f.* chain

ca-den-cia *f.* rhythm; cadence

ca-de-ra *f.* hip, hip joint

ca-de-te m. cadet

ca-du-co, a *adj.* lapse; to expire

caer(se) *v.* to fall

ca-fe m. coffee; cafe

ca-fe-i-na *f.* caffeine

ca-fe-tal *m.* coffee plantation

ca-fe-te-ri-a *f.* cafeteria; cafe

cai-da *f.* downfall; tumble

cai-man *m.* alligator

ca-ja *f.* cabinet; chest

ca-je-ro *m.* cashier; teller

ca-jis-ta *m.f.* typesetter

cal *f.* lime

ca-la *f.* cove

ca-la-ba-za *f.* pumpkin; gourd; squash

ca-la-bo-zo m. jail; underground prison cell

ca-la-dor m. mech. driller

ca-la-fa-te-ar *v.* to calk; caulk

ca-la-mar m. squid

ca-lam-bre m. cramp

ca-la-mi-dad *f.* calamity; misfortune

ca-la-mi-to-so *adj.* calamitous

ca-la-na *f.* character; nature

ca-lar(se) *v.* to swoop; to penetrate

cal-ce-te-ria *f.* hosiery

cal-ce-tin *m.* sock

cal-ci-fi-ca-ction *f.* calcification

cal-ci-fi-car(se) *v.* to calcify

cal-cio *m.* calcium

cal-co m. tracing

cal-co-ma-ni-a *f.* decal

cal-cu-la-dor, ra *m.f.* calculator

cal-cu-lar *v.* to estimate; calculate

cal-cu-lis-ta *m.f.* planner; calculator

cal-cu-lo *m.* calculation

cal-de-ra *f.* boiler

cal-do m. soup; broth; stock

ca-le-fac-tor m. heating; heat

ca-le-fac-tor m. heater

ca-len-da-rio *m.* calendar; schedule

ca-len-ta-dor *adj.* warming; heating

ca-len-tar(se) *v.* to heat or to warm

ca-lien-te *adj.* warm; hot

ca-li-na *f.* haze

ca-lip-so *m.* calypso

cal-ma *f.* calm

cal-man-te *adj.* sedative *m.* tranquilizer

cal-mar(se) *v.* to soothe; to calm; to settle

ca-lo-fri-o *m.* chill; feaver

ca-lor m. warmth; heat

ca-lo-ria *f.* calorie

ca-lo-ri-co *adj.* caloric

ca-lum-nia *f.* slander; calumny

ca-lum-nia-dor, ra *adj.* slanderous

ca-lu-ro-so *adj.* warm; hot

cal-va-rio *m. relig.* Clavary

cal-vi-cie *f.* baldness

cal-vo *adj.* bald

cal-za-da *f.* causeway; drive; highway; road

cal-zo-nes *m.* shoehorn

cal-zo-nes *m., pl.* trousers

ca-lla-do *adj.* silent; quiet

ca-llar(se) *v.* to keep quiet; hush

ca-lle *f.* street

ca-lle-jue-la *f.* alley

ca-llo *m.* callus; corn
ca-ma *f.* bed
ca-ma-da *f.* litter; brood
ca-ma-feo *m.* cameo
ca-ma-ra *f.* room; chamber
ca-ma-ra-da *m.,f.* comrade
ca-ma-re-ra *f.* waitress
ca-ma-re-ro *m.* waiter
ca-ma-ro-te *m.* cabin
cam-biar(se) *v.* to change; to alter
cam-bia-vi-a *m.* rail switch
cam-bio *m.* shift; change
cam-bis-ta *m.f.* broker, moneychanger
ca-me-le-ar *v. coll.* deceive
ca-me-lia *f.* camellia
ca-me-llo *m.* camel
ca-me-ro, a *adj.* double
ca-mi-lla *f.* stretcher
ca-mi-nar *v.* to walk; to travel
ca-mi-na-ta *f.* hike; walk
ca-mi-no *m.* route; road
ca-mion *m.* truck
ca-mio-ne-ro, a *m.f.* truck driver
ca-mio-ne-ta *f.* van
ca-mi-sa *f.* shirt
ca-mi-se-ta *f.* tee-shirt; undershirt
ca-mi-so-la *f.* camisole
ca-mi-son *m.* nightgown
ca-mo-rra *f. coll.* squabble
ca-mo-rre-ar *v. coll* to quarrel; squabble
cam-pa-men-to *m.* camp
cam-pa-na *f.* bell
cam-pa-ña *f.* campaign
cam-pe-si-no, -na *adj.* country; peasant
cam-pes-tre *adj.* rural
cam-pis-ta *m,f* camper
cam-po *m.* country; field
cam-po-san-to *m.* graveyard; cemetery
ca-mu-fla-je *m.* camouflage
ca-mu-flar *v.* to camouflage
ca-nal *m.* canal; channel
ca-na-le-te *m.* paddle
ca-nas-ta *f.* hamper; basket
can-ce-la-ción *f.* cancellation
can-ce-lar *v.* to cancel
can-cer *m.* cancer

can-ci-ller *m.* chancellor
can-ci-lle-ri-a *f.* chancellery
can-ción *f.* song
can-cio-ne-ro *m. mus.* songbook
can-cro *m. med.* cancer
can-da-do *m.* padlock
can-del-a *f.* candle
can-de-le-ro *m.* candlestick
can-di-da-to *m.* candidate
can-di-da-tu-ra *f.* candidacy
can-di-do *adj.* unsophisticated
ca-ne-la *f.* cinnamon
ca-ne-ion *m.* roof gutter
ca-ne-lo-nes *m., pl.* canneloni
ca-ne-su *m.* bodice; yoke
can-gre-jo *m.* crab
can-gu-ro *m.* kangaroo
ca-ni-bal *m.* cannibal
ca-ni-ca *f.* marble
ca-ni-no *adj.* canine
ca-ni-cu-la *f.* midsummer heat; dog days of summer
ca-ni-lla *f. anat.* shinbone
ca-ni-lli-ta *m.* newspaper boy
ca-ni-no, a *adj.& m.* canine
can-je *m.* trade; exchange
can-je-a-ble *adj.* exchange-able
can-je-ar *v.* to trade; exchange
ca-no, a *adj.* gray-haired
ca-noa *f.* canoe; rowboat
ca-non *m.* canon
can-sa-do *adj.* weary; tired; rundown
can-san-cio *m.* tiredness
can-sar(se) *v.* to weary; tire
can-ta-lu-po *m.* cantaloupe
can-tan-te *m.,f.* singer
can-tar *v.* to sing; chant *m.* song
can-te-ra *f.* pit; quarry
can-ti-dad *f.* quantity; amount
can-tim-plo-ra *f.* canteen
can-to *m.* singing; croak
can-tu-rrear *v.* to croon; hum
ca-ña *f.* cane; reed
ca-ño *m.* pipe; spout

ca-non *m.* cannon; barrel

ca-os *m.* chaos

ca-pa *f.* cape; coating; layer

ca-pa-ci-dad *f.* capacity; capability

ca-pa-taz *m.* foreman

ca-paz *adj.* roomy; capable

cap-cio-so *adj.* deceitful

ca-pe-llan *m.* chaplain

ca-pe-ru-za *f.* hood

ca-pi-lar *adj. & m.* capillary

ca-pi-la-ri-dad *f.* capillarity

ca-pi-lla *f.* chapel

ca-pi-llo *m.* baby bonnet; cap

ca-pi-ro-ta-zo *m.* flip as with the finger

ca-pi-tal *m.* capital

ca-pi-ta-lis-mo *m.* capitalism

ca-pi-ta-lis-mo *m.* capitalism

ca-pi-tan *m.* captain

ca-pi-to-lio *m.* capitol

ca-pi-tu-lo *m.* chapter

ca-po *m.* bonnet; hood

ca-pon *adj.* casterated

ca-pri-cho *m.* whim; fancy; quick

ca-pri-cho-so *adj.* temperamental; whimsical

cap-su-la *f.* capsule

cap-tu-ra *f.* capture; catch

ca-pu-cha *f.* hood

ca-pu-llo *m.* cocoon

ca-qui *m.* khaki

ca-ra *f.* face

ca-ra-col *m.* snail

ca-rac-ter *m.* nature; character

ca-rac-te-ris-ti-co, -ca *adj.* typical

ca-rac-te-ri-za-do, a *adj.* distinguished

ca-rac-te-ri-za-dor, ra *adj.* distinguishing

ca-rac-te-ri-zar *v.* to characterize

ca-ra-cu *m.* Amer. bone marrow

ca-ram-ba-no *m.* icicle

ca-ra-me-li-zar *v.* to cover with caramel

ca-ra-me-lo *m.* caramel

ca-ra-va-na *f.* caravan

car-bo-hi-dra-to *m.* carbohydrate

car-bon *m.* coal

car-bo-na-to *m.* carbonate

car-bo-no *m.* carbon

car-nun-co *m.* carbuncle

car-bu-ra-dor *m.* carburetor

car-bu-ran-te *m.* fuel

car-cel *f.* prison; jail

car-de-nal *m.* cardinal

car-dia-co *adj.* cardiac

ca-re-cer *v.* to lack

ca-ren-cia *f.* need; lack

ca-rey *m.* sea turtle

car-ga *f.* burden; load

car-ga-de-ro *m.* loading platform

car-ga-men-to *m.* cargo

car-gar(se) *v.* to burden; load

car-go *m.* charge; burden; load

ca-riar-se *v.* to decay

ca-ri-dad *f.* charity

ca-ri-no, a *m.* affection; love

ca-ri-ta-ti-vo *adj.* charitable

car-nal *adj.* carnal

car-na-val *m.* carnival

car-ne *f.* pulp; flesh; meat

car-ne-ar *v.* Amer. to slaughter

car-ni-ce-ria *f.* slaughter; bloodshed

car-ni-ce-ro *m.* butcher

car-pe-ta *f.* folder

car-pin-te-ria *f.* carpentry

car-pin-te-ro *m.* carpenter

ca-rre-ra *f.* career; race

ca-rre-ro *m.* carrier

ca-rre-ta-je *m.* cartage

ca-rre-te *m.* reel; spool; coil; bobbin

ca-rre-te-ra *f.* road; highway

ca-rro-za *f.* coach; chariot

ca-rrua-je *m.* carriage

ca-rru-sel *m.* merry-go-round

car-ta *f.* card; letter

car-ta-pa-cio *m.* notebook

car-tel *m.* poster

car-te-le-ra *f.* billboard

car-te-ra *f.* billfold; wallet

car-te-ro *m.* postman

car-ti-la-go *m.* gristle; cartilage

car-to-gra-fi-a f. mapmaking; cartography

car-to-gra-io, a m., f. mapmaker, catographer

car-ton m. cardboard

car-tu-cho m. cartridge

ca-sa f. home; house

ca-sa-ca f. dress coat

ca-sa-do, a adj. married

casar(se) v. wed; to marry

cas-ca-bel m. small bell

cas-ca-be-le-ar v. to jingle

cas-ca-do, a adj. cracked; decrepit

cas-ca-da f. cascade

cas-ca-jo m. gravel

cas-ca-ra f. hull; shell; skin; rind

ca-se-ta f. cottage

ca-se-te m.f. tape cartridge; cassette

cas-co-te m. rubble

ca-si adv. almost

ca-si-mir m. cashmere

ca-si-no m. casino

ca-so m. happening; case

cas-pa f. dandruff

cas-ta f. breed; caste; cast

cas-ta-ne-te-ar v. to chatter

cas-ti-dad f. chastity

cas-ti-gar v. to punish

cas-ti-llo m. castle

cas-tor m. beaver

cas-tra-cion f. castration

ca-sual adj. accidental; coincidental

ca-sua-li-dad f. coincidence; chance

ca-ta-le-jo m. small telescope; spyglass

ca-ta-lo-gar v. to catalog; catalogue

ca-tar v. to taste; to sample

ca-ta-ra-ta f. waterfall; cataract

ca-tas-tro-fe f. catastrophe

ca-te-dral f. cathedral

ca-te-go-ria f. category

ca-ter-va f. gang

ca-te-ter m. catheter

ca-tin-ga f. body odor

ca-tor-ce adj. fourteen

ca-tre m. cot made of canvas

cau-ce m. channel; riverbed; ditch

cau-cion f. bail; caution

cau-cho m. rubber; rubber tree or plant

cau-di-llo m. leader

cau-sa f. cause

cau-te-la f. cautiously

cau-te-la f. caution

cau-te-lo-so, a adj. cautions

cau-te-ri-zar v. captivating

cau-ti-ve-rio m. captivity

cau-ti-vo, a adj. & m.f captive

cau-to, a adj. cautions

ca-var v. to dig

ca-ver-na f. cave, cavern

ca-vial/viar m. caviar

ca-vi-dad f. cavity

ca-vi-la-cion f. rumination; pondering

ca-vi-lar intr. to ruminate; ponder

ca-za f. hunt game

ca-za-dor, ra adj. hunting

ca-zar v. to hunt

ca-zo m. ladle

ca-zue-la m. small shark

ce-bar v. to fatten

ce-bo-lla f. onion

ce-bra f. zebra

ce-ce-o m. lisp

ce-dro m. cedar

ce-du-la f. document

ce-fi-ro m. zephyr

ce-gar v. to blind

ce-gue-dad-ra f. blindness

ce-ja f. eyebrow

ce-jar intr. to back up

ce-la-da f. ambush

ce-la-dor, ra adj. vigilant; watchful

ce-lar v. to comply with something

cel-da f. cell

ce-le-bra-cion. f. celebration

ce-le-bran-te adj. celebrating

ce-le-brar v. to celebrate

ce-le-bre adj. famous; celebrated

ce-le-bri-dad *f.* celebrity
ce-le-ri-dad *f.* speed
ce-les-te *adj.* sky-blue
ce-les-tial *adj.* heavenly
ce-les-ti-na *f.* madam; procuress
ce-li-ba-to *m.* celibacy
ce-li-be *adj. & m.f.* celibate
ce-lo-tan *m.* cellophane
ce-lo-si-a *f.* latticework
ce-lo-so, a *adj.* zealous
ce-lu-la *f.* cell
ce-lu-loi-de *m.* celluloid
ce-lu-lo-so *adj.* cellulous
ce-llis-ca *f.* sleet
ce-men-te-rio *m.* cemetery
ce-men-to *m.* cement
ce-na *f.* supper; dinner
ce-na-gal *m.* swamp
ce-nar *intr.* to have dinner
cen-ca-rro *m.* cowbell
ce-ni-ce-ro *m.* ashtray
ce-nit *m.* zenith
cen-sor *m.* censor
cen-su-rar *v.* to censor
cen-te-lla *f.* flash
cen-te-lle-an-te *adj.* sparkling
cen-te-na *f.* one hundred
cen-te-nar *m.* one hundred
cen-ta-no *m.* rye
cen-te-si-mo *adj.* hundredth
cen-ti-gra-do *adj.* centigrade
cen-ti-me-tro *m.* centimeter
cen-ti-me-tro, a *adj.* hundredth
cen-ti-ne-la *m.f.* sentry
cen-to-lla *f.* spider crab
cen-tra-do, a *adj.* centered
cen-tral *adj.* central
cen-tra-li-zar *v.* to centralize
cen-trar *v.* to center
cen-tri-co *adj.* central
cen-tro *m.* core; middle; center
ce-nir *v.* to encircle; to bind; to be tight on
ce-no *m.* frown
ce-pa *f.* stump
ce-pi-llo *m.* brush
ce-ra *f.* wax
ce-ra-mi-ca *f.* ceramics

cer-ca *adv.* near; close
cer-ca *f.* fence
cer-ca-ni-a *f.* nearness *pl.* outskirts
cer-ca-no *adj.* near; close
cer-car *v.* to surround; to fence something in
cer-ce-nar *v.* to cut
cer-cio-rar *v.* to assure
cer-co *m.* circle
cer-da *f.* pig; sow
cer-do *m.* pig
cer-do-so *adj.* bristly
ce-real *m.* cereal
ce-re-bral *adj.* cerebral
ce-re-bro *m.* brain
ce-re-mo-nia *f.* ceremony
ce-re-mo-nial *m.* cermonial
ce-re-za *f.* cherry
ce-ri-lla *f.* match
ce-ro *m.* zero
ce-rra-do *adj.* shut
ce-rra-du-ra *f.* lock
ce-rrar(se) *v.* to close; seal
ce-rro-jo *m.* bolt
cer-ti-fi-ca-do *m.* certificate
cer-ti-fi-car *v.* to certify
cer-va-to *m.* fawn
cer-ve-za *f.* ale; beer
ce-sar *v.* to cease
ce-sion *f.* grant; cession
ces-ped *m.* grass; sod; lawn
ces-ta *f.* basket
ce-tri-no *adj.* sallow
ci-cli-co *adj.* cyclic
ci-clis-ta *m., f.* cyclist
ci-clo *m.* circle
ci-clon *m.* cyclone
ci-cu-ta *f.* hemlock
cie-go *adj.* sightless; blind
cie-lo *m.* heaven; sky
cien *adj.* hundred
cie-na-ga *f.* swamp
cien-cia *f.* science
cien-ti-fi-co *m.* scientist
cien-to *a., m.* hundred
cie-rre *m.* snap
cier-ta-men-te *adv.* certainly
cier-to, -ta *adj.* certain; sure
cier-vo *m.* hart; stag
ci-fra *f.* figure; cipher
ci-frar *v.* to cipher
ci-ga-rri-llo *m.* cigarette

ci-lin-dro *m.* cylinder
ci-ma *f.* crest; summit; top
cin-co *adj.* five
cin-cuen-ta *adj.* fifty
cí-ne *m.* movies
cin-ta *f.* reel; tape; ribbon
cin-to *m.* girdle
cin-tu-rón *m.* belt
ci-prés *m.* cypress
cir-co *m.* circus
cir-cu-la-ción *f.* circulation
cir-cu-lar *adj.* circular
cir-cu-lo *m.* circle
cir-cun-ci-dar *v.* to circumcise
cir-cun-ci-sión *f.* circumcision
ci-rio *m.* candle; taper
ci-rro *m.* cirrus
ci-rue-la *f.* plum
ci-ru-gía *f.* surgery
ci-ru-ja-no *m.* surgeon
cis-ne *m.* swan
ci-ta *f.* meeting; date; appointment
ci-ta-ción *f.* citation; subpena
ci-tar(se) *v.* to quote; summon
clu-dad *f.* town; city
ciu-da-da-no *m.* citizen
cí-vi-co *adj.* civic
ci-vil *adj.* civilian; civil
ci-vi-li-za-ción *f.* civilazation
cal-mor *m.* outcry; noise
cla-mo-ro-so *adj.* clamorous
clan *m.* clan
cla-ra-men-te *adv.* clearly
cla-ri-dad *f.* clearness; clarity
cla-ri-fi-ca-ción *f.* clarification
cla-ri-fi-car *v.* to clarify
cla-rín *m.* bugle
cla-ri-ne-te *m.* clarinet
cla-ro *adj.* clear; light; lucid
cla-se *f.* grade; class; sort
clá-si-co *adj.* classic; classical
cla-si-fi-ca-ción *f.* classification
cla-si-fi-car(se) *v.* to classify; class
cla-var(se) *v.* to nail; to

thrust; stick
cla-ve *adj.* key
cla-vel *m.* carnation
cla-vi-ja *f.* peg
cla-vo *m.* spike; nail
cle-men-cia *f.* mercy; clemency
cle-men-te *adj.* clement
cle-ri-cal *adj.* clerical
cle-ri-go *m.* priest; parson
cle-ro *m.* ministry; clergy
clien-te *m., f.* client; customer; patron
cli-ma *m.* climate
cli-max *m.* climax
clí-ni-ca *f.* clinic
clo-quear *v.* to cluck
clo-ro *m.* chlorine
coac-ción *f.* compulsion; constraint
coa-gu-la-ción *f.* coagulation
coa-gu-lar(se) *v.* to coagulate; clot
coa-li-cion *f.* coalition
co-bal-to *m.* cobalt
co-bar-de *adj.* cowardly
co-bra *f.* cobra
co-bra-dor, a *m.* conductor
co-brar(se) *v.* cash; receive
co-bre *m.* copper
co-bro *m.* recovery
co-caí-na *f.* cocaine
co-cer *v.* to bake; cook
co-cien-te *m.* quotient
co-ci-na *f.* kitchen; stove
co-ci-nar *v.* to cook
co-co *m.* coconut
co-co-dri-lo *m.* crocodile
coc-tel *m.* cocktail
co-che *m.* automobile
co-di-cia *f.* greed
codi-ciar *v.* to covet
co-di-cio-so *adj.* greedy
co-di-fi-car *v.* to codify
co-di-go *m.* code
co-do *m.* elbow
co-e-du-ca-ción *f.* coeducation
coe-tá-neo *m.* contemporary
co-fra-día *f.* gang
co-fre *m.* chest
co-ger *v.* get; choose; take
co-gi-da *f.* toss; catch

co-he-char v. to bribe
co-he-cho m. bribery
co-he-ren-te adj. coherent
co-he-te m. rocket
coin-ci-den-te adj. coincidental
coin-ci-dir v. to coincide
coi-to m. intercourse
co-jear v. to hobble
co-je-ra f. limp
co-jin m. cushion
co-jo adj. lame
col f. cabbage
co-la f. tail
co-la-bo-ra-ción f. collaboration
co-la-no-rar v. to collaborte
co-la-dor m. strainer
co-lap-so m. collapse
col-cha f. quilt; spread
col-chon m. mattress
co-lec-ción f. collection
co-lec-cio-nar v. to collect
co-le-ga f. colleague
co-le-gio m. academy; college; high school
col-ga-du-ra f. drape
co-li-brí m. hummingbird
có-li-co f. colic
co-li-flor f. cauliflower
co-li-na f. hill
col-me-nar f. hive; beehive
col-mi-llo m. fang; tusk
col-mo m. height; climax
co-lo-ca-ción f. location; situation
co-lo-car(se) v. to place; locate; put
co-lon m. colon
co-lo-nia f. colony
co-lo-nial adj. colonial
co-lo-no m. settler
co-lor m. color
co-lo-re-te m. rouge
co-lum-na f. pillar
co-lum-nis-ta m., f. columnist
co-lim-piar(se) v. to swing
co-lu-sion f. colusion
co-ma f. comma
co-ma-dre f. gossip
co-man-dan-te f. commander

co-man-dar v. to command
co-ma-to-so adj. comatose
com-ba f. bend
com-bar(se) v. to bend; sag
com-ba-te m. fight
com-ba-tir(se) v. to combat
com-bi-na-ción f. combination
com-bi-nar(se) v. to blend; combine
com-bus-ti-ble adj. combustible
com-pe-ler v. to compel
com-pen-sa-ción f. compensation
com-pe-ten-cia f. competence
com-pe-tir f. compilation
com-pi-lar v. to compile
com-pin-che m. chum
com-pla-cer(se) v. to please; humor
com-ple-men-to n. complement
com-ple-tar v. to complete
com-ple-to adj. full; absolute; thorough; complete
com-pli-ca-ción f. complication
com-ple-car(se) v. to involve
com-pli-ce m. accessory
com-po-ner(se) v. to make; compose
com-por-ta-mien-to m. behavior
com-por-tar(se) v. to behave
com-po-si-ciona f. composition
com-prar v. purchase; trade
com-pre-hen-sión f. prehesnion
com-pren-der v. understand
com-pren-si-vo adj. comprehensive
com-pre-sion f. compression
com-pri-mir v. to compress
com-pro-ba-ción f. proof
com-pro-bar v. to verify
com-pues-to m. compound
com-pul-sion f. compulsion
com-pu-ta-dor m. computer
com-pu-tar v. to compute

co-mun *adj.* common
con *prep* towards; with; by
con-ca-vi-dad *f.* hollow
con-ce-bir *v.* to conceive
con-ce-der *v.* allow; accord
con-ce-jo *m.* council
con-cen-tra-ción *f.* concentration
con-cen-trar(se) *v.* to concentrate
con-cep-ción *f.* conception
con-cep-to *m.* concept; notion
con-ce-sion *f.* allowance; concession
con-cien-cia *f.* conscience
con-cier-to *m.* concert
con-cluir(se) *v.* to end; conclude
con-cor-dar *v.* to tally; agree
con-cor-dia *f.* concord
con-cre-to *adj.* concrete
con-cu-bi-na *f.* concurence; turnout
con-cu-rrir *v.* to meet; concur
con-cur-san-te *m.,* *f.* participant
con-cur-so *m.* contest
con-da-do *m.* county
con-de *m.* earl; count
con-de-co-rar *v.* to decorate
con-de-na *f.* sentence
con-de-na-ción *f.* condemnation
con-de-sa *f.* countess
con-di-ción *f.* state; condition
con-di-ció-nal *adj.* conditional
con-di-ció-nar *v.* to condition
con-di-men-to *m.* condiment; seasoning
con-do-len-cia *f.* condolence
con-do-nar *v.* to condone
con-du-cir(se) *v.* to steer; lead; conduct; drive
con-duc-ta *f.* behavior
con-duc-to *m.* duct; conduit
co-nec-tar *v.* to connect
co-ne-ji-to *m.* bunny
co-ne-jo *m.* rabbit
co-ne-xion *f.* connection

con-fec-ción *f.* confection
con-fec-cio-nar *v.* to make up; concoct
con-fe-de-ra-ción *f.* confederation; confederacy
con-fe-ren-cia *f.* lecture; conference
con-fe-rir *v.* to grant; bestow
con-fe-sar(se) *v.* to confess; admit
con-fe-sion *f.* confession; avowal
con-fe-sio-na-rio *m.* confessional
con-fe-so *m.* confessor
con-fe-ti *m.* confetti
con-fia-ble *adj.* reliable
con-fian-za *f.* dependence; confidence
con-fiar *v.* trust; rely; confide
con-fi-den-cial *adj.* confidential
con-fi-gu-ra-ción *f.* configuration
con-fin *m.* confines; bound
con-fir-ma-ción *f.* corroboration
con-fir-mar *v.,* ratify; confirm
con-fis-ca-ción *f.* confiscation
con-fis-car *v.* to confiscate
con-fla-gra-ción *f.* conflagration
con-flic-to *m.* clash; conflict
con-for-mar(se) *v.* to adjust; conform
con-for-me *adj.* similar; agreeable
con-for-mi-dad *f.* conformity
con-for-tar *v.* to comfort
con-fron-ta-ción *f.* confrontation
con-fron-tar *v.* to confront
con-fun-dir(se) *v.* to confound; perplex; puzzle; baffle
con-fu-sion *f.* mess; jumble; confusion
con-fu-tar *v.* to disprove; confute
con-ge-la-ción *f.* frostbite
con-ge-lar(se) *v.* to freeze; congeal

con-ge-ni-to *adj.* congenital
con-ges-tion *f.* congestion
con-glo-me-ra-do *m.* conglomerate
con-gre-gar(se) *v.* to flock; assemble
con-gre-so *m.* convention; congress
con-je-tu-ra *f.* surmise; guess; conjecture
con-je-tu-rar *v.* conjecture
con-ju-gar(se) *v.* conjugate
con-jun-ción *f.* conjunction
con-jun-to *m.* whole; ensemble
con-ju-rar *v.* to conjure
con-me-mo-ra-ción *f.* commemoration
con-me-mo-rar *v.* to commemorate
con-me-mo-ra-ti-vo *adj.* memorial
con-mo-cion *f.* stir; concussion; commotion
con-mo-ve-dor *adj.* stirring
con-mo-ver(-se) *v.* to shake; move; thril
co-no *m.* cone
cons-truc-ti-vo *adj.* constructive
cons-truir *v.* to build; structure; construct
con-sue-lo *m.* consolation
con-sul-tar *v.* to consult
con-su-mar *v.* to carry out
con-su-mi-dor *m.* consumer
con-su-mir(se) *v.* to waste away; consume
con-su-mo *m.* consumption
con-sun-cion *f.* consumption
con-tac-to *m.* contact
con-ta-giar(se) *v.* to catch; infect
con-ta-gio *m.* contagion
con-ta-gio-so *adj.* catching
con-ta-mi-na-ción *f.* pollution; contamination
con-ta-mi-nar(se) *v.* to contaminate
con-tar(se) *v.* to number; count; relate; tell
con-tem-pla-ción *f.* contemplation

con-tem-plar *v.* to view; meditate
con-tem-po-ra-neo *adj.* contemporary
con-ten-der *v.* to strive; conten; contest
con-ten-dien-te *v.* contestant
con-te-ner(se) *v.* to hold; include; contain
con-te-ni-do *m.* content
con-ten-to *adj.* happy; contented
con-tes-ta-ción *f.* answer
con-tes-tar *v.* reply; answer
con-tien-da *f.* contest; strife; struggle
con-ti-guo *adj.* adjacent
con-ti-nen-tal *adj.* continental
con-ti-nen-te *m.* mainland; continent; container
con-tin-gen-cia *f.* contingency
con-ti-nua-ción *f.* continuation
con-ti-nuar *v.* to continue
con-ti-nuo *adj.* constant; perpetual; continuous
con-to-near(se) *v.* to strut
con-tor-no *m.* contour; outline
con-tra *prep.* versus; against *adv.* against
con-tra-ba-jo *m.* bass
con-tra-ban-dis-ta *m.*, *f.* smuggler
con-tra-ban-do *m.* smuggling; contraband
con-trac-ción *f.* contraction
con-tra-de-cir *v.* to contradict
con-tra-dic-ción *f.* contradiction
con-traer(se) *v.* to contract
con-tral-to *m.*, *f.* alto; contralto
con-tra-rie-dad *f.* snag; vexation
con-tra-rio *adj.* adverse; contrary
con-tras-tar *v.* contrast
con-tras-te *m.* contrast
con-tra-tiem-po *m.* upset; mishap

con-tra-to m. contract; agreement
con-tra-ven-ta-na f. shutter
con-tri-bu-ción f. task; contribution
con-tri-buir v. to contribute
con-trol m. control
con-tro-lar v. to control
con-tro-ver-sia f. controversy
con-tu-sion f. bruise; contusion
con-va-le-cen-cía f. convalescence
con-va-le-cer v. convalesce
con-va-le-cien-te m., f. convalescent
con-ve-nien-cia f. expediency
con-ve-nien-te adj. handy; fitting; convenient
con-ve-nir(se) v. agree; befit
con-ven-to m. abbey
con-ver-gir v. to converge
con-ver-sa-ción f. conversation
con-ver-sar v. to converse
con-ver-tir(se) v. to turn into
con-ve-xo adj. convex
con-vic-cion f. conviction
con-vi-da-do-m. guest
con-vi-dar(se) v. to invite
con-vi-te m. invitation
con-vo-ca-ción f. convocation
con-vo-car v. to summon
con-voy m. convoy
con-vul-sion f. convulsion
co-nac m. brandy
co-o-pe-ra-cion f. teamwork
co-o-pe-rar v. to cooperate
co-or-di-na-ción f. coordination
co-or-di-nar v. to coordinate
co-pa f. goblet
co-pe-te m. tuft
co-pia f. imitation; copy
co-piar v. to copy
co-pio-so adj. copious

co-que-ta f. coquette
co-que-tear v. to flirt
co-ral adj. choral
co-ra-zon m. heart
co-ra-zo-na-da f. hunch
cor-ba-ta f. tie
cor-cel m. steed
cor-che-te m. clasp
cor-cho m. cork
cor-de-ro m. lamb
cor-don m. cord
co-reo-gra-fo m. choreographer
cor-ne-ta f. bugler
cor-ni-sa f. cornice
co-ro m. chorus
co-ro-la f. corolla
co-ro-na f. crown
co-ro-nar v. to crown
co-ro-na-ria f. coronary
cor-pi-ño m. bodice
cor-po-ral adj. corporal
cor-po-reo adj. bodily
corps m., pl. corps
co-rral m. corral
co-rrea f. strap
co-rrec-ción f. propriety
co-rrec-to, -ta adj. right
co-rre-dor m. broker
co-rre-gir(se) v. stream; run
co-rre-ria f. foray
co-rres-pon-der(se) v. to concern
co-rrien-te adj. current
co-rroer(se) v. to erode
co-rrom-per(se) v. to rot
co-rro-sion f. corrosion
co-rro-si-vo adj. corrosive
co-rrup-ción f. corruption
cor-se m. corset
cor-ta-do adj. abrupt
cor-ta-du-ra f. slit
cor-tan-te adj. edged
cor-tar(se) v. chop; cut; clip
cor-te m. court
cor-tes adj. civil; polite
cor-te-sia f. civility
cor-ti-jo m. grange
cor-to adj. brief
co-sa f. affair
co-se-cha f. crop
co-ser v. to sew
cos-me-ti-co adj. cosmetic

cos-mos m. cosmos
cos-qui-llear v. to tickle
cos-ta f. cost
cos-tar v. to cost
cos-te m. price
cos-ti-lla f. rib
cos-to-so, -sa adj. expensive
cos-tum-bre f. custom
cos-tu-ra f. joint
co-ti-dia-no adj. daily
co-yo-te m. coyote
cra-neo m. skull
cra-ter m. crater
crea-cion f. creation
crea-dor m. creator
crear v. to make; create
cre-cer(se) v. to increase
cre-ci-mien-to m. growth
cre-cien-te m. crescent
cre-di-to m. credit
cre-do m. credo
cre-du-lo adj. credulous
creen-cia f. faith
creer(se) v. to think
crei-ble adj. plausible
cre-ma f. cream
cre-sa f. maggot
cres-po adj. crisp
cre-ta f. chalk
cria-da f. maid
criar(se) v. to raise; nurse
cri-men m. felony
crip-ta f. crypt
cri-sis f. breakdown
cri-sol m. crucible
cris-tal m. crystal; glass
cris-tia-nis-mo m. Christianity
Christo m. Christ
cri-te-rio m. criterion
cri-ti-ca f. censure; criticism
cri-ti-car v. to criticize
cri-ti-co, -ca adj. critical
cro-ma-ti-co adj. chromatic
cro-mo m. chrome
cro-ni-ca f. chronicle
cro-ni-co adj. chronic
cro-no-me-trar v. to tell time
cro-quet m. croquet
cro-que-ta f. croquette
cru-ce m. intersection
cru-ci-fi-car v. to crucify

cru-ci-fi-xion f. crucifixion
cru-do adj. crude; raw
cruel adj. heartless; cruel
cru-ji-do m. crack
cru-jir v. to crunch
cruz f. cross
cru-za-da f. crusade
cru-za-do, -da m. crusader
cru-zar(se) v. to cross
cua-dra-do m. square
cua-dran-te m. quadrant
cua-drar(se) v. to tally
cua-dri-lon-go adj. oblong
cua-dro m. square; picture
cua-ja-da f. curd
cual adv. as; pron. which
cua-li-dad f. quality
cual-quier adj. any; either
cuan adv. how
cuan-do prep. when; adv. when; since
cuan-ti-a f. amount
cuan-to adj. as much as
cuan-to adj. how much?
cua-ren-ta adj. forty
cua-ren-ta-vo adj. fortieth
cua-res-ma f. Lent
cuar-te-ar v. to cut up; to quarter
cuar-tel m. Mil. barracks
cuar-to m. quarter; fourth
cuar-zo m. quartz
cua-si adv. almost
cua-te adj. twin; alike
cua-tre-re-ar v. to rustle or steal
cua-tre-ro adj. to steal horses
cua-tro m. four
cua-tro-cien-tos adj. four hundred
cu-be-ta f. bucket
cu-bier-to f. casing; cover
cu-bil m. den
cu-bi-le-te m. tumbler
cu-bo m. pailful
cu-brir(se) v. to conceal; to cover
cu-ca-ra-cha f. cockroach
cu-co adj. cute
cu-cha-ra f. spoon
cu-cha-ra-da f. spoonful
cu-che-ta f. cabin

cu-chi-che-ar *intr.* to whisper
cu-chi-che-o *m.* whispering
cu-cha-ri-lla *f.* teaspoon
cu-chi-lla *m.* knife
cue-le *m.* collar
cuen-ta *f.* count; bill
cuen-ta-go-tas *m.* eyedropper
cuen-te-ro *adj.* gossipy
cuen-tis-ta *m.* storyteller
cuen-to *m.* tale
cuer-da *f.* cord
cuer-do *adj. & m.f.* sensible; sane person
cuer-no *m.* horn
cue-ro *m.* hide
cuer-pe-ar *intr.* to dodge something
cuer-po *m.* body
cuer-vo *m.* crow
cues-ta *f.* hill; slope
cues-tión *f.* count; bill
cues-tio-na-bel *adj.* debatable; questionable
cues-tio-nar *v.* to debate; discuss
cues-tio-na-rio *m.* questionaire
cue-va *f.* cave
cui-da-do *m.* heed
cui-da-dor *m.,f.* caretaker
cui-da-do-so *adj.* careful
cui-dar(se) *v.* to look after
cui-ta *f.* grief
cu-lan-tro *m.* coriander
cu-le-bra *f.* snake
cu-le-bri-lla *f.* MED. ringworm
cu-li-na-rio, a *adj.* culinary
cul-mi-na-ción *f.* culmination
cul-mi-nan-te *adj.* culminating
cul-mi-nar *v.* to culminate
cul-pa *f.* fault
cul-pa-bi-li-dad *f.* guilt
cul-pa-ble *adj.* guilty
cul-par *v.* to criticize; to accuse
cul-ti-va-cion *f.* cultivation
cul-ti-var *v.* farm; to cultivate
cul-ti-vo *m.* cultivation

cul-to *adj.* cultured
cul-tu-ra *f.* culture
cum-bre *f.* peak; top
cum-plea-nos *m.* birthday
cum-pli-do, -da *adj.* perfect; complete
cum-pli-dor *adj.* reliable; trustworthy
cum-pli-men-tar *v.* to compliment
cum-pli-mien-to *m.* fulfillment
cum-plir *v.* to accomplish
cun-dir *intr.* to expand; to spread
cu-na-da *f.* sister-in-law
cu-na-do *m.* brother-in-law
cu-ple *m.* popular song
cu-po *m.* quota
cu-pon *m.* coupon
cu-ra *f.* cure
cu-ra-ble *adj.* curable
cu-ra-cion *f.* treatment, cure
cu-ran-de-ro, a *m.,f.* quack
cu-rar(se) *v.* to heal; recover
cu-ria *f.* court
cu-rio-se-ar *intr.* to pry, snoop
cu-rio-si-dad *adj.* curiosity
cu-rio-so *adj.* curious
cu-rri-cu-lum vi-tae *m.* resume
cur-sar *v.* to study
cur-si *adj.* vulgar
cur-si-vo *adj.* cursive
cur-so *m.* course
cur-ti-do *m.* tanning as in leather
cur-ti-dor *m.* tanner
cur-tiem-bre *m.* tannery
cur-tir(se) *v.* to coarsen
cur-va *f.* bend; curve
cur-va-do, a *adj.* bent; curved
cur-var *v.* to curve
cur-va-tu-ra *f.* curvature
cus-to-dia *f.* keeping
cus-to-diar *v.* to protect; to watch over
cus-to-dio *adj. & m.* guardian
cu-ti-cu-la *f.* curicle
cu-tis *m.* complexion; skin

da-ble adj. feasible; possible

dac-ti-lo-gra-ti-a f. typewriting; typing

dac-ti-lo-gra-fo m.f. typist

da-di-va f. gift; present

da-di-vo-si-dad f. liberality; generosity

da-di-vo-so, a adj. lavish; generous

da-do m. die

dal-to-nis-mo m. colorblindness

da-ma f. lady

da-mi-se-la f. damsel

dam-ni-fi-car v. to harm; to damage

dam-ni-fi-ca-do, a adj. harmed; damaged

dan-za f. dance

da-ñar(se) v. to hurt; to damage

da-ni-no, -na adj. harmful; damaging

da-no m. damage

dar(se) v. to give; allow

dar-do m. arrow; dart

dar-se-na f. dock; inner harbor; port

da-ta f. items; date

da-tar v. to date

da-to m. fact

de prep. of; from; with

de-am-bu-lar intr. to roam or wander around

de-ba-jo adv. underneath; below

de-ba-te m. discussion; debate

de-ba-tir v. to discuss; to debate

de-be m. debit

de-ber v. to owe m. obligation or duty

de-bi-da-men-te adv. duly; properly

de-bi-do adj. fitting; due

de-bil adj. feeble; weak; faint

de-bi-li-dad f. weakness

de-bi-li-tar tr. & reflex to weaken

de-but m. opening; debut

de-bu-tan-te f. debutant adj.

beginning

de-ca-den-cia f. decline; decadence

de-ca-den-te adj. & m.f. decadent

de-ca-er v. to decay

de-cai-mien-to m. feebleness, weakness; dejection

de-ca-no m. dean

de-can-ta-ción f. pouring off

de-can-tar v. to pour off; to decant

de-ca-pi-tar v. to behead

de-cen-cia f. decency

de-ce-nio m. decade

de-cen-te adj. decent

de-cep-cion f. deception; disappointment

de-cep-cio-nar v. to disappoint

de-ce-so m. death; decease

de-ci-di-do, a adj. resolute; determined

de-ci-dir v. to resolve

de-ci-mal adj. decimal

de-cir v. to state; say

de-ci-sion f. decision; verdict; ruling

de-ci-si-vo adj. crucial; conclusive; decisive

de-cla-mar tr. & intri. to recite

de-cla-ra-ción f. declaration; statement; evidence

de-cla-ra-da-men-te adv. openly; manifestly

de-cla-rar(se) v. to propose; declare

de-cli-na-cion f. decline

de-cli-nar v. to decline; to refuse

de-cli-ve m. incline; slope

de-co-lo-ra-ción f. discoloration

de-co-lo-ran-te m. decolorant

de-co-lo-rar v. to fade; to discolor

de-co-mi-sar v. to seize; confiscation

de-co-ra-do m. scenery or set in a theater

de-co-ra-dor, ra adj.

ornamental; decorative

de-co-rar v. to decorate

de-co-ra-ti-vo, a adj. ornamental; decorative

de-co-ro m. honor; respect

de-co-ro-so, a adj. decent; honorable

de-cre-cer v. to diminish

de-cre-ci-mien-to m. decrease

de-cre-pi-to, -ta adj. aged; decrepit

de-cre-tar v. to decree; order

de-dal m. thimble

de-di-car(se) v. to devote

de-do m. finger

de-du-cir v. to conclude; deduce; subtract

de-fa-mar v. to defame

de-fec-ción f. defection

de-fec-to m. flaw; defect

de-fec-tuo-so, a adj. faulty; defective

de-fen-der v. to defend

de-fen-sa f. defense

de-fen-sor m. supporter

de-fe-ren-cia f. difference

de-fi-cien-cia f. lacking; deficient

de-fi-ni-ción f. definition; determination

de-fi-nir v. to define

de-for-mar(se) v. to loose shape

de-frau-da-ción f. cheating; fraud

de-frau-dar v. to cheat

de-fun-ción f. death; demise

de-ge-ne-rar v. to decline; to degenerate

de-go-lla-de-ro m. windpipe; throat

de-go-llar v. to cut the throat

de-gra-dar(se) v. to demean

de-gus-ta-ción f. sampling; tasting

dei-dad f. deify

de-ja-do, a adj. negligent; careless

de-jar(se) v. to quit; let

de-jo m. abandonmnet

del contr. of de and el

de-lan-ta adv. ahead; before; in front

de-lan-te-ro adj. forward; front

de-la-tar v. to inform; to denounce, expose

de-le-ga-ción f. delegation

de-le-gar v. to delegate

de-lei-ta-ble adj. enjoyable; delightful

de-lei-tar(se) v. to delight

del-ga-do adj. thin; slim

de-li-be-ra-do, a adj. intentional; deliberate

de-li-ca-do, -da adj. sensitive

de-li-cia f. pleasure; delight

de-lin-cuen-te adj. delinquent

de-li-ne-ar v. to outline; delineate

de-li-ran-te adj. delirious

de-li-rar v. to rave; to be delirious

de-man-da f. challenge; demand

de-man-dar v. to demand; to ask for

de-ma-sí-a f. surplus; more than what is needed

de-ma-sia-do adv. too much

de-me-ri-to m. demerit

de-mo-cra-cia f. democracy

de-mo-le-dor, ra adj. demolishing

de-mo-ler v. to demolish; to destroy

de-mo-li-ción f. destruction

de-mo-nio m. devil; demon

de-mo-ra f. wait; delay

de-mo-rar(se) v. to delay

de-mos-trar v. to display; to demonstrate

de-mos-tra-ti-vo, a adj. & m. demonstrative

de-mu-dar v. to change

de-ne-gar v. to reject; to refuse

de-no-da-do, a adj. bold

de-no-mi-na-ción f. denomination

de-no-mi-na-dor, ra adj. denominating

de-nos-tar v. to insult; to

abuse

de-no-tar v. to denote

den-si-dad f. density

den-so adj. thick; dense

den-ta-du-ra f. denture

den-tal adj. dental

den-te-lle-ar v. to bite; to nibble

den-te-ra f. jealousy; envy

den-ti-fri-co m. toothpaste

den-tis-ta m., f. dentist

den-tro adv. within; inside

de-nue-do m. courage; bravery

de-nues-to m. insult

de-nun-ciar v. to denounce

de-pa-rar v. to supply

de-par-ta-men-to m. office; department; section

de-par-tir v. to converse; to talk

de-pen-den-cia f. dependence; kinship; reliance

de-pen-der v. to depend

de-plo-rar v. deplore

de-po-ner v. depose; to put aside

de-por-ta-ción f. deportation

de-por-tar v. to exile; deport

de-por-te m. sport

de-po-si-tar v. to bank

de-pó-si-to m. deposit

de-pra-va-ción f. corruption

de-pra-va-do, a adj. corrupted

de-pra-var v. to deprave

de-pre-car v. to implore

de-pre-ca-to-rio adj. imploring

de-pre-ciar v. to depreciate

de-pre-dar v. to pillage

de-pre-sión f. slump; depression

de-pri-mi-do adj. depressed

de-pri-mir v. to depress

de-re-cho adj. right; upright

de-ri-var(se) v. to drift

der-ma-to-lo-gi-a f. dermatology

der-ma-to-lo-go m., f. dermatologist

de-rra-mar(se) v. to overflow; to spill

de-rri-bar v. to overthrow; to knock down

de-rro-char v. to waste

de-rro-che m. squandering

de-rro-tar v. to ruin

des-a-co-plar v. to disconnect

des-a-fiar v. to defy

des-a-fio m. challenge

des-a-gra-dar v. to displease

des-a-hu-ciar v. to evict

des-ai-re m. slight

des-a-len-tar v. to dishearten

des-a-ni-mar(se) v. dismay

des-a-ni-mo m. depression

des-a-pro-bar v. disapprove

des-a-rre-glar(se) v. derange

des-a-rre-glo m. disorder

des-a-rro-llar(se) v. to unfold

des-a-rro-llo m. development

des-a-so-sie-go m. unrest

de-sas-tre m. disaster

des-a-tar(se) v. to undo

des-a-ten-to adj. unthinking

des-a-ti-no m. blunder

des-a-yu-nar(se) v. breakfast

des-a-yu-no m. breakfast

des-ca-li-fi-car v. disqualify

des-can-sar v. to rest

des-can-so m. rest

des-ca-ra-do adj. brazen

des-car-gar(se) v. to unload

des-cen-den-te adj. downward

des-cen-der v. descent

des-ci-frar v. to decipher

des-co-lo-rar(se) v. fade

des-com-po-ner(se) v. to decompose

des-con-cer-tar(se) v. to embarrass

des-con-fiar v. to distrust

des-co-no-cer v. to disavow

des-con-ten-to m. discontent

des-con-ti-nuar v. to discontinue

des-cor-tés adj. impolite

des-co-ser(se) v. to come apart

des-cri-bir v. to describe

des-crip-ción f. description

des-cu-brir v. to find

des-cui-da-do adj. remiss

des-cui-dar v. to neglect
des-de prep. since; from
des-de-nar v. to disdain
des-di-cha f. unhappiness
de-sea-ble adj. elegible
de-sear v. hope; wish; desire
des-e-char v. to reject
des-em-bo-car v. to land
des-em-bol-sar v. disburse
des-en-cov-var v. to unbend
des-en-la-ce m. ending
de-seo m. craving
de-ser-tar v. to defect
de-ser-tor m. deserter
des-es-pe-rar v. to despair
des-fal-car v. to embezzle
des-fi-gu-rar v. to blemish; to disfigure
des-fi-le m. parade
des-ga-rrar(se) v. to tear
des-gas-te m. waste
des-gra-cia f. misfortune
des-gra-cia-do m. unfortunate
des-ha-cer(se) v. to unwrap
des-he-lar(se) v. to thaw
des-hi-dra-ta-ción f. dehydration
des-hon-ra f. disgrace
des-hon-rar v. to disgrace
des-i-gual adj. irregular
des-in-flar v. to deflate
des-in-te-res m. disinterest
de-sis-tir v. to desist
des-leal adj. disloyal
des-li-zar(se) v. to glide
des-lo-car(se) v. dislocate
des-lum-brar v. to blind
des-lus-trar(se) v. to dull
des-lus-tre m. tarnish
des-ma-yo m. swoon
des-mi-ga-jar(se) v. crumble
des-mon-tar(se) v. to dismantle
des-na-tar v. to skim
des-nu-dar(se) v. to undress
des-nu-do, a adj. nude; bare
des-nu-tri-ción f. malnutrition
des-o-be-de-cer v. to disobey
des-o-cu-pa-do adj. free
des-o-do-ri-zar v. deodorize
de-so-la-ción f. desolation

des-or-den m. mess
des-or-ga-ni-zar v. to disrupt
des-pa-cio adv. slowly
des-pa-char v. to speed
des-pe-dir(se) v. to dismiss; to see off
des-pei-na-do adj. unkempt
des-per-di-ciar v. to waste
des-per-tar(se) v. to awaken; to wake up
des-pier-to adj. awake
des-ple-gar(se) v. to unfold
des-po-jar(se) v. to strip
des-po-sar(se) v. to marry
des-pre-cia-ble adj. vile; worthless
des-pre-ciar(se) v. to scorn
des-pues adv. after; later
des-te-rrar v. to banish
des-te-tar(se) v. to wean
des-ti-lar v. to distill
des-tre-za f. dexterity; skill
des-truc-cion f. destruction
des-truir v. to destroy
des-u-nir v. to disunite
des-va-ne-cer(se) v. vanish
des-ver-gon-za-do adj. unabashed
des-viar(se) v. to divert; wander
de-ta-lla-do adj. elaborate
de-ta-llar v. to itemize
de-ta-lle m. detail
de-tec-ti-ve m. sleuth
de-ten-ción f. arrest
de-te-ner(se) v. to arrest
de-te-rio-rar(se) v. to decay
de-ter-mi-nar v. to decide
de-tes-tar v. to hate
de-tras adv. aback; behind
deu-da f. debt
de-va-nar v. to wind
de-vas-tar v. to devastate
de-vo-ción f. devotion
de-vol-ver v. to refund; return
de-vo-rar v. to devour
dia m. day
dia-blo m. devil
dia-co-no m. deacon
dia-frag-ma m. diaphragm
diag-nos-ti-car v. to diagnose
dia-gra-ma m. diagram
dia-lec-to m. dialect

dia-man-te m. diamond
dia-rio m. daily
di-bu-jan-te m. cartoonist
di-bu-jar v. to sketch
dic-cio-na-rio m. dictionary
di-ciem-bre m. December
dic-ta-dor m. dictator
dic-tar v. to dictate
di-cho m. remark; saying
die-ci-nue-ve adj. nineteen
die-cio-cho adj. eighteen
die-ci-séis adj. sixteen
die-ci-sie-te adj. seventeen
dien-te m. tooth
diez adj. ten
di-fe-ren-cia f. difference
dife-ren-te adj. different
di-fe-rir v. to defer
di-fí-cil adj. hard; difficult
di-fun-to adj. deceased
di-fu-so adj. widespread
di-ge-rir v. to digest
di-ges-tion f. digestion
di-gi-to m. digit
dig-ni-dad f. dignity
di-la-tar(se) v. to dilate
di-li-gen-te adj. diligent
di-luir v. to dilute
di-lu-viar v. to pour
di-men-sion f. dimension
di-nas-tia f. dynasty
di-ne-ro m. money
dios m. god
dio-sa f. goddess
di-plo-ma-cia f. diplomacy
di-rec-ción f. direction
di-rec-ta-men-te adv.
   straight
di-rec-to adj. straight
di-ri-gir(se) v. to lead; control
dis-cer-nir v. to discern
dis-ci-pli-na f. discipline
dis-ci-pli-nar v. discipline
dis-co m. record
dis-cre-par v. to disagree
dis-cre-to adj. discreet
dis-cul-pa f. excuse
dis-cul-par v. to excuse
dis-cu-sion f. discussion
dis-cu-tir v. to argue
di-se-mi-nar v. to spread
di-se-nar v. to design
dis-fraz m. costume

dis-fra-zar v. to disguise
dis-gus-tar(se) v. to annoy
dis-gus-to m. displeasure
dis-lo-ca-ción f. dislocation
di-sol-var(se) v. to dissolve
dis-per-sar(se0 v. to dispel
dis-po-ner(se) v. ready
dis-pues-to adj. willing
dis-pu-ta f. dispute
dis-pu-tar v. fight; quarrel
dis-tan-te adj. distant
dis-tin-guir v. distinguish
dis-traer(se) v. to divert; dis-
   tract
dis-tri-buir v. to distribute
dis-tur-bio m. trouble
di-sua-dir v. to deter
di-van m. couch
di-ver-gir v. to diverge
di-ver-sion f. amusement
di-ver-so adj. varied; different
di-vi-dir(se) v. to split; divide
di-vi-no adj. divine
di-vor-ciar(se) v. to divorce
do-blar(se) v. fold; double
do-ce adj. twelve
do-ce-na f. dozen
do-cil adj. meek
do-lar m. dollar
do-ler(se) v. to pain; hurt
do-lor m. ache; pain
do-mes-ti-car(se) v. to
   domesticate
do-min-go m. Sunday
do-nan-te m. donor
do-ñar v. to donate
don-de adv. where
dor-mir(se) v. to sleep
dos adj. two
dra-gon m. dragon
dra-ma-ti-co adj. dramatic
dro-ga f. drug
du-cha f. shower
du-char-se v. to shower
du-dar v. to hesitate; doubt
due-na f. owner; master
dul-ce m. candy
duo-de-ci-mo adj. twelfth
du-pli-car(se) v. duplicate
du-que-sa f. duchess
du-ra-de-ro adj. durable
du-ran-te prep. during
du-ro adj. stiff; hard

e-ba-no *m.* ebony
e-brie-dad *f.* inebriation
e-brio *m.* drunk
e-clec-ti-co *adj.* eclectic
e-cle-sias-ti-co *adj.* ecclesiastic
e-clip-sar *v.* eclipse
e-clip-se *m.* eclipse
e-co *m.* echo
e-co-lo-gia *f.* ecology
e-co-no-mia *f.* economy
e-co-no-mis-ta *m.* economist
e-co-no-mi-zar *v.* economize
e-cua-ción *f.* equation
e-cua-dor *m.* equator
e-cua-ni-me *adj.* impartial
e-cua-to-rial *adj.* equatorial
ec-ze-ma *m.* eczema
e-cha-da *f.* toss
e-char(se) *v.* throw; cast away
e-dad *f.* age
e-di-ción *f.* edition
e-dic-to *m.* edict
e-di-fi-car *v.* edify
e-di-tar *v.* edict
e-di-tor *m.* editor
e-di-to-rial *m.* editorial
e-du-ca-ción *f.* education
e-du-car *v.* instruct; teach; train; educate
e-fe-bo *m.* adolescent
e-fec-ti-vi-dad *f.* effectiveness
e-fec-to *m.* result; impact; effect
e-fec-tuar *v.* contrive; effect
e-fi-ca-cia *f.* efficacy
e-fi-cien-cia *f.* efficiency
e-fi-cien-te *adj.* efficient
e-fu-sion *f.* effusion
e-fu-si-vo *adj.* effusive
e-go *m.* ego
e-gre-sar *v.* graduate
e-je-cu-ción *f.* execution
e-je-cu-tar *v.* execute
e-je-cu-ti-vo *adj.* executive
e-jem-plar *m.* example
e-jem-pli-fi-car *v.* exemplify
e-jem-plo *m.* example
e-jer-cer *v.* exercise
e-jer-ci-cio *m.* drill; exercise; practice
e-jer-ci-to *m.* army

e-lec-to *adj.* elect
e-lec-to-ra-do *m.* electorate
e-lec-tri-ci-dad *f.* electricity
e-lec-tri-fi-car *v.* to electrify
e-lec-tro-cu-tar *v.* to electrocute
e-lec-trom *m.* electron
e-le-fan-te *m.* elephant
e-le-gan-cia *f.* grace
e-le-gan-te *adj.* elegant
e-le-gi-do *adj.* chosen
e-le-gir *v.* to choose; elect
e-le-men-tal *adj.* elementary; essential; elemental
e-le-va-ción *f.* elevation
e-le-va-do *adj.* high
e-le-var(se) *v.* to elevate; lift
e-li-mi-nar *v.* to eliminate
e-lip-se *f.* ellipse
e-lip-ti-co *adj.* elliptical
e-li-xir *m.* elixir
e-lo-cuen-cia *f.* eloquence
e-lo-cuen-te *adj.* eloquent
e-lo-giar *v.* to eulogize
e-lu-ci-dar *v.* to elucidate
e-lu-dir *v.* to elude
e-lla *pron., f.* she
e-llas *pl. pron., f.* them; they
e-llo *pron.* it
e-llos *pl. pron., m.* them; they
e-ma-nar *v.* to emanate
e-man-ci-par *v.* to emancipate
em-ba-ja-da *f.* embassy
em-ba-ja-dor *m.* ambassador
em-bal-sa-mar *v.* to embalm
em-ba-ra-za-da *adj.* pregnant
em-ba-ra-zo, -za *m.* embarrassment; pregnancy
em-bar-car(se) *v.* to embark
em-bar-que *m.* shipment
em-bas-tar *v.* to tack; quilt
em-be-ber *v.* to wet; absorb
em-be-le-cer *v.* to embellish
em-bes-tir *v.* to attack
em-blan-que-cer *v.* to bleach
em-ble-ma *m.* emblem
em-bo-lia *f.* embolism
em-bo-rra-char(se) *v.* to get drunk
em-bos-car *v.* to ambush
em-bo-ta-do, -da *adj.* dull
em-bo-tar *v.* to dull

em-bo-te-llar v. to bottle
em-bra-ve-cer v. to infuriate
em-bria-gar(se) v. to intoxicate
em-brion m. embryo
em-bro-llar v. to embroil
e-mer-gen-cia f. emergency
e-mi-gra-do m. emigrant
e-mi-grar v. to emigrate
e-mi-sa-rio m. emissary
e-mi-sion f. issue
e-mi-tir v. to give off; emit
e-mo-ción f. feeling; emotion
e-mo-cio-nar v. to affect
e-mo-ti-vo, -a adj. emotional
em-pal-mar v. to splice; join
em-pa-par(se) v. to drench; wet
em-pa-pe-la-do m. lining
em-pa-pe-lar v. to line with paper
em-pa-re-da-do m. recluse; captive; prisoner
em-pa-tar v. to tie
em-pa-te m. impediment; draw; connection
em-pe-ci-na-do adj. obstinate
em-pe-ci-nar v. to be obstinate
em-pe-llar v. to push
em-pe-no m. patron; pledge; insistence
em-peo-rar(se) v. to become worse
em-pe-ra-dor m. emperor
em-pe-ra-triz f. empress
em-pe-ro conj. however
em-pe-zar v. to start; begin
em-pí-ri-co adj. empirical
em-plas-tar v. to hamper; plaster
em-plas-to m. plaster
em-ple-a-do m. employee
em-ple-a-dor m. employer
em-ple-ar(se) v. to employ
em-pleo m. job; work
em-plu-mar v. to feater
em-po-bre-ci-do adj. impoverished
em-pren-der v. to begin
em-pre-sa f. company; business
em-pre-sa-rio m. director

em-pu-jar v. to thrust; push
em-pu-je m. push
e-mu-la-ción f. emulation
e-mul-sion f. emulsion
en prep. in
e-na-je-na-ble adj. alienable
e-na-je-na-ción f. alienation
e-na-je-nar v. to alienate
e-na-no m. dwarf
e-nar-de-cer v. to ignite
en-ca-be-za-mien-to m. heading; caption
en-ca-be-zar v. to enroll; to head
en-ca-jar v. to force; insert
en-ca-je m. insertion; lace
en-ca-lle-cer v. to develop a callous
en-can-di-lar v. to excite; stir
en-can-ta-do adj. happy; delighted
en-can-ta-dor adj. charming; enchanting
en-can-ta-mien-to m. enchantment
en-can-tar v. to charm; to enchant
en-can-to m. enchantment
en-ca-po-ta-do adj. cloudy
en-ca-po-tar v. to become overcasted
en-ca-ra-mar v. to elevate; to raise; to promote
en-ca-rar v. to confront
en-car-gar v. to advise; place in charge; request
en-car-go m. assignment; task; job
en-car-na-ción f. incarnation
en-car-nar v. to heal; to mix; to embody
en-car-ni-za-do adj. bloody
en-ca-rri-llar v. to guide
en-ce-fa-li-tis f. encephalitis
en-cen-de-dor m. lighter
en-cen-der(se) v. to ignite
en-ce-rar v. to polish
en-ce-rrar v. to confine
en-ci-clo-pe-dia f. encyclopedia
en-cie-rro m. closing; seclusion; enclosure
en-ci-ma adv. above

en-ci-ma de *adv.* upon
en-cin-ta *adj.* pregnant
en-co-co-rar *v.* to annoy
en-co-ger *v.* to shrink; contract; become smaller
en-co-gi-mien-to *m.* shrinkage; contraction
en-co-lar *v.* to glue
en-co-men-dar(se) *v.* to commend
en-co-miar *v.* to extol
en-co-nar *v.* to irritate; anger
en-con-trar(se) *v.* to find; encounter
en-cor-var *v.* to curve
en-cru-ci-ja-da *f.* intersection
en-cua-der-nar *v.* to bind
en-cua-drar *v.* to frame
en-cu-brir *v.* to hide
en-cuen-tro *m.* meeting; collision; encounter
en-cues-ta *f.* inquiry
en-cum-brar *v.* to honor; to lift; to raise
en-cur-tir *v.* to preserve
en-chi-la-da *f.* enchilada
en-chu-far *v.* to couple; to connect; to merge
en-chu-fe *m.* plug; connection; socket
en-de-ble *adj.* weak
en-de-mi-co *adj.* endemic
en-de-re-zar *v.* to direct; to straighten
en-di-bla-do *adj.* diabolical
en-di-bia *f.* endive
en-do-sa-ble *adj.* endorsable
en-do-san-te *m.* endorser
en-do-sar *v.* to endorse
en-do-so *m.* endorsement
en-dul-zar *v.* to make sweet
en-du-re-cer(se) *v.* to toughen
e-ne-mi-go *m.* enemy
e-ne-mis-tad *f.* animosity
en-ner-gia *f.* energy
e-ner-gi-co *adj.* energetic
e-ne-ro *m.* January
e-ner-va-ción *f.* enervation
e-ner-var *v.* to weaken
en-fa-dar *v.* to annoy; to make angry
en-fa-sis *m.* stress; emphasis

en-fer-mar *v.* to become ill
en-fer-me-dad *f.* sickness
en-fer-me-ra *f.* nurse
en-fer-mo *adj.* ill
en-fer-vo-ri-zar *v.* to encourage; to enliven
en-fi-lar *v.* to string; to point; direct
en-fo-car(se) *v.* to focus
en-fren-te de *adv.* in front of
en-friar(se) *v.* to cool
en-fu-re-cer *v.* to make furious; to infuriate
en-gan-char *v.* to persuade
en-gan-che *m.* hook
en-ga-na-di-zo *adj.* credulous
en-ga-nar(se) *v.* to fool; to deceive
en-ga-no *m.* mistake; trick; error; fraud
en-ga-no-so *adj.* tricking; deceitful; deceiving
en-gar-zar *v.* to curl; to mount; to thread
en-gas-te *m.* mounting
en-gen-drar *v.* to breed
en-gen-dro *m.* fetus
en-go-la-do *adj.* arrogant
en-go-lle-ta-do *adj.* proud
en-go-mar *v.* to glue
en-gor-de *m.* fattening
en-go-rro-so *adj.* troublesome
en-gra-nar *v.* to link; connect
en-gran-de-cer *v.* to praise; increase; heighten; augment; be promoted; exaggerate
en-gra-pa-do-ra *f.* stapler
en-gra-sa-do *m.* lubricant
en-gra-se *m.* lubricant
en-gre-í-do *adj.* arrogant
en-gro-sar *v.* to swell; to enlarge
en-ha-ci-nar *v.* to heap
en-he-brar *v.* to connect; to string; to link
en-hi-lar *v.* to arrange; guide; thread; order
e-nig-ma-ti-co *adj.* enigmatic
en-jam-brar *v.* to swarm
en-jam-bre *m.* swarm
en-ju-gar *v.* to settle; dry

en-jui-ciar v. to examine; to indict; to judge

en-jun-dia f. fat; grease; vitality

en-la-ce m. liaison; link; junction; connection

en-lar-dar v. to baste

en-la-zar v. to connect; to rope; to lace; to lasso

en-lo-que-cer v. to make insane; to drive crazy

en-lo-sa-dor m. tiler

en-lu-cir v. to plaster

en-lu-tar v. to sadden; darken

en-men-da-ble adj. amendable

en-men-da-ción f. amendment

en-ne-gre-cer v. to darken

en-no-ble-cer v. to ennoble

e-no-jar(se) v. to anger one

e-no-jo m. annoyance

e-no-jo-so, -sa adj. annoying

e-no-lo-go m. oenologist

e-nor-me adj. very large; enormous

e-nor-me-men-te adv. enormously

en-ra-ma-da f. arbor

en-ra-sar v. to smooth; level

en-re-da-dor m. gossip

en-re-dar(se) v. to mesh; mix

en-re-do m. muddle; snarl; mess

en-re-ve-sa-do adj. complicated

en-ri-que-cer(se) v. to enrich

en-ris-car v. to lift

en-ro-je-cer v. to turn red; to make red; to redden

en-ro-lar v. to recruit

en-ro-liar v. to involve; entangle

en-ros-car v. to twist

en-sa-la-da f. salad

en-sa-la-de-ra f. bowel for salad

en-sal-zar v. to exalt

en-sam-blar v. to connect

en-san-char v. to extend; to broaden; to expand

en-san-che m. expansion

en-sa-yar v. to practice; train

en-sa-yo m. test

en-sa-na-da f. inlet

en-se-nan-za f. tuition

en-se-nar v. to instruct; to tell; to teach

en-si-mis-ma-do adj. pensive

en-si-mis-ma-mien-to m. vanity; pensiveness

en-som-bre-cer v. to eclipse; to darken

en-sor-de-cer v. to make deaf

en-su-ciar(se) v. to make soiled

en-sue-no m. daydream

en-ta-bla-do m. floor

en-ta-llar v. to engrave; to carve; to groove

en-ten-de-dor, -a adj. sharp; expert

en-ten-der(se) v. to understand

en-ten-di-mien-to m. understanding

en-te-ra-men-te adv. totally; entirely

en-te-rar(se) v. to learn

en-te-re-za f. fortitude; integrity

en-te-ri-zo adj. entire

en-te-ro adj. whole; entire

en-ti-dad f. concern; entity

en-tie-rro m. funeral; burial; grave; internment

en-tin-ta-do m. inking

en-tin-tar v. to ink

en-to-mo-lo-gi-a f. entomolgy

en-to-nar v. to modulate; to intone

en-ton-ces adv. then

en-tor-no m. enviroment

en-tor-pe-cer v. to deaden; to obstruct; to dull

en-tra-da f. entrance

en-tram-par v. to snare; to trick; to entangle

en-tran-te adj. coming; next

en-tra-na-ble adj. beloved; close; dear

en-trar v. to go into; to enter

en-tre prep. among; between

en-tre-ca-no adj. graying

en-tre-cor-tar v. to interrupt

en-tre-ga f. delivery
en-tre-gar(se) v. to deliver to
en-tre-na-dor m. coach
en-tre-na-mien-to m. coaching
en-tre-nar v. to train
en-tre-ta-llar v. to impede; to carve; to engrave
en-tre-te-ner(se) v. to entertain
en-tre-te-ni-do adj. entertaining
en-tre-ver v. to surmise
en-tre-ve-ro m. jumble
en-tre-vis-tar v. to interview
en-tu-bar v. to put a tube into
en-tuer-to m. injustice
en-tur-biar v. to cloud
en-tu-sias-mar v. to enthuse
en-tu-sias-mo m. enthusiasm
e-nu-me-ra-ción f. enumeration
e-nu-me-rar v. to enumerate
e-nun-cia-ción f. enunciation
e-nun-ciar v. to enunciate
en-va-sar v. to package; to bottle
en-va-se m. packaging
en-ver-gar v. to fasten
en-via-do m. envoy
en-viar v. to send
en-vi-dia f. envy
en-vi-diar v. to envy
en-vi-djo-so adj. envious
en-ví-o m. dispatch; package; sending
en-vol-tu-ra m. wrapper
en-vol-ven-te adj. enveloping
en-vol-ver(se) v. to wrap up
en-ye-sar v. to plaster
en-zi-ma f. enzyme
e-on m. eon
e-pi-cen-tro m. epicenter
e-pi-co f. epic
e-pi-de-mia f. epidemic
e-pi-dé-mi-co adj. epidemic
e-pi-der-mi-co adj. epidermic
e-pi-glo-tis f. epiglottis
e-pi-lep-sia f. epilepsy
e-pi-lo-go m. epilogue
e-pi-so-dio m. episode

e-pi-te-lio m. epithelium
e-po-ca f. age; time period
e-po-pe-ya f. epic
e-qui-dad f. equity
e-qui-la-te-ro adj. equilateral
e-qui-li-bra-do adj. well-balanced; reasonable
e-qui-li-brar v. to balance
e-qui-li-brio adj. equilibrium
e-qui-li-bris-ta f. acrobat
e-qui-no adj. equine
e-qui-pa-je m. baggage
e-qui-par v. to equip
e-qui-pa-rar v. to compare
e-qui-po m. team
e-qui-ta-ti-vo adj. fair
e-qui-va-len-te adj. equivalent
e-qui-vo-ca-do adj. being wrong
e-qui-vo-car(se) v. to error
e-qui-vo-co adj. equivocal
er-bio m. erbium
e-rec-to adj. erect
e-rguir v. to lift up
e-ri-gir v. to erect
e-ro-sión f. erosion
e-ro-ti-co adj. erotic
e-rra-di-car v. to uproot; to eradicate
e-rra-do adj. mistaken
e-rran-te adj. errant
e-rrar(se) v. to wander; to miss; to roam; to fail
e-rro-ne-o adj. erroneous
e-rror m. error
e-ruc-to m. burp
e-ru-di-ción f. erudition
e-rup-ción f. eruption
e-sa adj. that
es-bel-to adj. slender
es-bo-zo m. outline
es-ca-bel m. footstool; stool
es-ca-bro-so adj. rough; rugged
es-ca-la f. range; ladder
es-ca-lar v. to climb; to scale
es-ca-le-ra f. stairs; staircase
es-cal-far v. to poach
es-ca-lo-nar v. to stagger
es-ca-par(se) v. to escape; to get away
es-car-pa-do, -a adj. short;

abrupt

es-ca-so *adj.* scarce

es-ce-na *f.* scene

es-cla-vi-zar *v.* to put into slavery

es-cla-vo, -a *m.* slave

es-co-ba *f.* broom

es-co-ger *v.* decide; choose

es-con-der(se) *v.* to hide

es-cor-pión *m.* scorpion

es-cri-bir *v.* to write

es-cu-char *v.* to listen

es-cue-la *f.* school

es-cul-pir *v.* to carve

es-cul-tu-ra *f.* sculpture

e-se *adj.* that; **e-sos** *pl.* those

e-sen-cial *adj.* essential

es-for-zar(se) *v.* to strive for

es-fuer-zo *m.* exertion; attempt

es-mal-te *m.* enamel

es-me-ral-da *f.* emerald

e-so *pron.* that

e-so-fa-go *m.* esophagus

es-pa-ciar(se) *v.* spread out

es-pa-cio *m.* space

es-pa-gue-ti *m.* spaghetti

es-pal-da *f.* back

es-pas-mo *m.* spasm

es-pas-ti-co *adj.* spastic

es-pe-cial *adj.* special

es-pe-cia-li-dad *f.* speciality

es-pe-cia-li-zar(se) *v.* to specialize

es-pe-ci-fi-car *v.* to specify

es-pe-ci-men *m.* specimen

es-pec-ta-dor *m.* witness

es-pe-jo *m.* mirror

es-pe-ra *f.* wait

es-pe-rar *v.* to hope; wait

es-piar *v.* to spy

es-pi-na *f.* spine

es-pi-na-zo *m.* backbone

es-pi-ni-lla *f.* shin

es-pi-ral *adj.* spiral

es-pi-rar *v.* to exhale

es-plen-di-do *adj.* splendid

es-plen-dor *m.* splendor

es-pon-ta-neo *adj.* spontaneous

es-po-sa *f.* wife

es-po-so *m.* husband

es-que-le-to *m.* skeleton

es-qui *m.* ski

es-quiar *v.* to ski

es-qui-na *f.* corner

es-ta *adj., f.* this

es-ta *pron., f.* this

es-ta-ble-cer(se) *v.* to settle; to establish

es-ta-ción *f.* station; season

es-ta-dio *m.* stadium

es-ta-do *m.* state

es-ta-llar *v.* to explode

es-tam-par *v.* to stamp

es-tam-pi-da *f.* stampede

es-tan-car(se) *v.* to stagnate

es-tan-dar-te *m.* standard

es-tar *v.* to lie; to be

es-ta-tua *f.* statue

es-ta-tu-ra *f.* stature

es-te *adj.* east

es-te *pron.* this; *pl.* these

es-te-ri-li-dad *f.* sterility

es-ti-bar *v.* to stow

es-ti-lo *m.* style

es-ti-mar(se) *v.* to estimate

es-ti-mu-lar *v.* to stimulate

es-ti-rar *v.* to stretch

es-to-ma-go *m.* stomach

es-tor-bar *v.* block; impede

es-tor-nu-dar *v.* to sneeze

es-tor-nu-do *m.* sneeze

es-tran-gu-lar *v.* to choke

es-tra-te-gia *f.* strategy

es-tra-ti-fi-car(se) *v.* to stratify

es-tre-char(se) *v.* to narrow

es-tre-lla *f.* star

es-tre-llar)se) *v.* smash into

es-tre-me-cer(se) *v.* to shake

es-tric-to *adj.* strict

es-tro-pa-jo *m.* mop

es-tro-pear(se) *v.* to ruin

es-truc-tu-ra *f.* form

es-truen-do *m.* thunder

es-tu-dian-te *m., f.* student

es-tu-diar *v.* to study

es-tu-dio *m.* studio

es-tu-fa *f.* stove

es-tu-pen-do *adj.* stupendous

es-tu-pi-do *adj.* stupid

es-ter-ño *adj.* eternity

e-ti-que-ta *f.* label

eu-fo-ria *f.* euphoria

e-va-cua-ción *f.* evacuation

e-va-cuar v. to evacuate
e-va-dir v. to avoid; dodge
e-va-lua-ción f. evaluation
e-va-po-ra-ción f. evaporation
e-va-po-rar(se) v. evaporate
e-va-sión f. evasion
e-vi-den-cia f. evidence
e-vi-den-te adj. obvious
e-vi-tar v. to shun
e-vo-car v. to evoke
e-o-lu-ción f. evolution
ex-ac-ta-men-te adv. exactly
ex-a-ge-ra-ción f. exaggeration
ex-a-ge-rar v. to exaggerate
ex-a-men m. test; quiz
ex-a-mi-nar(se) v. examine
ex-ca-va-ción f. excavation
ex-ce-der(se) v. to surpass
ex-ce-len-cia f. excellence
ex-ce-len-te adj. excellent
ex-cep-to prep. unless
ex-ci-tar(se) v. to arouse
ex-cla-ma-ción f. exclamation
ex-cla-mar v. to exclaim
ex-cluir v. to exclude
ex-clu-sión f. exclusion
ex-cu-sa f. excuse
ex-cu-sar v. to excuse
ex-ha-lar v. to exhale
ex-i-gir v. to require
ex-is-tir v. to exist
ex-pan-sión f. expansion
ex-pen-der v. to expend
ex-pe-rien-cia f. experience
ex-pe-ri-men-tar v. to experiment
ex-per-to m. expert
ex-pli-ca-ción f. explanation
ex-pli-car(se) v. to explain
ex-plo-ra-ción f. exploration
ex-plo-rar v. to explore
ex-por-ta-ción f. export
ex-por-tar v. to export
ex-pre-sar(se) v. tell; express
ex-pre-sión f. expression
ex-pul-sar v. to put out; expel
ex-ten-der(se) v. expand out
ex-te-rior adj. exterior
ex-tran-je-ro m. alien
ex-tra-ño adj. odd; strange
ex-tre-mo adj. extreme

fa-bri-ca f. mill
fa-bri-ca-ción f. manufacture
fa-bri-car v. to manufacture
fa-bu-la f. fiction; fable
fa-bu-lo-sa-men-te adv. fabulously
fa-bu-lo-so adj. fabulous
fac-ción f. feature; faction
fa-ce-ta f. facet
fa-cil adj. simple
fa-fi-li-dad f. chance; facility
fa-ci-li-tar v. to expedite; to facilitate
fac-ti-ble adj. feasible
fac-tor m. factor
fac-to-ri-a f. foundry; factory
fac-tu-ra-ción f. invoicing
fac-tu-rar v. to invoice
fa-cul-dad f. power
fa-cul-tar v. to empower
fa-cha f. appearance
fai-san m. pheasant
fa-ja f. sash; band
fa-ja-du-ra f. belting
fa-jar v. to belt; wrap
fa-lan-ge f. phalanx
fa-laz adj. deceptive
fal-da f. skirt
fal-don m. tail
fa-li-co adj. phallic
fal-se-dad f. untruth; lie
fal-si-fi-car v. to misrepresent
fal-so adj. dishonest
fal-ta f. fault; shortage; flaw; want; lack
fal-tar v. to fail; to need
fal-to adj. wanting; wretched; short
fa-llar v. to fail
fa-llo adj. judgment; void; decision; ruling
fa-ma f. fame
fa-me-li-co adj. famished
fa-mi-lia f. family
fa-mi-liar adj. familiar; casual; familial
fa-mo-so adj. well-known
fa-na-ti-zar v. to fanaticize
fan-fa-rron adj. showy; bragging
fan-go m. mud
fan-go-si-dad f. muddiness
fan-ta-se-ar v. to dream

fan-ta-sia f. fantasy

fan-tas-ti-co adj. bizarre; fanciful

fa-ran-du-la f. business; theater

fa-ra-on m. pharaoh

far-do m. bale; pack

fa-rin-ge f. pharynx

far-ma-ceu-ti-co m. pharmacist

far-ma-cia f. pharmacy

fa-ro m. beacon; light; lighthouse

fa-rol m. light; lantern

far-sa f. farce

fas-ci-na-ción f. fascination

fas-ci-nan-te adj. fascinating

fas-ci-nar v. to intrigue; to fascinate

fas-cis-ta m. fascist

fas-ti-diar(se) v. to hassel; to annoy; to bother

fas-ti-dio m. annoyance; repugnance

fas-ti-dio-so adj. annoying; tedious; bothersome

fas-to m. splendor

fas-tuo-si-dad f. splendor

fa-tal adj. fatal

fa-ta-li-dad f. fatality

fa-tal-men-te adv. unhappily; wretchedly

fa-ti-ga f. fatigue

fa-ti-gar(se) v. to fatigue; tire

fa-ti-go-so adj. tiring; fatigued; tired

fa-tuo m. fool

fau-na f. fauna

fa-vor m. favor

fa-vo-ra-ble adj. favorable

fa-vo-re-cer v. to favor; to help another; to support

fa-vo-ri-to adj. favorite

fe f. trust; faith

fe-bre-ro m. February

fe-bril adj. hectic

fe-cu-la f. starch

fe-cun-di-dad f. fertility

fe-cha f. date

fe-char v. to date

fe-de-ra-ción f. federation

fe-de-ral adj. federal

fe-de-ra-lis-ta adj. federalist

fe-de-rar v. to federate

fe-li-ci-dad f. bliss; happiness; felicity

fe-li-ci-ta-ción f. congratulation

fe-li-ci-tar v. to congratulate

fe-li-no adj. feline

fe-liz adj. happy

fel-po m. rug

fel-po-so adj. plush

fel-pu-do m. rug

fe-me-ni-no adj. feminine

fe-mi-nis-ta adj. feminist

fe-mur m. femur

fe-ne-cer v. to pass away; to settle; to finish

fe-no-bar-bi-tal m. phenobarbital

fe-nol m. phenol

feo adj. ugly

fe-ria f. fair; market

fe-ria-do adj. holiday

fe-ri-no, -a adj. ferocious; fierce

fer-men-ta-cion f. fermentation

fer-men-tar v. to ferment

fe-ro-ci-dad f. ferocity

fe-roz adj. fierce

fe-rre-o adj. iron

fe-rro-ca-rril m. railway

fer-til adj. rich

fer-ti-li-zan-te adj. fertilizing

fer-ti-li-zar v. to fertilize

fer-vi-do adj. fervid

fer-vor m. fervor

fes-te-jar v. to celebrate; to entertain; to court

fes-tin m. feast

fes-ti-val m. festival

fes-ti-vo, -va adj. merry; festive; witty

fe-tal adj. fetal

fe-ti-che m. fetish

fe-ti-dez f. fetidness

fe-to m. fetus

feu-dal adj. feudal

feu-da-lis-mo adj. feudalism

fia-ble adj. dependable

fia-dor m. bail

fian-za f. guarantor; security

fiar v. to entrust; to guaranty

fias-co m. fiasco

fi-bro-ma *m.* fibroma
fi-bro-so *adj.* stringy; fibrous
fic-ción *f.* fiction
fic-ti-cio *adj.* fictitious
fi-cha *f.* chip; token
fi-de-dig-no *adj.* trustworthy
fi-dei-co-mi-so *m.* trust
fi-de-li-dad *f.* accuracy; fidelity
fie-bre *f.* fever
fiel *adj.* true; loyal; honest; faithful; trustworthy
fiel-tro *m.* felt
fie-re-za *f.* ferocity; deformity; fierceness
fies-ta *f.* feast; party
fi-gu-ra *f.* shape; figure; character
fi-gu-ra-ción *f.* figuration
fi-gu-ra-do *adj.* figurative
fi-gu-rar *v.* to figure
fi-gu-ra-ti-vo *adj.* figurative
fi-ja-dor *adj.* fixative
fi-ja-men-te *adv.* firmly
fi-jar(se) *v.* to determine; set
fi-jo *adj.* permanent; set; steady; fixed
fi-la *f.* row; file; tier
fi-la-men-to *m.* filament
fi-lan-tro-po *m.* philanthropist
fi-la-te-lis-ta *m.* philatelist
fi-li-gra-na *f.* filigree
fil-mar *v.* to film
fil-mi-co *adj.* movie; film
fi-lo *m.* edge
fi-lo-lo-gi-a *f.* philology
fi-lo-so-fi-a *f.* philosophy
fi-lo-so-fo *m.* philosopher
fil-tra-ción *f.* filtration
fil-trar(se) *v.* to strain; filter
fil-tro *m.* filter
fin *m.* finish
fi-nal *adj.* ending; last; end; final
fi-na-li-dad *f.* finality
fi-na-lis-ta *m.* finalist
fi-na-li-zar *v.* to conclude
fi-nal-men-te *adv.* finally
fin-ca *f.* land; farm
fi-ne-za *f.* politeness; fineness; affection
fin-gir(se) *v.* pretend; sham

fi-ni-to *adj.* finite
fi-no *adj.* acute; fine; elegant; delicate
fir-ma *f.* firm
fir-ma-men-to *m.* firmament
fir-mar *v.* to sign something
fir-me *adj.* hard; strong; firm
fis-ca-li-zar *v.* to investigate; to oversee; to snoop
fi-si-co *adj.* physical
fi-sio-lo-gi-a *f.* physiology
fi-sio-lo-go *m.* physiologist
fi-sion *f.* fission
fis-tu-la *f.* fistula
fi-su-ra *f.* fissure
fla-co *adj.* skinny; gaunt
fla-ge-la-do *adj.* flagellate
fla-gran-te *adj.* flagrant
fla-me-ar *v.* to flame
flan-co *m.* side
fla-que-ar *v.* to weaken
fla-que-za *f.* weakness; leanness
flau-ta *f.* flute
flau-tin *m.* piccolo
flau-tis-ta *f.* flutist
fle-bi-tis *f.* phlebitis
fle-cha *f.* arrow
fle-ma *f.* phlegm
fle-te *m.* cargo; freight
fle-xi-bi-li-dad *f.* flexibility
fle-xi-ble *adj.* flexible
fle-xor *adj.* flexor
flo-je-dad *f.* laziness; debility
flo-je-ra *f.* carelessness
flo-jo *adj.* limp; weak
flor *f.* blossom; flower; bloom
flo-re-cer *v.* to bloom; prosper
flo-reo *m.* flourish
flo-ris-ta *m., f.* florist
flo-tar *v.* to float
fluc-tua-ción *f.* vaciation
fluc-tuar *v.* to fluctuate
flui-do *adj.* fluid
fluir *v.* to flow
fo-co *m.* focus
fo-li-cu-lo *m.* follicle
fo-lla-je *m.* foliage
fo-lle-to *m.* brochure
fo-men-tar *v.* to encourage
fon-ta-ne-ro *m.* plumber
for-jar *v.* to forge

r-ma *f.* shape; form
r-ma-ción *f.* formation
r-ma-li-dad *f.* formality
r-mar(se) *v.* make; shape
r-ta-le-cer(se) *v.* to fortify
r-ta-le-za *f.* fortress
r-tui-to *adj.* casual
r-tu-na *f.* fortune
r-zar *v.* to strain; force
-sil *m.* fossil
-to *f.* picture; photograph
-to-gra-fía *f.* photography
a-ca-sar *v.* to fail
ac-ción *f.* fraction
ac-tu-ra *f.* break; fracture
ac-tu-rar(se) *v.* to fracture
a-gil *f.* frail
an-ca-men-te *adv.* frankly
an-ces *adj.* French
an-co *adj.* open; candid
an-que-za *f.* frankness
a-ter-ni-dad *f.* fraternity
-se *f.* sentence
-cuen-cia *f.* frequency
-cuen-te *adj.* frequent
-gar *v.* to wash; scrub
-irse *v.* to fry
-nar *n.* brake
n-te *f.* front; forehead
s-co *adj.* fresh
c-ción *f.* friction
n-tal *adj.* frontal
n-te-ra *f.* border; limit
-tar(se) *v.* to chafe
n-cir *v.* to gather
s-tra-ción *f.* frustration
s-trar(se) *v.* to frustrate
-go *m.* fire
en-te *f.* spring; fountain
-ra *adv.* outside; off
r-te *m.* sturdy; strong
r-za *f.* power; force
gar-se *v.* to abscond
-gu-rar *v.* to gleam
mar *v.* to smoke
-da-ción *f.* foundation
-dar(se) *v.* to establish
-dir(se) *v.* to fuse
ria *f.* fury
rio-so *adj.* furious
tu-ro *m.* future

ga-ban *m.* topcoat
ga-bar-di-na *f.* gabardine
ga-bi-ne-te *m.* boudoir
ga-ce-la *f.* gazelle
ga-ce-ta *f.* gazette
ga-chí *f.* girl
ga-cho *adj.* floppy; bent
ga-fas *f.* glasses
ga-ga *adj.* foolish
gai-te-ro *adj.* gaudy
ga-jo *m.* section; bunch
ga-lac-ti-co *adj.* galactic
ga-la-na-men-te *adv.* elegantly
ga-la-ni-a *f.* elegance
ga-lan-te *adj.* gallant
ga-lan-te-o *m.* flirting; courting another
ga-len-te-ri-a *f.* generosity; grace
ga-lar-do-nar *v.* to reward
ga-la-xia *f.* galaxy
ga-le-on *m.* gallon
ga-le-ra *f.* galley
ga-le-ría *f.* gallery
ga-li-ma-ti-as *m.* nonsense
ga-lon *m.* gallon
ga-lo-pan-te *adj.* galloping
ga-lo-par *v.* to gallop
ga-lo-pe *m.* gallop
gal-va-ni-zar *v.* to galvanize
ga-llar-dí-a *f.* gallantry; grace; elegance
ga-llar-do *adj.* graceful; brave
ga-lle-ta *f.* cracker
ga-lli-na *f.* chicken; hen
ga-lli-ne-ro *m.* henhouse; coop
ga-llo *m.* cock; rooster
ga-ma *f.* gamut
gam-ba-do *adj.* bowlegged
gam-be-te-ar *v.* to prance
ga-na *f.* longing; appetite
ga-na-de-ro *m.* cattle
ga-na-do *m.* livestock
ga-nan-cia *f.* profit
ga-nar *v.* to earn; to win
gan-cho *m.* hook
gan-du-le-rí-a *f.* laziness
gan-glio *m.* ganglion
gan-go-so *adj.* nasal
gan-gre-na *f.* gangrene

ga-no-so *adj.* anxious

gan-so *m.* goose

ga-ra-ba-to *m.* grapple

ga-ra-je *m.* garage

ga-ran-tia *f.* warrant; guaranty

ga-ran-tir *v.* to defend; to guarantee

ga-ra-tu-sa *f.* compliment

gar-ban-zo *m.* chickpea

gar-be-ar *v.* to steal; to rob

gar-bi-llo *m.* sieve

gar-bo-so *adj.* graceful; generous

gar-fa *f.* claw

gar-ga-je-ar *v.* to spit

gar-gan-ta *f.* neck

gar-ga-ra *f.* gargling

gar-ga-ri-zar *v.* to gargle

gar-go-la *f.* gargoyle

gar-gue-ro *m.* trachea

ga-rra *f.* talon

ga-rra-fal *adj.* enormous

ga-rra-pa-ta *f.* mite

ga-rra-pi-nar *v.* to grab

ga-rron *m.* claw

ga-ruar *v.* to drizzle

gas *m.* gas

ga-sa *f.* guaze

ga-si-fi-car *v.* to gasify

ga-so-li-na *f.* gas

gas-ta-do, -a *adj.* threadbare; exhausted

gas-tar *v.* to exhaust; to spend; to squander; wear

gas-tri-co *adj.* gastric

gas-tri-tis *f.* gastritis *

gas-tro-no-mia *f.* gastronomy

gas-tro-no-mi-co *adj.* gastronomic

ga-te-ar *v.* to climb; to swipe

ga-ti-llo *m.* hammer

ga-to *m.* cat

ga-tu-no *adj.* catlike

gau-cho *adj.* gaucho

ga-ve-ta *f.* drawer

ga-vio-ta *f.* gull

ga-za-pi-na *f.* brawl

gaz-na-te *m.* windpipe; throat

gei-ser *m.* geyser

ge-la-ti-na *f.* gelatin

ge-ma *f.* gem

ge-mi-do *m.* groan

ge-ne-a-lo-gi-a *f.* genealogy

ge-ne-ra-cion *f.* generation

ge-ne-ral *m.* general

ge-ne-ra-li-dad *f.* generality

ge-ne-ra-li-za-cion *f.* generalization

ge-ne-ra-li-zar *v.* generalize

ge-ne-ra-ti-vo *adj.* generative

ge-ne-ri-ca-men-te *adv.* generically

ge-ne-ri-co *adj.* generic

ge-ne-ro-si-dad *f.* generosity

ge-ne-ro-so, -a *adj.* fine; generous

ge-nial *adj.* genial; inspired; pleasant

ge-nio *m.* genius; disposition

ge-no-ci-dio *m.* genocide

ge-no-ti-po *m.* genotype

gen-te *f.* nation; people

gen-til *adj.* genteel; excellent; polite

gen-ti-o *m.* mob

ge-nui-no *adj.* real; true; genuine

ge-o-fi-si-co *adj.* geophysical

ge-o-gra-fia *f.* geography

ge-o-gra-fo *m., f.* geographer

ge-o-lo-gia *f.* geology

ge-o-lo-go *m., f.* geologist

ge-o-me-tria *f.* geometry

ge-ra-nio *m.* geranium

ge-ren-te *m., f.* director

ge-ria-tri-co *adj.* geriatric

ger-ma-nio *m.* germanium

ger-men *m.* germ

ger-mi-na-cion *f.* germination

ger-mi-nar *v.* to germinate

ge-ron-to-lo-gia *f.* gerontology

ges-ta-cion *f.* gestation

ges-ti-cu-la-cion *f.* gesture; grimace

ges-ti-cu-lar *v.* to gesture

gey-ser *m.* geyser

gi-bar *v.* to curve

gi-bon *m.* gibbon

gi-gan-ta *f.* sunflower

gi-gan-te *m.* giant

gi-go-lo *m.* gigolo
gim-na-sia *f.* gymnastics
gim-nas-ta *f., m.* gymnast
gi-mo-te-ar *v.* to whine
gi-ne-co-lo-gía *f.* gynecology
gin-gi-vi-tis *f.* gingivitis
gi-rar *v.* rotate; spin; gyrate
gi-ra-to-rio *adj.* rotating
gi-ro *m.* rotation; turn
gi-ros-co-pio *m.* gyroscope
gi-ta-nes-co *adj.* gypsy-like
gla-cia-ción *f.* glaciation
gla-cial *adj.* glacial; icy
gla-ciar *adj.* glacial
gla-dia-dor *m.* gladiator
glan-du-la *f.* gland
gla-se-ar *v.* to glaze
glau-co-ma *m.* glaucoma
glo-bal *adj.* global
glo-bo *m.* globe
glo-glo *m.* gurgle
glo-ria *f.* glory
glo-ri-fi-ca-ción *f.* glorifica-
tion
glo-ri-fi-car(se) *v.* to glorify
glo-rio-so *adj.* glorious
glo-sa *f.* gloss
glo-sar *v.* to gloss
glo-sa-rio *m.* glossary
glo-tis *f.* glottis
glu-co-sa *f.* glucose
glu-ti-no-so *adj.* glutinous
go-ber-na-ción *f.* government
go-ber-na-dor *m.* governor
go-ber-nar *v.* to govern
go-bier-no *n.* government
go-la *f.* throat
golf *m.* golf
gol-fo *m.* golf
go-lo-si-na *f.* craving;
delicacy; longing
gol-pe *m.* blow; hit
gol-pear *v.* to slug; hit; beat
gol-pe-te-ar *v.* to pummel;
hit; to pound; to beat
go-ma *f.* rubber; gum; rubber band
go-mo-so *adj.* gummy
gón-do-la *f.* gondola
gon-do-le-ro *m.* gondolier
go-no-co-co *m.* gonococcus
gor-do *adj.* fat

gor-go-te-o *m.* gurgle
go-ri-la *m.* gorilla
go-te-o *m.* dripping
go-zar *v.* to enjoy; to rejoice
gra-bar *v.* to engrave
gra-cia *f.* kindness; charm;
pardon
gra-cio-so *adj.* funny;
charming; amusing
gra-do *m.* step; grade; stair
gra-dual *adj.* gradual
gra-fi-to *m.* graphite
gra-ma-ti-co *adj.* grammati-
cal
gra-na-te *m., adj.* garnet
gra-ni-to *adj.* granite
gran-je-ro *m., f.* farmer
gra-pa *f.* staple
gra-ti-fi-car *v.* to gratify
gra-ve *adj.* serious;
important; grave
gre-ga-rio *adj.* gregarious
gris *adj.* grey
gri-tar *v.* to yell; to cry
gri-to *m.* yell; scream
gro-se-ría *f.* roughness;
stupidity; vulgarity
gro-se-ro *adj.* vulgar; coarse
gro-tes-co *adj.* grotesque
grue-so *adj.* fat; coarse
gru-ñir *v.* to grumble; grunt
gru-po *m.* bunch
guan-te *m.* glove
guan-te-ro *m.* glove maker
gua-pe-tón *adj.* bold; flashy
gua-pe-za *f.* daring
gua-po *adj.* flashy; good-
looking
guar-da *f.* custody; guard
guar-dar(se) *v.* keep; guard
guar-dia *f.* guard
guar-dián *m., f.* guardian
guar-ne-cer *v.* border; supply
gu-ber-na-men-tal *adj.*
governmental
gue-rra *f.* war
gue-rre-ar *v.* to fight
guía *a m., f.* leader; guide
guiar *v.* to steer; to guide
gui-ta-rra *f.* guitar
gu-sa-no *m.* worm
gus-tar *v.* to like
gus-to *m.* zest; taste

ha-ber v. to have
ha-bil adj. skillful
ha-bi-li-dad f. ability; skill
ha-bi-ta-cion f. habitation; lodging
ha-bi-tar v. to dwell
ha-bi-tual adj. habitual
ha-bi-tuar v. to habituate
ha-bla f. speech
ha-bla-do adj. spoken
ha-bla-du-ri-a f. gossip; chatter
ha-blar v. to talk; to speak
ha-ce adv. ago
ha-cer(se) v. to act; to become; to force; compose
ha-cia prep. about; to
ha-cien-da f. ranch
ha-ci-na f. pile
ha-ci-nar v. to pile up
ha-da f. fairy
ha-do m. fate
ha-la-gue-no adj. promising; attractive; pleasing
ha-lar v. to tow something
hal-con m. falcon
hal-co-ne-ri-a f. falconry
hal-co-ne-ro m. falconer
ha-llar(se) v. to locate
ham-bre f. hunger
ham-brien-to adj. hungry; starved
ham-bur-gue-sa f. hamburger
ha-ra-po-so adj. tattered
ha-ren m. harem
har-tar v. to annoy; to stuff
has-ta prep. till
has-tiar v. to annoy; to sicken
he-bra f. filament; thread
he-chi-ce-ro m., f. charmer; sorceress; sorcerer
he-chi-zo m. charm; spell
he-der v. to stink; smell bad
he-dor m. stink
he-la-do m. ice cream
he-lar v. to freeze
he-li-cop-te-ro m. helicopter
he-lio m. helium
he-li-puer-to m. heliport
hem-bra f. female; woman
he-mo-fi-lia f. hemophilia
he-mo-glo-bi-na f. hemo-

globin
he-mo-rra-gia f. hemorrhage
hen-der(se) v. to crack
he-nil m. hayloft
he-no m. hay
he-pa-ti-tis f. hepatitis
her-ba-rio adj. herbal
he-re-di-ta-rio adj. hereditary
he-ren-cia f. heritage
he-ri-da f. wound
he-rir v. hurt; injure; wound
her-ma-na f. sister
her-man-dad f. sisterhood; brotherhood; league
her-ma-no m. brother
her-mo-se-ar v. to beautify
her-mo-so, -a adj. beautiful
her-nia f. hernia
he-roi-co adj. heroic
he-ro-i-na f. heroine
her-pes m. herpes
he-rre-ro m. blacksmith
he-rrin m. rust
he-rrum-brar v. to rust
her-vor m. boiling
he-si-ta-cion f. hesitation
he-si-tar v. to hesitate
he-xa-go-no adj. hexagonal
hi-ber-na-cion f. hibernation
hi-ber-nar v. to hibernate
hi-bri-do m. hybrid
hi-dra-ta-cion f. hydration
hi-dra-tar v. to hydrate
hi-dro-car-bu-ro m. hydrocarbon
hi-dro-fo-bia f. hydrophobia
hi-dro-ge-no m. hydrogen
hi-dro-te-ra-pia f. hydrotherapy
hi-dro-xi-do m. hydroxide
hie-dra f. ivy
hie-lo m. ice
hier-ba f. grass
hi-gie-ne f. hygiene
hi-gie-ni-co adj. hygienic
hi-ja f. daughter
hi-jas-tra f. stepdaughter
hi-jas-tro m. stepson
hi-jo m. son
hi-la-do-ra m., f. spinner
hi-lar v. to spin
hi-le-ro m. current
hi-lo m. filament; thread

hi-men m. hymen
him-no m. hymn
hin-char v. to exaggerate; to swell; to blow up
hi-no-jo m. knee
hi-per-bo-la f. hyperbola
hi-per-sen-si-ble adj. hypersensitive
hi-per-ter-mía f. hyperthermia
hip-no-sis f. hypnosis
hip-no-tis-mo m. hypnotism
hip-no-ti-zar v. to hypnotize
hi-po-con-drí-a f. hypochondria
hi-po-cre-si-a f. hypocrisy
hi-po-cri-ta f., m. hypocrite
hi-po-te-ca f. mortgage
hi-po-te-car v. to mortgage
hi-po-ter-mia f. hypothermia
his-te-ria f. hysteria
his-to-ria f. story; history
his-to-rial adj. historical
ho-ci-car v. smooch; nuzzle
hoc-key m. hockey
ho-gue-ra f. bonfire
ho-ja f. petal; leaf; sheet
ho-jo-so adj. leafy
hol-gan-za f. leisure
ho-lo-caus-to m. holocuast
hom-bre m. man
hom-bre-ra f. shoulder pad
hom-bri-llo m. yoke
hom-bro m. shoulder
ho-mi-ci-da adj. homicidal
ho-mi-ci-dio m. homocide
ho-mo-ge-nei-zar v. to homogenize
ho-mo-ni-mia f. homonymy
hon-do adj. intense; deep
hon-do-na-da f. gorge
ho-nes-ti-dad f. honesty
hon-go m. mushroom
ho-nor m. honor
ho-no-ra-ble adj. honorable
hon-ra-dez f. honesty
hon-ra-do adj. honest
hon-ra-so adj. honorable
ho-ra f. time; hour
hor-con m. pitchfork
ho-ri-zon-tal adj. horizontal
ho-ri-zon-te m. horizon
hor-mi-go-ne-ra f. cement

hor-mo-na f. hormone
hor-ne-ar v. to bake
hor-ne-ro f., m. baker
hor-ni-llo m. stove
hor-no m. oven
ho-ros-co-po m. horoscope
ho-rren-do adj. horrendous
ho-rri-ble adj. awful; horrible
ho-rri-do adj. horrid
ho-rri-fi-car v. to horrify
ho-rror m. terror; horror
hor-ti-co-la adj. horticultural
hor-ti-cul-tu-ra f. horticulture
hos-pi-tal m. hospital
hos-pi-ta-li-zar v. hospitalize
hos-te-rí-a f. hostel; inn
hos-ti-gar v. to harass; whip
hos-til adj. hostile
hos-ti-li-dad f. hostility
ho-tel m. hotel
hoy m. today
ho-ya f. hole
hue-co adj. deep; hollow
hue-lla f. print; footprint
huer-ta f. garden
hue-sa f. grave
hue-su-do adj. bony
hue-vo m. egg
huir(se) v. to flee; to escape; to avoid; to run from
hu-ma-nar v. to humanize
hu-ma-ni-dad f. humanity
hu-ma-ni-zar v. to humanize
hu-ma-no m. human
hu-me-ar v. to steam; smoke
hu-me-dad f. humidity
hu-me-do adj. humid
hu-me-ro m. humerus
hu-mil-dad f. humility
hu-mi-lla-cion f. humiliation
hu-mi-llan-te adj. humiliating
hu-mí-llo m. pride
hu-mo m. smoke
hu-mo-ris-mo m. wit
hu-mo-so adj. smoky
hun-dir v. ruin; sink; plunge
hu-ra-can m. hurricane
hur-gon m. poker
hu-ron m. ferret
hur-tar(se) v. to steal; take
hur-to m. robbery
hus-me-ar v. to pry
hus-me-o m. prying

i-bis f. ibis
i-ce-berg m. iceberg
i-co-no m. icon
i-co-no-gra-fí-a f. iconography
ic-te-ri-cia f. jaundice
ic-tio-lo-go m. ichthyologist
i-dea f. notion; thought; image; idea; picture
i-de-al m. ideal
i-de-a-lis-ta adj. idealist
i-de-a-li-zar v. to idealize
i-de-ar v. to invent; to plan; to design
i-den-ti-co adj. identical
i-den-ti-dad f. identity
i-den-ti-fi-ca-ble adj. identifiable
i-den-ti-fi-ca-cion f. identification
i-den-ti-fi-car v. to identify
i-de-o-lo-gí-co adj. ideological
i-di-lio m. idyll
i-dio-ma-tí-co adj. idiomatic
i-dio-sin-cra-sia f. idiosyncrasy
i-dio-ta f., m. idiot, adj. idiotic; foolish
i-do-la-trar v. to idolize
i-do-la-tri-a f. idolatry
i-do-lo m. idol
i-gle-sia f. church
ig-ni-cion f. ignition
ig-no-mi-nio-so adj. ignominious
ig-no-ran-cia f. ignorance
ig-no-ran-te adj. ignorant; unaware; uneducated
ig-no-to adj. undiscovered
i-gual adj. level; even; alike; like
i-gua-la-míen-to m. equalization
i-gua-lar v. to make equal; to equate; to smooth
i-gual-dad f. equality
i-gual-men-te adv. too; equally
i-gua-na m. iguana
i-la-cíon f. cohesiveness
i-le-gal adj. unlawful; illegal; against the law

i-le-ga-li-dad f. illegality
i-le-gi-ble adj. illegible
i-le-tra-do adj. illiterate
i-lo-gi-co adj. illogical
i-lu-mi-na-cion f. illumination
i-lu-mi-na-dor adj. illuminative
i-lu-mi-nar v. light; illuminate
i-lu-sion f. illusion
i-lu-so-rio adj. illusory
i-lus-tra-cion f. illustration
i-lus-tra-dor adj. illustrative
i-lus-trar v. to illustrate
i-lus-tre adj. illustrious
i-ma-gi-na-ble adj. imaginable
i-ma-gi-na-cion f. imagination
i-ma-gi-nar(se) v. to think up; to conceive
i-ma-gi-na-tí-vo adj. imaginative
i-ma-nar v. to magnetize
im-be-ci-li-dad f. imbecility
i-mi-ta-ble adj. imitable
i-mi-ta-cion f. imitation
i-mi-tar v. to imitate
im-pa-cién-cia f. impatience
im-pa-cien-te adj. impatient
im-par-cial adj. impartial
im-par-tir v. to concede
im-pa-si-ble adj. impassive
im-pe-ca-ble adj. impeccable
im-pe-di-men-to m. impediment
im-pe-dir v. to deter; hinder
im-pen-sa-ble adj. inimaginable; unthinkable
im-pe-rar v. to reign
im-per-do-na-ble adj. inexcusable
im-per-fec-cíon f. imperfection
im-pe-rial adj. imperial
im-per-me-a-bi-li-dad f. impermeability
im-per-me-a-ble m. raincoat
im-per-so-nal adj. impersonal
im-pe-ti-go m. impetigo
im-pe-tu m. energy; impetus
im-pe-tuo-so adj. impetuous; violent

n-pla-ca-ble *adj.* implacable
n-plan-tar *v.* to implant
n-pli-ca-cion *f.* implication; consequence
n-pli-car *v.* mean; implicate
n-plo-rar *v.* to invoke
n-po-ner *v.* to charge; to inspire; to inform
n-po-pu-lar *adj.* unpopular
n-por-ta-cion *f.* importation
n-por-tan-cia *f.* authority; importance
n-por-tan-te *adj.* important
n-por-tu-nar *v.* to importune
n-por-tu-no *adj.* inopportune
n-po-si-bi-li-dad *f.* impossibility
n-po-si-ble *adj.* impossible; difficult
n-pos-tor *m.* impostor
n-po-ten-cia *f.* impotence
n-prac-ti-ca-ble *adj.* unfeasible; impracticable
n-pre-ci-so *adj.* imprecise
n-preg-nar *v.* to impregnate
n-pre-sion *f.* impression
n-pre-sio-nan-te *adj.* impressive
n-pre-vis-to *adj.* unexpected; sudden
n-pri-mir *v.* to stamp; to print; to imprint
n-pro-ba-ble *adj.* improbable
n-pro-duc-ti-vo *adj.* unproductive
n-pro-vi-sa-cion *f.* improvisation
n-pu-den-cia *f.* impudence
n-pug-nar *v.* to impugn
n-pul-sar *v.* to drive; impel
n-pul-sion *f.* impulse
n-pul-so *m.* impulse
n-pu-ni-dad *f.* impunity
n-pu-re-za *f.* impurity
n-pu-ro *adj.* impure
nac-cion *f.* inaction
na-cep-ta-ble *adj.* unacceptable
nac-ti-vo *adj.* inactive
n-a-de-cua-do *adj.* inadequate

i-nad-ver-ten-cia *f.* carelessness; inadvertence
i-nal-te-ra-ble *adj.* unalterable
i-na-ne *adj.* insane
i-na-ni-dad *f.* inanity
i-na-pli-ca-ble *adj.* inapplicable
i-na-ten-cion *f.* inattention
i-na-ten-to *adj.* unattentive
in-ca-pa-ci-dad *f.* incapacity
in-ca-pa-ci-tar *v.* to incapacitate
in-ca-paz *adj.* unable; incapable
in-cen-dio *m.* fire
in-cen-ti-vo *m.* incentive
in-ces-to *m.* incest
in-cien-so *m.* incense
in-cier-to *adj.* vague; uncertain; doubtful
in-ci-ne-rar *v.* to incinerate
in-ci-sion *f.* incision
in-ci-tar *v.* to urge; to incite
in-cle-men-te *adj.* inclement
in-cli-na-cion *f.* slant; inclination; slope
in-cli-nar(se) *v.* to slant; to sway; to incline; persuade
in-cluir *v.* to contain; include
in-clu-sion *f.* inclusion
in-clu-si-vo *adj.* inclusive
in-co-he-ren-te *adj.* incoherent
in-co-mi-ble *adj.* inedible
in-com-pa-ti-ble *adj.* incompatible
in-com-ple-to *adj.* incomplete
in-con-clu-so *adj.* inconclusive
in-cons-tan-te *adj.* fickle
in-cor-po-ral *adj.* incorporeal
in-cor-po-rar *v.* incorporate
in-co-rrec-to *adj.* incorrect
in-co-rrup-to *adj.* incorrupt
in-cre-du-lo *adj.* incredulous
in-cre-i-ble *adj.* incredible
in-cre-men-tar *v.* to increase
in-cre-men-to *m.* increase
in-cre-par *v.* to reprimand
in-cri-mi-nar *v.* to incriminate
in-crus-tar *v.* to encrust

in-cu-ba-cion *f.* incubation
in-cu-bar *v.* to incubate
in-cul-car *v.* to inculcate
in-cu-ra-ble *adj.* incurable
in-cu-rrir *v.* to incur
in-de-cen-te *adj.* indecent
in-de-ci-sion *f.* indecision
in-de-ci-so *adj.* indecisive
in-de-fen-so *adj.* defenseless
in-de-le-ble *adj.* indelible
in-dem-ne *adj.* unhurt
in-de-pen-di-zar *v.* to liberate
in-de-se-a-ble *adj.* undersirable
in-di-ca-cion *f.* sign; indication; direction
in-di-car *v.* to show; indicate
in-di-fe-ren-te *adj.* indifferent
in-di-gen-cia *f.* indigence
in-di-gen-te *adj.* indigent
in-di-ges-tion *f.* indigestion
in-dig-nar *v.* to infuriate
in-dig-no *adj.* despicable
in-di-go *m.* indigo
in-di-rec-to *adj.* hint; indirect
in-dis-cre-cion *f.* indiscretion
in-dis-cu-ti-ble *adj.* indisputable
in-dis-tin-to *adj.* indistinct
in-di-vi-dual *adj.* individual
in-di-vi-duo *m.* individual
in-di-vi-si-ble *adj.* indivisible
in-do-cil *adj.* indocile
in-do-ci-li-dad *f.* unruliness
in-do-len-cia *f.* indolence
in-do-len-te *adj.* indolent
in-do-ma-ble *adj.* uncontrollable; untamable
in-do-mi-to *adj.* untamable; indomitable
in-duc-cion *f.* induction
in-du-cir *v.* to induce
in-du-da-ble *adj.* certain
in-dul-gen-te *adj.* indulgent
in-dus-tria *f.* industry
in-dus-trial *adj.* industrial
in-dus-tria-li-zar *v.* to become industrialize
in-dus-trio-so *adj.* industrious
i-ne-fa-ble *adj.* ineffable
i-ne-fi-caz *adj.* ineffective
i-nep-ti-tud *f.* ineptitude
i-nep-to *adj.* inept

i-ner-cia *f.* inertia
i-ner-te *adj.* inert
i-nes-pe-ra-do *adj.* unexpected
i-nes-ta-ble *adj.* unstable
i-ne-vi-ta-ble *adj.* inevitable
i-ne-xis-ten-te *adj.* nonexistent; not existing
i-nex-plo-ra-do *adj.* unexplored
in-fa-li-ble *adj.* infallible
in-fa-mar *v.* to slander
in-fa-mia *f.* infamy
in-fan-cia *f.* infancy
in-fan-te *m.* baby; infant
in-fan-til *adj.* childish; baby
in-far-to *m.* infarction
in-fa-tuar *v.* to become conceited
in-fec-cion *f.* infection
in-fec-cio-so *adj.* infectious
in-fec-tar(se) *v.* to infect
in-fe-liz *adj.* wretched
in-fe-ren-cia *f.* inference
in-fe-rior *adj.* under; inferior
in-fe-rio-ri-dad *f.* inferiority
in-fe-rir *v.* to inflict; to infer
in-fes-tar *v.* to infest
in-fiel *adj.* disloyal
in-fier-no *m.* hell
in-fil-trar *v.* to infiltrate
in-fi-mo *adj.* worst; lowest
in-fi-ni-to *m., adj.* infinite
in-fla-cion *f.* inflation
in-fla-ma-ble *adj.* inflammable
in-fla-mar *v.* to inflame
in-flar *v.* to inflate
in-fle-xi-ble *adj.* rigid; unyielding
in-fluen-cia *f.* influence
in-flue-ciar *v.* to influence
in-flu-jo *m.* influence
in-for-ma-cion *f.* information
in-for-mal *adj.* informal
in-for-mar(se) *v.* to report; to inform; to find out
in-for-me *adj.* formless
in-for-tu-nio *m.* misfortune
in-fra-rro-jo *adj.* infared
in-fre-cuen-te *adj.* infrequent
in-fruc-tuo-so *adj.* fruitless
in-fun-dir *v.* to arouse

in-fu-sión f. infusion
in-ge-nie-ría f. engineering
in-ge-nie-ro m. engineer
in-ge-nio-so adj. witty; clever
in-ge-rir v. to ingest
in-ges-tión f. ingestion
in-glés m. English
in-gra-to adj. thankless
in-gre-dien-te m. ingredient
in-gre-so m. entrance
in-ha-bi-li-dad f. incompetence
in-ha-lar v. to inhale
in-he-ren-te adj. inherent
in-hi-bir v. to inhibit
in-hu-ma-no adj. inhuman
ini-cia-ción f. initiation
ini-cial adj. initial
ini-ciar v. to initiate
ini-cio m. beginning
ini-gua-la-do adj. unequaled
ini-mi-ta-ble adj. inimitable
in-je-rir v. to insert
in-jer-to m. transplant
in-ju-ria f. injury
in-jus-ti-cia f. injustice
in-jus-to adj. unjust
in-ma-du-ro adj. immature
in-me-mo-rial adj. immemorial
in-men-so adj. immense
in-mer-sión f. immersion
in-mi-grar v. to immigrate
in-mi-nen-te adj. imminent
in-mo-des-to adj. immodest
in-mo-lar v. to immolate
in-mo-ral adj. immoral
in-mor-tal adj. immortal
in-mo-vi-ble adj. immovable
in-mó-vil adj. immobile
in-mun-do adj. filthy
in-mu-ni-dad f. immunity
in-mu-ni-zar v. to immunize
in-mu-ta-ble adj. immutable
in-no-ble adj. ignoble
in-no-va-ción f. innovation
in-no-var v. to innovate
ino-cen-cia f. innocence
ino-cen-te adj. innocent
ino-cu-lar v. to inoculate
ino-cuo adj. innocuous
ino-pe-ra-ble adj. inoperable
inor-gá-ni-co adj. inorganic

in-quie-tar v. to alarm
in-quie-tud f. uneasiness
in-qui-li-no m., f. tenant
in-qui-rir v. to probe
in-sa-no adj. insane
ins-cri-bir(se) v. to record; to engrave
ins-crip-ción f. record; inscription
in-sec-to m. insect
in-se-gu-ro adj. insecure
in-sen-si-ble adj. unfeeling; unconscious; insensible
in-ser-ción f. insertion
in-ser-tar v. to insert
in-sig-nia f. emblem
in-sin-ce-ro adj. insincere
in-sis-ten-te adj. insistent
in-sis-tir v. to insist
in-so-len-cia f. insolence
ins-pec-ción f. inspection
ins-pi-rar v. to inspire
ins-truc-ción f. instruction
ins-truir(se) v. to teach; to learn; to instruct
in-su-li-na f. insulin
in-sul-tar v. to insult
in-tac-to adj. together; intact
in-te-li-gen-cia f. intellect; intelligence
in-te-li-gen-te adj. smart; intelligent
in-ten-si-fi-car v. to intensify
in-te-re-sar(se) v. to concern
in-te-rior m. inside
in-ter-no adj. inside
in-te-rrup-ción f. interruption
in-ter-ve-nir v. to mediate; to intervene
in-ti-mo adj. intimate
in-tor-duc-ción f. introduction
in-va-dir v. to invade
in-va-sión f. invasion
in-ven-ción f. invention
in-ven-tar v. to contrive; to think up; to invent
in-ves-tir v. to invest
in-vier-no m. winter
ir(se) v. to depart; to leave
i-rre-gu-lar adj. irregular
is-la f. island
iz-quier-do, -a adj. left

ja-ba-li *m.* boar
a-ba-lí-na *f.* javelin
a-bon *m.* soap
a-bo-na-do *m.* wash
a-bo-nar *v.* to lather up
a-bo-ne-ro *m., f.* soapmaker
a-ca *f.* nag; pony
a-ca-re-ro *adj.* lively
a-co*m.* nag
jac-tan-cía *f.* arrogance;
  bragging; boast
jac-tan-ció-so *adj.* arrogant
jac-tar-se *v.* to brag
a-de *m.* jade
a-de-ar *v.* to gasp for air
a-diar *v.* to hoe
a-guar *m.* jaguar
a-lar *v.* to pull on
a-le-a *f.* jelly
a-le-ar *v.* to urge one
a-leo *m.* racket; uproar
a-lo-nar *v.* to mark
ja-más *adv.* never; ever;
  never again
jam-ba *f.* jamb
a-mel-go *m.* nag
a-mon *m.* ham
a-que *m.* check
a-que-ar *v.* to check
a-ra-be *m.* syrup
a-ra-near *v.* to carouse
jar-ca *f.* acacia
ar-din *m.* garden
ar-di-ne-ra *f.* gardener
ar-di-ne-ro *m.* gardener
a-rra *f.* mug; pitcher
a-rro *m.* flagon
a-rrón *m.* vase
as-pe *m.* jasper
au-la *f.* cell; cage
az-min *m.* jasmine
e-fa *f.* master; boss
e-fe *m.* head; boss; master
e-mi-que-ar *v.* to whine
en-gi-bre *m.* ginger
e-rar-quí-a *f.* hierarchy
e-re-mias *m., f.* complainer
er-ga *f.* jargon; slang
e-ri-gon-za *f.* gibberish
e-rin-gar *v.* to pester
e-rin-ga-zo *m.* injection
e-ro-glí-fi-co *m.* hieroglyph
er-sey *m.* sweater

ji-fía *f.* swordfish
jin-da *f.* fright
ji-ne-te *m.* equestrian;
  horseman
ji-ne-te-ar *v.* to ride a horse
i-par *v.* to pant
ji-ra *f.* excursion
ji-ra-fa *f.* giraffe
o-co-si-dad *f.* joke; wit
jo-co-so *adj.* jocular
o-cun-di-dad *f.* jocundity
o-fai-na *f.* washbowel
or-na-da *f.* trip
or-nal *m.* wage
o-ro-ba *f.* hump
o-ro-bar *v.* to annoy; bother
o-rrar *v.* to haul
o-ven *m.* youth
o-vial *adj.* jovial
o-ya *f.* gem; jewel
o-ye-ra *f.* box for jewelry
o-ye-ría *f.* jewelry store
o-ye-ro *m.* jeweler
u-bi-la-do *m., f* retired one
u-bi-lar(se) *v.* to retire
u-bi-leo *m.* jubilee
u-bi-lo *m.* joy
u-bi-lo-so *adj.* joyful
u-día *f.* bean
ue-go *m.* play; game
ué-ves *m.* Tuesday
uéz *m.* judge
u-gar *v.* to game; to play
u-gue-tear *v.* to play
u-gue-ton *adj.* playful
ui-cío *m.* verdict; judgment
u-lío *m.* July
un-co *m.* junk
u-nío *m.* June
un-ta *f.* union
un-ta-men-te *adv.* together
un-tar(se) *v.* to connect; join
un-to *adv.* together
u-ra-do *m.* jury
u-rar *v.* to vow; swear; curse
u-ris-ta *f.* jurist
us-ta-men-te *adv.* fairly
us-ti-cía *f.* justice
us-ti-fi-car *v.* to warrant
us-to *adj.* fair
u-ve-nil *adj.* youth
u-ven-tud *f.* youth
juz-gar *v.* to try; to judge

ki-lo *m.* kilogram
ki-lo-ci-clo *m.* kilocycle
ki-lo-gra-mo *m.* kilogram
ki-lo-me-tri-co *adj.* kilometric
ki-ló-me-tro *m.* kilometer
ki-lo-va-tio *m.* kilowatt
kirsch *m.* cherry-brandy
kum-mel *m.* cumin brandy

la *def. article* the
la-be-rin-to *m.* labyrinth
la-bia *f.* elloquence
la-bio *m.* lip
la-bor *f.* work
la-bo-ra-ble *adj.* working
la-bo-ral *adj.* labor
la-bo-rar *v.* to work
la-bo-ra-to-rio *m.* laboratory
la-bo-re-ar *v.* to work
la-bo-rio-so *adj.* arduous
la-bra-do, -da *adj.* plowed; cultivated; wrought
la-bra-dor, ra *adj.* farming *m.* farmer; peasant
la-bran-za *f.* farmland; farm
la-brar *v.* to carve; work; plow; cultivate; tool
la-ca *f.* shellac; lacquer; hair spray
la-ca-yo *m.* valet; attendant
la-ce-ra-cion *f.* laceration
la-ce-rar *v.* to injure; lacerate
la-ce-ria *f.* want; toil
la-cio *adj.* limp; straight
la-co-ni-co, -ca *adj.* laconic
la-cra *f.* scar
la-cre *m.* a sealing wax
la-cri-mó-ge-no, -na *adj.* tear producing
la-cri-mo-so, -sa *adj.* tearful; sad; sorrowful
lac-ta-cion *f.* nursing
lac-tan-cia *f.* lactation
lac-tar *v.* to suckle
lác-ti-co, -ca *adj.* lactic
lac-to-sa *f.* lactose
la-de-ar *v.* to tilt
la-de-o *m.* inclination
la-de-ra *f.* slope

la-di-no, -na *adj.* astute
la-do *m.* room; side; protection de next to; beside; along side
la-drar *v.* to snarl at something; to growl
la-dri-llo *m.* brick
la-dron *m.* robber
la-dro-ne-ri-a *f.* theft
la-gar-ti-ja *f.* a small lizard
la-gar-to *m.* lizard
la-go *m.* lake
lá-gri-ma *f.* tear
la-gri-me-ar *v.* to tear; to weep; to cry
la-gri-mo-so, -sa *adj.* tearful; watery
la-gu-na *f.* lagoon
lai-cal *adj.* laical
la-ja *f.* slab of stone
la-me-du-ra *f.* licking
la-men-ta-ble *adj.* lamentable
la-men-ta-ción *f.* lamentation
la-men-tar *v.* to be sorry for; to regret something
la-men-to *m.* lament
la-men-to-so, -sa *adj.* mournful
la-mer *v.* to lap up
la-me-ta-da *f.* lick
la-mi-do, -da *adj.* polished
la-mi-na-cion *f.* lamination
la-mi-nar *v.* to laminate
lám-pa-ra *f.* lamp
lam-pa-ri-lla *f.* little or small lamp
lam-pa-ron *m.* stain
lam-pi-ño, -ña *adj.* hairless
la-na *f.* wool
la-na-do, -na *adj.* fleecy
lan-ce *m.* argument; move; occurrence
lan-ce-ar *v.* to lance
lan-ce-ta *f.* lancet
lan-cha *f.* boat
lan-che-ro *m.* boatman
lan-chon *m.* barge
la-ne-ro, -ra *adj.* woolen
lan-gui-de-cer *v.* to languish
lan-gui-dez *f.* feebleness; lethargy

lán-gui-do, -da *adj.* languid

lan-guor *m.* languor

la-no-li-na *f.* lanolin

la-no-so, -sa *adj.* woolly

lan-za *f.* spear

lan-za-da *f.* wound due to a lance

lan-za-mien-to *m.* throwing

lan-zar *v.* to hurl; to fire; to release; to vomit; to throw; to shoot

lá-pi-da *f.* tombstone

la-pi-da-rio, -ria *adj.* concise; japidary

lá-piz *m.* pencil

lap-so, -sa *m.* interval; lapse

la-que-ar *v.* to varnish

lar-do *m.* fat; lard

lar-gar *v.* to let go; to dismiss; to release; to hurl; to throw

lar-go *adj.* lengthy; long; abundant

lar-gor *m.* length

lar-gue-za *f.* length

lar-gui-ru-cho, -cha *adj.* lanky

la-rin-ge *f.* larynx

la-rin-gi-tis *f.* laryngitis

lar-va *f.* larva

lar-val *adj.* larval

las *pron.* them; *art.* the

lá-ser *m.* laser

la-si-tud *f.* lassitude

la-so *adj.* weak; limp

lás-ti-ma *f.* compassion; shame; pity

las-ti-ma-du-ra *f.* wound

las-ti-mar *v.* to hurt; to offend; to injure

las-ti-me-ro, -ra *adj.* pitiful

la-ta *f.* can; tin can; pest

la-te-ar *v.* to bend

la-ten-te *adj.* latent

la-te-ral *adj.* lateral

la-ti-do *m.* beating; throbbing; beat

la-tien-te *adj.* throbbing

la-ti-gue-ar *v.* to whip; to crack the whip

la-tir *v.* to throb

la-ti-tud *f.* breadth; extent; width; scope

la-ti-tu-di-nal *adj.* latitudinal

la-to, -ta *adj.* wide

la-tón *m.* brass

la-to-ne-ro *m.* brassworker

la-to-so, -sa *adj.* bothersome

la-tro-ci-nio *m.* theft

lau-da-ble *adj.* laudable

lau-de *f.* tombstone

lau-do *m.* verdict

lau-rel *m.* bay; laurel

lau-re-o *adj.* laurel

la-va *f.* lava

la-va-ble *adj.* washable

la-va-da *f.* washing

la-va-de-ro *m.* laundry

la-va-do *m.* wash

la-va-dor *m.* washer

la-van-da *f.* lavender

la-van-de-ra *f.* laundrywoman

la-van-de-ro *m.* laundryman

la-va-pla-tos *m.* dishwasher

la-var *v.* to wash; to clean

la-va-ti-va *f.* enema

la-xar *v.* to slacken

la-xa-ti-vo *adj.* laxative

la-zar *v.* to rope

la-za-ri-no, -na *adj.* leprous

la-zo *m.* lasso; knot; trap; snare

le *pron.* him

le-al *adj.* faithful

le-al-tad *f.* loyalty

lec-ción *f.* lession

lec-tor, a *adj.* reading

lec-tu-ra *f.* reading

le-cha-da *f.* grout; whitewash

le-char *v.* to milk

le-che *f.* milk

le-che-río, -ría *adj.* dairy; milky

le-cho *m.* layer; bed

le-cho-so *adj.* milky

le-chu-ga *f.* lettuce

le-er *v.* to read

le-ga-ción *f.* legation

le-ga-do *m.* legacy

le-ga-jo *m.* file

le-gal *adj.* legal

le-ga-li-dad *f.* legality

le-ga-lis-ta *f.* legalist

le-ga-li-za-cion *f.* legalization

le-ga-li-zar *v.* to legalize

-**gar** v. to delegate; to bequeathe

-**gi-ble** adj. legible

-**gion** f. legion

-**gis-la-cion** f. legislation

-**gis-la-dor** m. legislator

-**gis-la-tu-ra** f. legislative

-**jos** adv. far away

n-**gua** f. language

-**on** m. lion

-**o-na** f. lioness

-**o-par-do** m. leopard

s **pron.** for them; for you

-**tal** adj. lethal

-**tra** f. letter

-**van-tar** v. to lift up; erect

y f. rule; law

-**be-ra-ción** f. liberation

-**be-ral** adj. liberal

-**ber-tad** f. freedom

bre adj. single; open; free

bro m. book

gar v. to commit; bind

-**mi-ta-ción** f. limitation

-**mi-ta-do** adj. limited

-**mi-tar** v. to restrict; limit

-**món** m. lemon

m-**piar** v. to clear; clean

m-**pie-za** f. neatness; cleaning

m-**pio** adj. pure; clean

-ne-a f. outline; line; boundary

s-**ta** f. list

s-**to** adj. ready

-**tro** m. liter

-**via-no, -na** adj. faithless; light

-**vi-dez** f. lividness

-**vi-do** adj. livid

o **def. article** the

o-a f. praise

o-a-ble adj. praiseworthy

o-ar v. to praise

o-ba f. the female wolf

o-bo m. the male wolf

o-bre-go adj. somber; dark

o-bu-lo m. lobe

o-ca-ción f. leasing

o-cal adj. local

o-ca-li-dad f. locality

o-ca-li-zar v. to find; to locate

lo-ción f. lotion

lo-co adj. crazy; extraordinary

lo-grar v. to take; obtain

lo-ro m. parrot

los pron. them; **art.** the

lu-ci-do adj. shining

lu-cir v. to illuminate; to light

lue-go adv. later; then

lu-na f. moon

lu-nar adj. iunar

lus-trar v. to shine

luz f. day; light

ma-ca-bro adj. funeral

ma-ca-dam m. macadam

ma-ca-rrón m. macaroon

ma-ce-ra-cion f. maceration

ma-ce-rar v. to macerate

ma-ce-ta f. flowerpot or holder

ma-ci-len-to, -ta adj. lean; thin; emaciated

ma-ci-zo, -za adj. solid

ma-cro-bio-ti-co f. macrobiotics

ma-cu-la f. spot

ma-cha-ca f. pounder

ma-cha-ca-dor, -ra adj. pounding

ma-cha-car v. to beat; to pound; to bother

ma-cha-con, -ona adj. tiresome f., m pest

ma-cha-da f. stupidity

ma-cha-do m. hatchet

ma-che-te m. machete

ma-che-te-ar v. to injure or cut with a machete

ma-cho adj. manly; male; tough; virile

ma-chu-ca-du-ra f. beating; bruising

ma-chu-car v. to beat

ma-de-ra f. timber; wood; lumber

ma-de-ra-da f. raft

ma-de-re-ri-a f. lumberyard

ma-de-re-ro, -ra adj. timber

ma-de-ro *m.* log
ma-dras-tra *f.* stepmother
ma-dre *f.* mom; mother
ma-dre-sel-va *f.* honeysuckle
ma-dri-gue-ra *f.* hole; burrow; lair
ma-dri-na *f.* bridesmaid; godmother; patroness
ma-dru-ga-dor, -ra *m., f* early riser
ma-dru-gar *v.* to anticipate; to get up early
ma-du-ra-cion *f.* ripening
ma-du-ra-dor, a *adj.* ripening
ma-du-rar *v.* to mature; to ripen; to maturate
ma-du-rez *f.* maturity, ripeness
ma-es-tre *m.* master
ma-es-tro, -tra *adj.* expert; teacher; *m.* mer
ma-gan-ce-ri-a *f.* trickery
ma-gia *f.* magic
má-gi-co, -ca *adj.* magic
ma-gis-tra-do *m.* magistrate
ma-gis-tral *adj.* imposing; masterful; magisterial
mag-na-te *m.* magnate
mag-ne-sia *f.* magnesia
mag-ne-sio *m.* magnesium
mag-né-ti-co, -ca *adj.* magnetic
mag-ne-tis-mo *m.* magnetism
mag-ne-to-fo-ni-co, -ca *adj.* magnetic
mag-ni-fi-ca-dor, -ra *adj.* magnifying
mag-ni-fi-car *v.* to exalt; to magnify; to glorify
mag-ni-fi-cen-cia *f.* magnificence
mag-ni-fi-cen-te *adj.* magnificent
mag-ní-fi-co, -ca *adj.* excellent; magnificent
mag-ni-tud *f.* size; importance; magnitude
mag-no-lia *f.* magnolia
ma-go, -ga *adj.* magic
ma-gu-llar *v.* to batter
ma-iz *m.* corn
ma-ja-de-ro, -ra *adj.* foolish

ma-ja-du-ra *f.* pounding
ma-jar *v.* to pound; to bother; to mash
ma-jes-tad *f.* grandeur; majesty
ma-jo, -ja *adj.* showy; attractive; flashy; nice
mal *adj.* bad; evil; disease
mal *adv.* wrongly; badly
ma-la-bar *v.* to juggle
ma-la-ba-ris-ta *m.* juggler
ma-la-cos-tum-bra-do, a *adj.* ill-mannered; have poor or bad habits; spoiled
ma-lan-drin, a *adj.* evil
ma-la-ria *f.* malaria
ma-la-ven-tu-ra *f.* misfortune
ma-la-ven-tu-ran-za *f.* misfortune
mal-ba-ra-tar *v.* to squander
mal-co-mer *v.* to eat badly or poorly
mal-co-mi-do *adj.* underfed
mal-con-ten-to, -ta *adj.* unhappy; rebellious
mal-cria-do, -da *adj.* ill-bred
mal-criar *v.* to spoil
mal-dad *f.* evil
mal-de-cir *v.* to slander; to curse
mal-di-ci-en-te *adj.* defaming; slandering *m., f.* curser; slanderer
mal-di-ción *f.* curse
mal-di-to, -ta *adj.* wicked; bad
ma-le-a-bi-li-dad *f.* malleability
ma-le-a-ble *adj.* malleable
ma-le-an-te *adj.* corrputing; wicked
ma-le-ar *v.* to ruin; to corrupt; to pervert
ma-le-di-cen-cia *f.* slander
ma-le-fi-cen-cia *f.* evil
ma-le-fi-cen-te *adj.* maleficent
ma-les-tar *m.* uneasiness; malaise
ma-le-ta *f.* suitcase; baggage; luggage
ma-le-vo-len-cia *f.* malevolence

nal-for-ma-cion f. malformation

nal-gas-tar v. to waste

nal-ha-da-do, -da adj. unfortunate

nal-he-rir v. to injure

nal-hu-mo-ra-do, -da adj. bad-tempered

nal-hu-mo-rar v. to irritate; to bother; to annoy

na-li-cia f. cunning; wickedness; slyness

na-li-cio-so, -sa adj. malicious; cunning

nal-lig-ni-dad f. malignancy

na-lig-no, -na adj. malignant

nal-mi-ra-do, -da adj. disfavored

na-lo adj. harmful; nasty; bad

na-lo-grar v. to fail; to lose; to waste

na-lo-gro m. failure

nal-pa-rar v. to harm; to damage

nal-quis-tar v. to estrange

nal-quis-to, -ta adj. unpopular

nal-so-nan-te adj. harsh

nal-tra-ta-mien-to m. mistreatment

nal-tra-tar v. to mistreat

nal-va-do, -da adj. wicked

nal-ver-sa-dor, -a m., f. embezzler

nal-ver-sar v. to embezzle

na-ma f. mommy

na-mar v. to nurse; to suck

na-ma-rio, -ia adj. mammary

na-me-lon m. nipple

na-na-da f. herd; bunch

na-na-de-ro, -a m., f. spring

na-nan-te adj. running

na-nar v. to flow

an-car v. to disable

an-ci-lla f. blemish

an-ci-llar v. to blemish

an-ci-par v. to enslave

an-co adj. one-armed; disabled

an-co-mu-nar v. to join together; to combine

man-co-mu-ni-dad f. union; association

man-cha f. blot; stain

man-char v. to stain; to spot; to soil

man-da f. bequest

man-da-do m. errand; task; order

man-da-mien-to m. command; order

man-dar v. to leave; to order

man-da-ri-na f. mandarin orange

man-da-to m. trust; command; order

man-di-bu-la f. mandible

man-do m. leadership; power

man-do-lin f. mandolin

man-dria adj. timid; worthless; useless

man-dril m. mandrill

ma-ne-ar v. to hobble around

ma-ne-ja-ble adj. manageable

ma-ne-jar v. to handle; to manage

ma-ne-jo m. operation; handling; management

ma-ne-ra f. style; way; manner; type

man-ga f. strainer; hose

man-ga-ne-so m. manganese

man-gar v. to swipe; to mooch

man-gos-ta f. mongoose

man-gue-ar v. to startle

man-gue-ra f. garden hose

man-gui-ta f. cover

ma-ni m. peanut

ma-ni-a f. habit; craze

ma-ni-a-co, -ca adj. maniac

ma-ni-fes-ta-ción f. manifestation

ma-ni-fes-tar v. to reveal; to manifest

ma-ni-fies-to, -ta adj. manifest

ma-ni-lla f. bracelet

ma-ni-pu-la-ción f. manipulation

ma-ni-pu-la-dor, a m. manipulator

ma-ni-pu-lar v. to manipulate; to manage

ma-ni-quí m. mannequin

ma-no f. hand

ma-no-jo m. handful; bunch

ma-no-se-ar v. to touch

man-so, -sa adj. mild; tame

man-ta f. shawl; blanket

man-te-ca f. fat; lard

man-tel m. tablecloth

man-te-nen-cia f. support; maintenance

man-te-ner v. to support; to keep; to feed; to maintain

man-te-ni-mien-to m. support; sustenance

man-te-que-rí-a f. dairy

man-te-que-ro m. dairyman

man-te-qui-lla f. butter

man-to m. mantle; robe; cloak; cover

ma-nual adj. manual

ma-nu-fac-tu-rar v. to manufacture

ma-nu-ten-ción f. maintenance

man-za-na f. apple

man-za-nar v. apple orchard

man-za-no m. apple tree

ma-ña f. dexterity; skill

ma-ña-na f. morning

ma-ne-ar v. to manage

ma-ñe-ro adj. shrewd

ma-pa f. map

ma-pa-che m. raccoon

ma-que-ar v. to varnish

ma-qui-na f. machine

ma-qui-na-ción f. machination

ma-qui-na-dor m., f. schemer

ma-qui-nar v. to scheme

ma-qui-nis-ta m. machinist

mar m. sea; tide

ma-ra-ton m. marathon

ma-ra-vi-lla f. marvel; astonishment; wonder

ma-ra-vi-llar v. to astonish; to be amazed

ma-ra-vi-llo-so, -sa adj. marvelous

mar-ca f. brand; mark; stamp; trademark

mar-ca-do adj. notable

mar-ca-dor, -ra adj. marking

mar-car v. to stamp; to mark; to note

mar-cial adj. military; martial

mar-co m. mark; standard

mar-cha f. march; velocity; speed; progress

mar-char v. to run; walk

mar-chi-tar v. to weaken; to wilt; to languish

mar-chi-to, -ta adj. wilted

ma-re-ar v. to sail; to bother

ma-re-ja-da f. turbulence

ma-re-o m. nausea

mar-ga-ri-na f. margarine

mar-ga-ri-ta f. daisy

mar-gen m. fringe; margin

mar-gi-nal adj. marginal

mar-gi-nar v. to marginate

ma-ri-dar v. to wed

ma-ri-do m. spouse

ma-ri-nar v. to marinate

ma-ri-ne-ría f. sailoring

ma-ri-ne-ro, -ra adj. marine; seaworthy

ma-ri-no adj. marine

ma-ri-po-sa f. butterfly

ma-ri-qui-ta f. ladybug

ma-ris-cal m. marshal

ma-ris-co m. crustacean

ma-ri-tal adj. marital

ma-rí-ti-mo, -ma adj. maritime

már-mol m. marble

mar-qués m. marquis

ma-rra-no adj. filthy

ma-rrar v. to fail; to miss something

ma-rrón adj. brown

ma-rru-lle-ro, -ra m., f. conniver

mar-so-pa f. porpoise

mar-su-pial adj. marsupial

mar-tes m. Tuesday

mar-ti-llar v. to hammer

mar-ti-llo m. hammer

már-tir m., f. martyr

mar-ti-rio m. martyrdom

mar-zo m. March

mas adv. rather; more

ma-sa-crar v. to massacre

ma-sa-cre *m.* massacre
ma-sa-je *m.* massage
ma-sa-jis-ta *m.* masseur
mas-car *v.* to chew
más-ca-ra *f.* disguise
mas-ca-ra-da *f.* masquerade
mas-co-ta *f.* mascot
mas-cu-li-ni-dad *f.* masculinity
mas-cu-li-no *adj.* manly; male
ma-si-vo, -va *adj.* massive
mas-ti-car *v.* to masticate; to ruminate
más-til *m.* mast
mas-toi-des *adj.* mastoid
ma-ta *f.* shrub
ma-ta-dor, -ra *m.*, *f.* killer
ma-ta-fue-go *m.* fire extinguisher
ma-tan-za *f.* massacre; killing; slaughtering
ma-tar *v.* to extinguish; to kill; to slaughter
ma-ta-ri-fe *m.* slaughterer
ma-ta-se-llar *v.* to cancel
ma-te-má-ti-co, -ca *adj.* mathematical
ma-te-ria *f.* matter
ma-te-rial *adj.* material
ma-te-ria-li-dad *f.* materiality
ma-te-ria-lis-ta *adj.* materialistic
ma-ter-nal *adj.* maternal
ma-ter-ni-dad *f.* maternity
ma-ter-no *adj.* motherly
ma-ti-nal *adj.* morning
ma-tiz *m.* tint
ma-ti-zar *v.* to tint
ma-tre-ro, -ra *adj.* shrewd
ma-triar-ca-do *m.* matriarchy
ma-triar-cal *adj.* matriarchal
ma-tri-ci-dio *m.* matricide
ma-trí-cu-la *f.* list
ma-tri-cu-la-ción *f.* registration
ma-tri-cu-lar *v.* to natriculate
ma-tri-mo-nial *adj.* matrimonial
ma-tri-mo-nio *m.* matrimony
ma-triz *f.* uterus
ma-tro-na *f.* matron
ma-tro-nal *adj.* matronly

ma-xi-ma-men-te *adv.* chiefly
ma-xi-me *adv.* principally
má-xi-mo *adj.* maximum
ma-yo *m.* May
ma-yo-ne-sa *f.* mayonnaise
ma-yor *adj.* greatest; larger; older
ma-yo-ría *f.* majority
ma-yo-ri-dad *f.* majority
ma-yus-cu-lo, -la *adj.* important; capital
maz-mo-rra *f.* dungeon
ma-zo *m.* bunch
me *pron.* me
me-cá-ni-co, -ca *adj.* mechanical
me-ca-ni-zar *v.* to mechanize
me-ce-do-ra *f.* rocking chair
me-cer *v.* to sway; to rock
me-cha *f.* match; wick
me-che-ra *f.* shoplifter
me-chón *m.* tuft
me-da-lla *f.* medal
me-da-llon *m.* medallion
me-dia *f.* stocking
me-dia-dor, -ra *m.*, *f.* mediator
me-dia-ne-ro, -ra *adj.* mediating
me-dia-no-che *f.* midnight
me-diar *v.* to intercede
me-di-ca-cion *f.* medication
me-di-car *v.* to medicate
me-di-ci-na *f.* medicine
me-di-ci-nal *adj.* medicinal
me-di-ci-nar *v.* to cure or treat with medicine
me-di-co, -ca *m.*, *f.* doctor
me-di-da *f.* measurement
me-die-val *adj.* medieval
me-dio *adj.* middle; half
me-dio-cre *adj.* mediocre
me-dio-cri-dad *f.* mediocrity
me-dio-dí-a *m.* noon
me-dir *v.* to weigh; measure
me-di-ta-ción *f.* meditation
me-di-tar *v.* to meditate
me-di-ta-ti-vo, -va *adj.* meditative
me-dium *m.* medium
me-drar *v.* to thrive; prosper

me-dro-so, -sa *adj.* timorous
me-du-la *f.* medulla
me-du-sa *f.* jellyfish
me-gá-fo-no *m.* megaphone
me-ga-tón *m.* megaton
me-ji-lla *f.* cheek
me-jor *adj.* superior; better
me-jo-ra *f.* betterment
me-jo-rar *v.* to make better
me-jo-ría *f.* improvement
me-lan-có-li-a *f.* melancholy
me-la-za *f.* molasses
me-lin-dre-ria *f.* affectation
me-lo-co-tón *m.* peach
me-lo-co-to-ne-ro *m.* peach tree
me-lo-dia *f.* tune
me-ló-di-co *adj.* tuneful
me-lo-dio-so, -sa *adj.* melodious
me-lo-dra-ma *m.* melodrama
me-lo-dra-ma-ti-co, -ca *adj.* melodramatic
me-lón *m.* melon
me-lo-te *m.* molasses
me-llar *v.* to nick; to chip
mem-bra-na *f.* membrane
me-mo-ra-ble *v.* memorable
me-mo-rar *v.* to recall
me-mo-ria *f.* remembrance; memory
me-mo-rial *m.* memorial
me-mo-ri-za-cion *f.* memorization
me-mo-ri-zar *v.* to memorize
men-ción *f.* mention
men-cio-nar *v.* to mention
me-ne-ar *v.* to sway
men-gua *f.* poverty
men-gua-do *adj.* decreased; timid
men-guar *v.* to wane; to diminish
me-nin-gi-tis *f.* meningitis
me-no-pau-sia *f.* menopause
me-nor *adj.* lesser; least; less; younger
me-nos *adv.* least; less
me-nos-ca-bar *v.* to impair
me-nos-ca-bo *m.* damage; diminishing
me-nos-pre-cia-ble *adj.* despicable
me-nos-pre-cio *m.* underestimation; contempt
men-sa-je *m.* message
men-sa-je-ro, -ra *adj.* messenger
men-sual *adj.* monthly
men-su-ra *f.* measurement
men-su-ra-ble *adj.* mensurable
men-su-rar *v.* measure
men-ta *f.* mint
men-ta-do, -da *adj.* reowned
men-tal *adj.* mental
men-ta-li-dad *f.* mentality
men-tar *v.* mention
men-te *f.* intellect; intelligence
men-tir *v.* to lie
men-ti-ra *f.* falsehood
men-ti-ro-so, -sa *adj.* lying
men-tor *m.* mentor
me-nu-do *adj.* little; insignificant
mer-ca-de-o *m.* marketing
mer-ca-do *m.* marketplace
mer-can-te *adj.* merchant
mer-can-til *adj.* mercantile
mer-car *v.* to buy
mer-ced *f.* gift
mer-ce-na-rio, -ria *adj.* mercenary
mer-cu-rial *adj.* mercurial
mer-cu-rio *m.* mercury
me-re-ci-mien-to *m.* worth
me-ri-dia-no, -na *adj.* meridian
me-rien-da *f.* snack
mé-ri-to *m.* value; worth
me-ri-to-rio, -ria *adj.* meritorious
mer-mar *v.* to diminish
me-ro, -ra *adj.* pure
me-ro-de-ar *v.* plunder
mes *m.* month
me-sa *f.* table
me-són *m.* tavern
me-so-ne-ro, -ra *m.*, *f.* innkeeper
me-su-ra *f.* moderation
me-su-ra-do, -da *adj.* moderate
me-ta-bo-li-co, -ca *adj.*

metabolic

me-ta-bo-lis-mo *m.* metabolism

me-tá-fo-ra *f.* metaphor

me-ta-fó-ri-co, -ca *adj.* metaphoric

me-tal *m.* metal

me-tá-li-co *adj.* metallic

me-ta-li-zar *v.* to metalize

me-ta-mor-fi-co, -ca *adj.* metamorphic

me-ta-no *m.* methane

me-te-o-ri-co, -ca *adj.* meteoric

me-te-o-ri-to *m.* meteorite

me-te-o-ro *m.* meteor

me-te-o-ro-lo-gi-a *f.* meteorology

me-te-o-ro-lo-gis-ta *m., f.* meteorologist

me-ter *v.* to insert into; to cause

me-ti-cu-lo-so, -sa *adj.* meticulous

me-ti-lo *m.* methyl

me-tó-di-co, -ca *adj.* methodical

me-to-do *m.* method

me-to-do-lo-gi-a *f.* methodology

me-tri-co *adj.* metric

me-tro-po-li-ta-no, -na *adj.* metropolitan

mez-cla-dor *m.* blending

mez-clar *v.* to mingle; blend

mez-quin-dad *f.* miserliness

mez-qui-no, -na *adj.* petty; wretched; miserly

mez-qui-ta *f.* mosque

mi *pron.* me

ni-cro-bio *m.* microbe

ni-cro-bio-lo-gia *f.* microbiology

ni-cro-fil-me *m.* microfilm

ni-cró-fo-no *m.* microphone

ni-cros-có-pi-co, -ca *adj.* microscopic

ni-cros-co-pio *m.* microscope

nie-do *m.* dread

nie-do-so, -sa *adj.* cowardly

niel *f.* honey

niel-ga *f.* alfalfa

miem-bro *m.* member

mien-tras *adv.* meanwhile *conj.* while

miér-co-les *m.* Wednesday

mies *f.* grain

mi-ga *f.* substance; scrap

mi-gra-ción *f.* migration

mi-gra-na *f.* migraine

mil *adj.* thousand

mi-la-gro *m.* miracle

mi-la-gro-so *adj.* miraculous

mi-li-cia *f.* militia

mi-li-cia-no, -na *adj.* military

mi-li-gra-mo *m.* milligram

mi-li-li-tro *m.* milliliter

mi-li-me-tro *m.* millimeter

mi-li-tar *f.* soldier

mi-lla *f.* mile

mi-llón *m.* million

mi-mar *v.* to fondle; pamper

mi-mi-co, -ca *adj.* mimic

mi-mo-so *adj.* spoiled

mi-na *f.* mine

mi-na-dor *adj.* mining

mi-nar *v.* to mine

mi-ne-ral *adj.* mineral

mi-ne-ra-lo-gis-ta *m.* mineralogist

mi-ne-ri-a *f.* mining

mi-nia-tu-ra *f.* miniature

mi-nia-tu-ris-ta *m., f.* miniaturist

mi-ni-fal-da *f.* miniskirt

mi-ni-mi-zar *v.* to minimize

mi-ni-mo, -ma *adj.* least; minimal; minute

mi-nis-te-rial *adj.* ministerial

mi-nis-te-rio *m.* ministry

mi-nis-tro *m.* minister

mi-no-rar *v.* to reduce

mi-no-ria *f.* minority

mi-no-ri-ta-rio *adj.* minority

mi-nu-cio-so, -sa *adj.* minute

mi-nús-cu-lo, -la *adj.* tiny; small

mi-nu-ta *f.* record; note

mi-nu-to *m.* minute

mi-o, -a *adj.* mine

mio-pe *adj.* myopic

mio-pi-a *f.* myopia

mi-ra *f.* sight; intention

mi-ra-do, -da *adj.* regarded; cautious

mi-ra-dor *adj.* watching
mi-rar *v.* to watch; to look at; to observe
mi-ra-sol *m.* sunflower
mi-rí-a-da *f.* myriad
mir-lo *m.* blackbird
mis-ce-lá-ne-o, -a *adj.* miscellaneous
mi-se-ra-ble *adj.* miserable; poor; miserly
mi-se-ria *f.* suffering; miserliness; misery
mi-sil *m.* missile
mi-sión *f.* mission
mi-sio-nal *adj.* missionary
mis-mo *adj.* likewise; same thing
mis-te-rio *m.* mystery
mis-te-rio-so *adj.* mysterious
mís-ti-co, -ca *adj.* mystic
mis-ti-fi-car *v.* to mystify
mis-tu-ra *f.* mixture
mi-tad *f.* half
mi-ti-ga-cion *f.* mitigation
mi-ti-gar *v.* to mitigate
mi-to *m.* myth
mi-ton *m.* mitt
mi-tra *f.* miter
mix-to, -ta *adj.* mixed
mix-tu-ra *f.* mixture
mix-tu-rar *v.* to mix up
mo-bi-lia-rio, -ria *adj.* movable
mo-bla-je *m.* furnishing
mo-blar *v.* to furnish
mo-ce-dad *f.* youth
mo-ción *f.* motion
mo-cho, -cha *adj.* hornless
mo-da *f.* fashion
mo-de-lo *m.* model
mo-de-ra-ción *f.* moderation
mo-de-ra-do *adj.* moderate
mo-de-rar *v.* to regulate; to restrain
mo-der-ni-za-ción *f.* modernization
mo-der-ni-zar *v.* to modernize
mo-der-no *adj.* modern
mo-des-tia *f.* modesty
mó-di-co, -ca *adj.* moderate
mo-di-fi-ca-ción *f.* modification

mo-di-fi-ca-dor *adj.* modifying
mo-di-fi-car *v.* to modify
mo-dis-te-ri-a *f.* shop for dresses
mo-do *m.* way
mo-do-so, -sa *adj.* well-mannered
mo-du-la-cion *f.* modulation
mo-du-la-dor, -ra *m., f.* modulator
mo-jar *v.* to drench; to dip; to wet
mol-de *m.* pattern; mold
mol-de-ar *v.* to shape
mo-lé-cu-lar *adj.* molecular
mo-ler *v.* to grind
mo-les-tar *v.* to annoy; to disrupt
mo-les-tia *f.* annoyance; trouble
mo-les-to *adj.* bothered; annoying
mo-men-to *m.* moment
mo-na *f.* a female monkey
mo-nas-te-rio *m.* monastery
mo-ni-tor *m.* monitor
mo-no *m.* male monkey
mo-no-gra-ma *m.* monogram
mons-truo *m.* monster
mons-truo-so *adj.* monstrous
mon-ta-ña *f.* mountain
mon-tar *v.* to mount
mo-nu-men-to *m.* monument
mo-ral *f.* morale
mo-ra-li-dad *f.* morality
mo-ra-li-zar *v.* to moralize
mo-rar *v.* to dwell; to live
mór-bi-do *adj.* morbid
mo-re-no *adj.* brown
mor-fi-na *f.* morphine
mo-rir *v.* to kill
mor-tal *adj.* fatal; mortal
mor-ta-li-dad *f.* mortality
mor-tuo-rio *m.* mortuary
mos-ca *f.* fly
mos-qui-to *m.* mosquito
mos-ta-za *f.* mustard
mos-trar *v.* to exhibit; to appear; to show
mo-tor *m.* engine

mo-ver v. to move
mo-vi-mien-to m. movement
mu-cha-cha f. girl
mu-cha-cho m. boy
mu-cho adj. many; a lot
muer-te f. death
muer-to adj. dead
mu-jer f. female; woman
múl-ti-ple adj. multiple
mul-ti-pli-car v. to multiply
mun-do m. world
mu-ni-ci-pal adj. municipal
mu-ñe-ca f. wrist; doll
mús-cu-lo m. muscle
mú-si-ca f. music
mu-si-cal adj. musical
mus-lo m. thigh
muy adv. much; greatly

na-bo m. turnip; mast
na-ca-ri-no adj. narcreous
na-cer v. to rise; to be born;
  to be concieved
na-ci-do, -da adj. born
na-cien-te adj. recent;
  growing; initial; nascent
na-ci-mien-to m. hatching;
  origin; birth; spring
na-ción f. nation
na-cio-nal adj. domestic; national
na-cio-na-li-dad f. nationality
na-cio-na-lis-ta m., f. nationalist
na-cio-na-li-za-cion f. nationalization
na-cio-na-li-zar v. to nationalize
na-da pron. no; not
  anything; none; nothing
na-da-dor m., f. swimmer
na-dar v. to swim
na-die pron. no one; nobody
nai-pe m. playing card
nal-ga f. behind; buttocks
na-ran-ja f. orange
na-ran-jal m. orange grove
na-ran-je-ro adj. orange
na-ran-jo m. orange tree

nar-có-ti-co, -ca adj. narcotic
nar-co-ti-zar v. to narcotize
na-riz f. nostril; nose
na-rra-cion f. narration; narrative
na-rra-dor, -ra adj. narrative
na-rrar v. to narrate
na-rra-ti-vo, -va adj. narrative
na-ta-ción f. swimming
na-tal adj. natal
na-ta-li-dad f. natality
Na-ti-vi-dad f. Christmas
na-ti-vo adj. inborn; native
na-to, -ta adj. natural
na-tu-ra f. nature
na-tu-ral adj. native; innate;
  natural
na-tu-ra-le-za f. nature
na-tu-ra-li-dad f. naturalness
na-tu-ra-li-za-ción f. naturalization
nau-fra-gar v. to shipwreck
náu-fra-go, -ga adj. shipwrecked
náu-se-a f. nausea
nau-se-ar v. to feel
  nauseous
náu-ti-co, -ca adj. nautical
na-val adj. naval
na-ve-ga-ble adj. navigable
na-ve-ga-cion f. navigation
na-ve-gar v. to sail
Na-vi-dad f. Christmas
na-ví-o m. vessel; boat
ne-bli-na f. fog
ne-bli-no-so, -sa adj. foggy
ne-bu-lo-si-dad f. haziness
ne-ce-dad f. nonsense
ne-ce-sa-rio adj. necessary
ne-ce-si-dad f. need;
  poverty; necessity
ne-ce-si-ta-do, -da adj. poor;
  needy
ne-ce-si-tar v. to want; to
  require; to need
ne-cio, -cia adj. foolish;
  stubborn
ne-cro-lo-gí-a f. necrology
nec-tar m. nectar
nec-ta-ri-na f. nectarine
ne-fri-tis f. nephritis
ne-ga-ble adj. refutable

ne-ga-ción f. denial; refusal; negation

ne-gar v. to refuse; to deny; to forbid

ne-ga-ti-vi-dad f. negativity

ne-gli-gen-cia f. disregard; negligence

ne-go-cia-ble adj. negotiable

ne-go-cia-ción f. negotiation; transaction

ne-go-ciar v. to deal; to negotiate

ne-go-cio m. job; work; business; transaction

ne-gro, -a adj. black

ne-gru-ra f. darkness

ne-gruz-co, -ca adj. dark

ne-ne, -na m., f. baby

ne-nu-far m. water lily

ne-ó-fi-to, -ta m., f. neophyte

ne-on m. neon

ne-o-na-to m. neonate

ner-vo m. nerve

ner-vio-si-dad f. nervousness

ner-vio-so, -sa adj. nervous

ner-vo-si-dad f. nervousness

ne-to, -ta adj. simple; pure

neu-má-ti-co, -ca adj. pneumatic

neu-ro-ci-ru-gí-a f. neurosurgery

neu-ro-lo-go m. neurologist

neu-ro-ti-co, -ca adj. neurotic

neu-to-nio m. newton

neu-tral adj. neutral

neu-tra-li-dad f. neutrality

neu-tra-li-zar v. to neutralize

neu-tro, -a adj. neutral

neu-trón m. neutron

ne-va-do, -da adj. snow-covered

ne-var v. to snow

ne-ve-ra f. refrigerator

ne-xo m. link

ni conj. neither; nor

ni-co-ti-na f. nicotine

ni-cho m. vault; recess

ni-dal m. nest

ni-do m. nest; liar; den

nei-bla f. mist

nie-ta f. granddaughter

nie-to m. grandson

nie-ve f. snow

ni-hi-lis-ta adj. nihilistic

ni-lon m. nylon

nim-bo m. halo

ni-mio, -a adj. insignificant

nin-fa f. nymph

nin-fe-a f. water lily

nin-fo m. dandy

nin-fo-ma-ni-a f. nymphomania

nin-gu-no, -na adj. no; none

ni-ne-rí-a f. childish

ni-nez f. infancy; childhood

ni-no, -na m. f. child

ní-quel m. nickel

ni-que-lar v. to nickel

ni-ti-do, -da adj. clear

ni-tra-to m. nitrite

ni-tri-to m. nitrite

ni-tro-ge-no m. nitrogen

ni-tro-gli-ce-ri-na f. nitroglycerin

ni-vel m. height; standard

ni-ve-lar v. to make level

no adv. no

no-ble adj. honorable; noble

no-ble-za f. nobleness; nobility

no-ción f. notion

no-ci-vi-dad f. noxiousness

no-ci-vo, -va adj. noxious

noc-tur-nal adj. nocturnal

noc-tur-no, -na adj. sad; nocturnal

no-che f. night

no-du-lo m. nodule

no-gal m. walnut

no-ma-da adj. nomadic

nom-bra-mein-to m. nomination; naming

nom-brar v. to name; to nominate

nom-bre m. name

no-men-cla-tu-ra f. nomenclature

no-mi-na f. roll

no-mi-na-ción f. nomination

no-mi-nal adj. nominal

no-mi-nar v. to nominate

non adj. uneven

no-na-da f. trifle

no-no, -na adj. ninth

nor-ma f. rule

nor-mal adj. normal

nor-ma-li-dad f. normality

nor-ma-li-za-cion f. normalization

nor-ma-li-zar v. to normalize

no-ro-es-te m. northwest

nor-te m. north

nos pron. us

no-ta-ble adj. outstanding; notable

no-tar v. to observe; note

no-ti-fi-car v. to notify

no-ve-no adj. ninth

no-ven-ta adj. ninety

no-via f. girlfriend

no-vio m. boyfriend

nu-bo-si-dad f. cloudiness

nu-ca f. nape

nues-tro adj. our

nue-ve adj. nine

nue-vo adj. new

nú-me-ro m. number

nun-ca adv. not ever

nu-trir v. to feed

ña-me m. yam

ña-pa f. tip; bonus

ña-que m. junk

ñe-que m. vigor; adj. strength

ño-ñe-ria f. timidity

ño-ñez f. bashfulness

ño-ño -a adj., m., f. timid; bashful

ñu-do m. knot

o conj. or

o-a-sis m. oasis

ob-ce-ca-da-men-to adv. blindly

ob-ce-car v. to blind

o-be-de-cer v. to obey

o-be-dien-cia f. obedience

o-be-dien-te adj. obedient

o-ber-tu-ra f. overture

o-be-si-dad f. obesity

o-bi-ce m. obstacle

o-bis-po m. bishop

ob-je-ción f. objection

ob-je-ta-ble adj. objectionable

ob-je-tar v. to object

ob-je-ti-var v. to objectify

ob-je-ti-vi-dad f. objectivity

ob-je-ti-vo adj. objective

ob-je-to m. theme; object

o-bli-cuo, -cua adj. oblique

o-bli-ga-ción f. responsibility; obligation

o-bli-gar v. to force; to oblige; to favor

o-bli-ga-to-rio, -ria adj. obligatory

o-blon-go, -ga adj. oblong

o-bo-e m. oboe

o-bra f. work; labor

o-brar v. to act; to work

o-bre-ro, -ra adj. working

obs-ce-ni-dad f. obscenity

obs-ce-no, -na adj. obscene

ob-se-quio m. present; kindness; gift

ob-se-quio-so, -sa adj. obsequious; attentive

ob-ser-va-ción f. observation

ob-ser-va-dor, -ra adj. observing m., f. observer

ob-ser-van-cia f. observance

ob-ser-var v. to watch; to observe

ob-se-sión f. obsession

ob-se-sio-nan-te adj. obsessive

ob-se-sio-nar v. to obsess about someting

ob-se-so, -sa adj. obsessive

obs-ta-cu-li-zar v. to hinder

obs-ta-cu-lo m. obstacle

obs-tan-te adj. obstructing

obs-tar v. to hinder; to obstruct something

obs-ti-na-ción f. obstinacy

obs-ti-na-do, -da adj. obstinate

obs-truc-ción f. obstruction

obs-truir v. to obstruct

ob-ten-ción f. obtaining

ob-te-ner v. to get; to have; to obtain

ob-tu-so, -sa *adj.* obtuse
ob-viar *v.* to prevent
ob-vio, -via *adj.* obvious
o-ca-sión *f.* cause; occasion; circumstance
o-ca-sio-nar *v.* to cause; to provoke; to occasion
oc-ci-den-tal *adj.* occidental
oc-ci-pi-tal *adj.* occipital
o-cé-a-no *m.* ocean
o-ce-a-no-gra-fí-a *f.* oceanography
o-ce-a-no-grá-fi-co, -ca *adj.* oceanographic
o-cio *m.* leisure; idleness
oc-ta-vo *adj.* eighth
oc-te-to *m.* octet
oc-to-ge-si-mo *adj.* eightieth
oc-to-go-nal *adj.* octagonal
oc-to-go-no, -na *adj.* octagonal
oc-tu-bre *m.* October
o-cul-tar *v.* to conceal; to silence; to hide
o-cu-lis-ta *m., f.* oculist
o-cul-ta-men-te *adv.* secretly
o-cul-tar *v.* to conceal; to silence; to hide
o-cul-tis-mo *m.* occultism
o-cul-to, -ta *adj.* concealed; occult
o-cu-pa-ción *f.* trade; occupation; job
o-cu-pa-do *adj.* occupied
o-cu-pan-te *adj.* occupying
o-cu-par *v.* to fill; to occupy; to employ; to pay attention to something
o-cu-rren-cia *f.* occurrence
o-cu-rrir *v.* to happen; to take place
o-chen-ta *adj.* eighty
o-chen-ta-vo, -va *adj.* eightieth
o-cho *adj.* eight
o-cho-cien-tos *adj.* eight hundred
o-da *f.* ode
o-da-lis-ca *f.* odalisque
o-diar *v.* to loathe
o-dio *m.* loathing
o-dio-so, -sa *adj.* odious
o-di-se-a *f.* odyssey

o-don-to-lo-go, -ga *m., f.* odontologist
o-es-te *m.* west
o-fen-der *v.* to hurt; offend
o-fen-sa *f.* offense
o-fen-si-vo, -va *adj.* offensive
o-fen-sor *adj.* offending
o-fer-tar *v.* to tender
o-fi-cial *m.* officer
o-fi-cia-li-dad *f.* officers
o-fi-cian-te *m.* officiant
o-fi-ci-na *f.* office
o-fi-ci-nis-ta *m., f.* office clerk
o-fi-cio *m.* work; office
o-fi-cio-so *adj.* obliging; diligent
o-fre-ci-mien-to *m.* offering
o-fren-da *f.* gift
o-fren-dar *v.* to give an offering for
of-tal-mo-lo-gi-a *f.* ophthalmology
of-tal-mo-lo-go *m.* ophthalmologist
o-fus-ca-cion *f.* confusion; dazzling
o-fus-car *v.* to bewilder; to blind
o-í-do *m.* ear
o-ír *v.* to listen; to hear; to attend
o-jal *m.* bottonhole
o-je-a-da *f.* glimpse
o-je-ri-za *f.* grudge
o-jo *m.* eye
o-jo-ta *f.* sandal
o-le-a-da *f.* wave
o-le-a-je *m.* waves
o-ler *v.* to smell
ol-fa-to *m.* instinct
ol-fa-to-rio, -ria *adj.* olfactory
o-li-va *f.* olive
o-li-var *m.* olive grove
o-li-vo *m.* olive tree
ol-mo *m.* elm tree
o-lor *m.* smell
o-lo-ro-so, -sa *adj.* fragrant
ol-vi-da-do, -da *adj.* forgetful; ungrateful
ol-vi-dar *v.* to omit; to forget; to leave out

ol-vi-do *m.* forgetfulness

o-lla *f.* kettle

om-bli-go *m.* navel

o-mi-sión *f.* omission

o-mi-tir *v.* to omit

óm-ni-bus *m.* omnibus

om-ni-po-ten-cia *f.* omnipotence

om-ni-po-ten-te *adj.* omnipotent

on-ce *adj.* eleven

on-ce-no *adj.* eleventh

on-co-lo-gí-a *f.* oncology

on-de-ar *v.* to flutter; to ripple

on-du-la-ción *f.* undulation

on-du-larv. to undulate

o-ne-ro-so, -sa *adj.* onerous

o-nix *f.* onyx

o-no-ma-to-pe-ya *f.* onomatopoeia

on-za *f.* ounce

on-za-vo *adj.* eleventh

o-pa *adj.* foolish

o-pa-ci-dad *f.* opacity

o-pa-co, -ca *adj.* opaque

ó-pa-lo *m.* opal

op-ción *f.* option

op-cio-nal *adj.* optional

ó-pe-ra *f.* opera

o-pe-ra-ción *f.* operation

o-pe-ran-te *adj.* operating

o-pe-rarv. to operate

o-pe-ra-ti-vo, -va *adj.* operative

o-pi-nión *f.* opinion

o-pio *m.* opium

o-po-ner *v.* to oppose

o-por-tu-na-men-te *adv.* opportunely

o-por-tu-ni-dad *f.* chance

o-por-tu-nis-ta *adj.* opportunist

o-por-tu-no, -na *adj.* opportune; fitting

o-po-si-ción *f.* opposition

o-po-si-tor, -ra *m., f.* opponent

o-pre-sión *f.* opression

o-pre-si-vo, -va *adj.* oppressive

o-pre-so, -sa *adj.* oppressed

o-pri-mi-do, -da *adj.* oppressed

o-pri-mir *v.* to press; to oppress

o-pro-bio *m.* disgrace

o-pro-bio-so, -sa *adj.* disgraceful

op-tar *v.* to select

óp-ti-co, -ca *adj.* optical

op-ti-mis-ta *adj.* optimistic

op-ti-mo, -ma *adj.* optimal

op-to-me-tra *m., f.* optometrist

op-to-me-trí-a *f.* optometry

o-pues-to *adj.* contrary; opposite

o-pu-len-cia *f.* opulence

o-ra *conj.* now

o-ra-ción *f.* oration; speech; sentence

o-rá-cu-lo *m.* oracle

o-ral *adj.* oral

o-ran-gu-tan *m.* orangutan

o-rar *v.* to speak

o-ra-to-rio, -ria *adj.* oratorical

or-be *m.* orb

or-den *m.* order

or-de-na-ción *f.* ordination; ordering

or-de-na-da *f.* ordinate

or-de-nar *v.* to command; to arrange; to put into order

or-de-nar *v.* to milk

or-di-nal *adj.* ordinal

or-di-na-riez *f.* commonness

or-di-na-rio *adj.* ordinary; uncouth; coarse

o-re-ar *v.* to ventilate

or-fa-na-to *m.* orphanage

or-fe-li-na-to *m.* orphanage

or-gá-ni-co *adj.* organic

or-ga-nis-mo *m.* organism

or-ga-nis-ta *m., f.* organist

or-ga-ni-za-dor, -ra *m., f.* organizer

or-ga-ni-zar *v.* to organize

ór-ga-no *m.* organ

or-gu-llo *m.* conceit

o-rien-ta-ción *f.* orientation

o-rien-tal *adj.* oriental

o-rien-tar *v.* to orient

o-ri-fi-cio *m.* opening

o-ri-gen m. source
o-ri-gi-nal adj. authentic; original; new
o-ri-gi-na-li-dad f. originality
o-ri-gi-nar v. to originate
o-ri-gi-na-ria-men-te adv. originally
o-ri-lla f. edge
o-ri-llar v. to edge
o-rin m. rust
o-ri-nal m. urinal
o-ri-nar v. to urinate
or-lar v. to edge
or-na-men-tal adj. ornamental
or-na-men-tar v. to ornament; to decorate
or-na-men-to m. ornament
or-nar v. to embellish
or-ni-to-lo-gi-a f. ornithology
or-ni-to-lo-go m., f. ornithologist
o-ro m. gold
or-ques-ta f. orchestra
or-ques-ta-cion f. orchestration
or-ques-tal adj. orchestral
or-ques-tar v. to orchestrate
or-qui-de-a f. orchid
or-ti-ga f. nettle
or-to-do-xo, -xa adj. orthodox
or-to-gra-fi-a f. orthographic
or-to-pe-di-co, -ca adj. orthopedic
or-to-pe-dis-ta m., f. orthopedist
o-ru-ga f. caterpillar
o-ru-jo m. residue
os pron. you
o-sa-di-a f. audacity
o-sa-do, -da adj. daring
o-sa-men-ta f. bones
o-sar v. to dare
os-ci-la-ción f. wavering; swinging
os-ci-lar v. to oscillate; to swing
os-cu-lo m. kiss
os-cu-re-cer v. to dim; to obscure; to shade
os-cu-re-ci-mien-to m. darkening

os-cu-ri-dad f. haziness; obscurity
os-cu-ro, -ra adj. unclear; dark; obscure
o-si-fi-car-se v. to ossify
os-mo-sis f. osmosis
o-so m. bear
os-ten-si-ble adj. ostensible
os-ten-ta-cion f. ostentation
os-ten-tar v. to flaunt; to show
os-te-o-lo-go, -ga m., f. osteologist
os-tra f. oyster
os-tra-cis-mo m. ostracism
o-te-ar v. to survey
o-to-ñal adj. autumnal
o-to-ño m. autumn
o-tor-gar v. to give
o-tro adj. other
o-va-ción f. ovation
o-va-cio-nar v. to give another an ovation
o-val adj. oval
o-va-lo m. oval
o-va-rio m. ovary
o-ve-ja f. the female sheep
o-ver-tu-ra f. overture
o-vi-llo m. snarl; ball
o-vi-no m. ovine
o-vu-la-cion f. ovulation
o-vu-lar adj. ovular
o-xi-da-cion f. oxidation
o-xi-dar v. to oxidize
ó-xi-do m. oxide
o-xi-ge-na-do, -da adj. oxygenated
o-xi-ge-nar v. to give oxygen to; to oxygenate
o-xi-ge-no m. oxygen
o-yen-te adj. listening m., f. listener
o-zo-no m. ozone

pa-be-llón m. banner; pavilion
pa-bi-lo m. candle wick
pa-bu-lo m. pabulum; support

pa-cer v. to graze
pa-cien-cia f. patience
pa-cien-te adj. patient
pa-ci-fi-ca-cion f. pacification
pa-ci-fi-ca-dor, -ra m., f. pacifier
pa-ci-fi-car v. to pacify
pa-ci-fi-co adj. pacific
pa-ci-fis-ta adj. pacifist
pa-cho-rra f. sluggishness
pa-de-cer v. to bear; to suffer; to endure
pa-dras-tro m. stepfather
pa-dre m. dad; father
pa-dri-llo m. stallion
pa-dri-no m. godfather
pa-ga f. payment
pa-ga-de-ro, -ra adj. payable
pa-ga-no, -na adj. pagan
pa-gar v. to repay; pay for
pa-gi-na f. page
pa-gi-nar v. to paginate
pa-go adj. paid
pais m. land
pai-sa-je m. landscape
pai-sa-jis-ta adj. landscape
pa-ja f. straw
pa-jar m. barn
pa-ja-re-ra f. cage for birds
pa-ja-re-ri-a f. bird store
pa-ja-ro m. bird
pa-la- f. blade; spade; shovelful
pa-la-bra f. word
pa-la-bre-o m. chatter
pa-la-cie-go, -ga adj. magnificent
pa-la-cio m. palace
pa-la-da f. shovelful
pa-la-de-ar v. to relish
pa-la-dio m. palladium
pa-la-fre-ne-ro m. groom
pa-lan-ca f. shaft; lever
pa-lan-ga-na f. washbasin
pa-le-ar v. to shovel
pa-le-on-to-lo-gi-a f. paleontology
pa-le-ta f. trowel; palette
pa-lia-ti-vo, -va adj. palliative
pa-li-dez f. pallor
pá-li-do, -da adj. pallid
pa-li-to m. small stick

pa-li-za f. thrashing
pal-ma f. palm
pal-ma-do, -da adj. palm-shaped
pal-mar m. palm grove
pal-me-a-do, -da adj. palm-shaped
pal-me-ar v. to applaud
pal-me-ra f. palm tree
pal-mo m. palm
pal-mo-te-ar v. to applaud
pa-lo m. pole; handle
pa-lo-ma f. pigeon
pa-lo-mi-ta f. popcorn
pa-lo-te m. drumstick
pal-pa-ble adj. palpable
pal-par v. to feel
pal-pi-ta-cion f. palpitation
pal-pi-tan-te adj. palpating
pal-pi-tar v. to palpitate; to beat
pal-ta f. avocado
pa-lu-dis-mo m. malaria
pa-lur-do, -da m., f. boor
pam-pa f. pampa
pan m. bread
pa-na f. corduroy
pa-na-de-rí-a f. bakery
pa-na-de-ro, -ra m., f. baker
pa-nal m. honeycomb
pan-cre-as m. pancreas
pan-cre-a-ti-co, -ca adj. pancreatic
pa-cho, -cha adj. unruffled
pan-da f. panda
pan-de-mo-nio m. pandemonium
pan-de-ro m. tambourine
pan-di-lla f. gang
pan-fle-to m. pamphlet
pá-ni-co, -ca m., adj. panic
pa-no-ra-ma f. panorama
pa-no-ra-mi-co, -ca adj. panoramic
pan-ta-ló-nes m. slacks; pants
pan-ta-lla f. movie screen; lamp shade
pan-ta-no m. difficulty
pan-te-on m. pantheon
pan-te-ra f. panther
pan-to-mi-ma f. pantomine
pan-to-rri-lla f. calf

pa-no *m.* cloth
pa-no-le-ta *f.* scarf
pa-no-lon *m.* shawl
pa-nue-lo *m.* kerchief
pa-pá *f.* potato
pa-pa-ga-yo *m.* parrot
pa-pal *adj.* papal
pa-pa-ya *f.* papaya
pa-pel *m.* paper
pa-pe-le-ro, -ra *adj.* paper
pa-pe-le-ta *f.* card
pa-pe-ra *f.* goiter
pa-pi-la *f.* papilla
pa-pi-ro *m.* papyrus
pa-que-te *m.* packet; pack; package
pa-que-te-ri-a *f.* elegance
pa-qui-der-mo *m.* pachyderm
par *adj.* paired; equal
pa-ra *prep.* for; to; towards
pa-ra-bo-la *f.* parable
pa-ra-bri-sas *m.* windshield
pa-ra-ca-i-das *f.* parachute
pa-ra-di-sia-co, -ca *adj.* heavenly
pa-ra-do, -da *adj.* stopped; stationary; idle
pa-ra-do-ja *f.* paradox
pa-ra-do-ji-co, -ca *adj.* paradoxical
pa-ra-fi-na *f.* paraffin
pa-ra-guas *m.* umbrella
pa-ra-i-so *m.* paradise
pa-ra-je *m.* area
pa-ra-le-lo *m.* parallel
pa-ra-le-lo-gra-mo *m.* parallelogram
pa-ra-li-sis *f.* paralysis
pa-ra-li-ti-co, -ca *adj.* paralytic
pa-ra-li-za-cion *f.* paralyzation
pa-ra-li-zar *v.* to paralyze
pa-ra-me-di-co, -ca *adj.* paramedical
pa-ra-me-tro *m.* parameter
pa-ra-no-ia *f.* paranoia
pa-ra-noi-co, -ca *adj.* paranoid
pa-ra-ple-ji-co, -ca *adj.* paraplegic

pa-rar *v.* to halt; to check; to stop
pa-ra-si-ti-co, -ca *adj.* parasitic
pa-ra-si-to, -ta *adj.* parasitic
pa-ra-sol *m.* parasol
par-ce-la *f.* parcel
par-cial *adj.* partial
par-cia-li-dad *f.* partiality
par-do *adj.* brown
pa-re-ar *v.* to pair
pa-re-cer *m.* view; appearance
pa-re-ci-do *adj.* similar
pa-red *f.* wall
pa-re-jo, -ja *adj.* equal; smooth; alike
pa-ren-te-la *f.* relatives
pa-ren-tes-co *m.* kinship
pa-ren-te-sis *m.* parenthesis
pa-ri-dad *f.* parity
pa-ri-ta-rio, -ria *adj.* joint
par-la-men-ta-rio *adj.* parliamentary
par-la-men-to *m.* parliament
par-lar *v.* to chatter
par-lo-te-o *m.* chatter
pa-ro *m.* unemployment
pa-ro-dia *f.* parody
pa-ro-diar *v.* to parody
pa-ro-dis-ta *m., f.* parodist
pa-ro-xis-mo *m.* paroxysm
par-pa-de-ar *v.* to twinkle
pár-pa-do *m.* eyelid
par-que *m.* park
par-que-o *m.* parking
par-que-dad *f.* moderation
pa-rra *f.* grapevine
pa-rra-fo *m.* paragraph
pa-rri-ci-dio *m.* parricide
pa-rro-quial *adj.* parochial
par-si-mo-nia *f.* moderation
par-si-mo-nio-so, -sa *adj.* parsimonious
par-te *f.* share; part
par-te-ra *f.* midwife
par-ti-cion *f.* partition
par-ti-ci-pa-cion *f.* participation
par-ti-ci-par *v.* to inform
par-ti-ci-pe *adj.* participating
par-ti-cu-la *f.* particle
par-ti-cu-lar *adj.* particular

par-ti-cu-la-ri-dad f. peculiarity

par-ti-cu-lar-men-te adv. particularly

par-ti-dis-ta adj. party

par-ti-da f. group; leaving; departure

par-ti-do m. party

par-tir v. to depart; to leave

par-ti-ti-vo, -va adj. partitive

par-ti-tu-ra f. score

pa-sa-di-zo m. passage

pa-sa-do m. past

pa-sa-dor adj. passing

pa-sa-je m. passage

pa-sa-por-te m. passport

pa-sar v. to elapse; to occur; to happen

pa-sa-tiem-po m. pastime

pa-se m. pass

pa-se-o m. stroll; outing

pa-sión f. passion

pa-so m. footstep; pace

pas-ta f. paste

pas-tel m. cake

pas-teu-ri-zar v. to pasteurize

pas-teu-ri-za-cion f. pasteurization

pas-to m. pasture; grass

pa-ta f. foot; leg; paw; female duck

pa-ta-da f. kick

pa-ta-ta f. potato

pa-te-ar v. to kick

pa-ten-tar v. to register

pa-ten-te adj. patent; evident; obvious

pa-ter-nal adj. paternal

pa-ter-ni-dad f. paternity

pa-ti-llas f. sideburns

pa-tín m. skate

pa-ti-nar v. to skate

pa-tio m. patio

pa-to m. duck

pa-to-lo-gía f. pathology

pa-to-lo-go, -ga m., f. pathologist

pa-triar-ca m. patriarch

pa-trio-ta m., f. patriot

pa-trió-ti-co, ca adj. patriotic

pa-tro-ci-nar v. to patronize

pa-trón m. host

pa-tro-nal adj. management

pa-tro-na-to m. patronage

pa-tru-llar v. to patrol

pau-la-ti-no, -na adj. gradual

pau-sa f. interruption

pau-ta f. rule

pa-va-da f. foolishness

pa-vi-men-ta-cion f. paving

pa-vi-men-to m. pavement

pa-vo m. turkey

pa-vor m. terror

pa-vu-ra f. terror

pa-ya-so m. clown

paz f. peace

paz-gua-to, -ta adj. foolish

pe-car v. to sin

pe-ce-ra f. aquarium

pec-ti-na f. pectin

pec-to-ral adj. pectoral

pe-cu-liar adj. peculiar

pe-cu-lia-ri-dad f. peculiarity

pe-cu-lio m. peculium

pe-cu-nia f. money

pe-char v. to pay

pe-cho m. breast; chest

pe-dal m. pedal

pe-da-le-o m. pedaling

pe-dan-te-rí-a f. pedantry

pe-da-zo m. bit; piece

pe-der-nal m. flint

pe-des-tal m. pedestal

pe-des-tre adj. pedestrian

pe-dia-trí-a f. pediatrics

pe-dí-cu-lo m. peduncle

pe-di-gre-e m. pedigree

pe-dir v. to order; to beg; to charge

pe-dre-go-so, -sa adj. rocky

pe-dris-ca f. hail

pe-dún-cu-lo m. peduncle

pe-ga-di-zo, -za adj. catching

pe-ga-jo-so, -sa adj. catching; adhesive

pe-gar v. to glue; to attach; to cleave

pei-na-do m. hairdresser

pei-ne m. comb

pe-la-do, -da adj. bare; bald

pe-la-du-ra f. peeling

pe-la-gra f. pellagra

pe-lar v. to peel; to cut

pe-le-a-dor adj. fighting

pe-li-ca-no m. pelican
pe-li-cu-la f. film; movie
pe-li-gro m. danger
pe-li-gro-so adj. dangerous
pe-lo m. fur; hair
pe-lo-ta f. ball
pel-tre m. pewter
pe-lu-ca f. wig
pel-vis f. pelvis
pe-lliz-car v. to nibble
pe-llon m. sheepskin
pe-ña f. anxiety; penalty; distress
pe-na-cho m. crest
pe-na-do, -da adj. grieved
pe-na-li-zar v. to penalize
pe-nar v. to punish
pen-den-ciar v. to quarrel; to argue
pen-der v. to hover
pen-dien-te adj. hanging
pe-ne-tra-ble adj. penetrable
pe-ne-tra-ción f. penetration
pe-ne-tran-te adj. piercing; penetrating
pe-ne-trar v. to pierce; to penetrate
pe-ni-ci-li-na f. penicillin
pe-nin-su-la f. peninsula
pe-ni-que m. penny
pe-ni-ten-cia f. penitence
pe-ni-ten-te adj. penitent
pe-no-so adj. grievous; wearing
pen-sa-mien-to m. thought
pen-san-te adj. thinking
pen-sar v. to think about
pen-sa-ti-vo adj. thoughtful; pensie
pen-sio-nar v. to pension
pen-to-tal m. pentothal
pe-ña f. circle
pe-nas-co-so, -sa adj. rocky
pe-or adj. worse
pe-pi-no m. cucumber
pep-ti-co, -ca adj. peptic
pe-que-ño adj. tiny; small
pe-ra f. pear
pe-ral m. pear tree
per-cep-ción f. perception
per-cep-ti-vo, -va adj. perceptive

per-ci-bir v. to sense; to recieve
per-cu-dir y. to dull
per-cu-sión f. percussion
per-cu-tir v. to percuss
per-cha f. hanger; prop
per-der v. to waste; to lose
per-di-da f. waste
per-di-do adj. missing
per-diz f. partridge
per-dón m. pardon
per-do-nar v. to remit; to excuse; to pardon
per-du-rar v. to last
pe-re-cer v. to perish
pe-re-gri-na-cion f. pilgrimage
pe-re-jil m. parsley
pe-ren-ne adj. perennial
pe-re-za f. laziness
pe-re-zo-so, -sa adj. lazy
per-fec-ción f. perfection
per-fec-cio-nar v. to make something perfect
per-fec-cio-nis-ta adj. perfectionist
per-fec-to adj. perfect
pér-fi-do, -da adj. unfaithful
per-fi-lar v. to profile
per-fo-ra-ción f. perforation
per-fo-ra-dor adj. perforating
per-fo-rar v. to perforate
per-fu-mar v. to perfume
per-fu-me m. perfume
per-fu-me-ri-a f. perfumery
pe-ri-car-dio m. pericardium
pe-ri-cia f. skill
pe-ri-co m. parakeet
pe-ri-me-tro m. perimeter
pe-rio-di-ca-men-te adv. periodically
pe-rio-di-co m. periodical
pe-rio-dis-mo m. journalism
pe-rio-dis-ta m., f. journalist
pe-rio-do m. period
pe-ris-to-le f. peristalsis
pe-ri-qui-to m. parakeet
pe-ris-co-pio m. periscope
pe-ri-to-ne-o m. peritoneum
per-ju-di-car v. to harm
per-ju-di-cial adj. harmful
per-ju-rio m. perjury
per-la f. pearl

per-ma-ne-cer v. to remain
per-ma-nen-te adj. permanent
per-mi-si-ble adj. permissible
per-mi-si-vo adj. permissive
per-mi-so m. consent
per-mi-tir v. to allow; to give; to permit
per-mu-tar v. to exchange
per-ni-cio-so, -sa adj. pernicious
per-no m. pin
pe-ro conj. but
pe-ro-ne m. fibula
pe-ró-xi-do m. peroxide
per-pe-tra-ción f. perpetuation
per-pe-tuar v. to perpetuate
per-ple-ji-dad f. perplexity
per-ple-jo, -ja adj. perplexed
pe-rro m. dog
per-se-cu-ción f. persecution
per-se-guir v. to follow; to hound; to pursue
per-se-ve-ran-cia f. perseverance
per-se-ve-ran-te adj. persevering
per-sia-na f. blind
per-sig-nar v. to cross
per-sis-ten-cia f. persistence
per-sis-tir v. to persist
per-so-na f. person
per-so-na-li-dad f. personality
per-so-na-li-zar v. to personalize
per-so-ni-fi-ca-ción f. personification
pers-pec-ti-va f. perspective
per-sua-dir v. to persuade
per-sua-sión f. persuasion
per-sua-si-vo, -va adj. persuasive
per-te-ne-cer v. to belong
per-te-ne-cien-te adj. pertaining
per-ti-nen-cia f. relevancy
per-ti-nen-cia f. relevance
per-ti-nen-te adj. relevant
per-tre-char v. to equip
per-tur-ba-ción f. disturbance

per-tur-bar v. to upset
per-ver-si-dad f. perversity
per-ver-sion f. perversion
per-ver-ti-do, -da adj. perverted
pe-sa-di-lla f. nightmare
pe-sa-do adj. dull; heavy; boring
pe-sar v. to grieve
pes-ca f. fishing
pes-ca-de-ri-a f. fish market
pes-ca-di-lla f. whiting
pes-ca-do m. fish
pes-ca-dor m. fisherman
pes-car v. to fish
pe-se-bre f. manger
pe-si-mis-ta adj. pessimistic
pe-so m. weight
pes-que-ro, -ra adj. fishing
pes-ta-ña f. eyelash
pes-ta-ñe-ar v. to wink
pes-ta-ne-o m. winking
pes-te f. plague
pé-ta-lo m. petal
pe-ti-ción f. petition
pé-tre-o, -a adj. rocky
pe-tri-fi-car v. to petrify
pe-tró-le-o m. petroleum
pe-tu-lan-cia f. arrogance
pe-tu-lan-te adj. arrogant
pe-tu-nia f. petunia
pez m. fish
pia-nis-ta m., f. pianist
pia-no m. piano
piar v. to chirp
pi-can-te adj. spicy
pi-car v. to sting; to chip; to bite
pi-ca-res-co, -ca adj. mischievous
pi-ca-ro, -ra adj. wicked; sly
pi-ca-zon f. itching
pi-co m. spout; beak
pi-cor m. itching
pi-co-te-ar v. to pick; to peck
pic-tó-ri-co, -ca adj. pictorial
pie m. foot
pie-dra f. stone
piel f. fur; skin
pier-na f. leg
pie-za f. piece
pi-fiar v. to miscue
pig-men-tar v. to pigment**

pig-me-o *adj.* pygmy
pi-ja-ma *m.* pajamas
pi-lar *m.* pillar
pi-le-ta *f.* sink
pi-lo-tar *v.* to pilot
pi-lo-to *m.* pilot
pi-llar *v.* to plunder
pi-llue-lo, -lla *adj.* mischievous
pi-men-ton *m.* paprika
pi-mien-ta *f.* pepper
pim-pan-te *adj.* spruce; graceful
pi-na-cu-lo *m.* pinnacle
pi-nar *m.* pine grove
pin-cel *m.* brush
pin-cha-du-ra *f.* puncture
pin-char *v.* to puncture
pin-cha-zo *m.* puncture
pin-gui-no *m.* penguin
pi-ño *m.* pine
pin-tar *v.* to paint
pin-to, -ta *adj.* speckled
pin-tor, -ra *m., f.* painter
pin-to-res-co, -ca *adj.* picturesque
pin-tu-ra *f.* painting
pi-ña *f.* pine cone
pio-jo *m.* louse
pio-la *f.* cord
pi-pa *f.* barrel
pi-per-min *m.* peppermint
pi-pe-ta *f.* pipette
pi-que-ta *f.* pick
pi-que-te *m.* picket
pi-ra-mi-dal *adj.* pyramidal
pi-rá-mi-de *f.* pyramid
pi-ra-ta *m.* pirate
pi-ri-ta *f.* pyrites
pi-rue-ta *f.* pirouette
pi-sa-da *f.* footprint
pi-sar *v.* to walk upon
pis-ci-na *f.* swimming pool
pi-so *m.* story; flat
pi-són *m.* tamper
pi-so-te-ar *v.* to trample
pis-ta *f.* runway; trail
pis-ta-cho *m.* pistachio
pis-to-la *f.* pistol
pis-tón *m.* piston
pi-ti-do *m.* whistling
pi-ti-llo *m.* cigarette
pi-to *m.* whistle

pi-tón *m.* python
pi-to-ni-sa *f.* pythoness
pi-tui-ta-rio, -ria *adj.* pituitary
pi-vo-te *m.* pivot
pla-ca *f.* plaque
pla-ce-bo *m.* placebo
pla-cen-ta *f.* placenta
pla-cen-te-ro, -ra *adj.* placenta
pla-cer *m.* gratification; pleasure
plá-ci-do *adj.* placid
pla-gar *v.* to plague
plan *m.* scheme; plan
plan-cha *f.* sheet
plan-cha-do, -da *adj.* ironing
plan-char *v.* to iron
pla-ne-ar *v.* to plan
pla-ne-ta *f.* planet
pla-ne-ta-rio, -ria *adj.* planetary
pla-ni-cie *f.* plain
pla-ni-fi-ca-cion *f.* planning
pla-ni-fi-car *v.* to plan
pla-no *adj.* level
plan-ta *f.* plant
plan-ta-cion *f.* plantation
plan-tar *v.* to plant
plan-te-ar *v.* to start; to expound
pla-ña-do *m.* lament
plas-ma *f.* plasma
plas-mar *v.* to mold
plás-ti-co, -ca *adj.* plastic
plas-ti-fi-car *v.* to shellac something
pla-ta *f.* silver
pla-ta-for-ma *f.* platform
plá-ta-no *m.* banana
pla-te-ar *v.* to silver-plate
pla-te-ro *m.* silversmith
pla-ti-car *v.* to talk
pla-ti-no *m.* platinum
pla-to *m.* dish; plate
pla-to-ni-co, -ca *adj.* platonic
plau-si-ble *adj.* plausible
pla-ya *f.* beach
pla-ye-ro, -ra *adj.* beach
ple-ga-ble *adj.* collapsible
ple-ga-do *m.* folding
ple-gar *v.* to fold; to bend; to pleat

pleu-re-si-a *f.* pleurisiy
pli-sa-do *m.* pleat
plo-me-ro *m.* plumber
plo-mo, -ma *adj.* leaden
plu-ma *f.* pen; feather
plu-ral *adj.* plural
plu-ra-li-dad *f.* plurality
plu-ra-li-zar *v.* to pluralize
plu-to-nio *m.* plutonium
po-bla-ción *f.* population
po-bla-do *m.* population
po-blar *v.* to populate
po-bre *adj.* poor
po-bre-za *f.* poverty
po-ción *f.* potion
po-co *adv.* little
po-dar *v.* to prune
po-der *v.* to be able; can
po-de-rí-o *m.* power
po-di-a-tra *m.* podiatrist
poe-ma *m.* poem
po-e-sí-a *f.* poetry
po-e-ta *m.* poet
poé-ti-co *adj.* poetical
po-e-ti-sa *f.* poetess
po-ker *m.* poker
po-lar *adj.* polar
po-la-ri-za-ción *f.* polarization
po-la-ri-zar *v.* to polarize
po-len *m.* pollen
po-li-cí-a *f.* constable; police
po-li-cial *adj.* police
po-li-fo-ní-a *f.* polyphony
po-lí-go-no *m.* polygon
po-li-lla *f.* moth
po-li-ni-za-ción *f.* pollination
po-li-no-mio *m.* polynomial
pó-li-po *m.* polyp
po-lí-ti-ca *f.* policy
po-lí-ti-co *adj.* political
po-li-ti-zar *v.* to politicize
po-lo *m.* pole
pol-trón, -na *adj.* lazy
po-lu-ción *f.* pollution
pol-vo *m.* powder; dust
pól-vo-ra *f.* powder
po-llo *m.* chicken
po-ma-da *f.* pomade
pom-pa *f.* pomp
pom-po-si-dad *f.* pomposity
pom-po-so, -sa *adj.* pompous

pon-che *m.* punch
pon-cho *m.* poncho
pon-de-ra-ble *adj.* ponderable
pon-de-rar *v.* to consider
po-ner *v.* to place; to don
pon-ti-fi-cal *adj.* pontifical
pon-ti-fi-car *v.* to pontificate
pon-zo-ño-so, -sa *adj.* poisonous
po-pu-la-cho *m.* populace
po-pu-lar *adj.* popular
po-pu-la-ri-dad *f.* popularity
po-pu-la-ri-zar *v.* to popularize
po-pu-rrí *m.* potpourri
po-quer *m.* poker
por *prep.* from; via; for
por-cen-ta-je *m.* percentage
por-cen-tual *adj.* percentage
por-ción *f.* part; portion
por-che *m.* porch
por-fia-do, -da *adj.* stubborn
po-ro-si-dad *f.* porosity
po-ro-so, -sa *adj.* porous
por-qué *conj.* because
por-qué *m.* reason
por-tal *m.* porch
por-tá-til *adj.* portable
por-ten-to-so, -sa *adj.* marvelous
por-ve-nir *m.* future
po-sar *v.* to rest; to lodge
pos-da-ta *f.* postscript
po-se-er *v.* to have
po-se-í-do, -da *adj.* possessed
po-se-sión *f.* dependency; possession
po-se-si-vo, -va *adj.* possessive
po-se-so, -sa *adj.* possessed
pos-fe-cha *f.* postdate
po-si-bi-li-dad *f.* possibility
po-si-bi-li-tar *v.* to make something possible
po-si-ble *adj.* possible
po-si-ción *f.* place; status
po-si-ti-vo, -va *adj.* positive
pos-po-ner *v.* to postpone
pos-ta *f.* slice
pos-tal *adj.* postal
pos-te *m.* post

pos-ter-ga-cion *f.* postponement

pos-te-gar *v.* to postpone

pos-te-rior *adj.* posterior

pos-te-rio-ri-dad *f.* posteriority

pos-ti-zo, -za *adj.* artificial

pos-to-pe-ra-to-rio, -ria *adj.* postoperative

pos-tor *m.* bidder

pos-trar *v.* to debilitate; to humiliate

pos-tre *m.* dessert

pos-tre-mo, -ma *adj.* final

pos-tre-ro, -ra *adj.* final

pos-tu-ra *f.* posture

po-ta-ble *adj.* potable

po-ta-sio *m.* potassium

po-te *m.* pot

po-ten-cia *f.* potency

po-ten-cial *adj.* potential

po-ten-ta-do *m.* potentate

po-ten-te *adj.* potent; powerful

po-trar *v.* to frolic

po-tre-ro *m.* pasture

po-tri-llo *m.* colt

po-tro *m.* colt

prác-ti-ca *f.* custom; practice

prac-ti-car *v.* to practice

prác-ti-co *adj.* practical

pra-de-ra *f.* meadow

pra-do *m.* meadow

pre-ám-bu-lo *m.* preamble

pre-ca-rio, -ria *adj.* precarious

pre-cau-ción *f.* precaution

pre-ca-vi-do, -da *adj.* cautious

pre-ce-den-te *adj.* preceeding

pre-ce-der *v.* to forego

pre-cep-to *m.* precept

pre-cep-tor, -ra *m., f.* tutor

pre-cia-do, -da *adj.* precious

pre-cin-ta-do, -da *adj.* sealed

pre-cin-tar *v.* to stamp

pre-cio *m.* fare; cost; price

pre-cio-si-dad *f.* beauty

pre-cio-so *adj.* precious

pre-ci-pi-ta-ción *f.* precipitation

pre-ci-pi-tar *v.* to hasten

pre-ci-sa-men-te *adj.* precisely

pre-ci-sar *v.* to set; to explain

pre-ci-sión *f.* precision

pre-co-ci-dad *f.* precocity

pre-cog-ni-cion *f.* precondition

pre-con-ce-bir *v.* to preconceive

pre-co-ni-zar *v.* to recommend something

pre-coz *adj.* precocious

pre-de-ce-sor, -ra *m., f.* predecessor

pre-de-cir *v.* to foretell

pre-des-ti-na-cion *f.* predestination

pre-de-ter-mi-nar *v.* to predetermine

pre-di-ca *f.* sermon

pre-di-ca-do *m.* predicate

pre-di-car *v.* to preach

pre-dic-ción *f.* prediction

pre-di-lec-to, -ta *adj.* favorite

pre-dio *m.* property

pre-dis-po-ner *v.* to predispose

pre-dis-po-si-cion *f.* predisposition

pre-do-mi-nan-te *adj.* predominant

pre-do-mi-nar *v.* to prevail

pre-do-mi-nio *m.* predominant

pre-es-co-lar *adj.* preschool

pre-fa-bri-ca-do, -da *adj.* prefabricated

pre-fa-bri-car *v.* to prefabricate

pre-fa-cio *m.* preface

pre-fec-tu-ra *f.* prefecture

pre-fe-ren-te *adj.* preferable

pre-fe-ren-te-men-te *adv.* preferably

pre-fe-ri-do *adj.* preferred

pre-fe-rir *v.* to prefer

pre-go-nar *v.* to divulge; to proclaim

pre-gun-ta *f.* question

pre-gun-tar *v.* to ask; to question

pre-his-to-ria *f.* prehistory
pre-his-to-ri-co, -ca *adj.* prehistoric
pre-juz-gar *v.* to prejudge
pre-lu-dio *m.* prelude
pre-ma-tu-ro-, -ra *adj.* premature
pre-me-di-ta-cion *f.* premeditation
pre-me-di-ta-da-men-te *adv.* deliberately
pre-me-di-tar *v.* to premeditate
pre-miar *v.* to reward
pre-mio *m.* prize
pre-mi-sa *f.* premise
pre-mo-ni-cion *f.* premonition
pre-mu-ra *f.* urgency
pre-na-tal *adj.* prenatal
pren-da *f.* token; guaranty
pren-der *v.* to catch
pren-sa *f.* press
pren-sar *v.* to press
pre-nup-cial *adj.* prenuptial
pre-ñez *f.* pregnancy
pre-o-cu-pa-cion *f.* concern
pre-o-cu-par *v.* to mind; to preoccupy
pre-pa-rar *v.* to ready; fix
pre-pon-de-ran-te *adj.* preponderant
pre-po-si-cion *f.* preposition
pre-po-ten-cia *f.* prepotency
pre-po-ten-te *adj.* prepotent
pre-pu-cio *m.* prepuce
pre-sa *f.* victim; capture
pres-cin-den-cia *f.* omission
pres-cin-di-ble *adj.* nonessential
pres-cin-dir *v.* to ignore
pres-cri-bir *v.* to prescribe
pre-sen-cia *f.* presence
pre-sen-ciar *v.* to witness
pre-sen-ta-cion *f.* presentation
pre-sen-tar *v.* to introduce; to feature
pre-sen-te *adj.* current
pre-ser-va-cion *f.* preservation
pre-ser-var *v.* to preserve
pre-ser-va-ti-vo, -va *adj.* preservative

pre-si-den-cia *f.* presidency
pre-si-den-cial *adj.* presidential
pre-si-den-ta *f.* president
pre-si-den-te *m.* president
pre-si-dia-rio *m.* convict
pre-si-dio *m.* prison
pre-si-dir *v.* to preside
pre-sion *f.* pressure
pre-sio-nar *v.* to press
pres-ta-cion *f.* services
pres-ta-dor, -ra *adj.* lending
pres-ta-men-te *adj.* quickly
prés-ta-mo *m.* lending
pres-tar *v.* to loan
pres-te-za *f.* promptness
pres-ti-gio *m.* prestige
pres-ti-gio-so, -sa *adj.* prestigious
pres-to, -ta *adj.* prompt
pre-su-mi-ble *adj.* presumable
pre-su-mir *v.* to presume
pre-sun-cion *f.* presumption
pre-sun-tuo-so, -sa *adj.* presumptuous
pre-su-po-ner *v.* to presuppose
pre-su-po-si-cion *f.* presupposition
pre-su-pues-ta-rio, -ria *adj.* budgetary
pre-su-ri-zar *v.* to pressurize
pre-ten-cio-so, -sa *adj.* pretentious
pre-ten-der *v.* to attempt; to pretend
pre-ten-dien-te *adj.* pretending to
pre-ten-sion *f.* desire
pre-ten-sio-so, -sa *adj.* pretentious
pre-va-le-cer *v.* to prevail
pre-va-le-cien-te *adj.* prevailing
pre-va-ler *v.* to prevail
pre-ven-cion *f.* prevention
pre-ve-nir *v.* to prepare; to prevent
pre-ven-ti-vo, -va *adj.* preventive
prez *m.* glory

pri-ma, -mo *f., m.* cousin
pri-ma-rio, -ria *adj.* primary
pri-ma-te *m.* primate
pri-ma-ve-ra *f.* spring
pri-me-ro *adj.* prime; first
pri-mi-ti-vo *adj.* primitive
pri-mo-ro-so *adj.* delicate; exquisite
prin-ce-sa *f.* princess
prin-ci-pa-do *m.* principality
prin-ci-pal *adj.* leading; master; principal
prin-ci-pal-men-te *adv.* principally
prin-ci-pe *m.* prince
prin-ci-pes-co, -ca *adj.* princely
prin-ci-pian-te, -ta *adj.* beginning
prin-ci-piar *v.* to begin
prin-ci-pio *m.* beginning
prin-go-so, -sa *adj.* greasy
prio-ri-dad *f.* priority
pri-sa *f.* haste
pri-sion *f.* prison
pri-sio-ne-ro, -ra *m., f.* prisoner
pris-ma *m.* prism
pris-ti-no, -na *adj.* pristine
pri-va-do *adj.* private
pri-va-ti-zar *v.* to privatize
pri-vi-le-gio *m.* privilege
pro-ba-bi-li-dad *f.* probability
pro-ba-ble *adj.* probable
pro-bar *v.* to prove; to try
pro-bi-dad *f.* probity
pro-ble-ma *m.* problem
pro-ble-má-ti-co, -ca *adj.* problematic
pro-bo, -ba *adj.* upright
pro-ce-di-mien-to *m.* procedure
pro-ce-sar *v.* to prosecute
pro-ce-sión *f.* procession
pro-ce-so *m.* action
pro-cla-ma-cion *f.* proclamation
pro-cla-mar *v.* to announce; to proclaim
pro-cre-a-cion *f.* procreation
pro-cre-ar *v.* to produce; to procreate
pro-di-gar *v.* to waste

pró-di-go *adj.* lavish; spendthrift
pro-di-gio-so, -sa *adj.* marvelous
pro-duc-cion *f.* turnout; production
pro-du-cir *v.* to yield; to produce
pro-duc-ti-vi-dad *f.* productivity
pro-duc-ti-vo, -va *adj.* productive
pro-duc-to, -ta *m.* product
pro-fa-nar *v.* to disgrace
pro-fe-sar *v.* to teach; to practice
pro-fe-sion *f.* vocation; job; profession
pro-fe-sio-nal *adj.* professional
pro-fe-sor, -ra *m., f.* professor; teacher
pro-fi-la-xis *f.* prophylaxis
pro-fun-di-dad *f.* profundity
pro-fun-do, -da *adj.* profound; deep
pro-fu-sion *f.* profusion
pro-du-so, -sa *adj.* profuse
pro-gra-ma *m.* program
pro-gra-ma-cion *f.* programming
pro-gra-mar *v.* to program
pro-gre-sar *v.* to progress
pro-gre-sion *f.* progress
pro-gre-sis-ta *adj.* progressive
pro-gre-so *m.* progress
pro-hi-bi-cion *f.* prohibition
pro-hi-bi-do, -da *adj.* forbidden
pro-hi-bir *v.* to prohibit something
pro-hi-bi-ti-vo, -va *adj.* prohibitive
pro-li-fe-ra-cion *f.* proliferation
pro-li-fe-rar *v.* to proliferate
pro-lí-fi-co, -ca *adj.* prolific
pró-lo-go *m.* prologue
pro-lon-ga-do, -da *adj.* prolonged
pro-lon-gar *v.* to lengthen
pro-me-dio *m.* average

pro-me-sa f. vow; promise

pro-me-te-dor, -ra adj. promising

pro-me-ter v. to promise

pro-mi-nen-te adj. prominent

pro-mi-so-rio, -ria adj. promising

pro-mo-ción f. promotion

pro-mo-cio-nar v. to promote

pro-mo-ve-dor, -ra adj. promoter; promoting

pro-mo-ver v. to promote

pro-no, -na adj. prone

pro-nom-bre m. pronoun

pro-no-mi-nal adj. pronominal

pro-nos-ti-car v. to predict

pron-ti-tud f. promptness

pron-to adj. prompt

pro-nun-cia-ción f. pronunciation

pro-nun-ciar v. to pronounce

pro-pa-ga-ción f. propagation

pro-pa-lar v. to divulge

pro-pen-so, -sa adj. prone

pro-pie-dad f. estate

pro-pi-na f. gratuity

pro-pio adj. proper

pro-po-ne-dor, -ra adj. proposing

pro-po-ner v. to intend

pro-por-ción f. proportion

pro-por-cio-nal adj. proportional

pro-po-si-ción f. motion; proposition

pro-pó-si-to m. purpose; intention

pro-pues-ta f. proposal

pro-pug-nar v. to advocate

pro-pul-sar v. to push

pro-pul-sión f. propulsion

pro-rra-te-ar v. to prorate

pró-rro-gar v. to extend

pro-sa f. prose

pro-sia-co, -ca adj. prosaic

pros-cri-bir v. to proscribe

pros-crip-ción f. proscription

pros-pec-to m. prospectus

pros-pe-rar v. to thrive; to prosper

pros-pe-ri-dad f. prosperity

pros-pe-ro, -ra adj. prosperous

prós-ta-ta f. prostate

pros-ti-tu-ción f. prostitution

pro-tec-ción f. protection

pro-tec-tor, -ra adj. supporting; protective

pro-te-ger v. to defend; to protect

pro-te-í-na f. protein

pro-tes-ta f. protest

pro-tes-tar v. to profess

pro-tes-to m. protest

protón m. proton

pro-to-ti-po m. prototype

pro-to-zo-a-rio m. protozoan

pro-ve-cho m. profit; benefit

pro-ve-cho-so adj. profitable

pro-veer v. to cater; to fill; to provide

pro-vi-den-cial adj. providential

pro-vi-sión f. provision

pro-vo-ca-ción f. provocation

pro-vo-car v. to antagonize

próx-i-mo adj. near

pru-den-cia f. prudence

psi-co-lo-gia f. psychology

pu-bli-ca-ción f. publication

pu-bli-car v. to publish

pú-bli-co m. public

pue-blo m. nation; town

puer-ta f. entrance

pues conj. then; for

pul-gar m. thumb

pu-lir v. to shine; to polish

pul-món m. lung

pun-ta f. point

pun-to m. dot; point

pu-ro adj. pure

púr-pu-ra f. purple

quan-tum m. quantum

que pron. that; whom

qué adj. what; which

que-bra-cho m. quebracho

que-bra-da f. gap; ravine

que-bra-di-zo, -za *adj.* fragile

que-bra-do *adj.* rough; broken; bankrupt

que-bra-du-ra *f.* rupture; fracture; crack

que-bra-jar *v.* to crack

que-bran-ta-dor, -ra *adj.* crushing; breaking

que-bran-ta-mien-to *m.* cracking; deterioration; breaking

que-bran-tar *v.* to crush; to break; to weaken

que-bran-to *m.* sorrow; loss

que-brar *v.* to break

que-da-men-te *adv.* calmly

que-dar *v.* to stay; to be; to remain

que-do, -da *adj.* calm

que-jar-se *v.* to complain; to whine

que-ji-do *m.* groan

que-jo-so *adj.* complaining

que-ma *f.* burning

que-ma-de-ro *m.* incinerator

que-ma-do, -da *adj.* burnt; burned out

que-ma-dor, -ra *adj.* burning

que-mar *v.* to heat up; to burn

que-ma-zón *f.* burning

que-re-lla *f.* lament; quarrel

que-re-llan-te *adj.* complaining

que-rer *v.* to desire; to want *m.* love; affection

que-ri-do, -da *adj.* beloved

que-so *m.* cheese

quie-bra *f.* crack

quien *pron.* who

quie-to, -ta *adj.* quiet

quí-mi-ca *f.* chemistry

quí-mi-co *adj.* chemical

quin-ce *adj.* fifteen

quin-to *adj.* fifth

qui-tar *v.* to forbid; to remove; to take away

rá-ba-no *m.* radish

ra-bi *m.* rabbi

ra-bia *f.* rabies

ra-biar *v.* to have rabies

ra-bi-no *m.* rabbi

ra-bio-so *adj.* furious

ra-bo *m.* stem; tail

ra-cial *adj.* racial

ra-ci-mo *m.* bunch; cluster

ra-ción *f.* allowance; ration

ra-cio-nal *adj.* rational

ra-cio-na-li-dad *f.* rationality

ra-cio-na-lis-mo *m.* rationalism

ra-cio-na-lis-ta *adj.* rationalist

ra-cio-na-li-zar *v.* to rationalize about

ra-cio-nar *v.* to ration

ra-cha *f.* gust

ra-da *f.* bay

ra-dar *m.* radar

ra-dia-ción *f.* radiation

ra-diac-ti-vi-dad *f.* radioactivity

ra-diac-ti-vo, -va *adj.* radioactive

ra-dia-dor *m.* radiator

ra-dial *adj.* radial

ra-dian-te *adj.* radiant

ra-diar *v.* to radiate

ra-di-cal *adj.* radical

ra-dio *m.* radio; radius

ra-dio-di-fun-dir *v.* to broadcast

ra-dio-gra-fí-a *f.* radiography

ra-dio-gra-ma *f.* radiogram

ra-dio-lo-gi-a *f.* radiology

ra-dio-lo-go, -ga *m., f.* radiologist

ra-dios-co-pia *f.* radioscopy

ra-er *v.* to scrape

raid *m.* raid

ra-i-do, -da *adj.* worn

ra-já *f.* splinter; crack

ra-ja-do, -da *adj.* cracked

ra-ja-du-ra *f.* crack

ra-jar *v.* to sliver; crack

ra-lo, -la *adj.* thin

ra-llar *v.* to grate

ra-ma *f.* branch

ra-ma-da *f.* grove

ra-mal *m.* flight; strand

ram-bla f. boulevard
ra-mi-fi-ca-cion f. ramification
ra-mi-fi-car-se v. to branch
ra-mi-lle-te m. cluster
ra-mo m. bouquet
ra-mo-ne-ar v. to graze
ram-pa f. ramp
ra-na f. frog
ran-ci-dez f. rancidity
ran-cio adj. rancid
ran-cho m. farm
ra-pa-ci-dad f. rapacity
ra-par v. to crop; to shave
ra-pi-da-men-te adv. rapidly
ra-pi-do adj. fast; express; rapid
rap-so-dia f. rhapsody
rap-to m. rapture
ra-que-ta f. racket
ra-qui-tis-mo m. rickets
ra-ra-men-te adv. rarely
ra-re-za f. rarity
ra-ro adj. rare; bizarre; odd
ra-sar v. to brush
ras-ca-cie-los m. skyscraper
ras-ca-du-ra f. scratch
ras-car v. to scrape
ras-ca-zon f. itch
ras-ga-du-ra f. tear
ras-gar v. to tear
ras-go m. feature; trait
ras-gon m. tear
ras-gu-ñar v. to scratch
ras-gu-ño m. scratch
ra-so, -sa adj. level; flat
ras-pa-dor m. scraper
ras-pa-du-ra f. rasping
ras-pan-te adj. abrasive
ras-par v. to erase; to scrape
ras-tra f. trail
ras-tre-ar v. to trail
ras-tri-llo m. rake
ra-su-ra f. shaving
ra-su-rar v. to shave
ra-ta f. rat
ra-te-ro, -ra m., f. thief
ra-ti-fi-ca-cion f. ratification
ra-ti-fi-car v. to ratificar
ra-ti-fi-ca-to-rio, -ria adj. ratifying
ra-to m. while
ra-ton m. mouse

ra-ya f. stripe; line
ra-yar v. to rule; to streak
ra-yo m. beam; ray
ra-yon m. rayon
ra-za f. race
ra-zon f. cause
ra-zo-na-ble adj. rational; reasonable
ra-zo-na-do, -da adj. reasoned
ra-zo-nar v. to reason
re-ac-cion f. reaction
re-ac-cio-nar v. to react
re-ac-ti-va-cion f. reactivation
re-ac-ti-var v. to reactivate
re-a-dap-ta-cion f. readaptation
re-a-dap-tar v. to readapt
re-a-fir-mar v. to reaffirm
re-a-jus-tar v. to readjust
re-a-jus-te m. readjustment
real adj. true; real; royal
re-a-le-za f. royalty
rea-li-dad f. reality
rea-lis-ta adj. realistic
re-a-li-za-dor, -ra adj. fulfilling
rea-li-zar v. to accomplish; to fulfil; realize
re-al-zar v. to enhance
re-a-ni-mar v. to reanimate
re-a-nu-da-cion f. resumption
re-a-nu-dar v. to resume
re-a-pa-re-cer v. to reappear
rea-ta f. rope
re-a-vi-var v. to revive
re-ba-ja f. reduction
re-ba-jar v. to reduce
re-ba-na-da f. slice
re-ba-nar v. to slice
re-ba-ño m. flock
re-be-lar-se v. to rebel; to revolt
re-bel-de adj. rebel
re-be-lion f. revolt
re-bor-de m. border
re-bo-tar v. to bounce
re-buz-no m. braying
re-ca-bar v. to request
re-ca-do m. message
re-ca-er v. to relapse

re-cal-car v. to squeeze
re-ca-len-ta-mien-to m. reheating
re-ca-len-tar v. to reheat
re-ca-pa-ci-tar v. to reconsider
re-ca-pi-tu-la-cion m. recapitulation
re-ca-pi-tu-lar v. to recapitulate
re-car-gar v. to overload; to reload
re-cau-dar v. to collect
re-cau-do m. collection
re-ce-lar v. to suspect
re-ce-lo m. jealousy; mistrust; suspicion
re-ce-lo-so, sa adj. suspicious
re-cep-cion f. reception
re-cep-cio-nis-ta m., f. receptionist
re-cep-ta-cu-lo m. receptacle
re-cep-ti-vi-dad f. receptivity
re-cep-ti-vo adj. receptive
re-ce-sion f. recession
re-ce-tar v. to prescribe
re-ci-bi-dor, -ra adj. receiving
re-ci-bi-mien-to m. reception
re-ci-bir v. to accept; receive
re-ci-bo m. receipt
re-ci-clar v. to recycle
re-cien adv. recently
re-cien-te adj. recent
re-cien-te-men-te adv. recently
re-cio, -cia adj. severe; strong
re-ci-pro-car v. to reciprocate
re-ci-pro-ci-dad f. reciprocity
re-ci-ta-cion f. recitation
re-ci-tar v. to recite
re-cla-ma-cion f. complaint
re-cla-ma-dor adj. claiming
re-cla-mar v. to reclaim
re-cli-nar v. to rest on
re-cluir v. to imprison
re-clu-sion f. imprisonment
re-clu-so m. recluse
re-clu-ta f. recruitment

re-clu-ta-mien-to m. recruitment
re-clu-tar v. to recruit
re-co-brar v. to regain; to recover
re-co-bro m. recovery
re-co-do m. bend
re-co-ge-dor, -ra adj. collecting
re-co-ger v. to collect; to gather; to shorten
re-co-gi-mien-to m. retirement
re-co-lec-ción f. collection
re-co-lec-tar v. to gather
re-co-men-da-ble adj. recommendable
re-co-men-da-cion f. recommendation
re-co-men-dar v. to recommend
re-com-pen-sa f. to reward
re-com-pen-sar v. to compensate
re-con-ci-lia-ble adj. reconcilalbe
re-con-ci-lia-ción f. reconciliation
re-con-ci-liar v. to reconcile
re-con-for-tar v. to comfort
re-co-no-cer v. to acknowledge
re-co-no-ci-do, -da adj. gratitude; recognition
re-con-quis-tar v. to recover
re-con-si-de-rar v. reconsider
re-cons-ti-tuir v. to reconstitute
re-cons-truc-cion f. reconstruction
re-cons-truir v. to reconstruct
re-con-tar v. to recount
re-co-pi-la-cion f. compilation
re-co-pi-la-dor m. compiler
re-co-pi-lar v. to compile
re-cor-da-cion f. memory
re-cor-dar v. to remember
re-co-rrer v. to travel
re-cor-tar v. to reduce
re-cre-a-ción f. recreation
re-cre-ar v. to re-create
re-crea-ti-vo adj. recreational

re-cre-o m. recreation

re-cri-mi-na-sion f. recrimination

re-cru-de-ci-mien-ti m. worsening

rec-tal adj. rectal

rec-ta-men-te adv. justly

rec-tan-gu-lar adj. rectangle

rec-tán-gu-lo adj. rectangular

rec-ti-fi-ca-cion f. rectification

rec-ti-fi-car v. to recify

rec-ti-tud f. honesty

rec-to adj. right; upright

re-cu-brir v. tocover

re-cuen-to m. recount

re-cuer-do m. memory; remembrance

re-cu-la-da f. backing up

re-cu-pe-ra-ble adj. recoverable

re-cu-pe-ra-cion f. recovery

re-cu-pe-rar v. to recover

re-cu-rren-te adj. recurrent

re-cu-rrir v. to return

re-cur-so m. remedy; resource

re-cu-sa-cion f. rejection

re-cu-sar v. to refuse

re-cha-za-mien-to m. rejection

re-cha-zar v. to reject; rebuff

re-cha-zo m. rejection

re-chi-fla f. hissing

re-chi-flar v. to hiss

re-dac-cion f. writing

re-dac-tar v. to edit

ra-da-da f. roundup

re-de-ci-lla f. mesh

re-den-cion f. redemption

re-dil m. fold

re-di-mir v. to redeem

ré-di-to m. rent

re-di-tuar v. to yield

re-do-blar v. to fold

re-don-dez f. roundness

re-don-do, -da adj. round

re-duc-cion f. reduction

re-du-ci-do adj. reduced

re-du-cir v. to shorten; reduce

re-duc-tor, -ra adj. reducing

re-dun-dan-cia f. redundancy

re-dun-dan-te adj. redundant

re-dun-dar v. to overflow

re-e-le-gir v. to reelect

re-em-bol-sa-ble adj. reimbursable

re-em-bol-sar v. to reimburse

re-em-bol-so m. reimbursement

re-em-pla-zar v. to replace

re-em-pla-zo m. substitution

re-en-car-na-cion f. reincarnation

re-es-truc-tu-ra-cion f. restructuring

re-es-truc-tu-rar v. to restructure

re-fec-to-rio m. refectory

re-fe-ren-cia f. refernce

re-fe-ren-te adj. referring

re-fe-rir v. to refer; to tell

re-fi-na-do, -da adj. refined

re-fi-na-mien-to m. refinement

re-fi-nar v. to refine

re-fi-ne-rí-a f. refinery

re-fle-jar v. to speculate; to reflect

re-fle-xión f. reflection

re-fle-xi-vo, -va adj. reflective

re-for-ma f. reform

re-for-ma-cion f. reformation

re-for-mar v. to reform

re-for-ma-to-rio, -ria adj. reformatory

re-for-mis-ta adj. reformist

re-for-za-do, -da adj. reinforced

re-for-zar v. to reinforce

re-frac-ción f. refraction

re-frac-tar v. to refract

re-fre-nar v. to restrain

re-fres-can-te adj. refreshing

re-fres-car v. to refresh

re-fres-co m. refreshment

re-fri-ge-ra-cion f. refrigeration

re-fir-ge-ra-dor m. refrigerator

re-fri-ge-rar v. to refrigerate
re-fri-to, -ta adj. refried
re-fuer-zo m. reinforcement
re-fu-gia-do, -da adj. refugee
re-fu-gio m. shelter; refuge
re-ful-gen-te adj. refulgent
re-fun-fu-nar v. to grumble
re-fun-fu-no m. grumble
re-fu-ta-cion f. rebuttal
re-fu-tar v. to rebut
re-ga-la-do, -da adj. easy; dainty
re-ga-lar v. to give away
re-ga-liz m. licorice
re-ga-lo m. present
re-ga-ñar v. to argue
re-gar v. to bathe
re-ga-zo m. lap
re-ge-ne-ra-cion f. regeneration
re-ge-ne-ra-dor, -ra m., f. regenerator
re-ge-ne-rar v. to regenerate
re-gen-tar v. to direct
ré-gi-men m. regimen
re-gi-men-tar v. to regiment
re-gio, -gia adj. regal
re-gión f. area; region
re-gio-nal adj. regional
re-gio-na-lis-mo m. regionalism
re-gir v. to govern
re-gis-tra-dor, -ra m., f. register; registering
re-gis-trar v. to record; to register
re-gis-tro m. search; registration; registry; register
re-gla f. rule
re-gla-men-ta-cion f. regulation
re-gla-men-tar v. to regulate
re-glar v. to regulate
re-go-ci-jo m. joy
re-go-de-o m. pleasure
re-gre-sar v. to return
re-gre-sion f. regression
re-gre-si-vo adj. regressive
re-gre-so m. return
re-gue-ro m. trail; stream
re-gu-la-ción f. regulation

re-gu-la-dor m. regulator
re-gu-lar adj. regular
re-gu-la-ri-dad f. regularity
re-gu-la-ri-zar v. to regularize
re-gu-lar-men-te adv. regularly
re-gur-gi-ta-cion f. regurgitation
re-gur-gi-tar v. to regurgitate
re-ha-bi-li-ta-cion f. rehabilitation
re-ha-bi-li-tar v. to rehabilitate
re-ha-cer v. to remake
re-ho-gar v. to brown
re-huir v. to avoid
re-hu-sar v. to refuse
re-im-pri-mir v. to reprint
rei-na f. queen
rei-na-do m. reign
rei-nan-te adj. ruling
rei-nar v. to reign
re-in-ci-den-te adj. relapsing
re-in-ci-dir v. to relapse
re-in-cor-po-ra-cion f. reincorporation
re-in-cor-po-rar v. to reincorporate
re-in-gre-sar v. to re-enter something
rei-no m. kingdom
re-ins-ta-la-cion f. reinstallation
re-ins-ta-lar v. to reinstall
re-in-te-gra-cion f. reintegration
re-in-te-grar v. to reintegrate
re-in-te-gro m. reintegration
re-ir(se) v. to laugh
rei-te-ra-cion f. reiteration
rei-te-rar v. to reiterate
rei-te-ra-ti-vo, -va adj. reiterative
rei-vin-di-car v. to recover
re-jun-tar v. to gather
re-ju-ve-ne-cer v. to rejuvenate
re-la-cion f. account; relation
re-la-cio-na-do, -da adj. related
re-la-cio-nar v. to relate
re-la-ja-ción f. relaxation

re-la-ja-do, -da adj. relaxed
re-la-jar v. to relax
re-la-mar v. to lick
re-lám-pa-go m. lightning
re-lám-pa-gue-o m. lightning
re-lap-so, -sa adj. relapsed
re-la-tar v. to narrate
re-la-ti-vi-dad f. relativity
re-la-ti-vo, -va adj. relative
re-la-to m. story; narration
re-le-gar v. to relegate
re-le-var v. to relieve; to praise
re-li-ca-rio m. reliquary
re-li-ve m. relief
re-li-gión f. religion
re-li-gio-si-dad f. religiosity
re-li-gio-so adj. religious
re-loj m. watch; clock
re-lo-je-ri-a f. clockmaking
re-lo-je-ro, -ra m., f. watchmaker
re-lu-cir v. to shine
re-lum-bran-te adj. dazzling
re-lum-brar v. to dazzle
re-lle-nar v. to refill
re-ma-llar v. to mend
re-mar v. to row
re-ma-tar v. to use up
re-ma-te m. conclusion
re-me-dar v. to mimic
re-me-dia-ble adj. remediable
re-me-diar v. to cure; to remedy
re-mem-bran-za f. remembrance
re-me-mo-ra-cion f. remembrance
re-me-mo-rar v. to remember something
re-men-dar v. to mend; to repair
re-mem-dón, -na m., f.
re-mi-sión f. remission
re-mi-so, -sa adj. remiss
re-mi-tne-te adj. remitting
re-mi-tir v. to forgive; to remit; to diminish
re-mo m. oar
re-mo-la-cha f. beet
re-mol-car v. to tow
re-mo-lo-ne-ar v. to loaf

re-mol-que m. tow truck
re-mon-tar v. to remount; to surmount
re-mor-di-mien-to m. remorse
re-mo-to adj. faraway
re-mo-ver v. to remove; to move; to dismiss
re-mo-zar v. to rejuvenate
re-mu-ne-ra-ción f. remuneration
re-mu-ne-rar v. to remunerate
re-mu-ne-ra-ti-vo, -va adj. remunerative
re-na-ci-mien-to m. revival
re-nal adj. renal
ren-ci-lla f. quarrel
ren-cor m. spite; bitterness; rancor
ren-co-ro-so adj. bitter; resentful
ren-di-do adj. submissive; obsequious
ren-di-mien-to m. submissiveness; yield
ren-dir v. to yield; to surrender; to defeat
ren-gue-ar v. to limp
re-no m. reindeer
re-nom-bra-do, -da adj. renowned
re-nom-bre m. renown
re-no-va-ción f. renovation
re-no-va-do adj. renewed
re-no-var v. to renovate; to reform
ren-ta f. interest; rent; income
ren-ta-ble adj. profitable
ren-tar v. to rent
re-nuen-cia f. reluctance
re-nuen-te adj. reluctant
re-nun-cia f. renunciation
re-nun-cia-cion f. renunciation
re-nun-ciar v. to reject; to surrender; to waive; to renounce
re-ñi-dor, -ra adj. quarrelsome
re-ñir v. to fight; to quarrel with another

re-or-ga-ni-za-cion f. reorganization

re-or-ga-ni-zar v. to reorganize

re-pa-ra-ción f. repair

re-pa-ra-dor, -ra m., f. repairer

re-pa-rar v. to mend; repair

re-pa-ro m. protection; objection

re-par-ti-ción f. sharing

re-par-ti-dor, -ra m., f. distributor

re-par-tir v. to share; to apportion; to divide

re-par-to m. delivery

re-pa-sar v. to review; to revise

re-pa-so m. review

re-pa-tria-ción f. repatriation

re-pa-triar v. to repatriate

re-pe-len-te adj. repellent

re-pe-ler v. to repel

re-pen-te m. start

re-pen-ti-no, -na adj. repercussion

re-per-cu-sión f. repercussion

re-per-cu-tir v. to reverberate

re-per-to-rio m. repertoire

re-pe-ti-ción f. repetition

re-pe-tir v. to repeat

re-pe-ti-ti-vo, -va adj. repetitive

re-pi-que-te-ar v. to beat; to ring

re-pi-sa f. shelf

re-plan-tar v. to replant

re-plan-te-ar v. to restate

re-ple-to, -ta adj. full

ré-pli-ca f. answer

re-pli-car v. to reply; to respond

re-po-bla-ción f. repopulation

re-po-blar v. to repopulate

re-po-llo m. cabbage

re-po-ner v. to replace; to revive

re-por-tar v. to bring

re-por-te-ro, -ra adj. reporting

re-po-sa-do adj. quiet

re-po-sar v. to lie

re-po-si-ción f. reposition

re-po-so m. repose

re-pren-der v. to reprimand

re-pren-sión f. reprimand

re-pre-sa-lia f. reprisal

re-pre-sen-ta-ción f. representation

re-pre-sen-tan-te adj. representing

re-pre-sen-tar v. to represent; to appear to be

re-pre-sen-ta-ti-vo, -va adj. representative

re-pre-sión f. repression

re-pre-si-vo, -va adj. repressive

re-pri-men-da f. reprimand

re-pri-mir v. to repress

re-pro-char v. to reproach

re-pro-che m. rebuke; reproach

re-pro-duc-ción f. reproduction

re-pro-du-cir v. to reproduce

rep-tar v. to crawl

rep-til m. reptile

re-pú-bli-ca f. republic

re-pu-bli-ca-no, na adj. republican

re-pu-dia-ción f. repudiation

re-pu-diar v. to repudiate

re-pug-nan-cia f. repugnance

re-pug-nan-te adj. repugnant

re-pul-gar v. to hem

re-pul-sar v. to reject

re-pul-sión f. repulsion

re-pul-si-vo, -va adj. repulsive

re-pun-tar v. to turn

re-pun-te adj. turning

re-que-brar v. to break something again

re-que-ri-mien-to m. requirement

re-que-rir v. to want; to require

re-quiem m. requiem

re-qui-sar v. to requisition

re-qui-si-ción f. requisition

re-qui-si-to m. requirement
re-sa-la-do, -da adj. charming
re-sar-cir v. to indemnify
res-ba-lar v. to glide
res-ca-tar v. to rescue; to recover
res-ca-te m. rescue
res-cin-dir v. to rescind
res-ci-sion f. rescission
re-sen-ti-do, -da adj. resentful
re-sen-ti-mien-to m. resentment
re-sen-tir-se v. to feel hurt
re-se-ña f. account; inspection
re-se-ñar v. to review; to inspect
re-ser-va f. reserve
re-ser-va-ción f. reservation
re-ser-va-do, -da adj. reserved; confidential
re-ser-var v. to reserve
res-fria-do m. cold
res-friar v. to cool
res-guar-dar v. to protect
res-guar-do m. guard; protection
re-si-den-cia f. residence
re-si-den-cial adj. residential
re-si-den-te m., f. resident
re-si-dir v. to live; reside
re-si-duo m. residue
re-sig-na-ción f. resignation
re-sis-ten-cia f. endurance; resistance
re-sis-ten-te adj. resistant
re-sis-tir v. to oppose; to resist
re-so-lu-ción f. resolution
re-so-lu-to, -ta adj. resolute
re-sol-ver v. to settle; to solve; to resolve
re-so-nan-cia f. resonance
re-so-nan-te adj. resounding
re-so-nar v. to resound
res-so-pli-do m. puffing
res-pal-dar v. to back something or someone
res-pal-do m. back
res-pec-ti-vo adj. respective
res-pec-to m. respect

res-pe-ta-ble adj. respectable
res-pe-tar v. to respect
res-pe-to m. respect
res-pe-tuo-so, -sa adj. respectful
res-pi-ra-ción f. respiration
res-pi-ra-dor m. respirator
res-pi-rar v. to inhale and exhale; to breath
res-pi-ro m. respite
res-plan-dor m. glow; brightness
res-pon-der v. to reply; to respond
res-pon-sa-ble adj. responsible
res-pues-ta f. answer; response
res-que-brar v. to crack
res-que-mor m. remorse
res-ta-ble-cer v. to reestablish
res-ta-ble-ci-mien-to m. reestablishment
res-ta-llar v. to crack
res-tau-ra-ción f. restoration
res-tau-ra-dor, -ra m., f. restorer
res-tau-ran-te m. restaurant
res-tau-rar v. to restore
res-ti-tu-ción f. restitution
res-to m. remainder
res-tric-ción f. restriction
res-tric-ti-vo, -va adj. restrictive
res-trin-gir v. to restrict
re-su-ci-tar v. to resuscitate
re-sul-ta f. result
re-sul-ta-do m. issue; result
re-sul-tar v. to result
re-su-mir v. to summarize
re-sur-gir v. to reappear
re-su-rrec-ción f. resurrection
re-tar-dar v. to delay
re-ten-ción f. retention
re-te-ner v. to keep; to retain
re-ti-na f. retina
re-ti-ni-tis f. retinitis
re-ti-ra-da f. retreat
re-ti-ra-do, -da adj. retired
re-ti-rar v. to retire; to

withdraw; to retract
re-ti-ro m. retreat; withdrawal
re-to m. challenge
re-to-ñar v. to sprout
re-tor-cer v. to twist
re-tor-ci-do, -da adj. twisted
re-tor-ci-mien-to m. twisting
re-tó-ri-co, -ca adj. rhetorical
re-tor-nar v. to return
re-to-zar v. to frolic
re-to-zo m. frolic
re-to-zon, -ona adj. frolicsome
re-trac-ción f. retraction
re-trac-tar v. to recant; to retract
re-trac-til adj. retractable
re-tra-er v. to dissuade
re-tra-i-do, -da adj. withdrawn
re-trai-mien-to m. seclusion
re-trans-mi-tir v. to retransmit
re-tra-sar v. to delay
re-tra-to m. portrait
re-tre-ta f. retreat
re-tri-bu-ción f. retribution
re-tri-bu-ir v. to reward
re-tro-ac-ti-vo, -va adj. retroactive
re-tro-gra-do, -da adj. retrograde
re-tros-pec-ción f. retrospection
re-tum-bar v. to resound
reu-ma-ti-co adj. rheumatic
reu-ma-tis-mo m. rheumatism
reu-nión f. meeting; reunion
reu-nir v. to gather; to mass; to meet
re-va-li-da-ción f. revalidation
re-va-li-dar v. to revalidate
re-va-lo-ri-zar v. to revalue
re-van-cha f. revenge
re-ve-la-ción f. revelation
re-ve-la-dor, -ra adj. revealing
re-ve-lar v. to betray; to reveal
re-ven-der v. to resell
re-ven-tar v. to blow; to

burst
re-ven-tión m. burst
re-ver v. to review
re-ver-be-rar v. to reverberate
re-ve-ren-cia f. reverence
re-ve-ren-ciar v. to revere
re-ve-ren-do, -da adj. reverend
re-ve-ren-te adj. respectful
re-ver-so m. reverse
re-ver-tir v. to revert
re-ves-tir v. to cover
re-vi-sar v. to review
re-vi-sión f. revision
re-vi-sor, -ra m., f. inspector
re-vis-ta f. magazine
re-vis-te-ro, -ra m., f. reviewer
re-vi-ta-li-zar v. to revitalize
re-vi-vi-fi-car v. to revive
re-vi-vir v. to revive
re-vo-ca-ción f. revocation
re-vo-car v. to repeal; to revoke
re-vol-con m. fall
re-vo-lo-te-ar v. to flutter
re-vo-lu-ción f. revolution
re-vo-lu-cio-nar v. to revolutionize
re-vo-lu-cio-na-rio adj. revolutionary
re-vol-ver v. to revolve; to mix; to shake
re-vol-ver m. revolver
re-vo-que m. plaster
re-vue-lo m. commotion
rey m. king
re-zar v. to pray; to say something
re-zon-gar v. to grumble
ri-be-ra f. shore
ri-be-te-a-do adj. trimmed
ri-be-te-ar v. to hem
ri-ca-men-te adv. richly
ri-co adj. wealthy; rich
ri-di-cu-la-men-te adv. ridiculously
ri-di-cu-li-zar v. to ridicule
ri-di-cu-lo adj. ridiculous
riel m. rail
rien-da f. rein
ries-go m. danger; risk

ri-fa f. raffle
ri-far v. to raffle off
ri-fle m. rifle
ri-gi-do adj. stiff; rigid
ri-gor m. rigor
ri-gu-ro-so adj. severe; rigorous
ri-ma f. rhyme
ri-mar v. to rhyme
rim-bom-ban-te adj. echoing
rin-cón m. corner
ri-no-ce-ron-te m. rhinoceros
ri-ña f. quarrel
ri-ñón m. kidney
río m. river
ri-que-za f. riches
ri-sa f. laughter
ri-si-ble adj. laughable
ris-tra f. string
ri-sue-ño, -na adj. smiling
rít-mi-co adj. rhythmical
ri-to m. ceremony
ri-tual m. ritual
ri-val m. rival
ri-va-li-dad f. rivalry
ri-va-li-zar v. to rival
ri-zar v. to curl up
ro-bar v. to steal
ro-ble m. oak
ro-bo m. robbery
ro-bus-te-cer v. to make strong; to strengthen
ro-bus-to adj. hardy; strong
ro-ciar v. to sprinkle
ro-cin m. donkey
ro-cí-o m. sprinkle
ro-dar v. to tumble; to roll
ro-de-ar v. to circle; to ring
ro-de-o m. to go around
ro-de-te m. bun
ro-di-lla f. knee
ro-e-dor, -ra adj. gnawing
ro-er v. to gnaw
ro-gar v. to request; to pray
ro-jo adj. red
ro-llo m. roll
ro-ma-no, -na adj. Roman
ro-mán-ti-co adj. romantic
ro-me-ro m. rosemary
rom-bo m. rhombus
rom-per v. to smash; to break
ron m. rum

ron-car v. to snore
ron-co, -ca adj. hoarse
ron-que-ra f. hoarseness
ro-no-so, -sa adj. filthy
ro-pa f. clothing
ro-pe-ro m. closet
ro-sa f. rose
ro-sa-do, -da adj. pink
ro-sal m. rosebush
ro-sa-le-da f. rose garden
ros-bif m. roast beef
ros-ca f. circle
ros-tro m. face
ro-ta-ción f. rotation
ro-ta-to-rio, -ria adj. rotating
ro-ton-da f. rotunda
ro-tor m. rotor
ro-tu-la-do m. label
ro-tu-la-dor, -ra adj. labeling
ro-tu-lar v. to label
ro-za-mien-to m. rubbing
ro-zar v. to scrape; to skim
ru-be-o-la f. rubella
ru-bí m. ruby
ru-bi-cun-do, -da adj. ruddy
ru-bio adj. blonde
ru-bor m. blush
ru-bo-ri-zae-se v. to blush
ru-da f. rue
ru-de-za f. rudeness
ru-di-men-tal adj. rudimentary
ru-di-men-ta-rio, -ria adj. rudimentary
ru-di-men-to m. rudiment
ru-do, -da adj. rude
rue-da f. wheel
rue-do m. hem; edge
rue-go m. request
ru-gi-do m. roar
ru-gi-dor, -ra adj. roaring
ru-go-so, -sa adj. winkled
rui-do m. sound; rattle; noise
rui-do-so, -sa adj. noisy
ruin adj. poor; despicable
rui-na f. ruin
rui-nar v. to ruin
rum-bo m. direction
ru-mor m. rumor
rup-tu-ra f. rupture
ru-ral adj. rural
ru-ti-lar v. to shine
ru-ti-na f. route

sá-ba-do *m.* Saturday
sá-ba-na *f.* sheet for a bed
sa-ber *v.* to inform; to know
sa-bi-do, -da *adj.* known
sa-bi-du-rí-a *f.* knowledge
sa-bio, -bia *adj.* learned
sa-ble *m.* saber
sa-bor *m.* flavor; taste
sa-bo-re-ar *v.* to taste
sa-bo-ta-je *m.* sabotage
sa-bo-te-a-dor, -ra *adj.* sabotaging
sa-bo-te-ar *v.* to sabotage
sa-bro-so *adj.* delightful
sa-ca-cor-chos *m.* corkscrew
sa-ca-pun-tas *m.* pencil sharpener
sa-car *v.* to pull out; to get out
sa-ca-ri-na *f.* saccharin
sa-cer-do-cio *m.* priesthood
sa-cer-do-te *m.* priest
sa-cer-do-ti-sa *f.* priestess
sa-co *m.* bag
sa-cra-men-to *m.* sacrament
sa-cri-fi-car *v.* to sacrifice
sa-cri-fi-cio *m.* sacrifice
sa-cri-le-gio *m.* sacrilege
sa-cro *adj.* sacred
sa-cu-di-da *f.* tremor; shake
sa-cu-dir *v.* to beat; to tug
sá-di-co, -ca *adj.* sadistic
sa-ga *f.* saga
sa-ga-ci-dad *f.* sagacity
sa-gaz *adj.* sagacious
sa-gra-do, -da *adj.* sacred
sa-ke *m.* sake
sal *f.* salt
sa-la *f.* living room of a house
sa-la-do, -da *adj.* salted; salty
sa-la-man-dra *f.* salamander
sa-laz *f.* salacious
sal-chi-chon *m.* sausage
sal-dar *v.* to pay off something
sal-do *m.* payment
sa-le-ro *m.* saltshaker
sa-li-da *f.* exit; solution
sa-lien-te *adj.* salient
sa-li-no, -na *adj.* saline

sa-lir *v.* to get out; to leave
sa-li-va *n.* saliva
sa-li-val *adj.* salivary
sa-li-var *v.* to salivate
sal-mo, -n *m.* psalm
sal-món *m.* salmon
sa-lo-bre *adj.* briny
sal-pi-car *v.* to splash
sal-pi-men-tar *v.* to season
sal-sa *f.* sauce
sal-ta-dor *m.* jumper
sal-ta-mon-tes *m.* grasshopper
sal-tar *v.* to jump; to leap; to bounce
sal-te-ar *v.* to skip
sal-to *m.* jump
sa-lu-bre *adj.* healthful
sa-lud *f.* health
sa-lu-da-ble *adj.* healthy
sa-lu-dar *v.* to salute
sa-lu-ta-cion *f.* greeting
sal-va-ción *f.* salvation
sal-va-guar-dar *v.* to safeguard
sal-va-guar-dia *f.* safeguard
sal-va-ja-da *f.* savagery
sal-va-je *adj.* untamed; wild; uncivilized
sal-var *v.* to avoid; to save; to cover
sal-via *f.* sage
sal-vo *adj.* safe
sa-an-men-te *adv.* sincerely
sa-nar *v.* to heal
san-ción *f.* sanction
san-cio-nar *v.* to sanction
san-da-lia *f.* sandal
san-da-lo-m *m.* sandalwood
san-dez *f.* nonsense
san-dí-a *f.* watermelon
sa-ne-a-mien-to *m.* sanitation
sa-ne-ar *v.* to right
san-grar *v.* to bleed
san-gre *f.* blood
san-grí-a *f.* sangria
san-grien-to *adj.* bloody
san-gui-jue-la *f.* leech
san-gui-na-rio, -ria *adj.* cruel
sa-ni-dad *f.* healthiness
sa-ni-ta-rio, -ria *adj.* sanitary
sa-no *adj.* unharmed;

wholesome
san-ti-dad f. sanctity
san-ti-fi-car v. to sanctify
san-to adj. blessed
san-tua-rio m. sanctuary
sa-pien-cia f. wisdom
sa-pien-te adj. wise
sa-po m. toad
sa-que-ar v. to plunder
sa-que-o m. plundering
sa-ram-pión m. measles
sar-cas-mo m. sarcasm
sar-cás-ti-co adj. sarcastic
sar-di-na f. sardine
sar-dó-ni-co, -ca adj. sardonic
sar-gen-to m. sergeant
sar-no-so, -sa adj. scabby
sa-rro m. crust
sar-ta f. string
sa-sa-fras m. sassafras
sa-té-li-te m. satellite
sa-ten m. satin
sa-ti-na-do, -da adj. satiny
sá-ti-ra f. satire
sa-tí-ri-co, -ca adj. satirical
sa-ti-ri-zar v. to satirize
sá-ti-ro m. satyr
sa-tis-fac-ción f. satisfaction
sa-tis-fa-cer v. to satisfy
sa-tis-fac-to-rio, -ria adj. satisfactory
sa-tu-ra-ción f. saturation
sa-tu-ra-do, -da adj. saturated
sa-tu-rar v. to saturate
sa-xó-fo-no m. saxophone
sa-zón f. season
sa-zo-na-do adj. flavorful
sa-zo-nar v. to season
se pron. herself; oneself; yourself; himself
se-bá-ce-o, -a adj. sebaceous
se-bo m. fat
se-bo-rre-a f. seborrhea
se-ca-do m. drying
se-ca-do-ra f. clothes dryer
se-can-te adj. drying
se-car v. to dry
sec-ción f. section
sec-cio-nar v. to section

se-ce-sión f. secession
se-ce-sio-nis-ta adj. secessionist
se-co adj. dried
se-cre-ción f. secretion
se-cre-ta-men-te adv. secretly
se-cre-ta-ria f. secretary
se-cre-ta-rio m. secretary
se-cre-te-ar v. to whisper
se-cre-te-o m. whispering
se-cre-to m. secret
sec-ta-rio, -ria adj. sectarian
sec-tor m. sector
sec-to-rial adj. sectorial
se-cue-la f. consequence
se-cuen-cia f. sequence
se-cues-trar v. to kidnap
se-cues-tro m. kidnapping
se-cu-lar adj. secular
se-cu-la-ri-zar v. to secularize
se-cun-dar v. to second
se-cun-da-rio, -ria adj. secondary
sed f. thirst
se-da f. silk
se-dan-te adj. sedative
se-dar v. to soothe
se-dar v. to sedate
se-da-ti-vo adj. sedative
se-den-ta-rio, -ria adj. sedentary
se-di-ción f. sedition
se-dien-to, -ta adj. thirsty
se-di-men-to m. sediment
se-do-so adj. silky
se-duc-ción f. seduction
se-du-cir v. to seduce
se-duc-ti-vo, -ra adj. seductive
se-ga-dor, -ra adj. seductive
se-gar v. to mow; to harvest
se-glar adj. secular
seg-men-ta-ción f. segmentation
seg-men-to m. segment
se-gre-ga-ción f. segregation
se-gre-ga-cio-nis-ta adj. segregationist
se-gre-gar v. to segregate
se-gui-da-men-te adv. con-

tinuously
se-gui-do *adj.* consecutive
se-gui-dor, -ra *m., f.* follower
se-guir *v.* to chase; to follow; to watch
se-gún *prep.* according to
se-gun-do *adj.* second
se-gur *m.* sickle
se-gu-ra-men-te *adv.* probably
se-gu-ri-dad *f.* safety
se-gu-ro *adj.* sure; certain
seis *adj.* six
seis-cien-tos, -tas *adj.* six hundred
se-lec-ción *f.* selection
se-lec-cio-nar *v.* to select
se-lec-ti-vo, -va *adj.* selective
se-lec-to, -ta *adj.* select
sel-va *f.* woods
se-llar *v.* to stamp
se-llo *m.* stamp
se-ma-na *f.* week
se-ma-nal *adj.* weekly
se-ma-nal-men-te *adv.* weekly
se-ma-na-rio, -ria *adj.* weekly
se-man-ti-co, -ca *adj.* semantic
sem-bra-dor, -ra *adj.* sowing
sem-brar *v.* to sow
se-me-jan-te *adj.* similar
se-me-jan-za *f.* similarity
se-men-tar *v.* to seed
se-mes-tral *adj.* semiannual
se-mes-tre *m.* semester
se-miau-to-ma-ti-co, -ca *adj.* semiautomatic
se-mi-cir-cu-lar *adj.* semicircular
se-mi-cir-cu-lo *m.* semicircle
se-mi-fi-na-lis-ta *adj.* semifinalist
se-mi-lla *f.* seed
se-mi-lle-ro *m.* nursery for plants
se-mi-nal *adj.* seminal
se-mi-na-rio *m.* seminary
se-mi-na-ris-ta *m.* seminarian
se-mo-la *f.* semolina

sem-pi-ter-no, -na *adj.* everlasting
se-na-do *m.* senate
se-na-dor *m.* senator
sen-ci-lla-men-te *adv.* simply
sen-ci-llez *f.* simplicity
sen-ci-llo, -lla *adj.* simple; easy
sen-da *f.* path; trail
se-nil *adj.* senile
se-no *m.* cavity; hollow
sen-sa-ción *f.* sensation
sen-se-cio-nal *adj.* sensational
sen-sa-cio-na-lis-ta *adj.* sensational
sen-sa-to *adj.* sensible
sen-si-bi-li-dad *f.* sensibility; sensitiveness
sen-si-bi-li-zar *v.* to sensitize
sen-si-ble *adj.* sentimental; sensitive
sen-si-ble-ri-a *f.* sentimentality
sen-si-ti-vo, -va *adj.* sensitive
sen-so-rio, -ria *adj.* sensorial
sen-sual *adj.* sensual
sen-sua-li-dad *f.* sensuality
sen-ta-do, -da *adj.* settled; seated
sen-tar *v.* to sit
sen-ten-cia *f.* sentence
sen-ten-ciar *v.* to sentence
sen-ten-cio-so, -sa *adj.* sententious
sen-ti-do, -da *adj.* heartfelt
sen-ti-men-tal *adj.* sentimental
sen-ti-mien-to *m.* sentiment
sen-tir *v.* to feel; to sense; to experience
se-ña *f.* signal; sign
se-ñal *f.* sign
se-ña-lar *v.* to point; to determine
se-ña-li-zar *v.* to put up signs
se-ñe-ro *adj.* solitary
se-ñor *adj.* Mr.; Mister
se-ño-ri-o *m.* domain; solemnity

e-ño-ri-ta f. lady; girl
e-ño-ri-to m. boy; young man
e-ñue-lo m. trap; bait
e-pa-ra-ción f. separation
e-pa-ra-da-men-te adv. separately
e-pa-ra-do adj. separated
e-pa-rar v. to divide
e-pa-ra-tis-ta m. separatist
e-pe-lio m. burial
ep-ti-co, -ca adj. septic
ep-tiem-bre m. September
ep-ti-mo adj. seventh
ep-tua-ge-na-rio, -ria adj. septuagenarian
ep-tua-ge-si-mo, -ma adj. seventieth
e-pul-tar v. to bury
e-pul-to, -ta adj. buried
e-pul-tu-ra f. burial
e-que-dad f. dryness
e-quí-a f. drought
er v. to be; to come from
e-ra-fin m. angel
e-re-nar v. to calm
e-re-na-ta f. serenade
e-re-ni-dad f. serenity
e-re-no, -na adj. calm
e-rial adj. serial
e-ria-men-te adv. seriously
e-rie f. series
e-rie-dad f. seriousness
e-rio adj. serious
r-món m. sermon
r-mo-ne-ar v. to lecture
r-pien-te f. snake
e-rra-do, -da adj. sawed
e-rra-ní-a f. mountains
e-rre-rí-a f. sawmill
e-rru-cho m. saw
r-vi-cio m. help; service
r-vi-dor, -ra m., f. servant
r-vil adj. servile
r-vi-lle-ta f. napkin
r-vir v. to serve
e-sa-mo m. sesame
e-sen-ta adj. sexty
e-sen-ta-vo, va adj. sixtieth
e-go m. slant
e-so m. brain

se-su-do, -da adj. wise
se-te-cien-tos, -tas adj. seven hundred
se-ten-ta adj. seventy
se-ten-ta-vo, -va adj. seventieth
se-tiem-bre m. September
seu-dó-ni-mo, -ma m. pseudonym
se-ve-ra-men-te adv. relentlessly; severly
se-ve-ri-dad f. graveness; severity
se-ve-ro, -ra adj. unyielding; severe
se-xa-ge-si-mo, -ma adj. sixtieth
sex-te-to m. sextet
sex-to adj. sixth
se-xual adj. sexual
se-xua-li-dad f. sexuality
si conj. if; adv. yes
si-bi-lan-te adj. sibilant
si-co-mo-ro m. sycamore
sie-ga f. harvesting
siem-bra f. sowing
siem-pre adv. forever; always
sien f. temple
sie-rra f. saw
sier-vo m. servant; serf
sies-ta f. nap in the afternoon
sie-te adj. seven
si-fi-lis f. syphilis
si-fi-lí-ti-co, -caadj. syphilitic
si-gi-lo m. secrecy
si-gla f. acronym
si-glo m. century
sig-ni-fi-ca-ción f. significance
sig-ni-fi-ca-do, -da adj. significant
sig-ni-fi-can-te adj. significant
sig-ni-fi-car v. to signify; to indicate
sig-ni-fi-ca-ti-vo, -va adj. significant
sig-no m. sign
si-guien-te adj. next
sí-la-ba f. syllable
si-la-be-ar v. to syllable
si-la-be-o m. syllabication

sil-ba-to m. whistle
sil-bi-do m. whistle
si-len-cia-dor m. silencer
si-len-ciar v. to silence
si-len-cio m. silence
si-len-cio-so adj. silent
si-li-co-na f. silicone
si-lo m. silo
si-lo-gis-ti-co, -ca adj. syllogistic
si-lue-ta f. outline
sil-ves-tre adj. wild
sil-vi-cul-tor m. forester
si-lla f. chair
si-llín m. seat
si-llón m. armchair
sim-bio-sis f. symbiosis
sim-bió-ti-co, -ca adj. symbiotic
sim-bo-li-zar v. to symbolize
sím-bo-lo m. symbol
si-me-trí-a f. symmetry
si-mé-tri-co, -ca adj. symmetric
si-mien-te f. seed
sí-mil adj. similar
si-mi-lar adj. similar
si-mi-li-tud f. similarity
sim-pa-tí-a f. congeniality; affection
sim-pá-ti-co, -ca adj. pleasant
sim-pa-ti-zan-te adj. sympathizing
sim-ple adj. simple
sim-ple-za f. simplicity
sim-pli-ci-dad f. simplicity
sim-pli-fi-ca-cion f. simplification
sim-pli-fi-car v. to simplify
sim-po-sio m. symposium
si-mu-la-cion f. pretense
si-mu-la-dor, -ra m., f. simulator
si-mul-tá-ne-o, -a adj. simultaneous
sin prep. without
si-na-go-ga f. synagogue
sin-ce-ri-dad f. sincerity
sin-ce-ro, -ra adj. sincere
sin-co-pa f. syncope
sin-co-pa-do, -da adj. syncopated

sin-co-pe m. syncope
sin-cro-ni-a f. synchrony
sin-cro-ni-za-cion f. synchronization
sin-cro-ni-zar v. to synchronize
sin-di-ca-li-za-cion f. unionization
sin-di-ca-li-zar v. to unionize
sin-dro-me m. syndrome
si-ner-gia f. synergy
sin-fo-ni-a f. symphony
sin-fo-ni-co, -ca adj. symphonic
sin-gu-lar adj. single
sin-gu-la-ri-zar v. to distinguish
sin-nú-me-ro m. countless
si-no conj. but; fate
si-no-ni-mia f. synonymy
si-no-ni-mo, -ma adj. synonymous
si-nop-sis f. synopsis
si-nóp-ti-co, -ca adj. synoptic
sin-ta-xis m. syntax
sin-te-sis f. synthesis
sin-te-ti-co, -ca adj. synthetic
sin-te-ti-za-dor m. synthesizer
sin-te-ti-zar v. to synthesize
sin-to-ma m. symptom
sin-to-ma-ti-co, -ca adj. symptomatic
sin-to-ni-zar v. to tune
si-nuo-si-dad f. sinuosity
si-nuo-so, -sa adj. sinuous
si-qui-a-tra m., f. psychiatrist
si-quia-tri-a f. psychiatry
si-qui-co adj. psychic
si-quie-ra adv. at least
sir-vien-ta f. maid
sir-vien-te m. servant
sis-mi-co, -ca adj. seismic
sis-mo m. earthquake
sis-mo-gra-fo m. seismograph
sis-te-ma m. system
sis-te-ma-ti-za-cion f. systematization
sis-te-ma-ti-zar v. to systematize

is-to-le f. systole
i-tio m. place
i-to, -ta adj. situated
i-tua-ción f. situation
i-tuar v. to place
o-ba-co m. armpit
o-bar v. to thrash; to knead
o-be-o m. strap
o-be-ra-ní-a f. sovereignty
o-be-ra-no, -na adj. sovereign
o-ber-bio, -bia adj. superb
o-bor-nar v. to bribe another
o-bor-no m. bribery
o-bra f. excess
o-bra-do, -da adj. plenty
o-bran-te adj. surplus
o-brar v. to surpass
o-bre prep. over; on; above
o-bre-a-bun-dan-cia f. superabundance
o-bre-a-bun-dan-te adj. superabundant
o-bre-car-ga f. overload
o-bre-car-gar v. to overload
o-bre-ce-jo m. frown
o-bre-co-ger v. to scare
o-bre-cu-bier-ta f. cover
o-bre-en-ten-di-do, -da adj. understood
o-bre-ex-ci-tar v. to overexcite
o-bre-lle-nar v. to overfill
o-bre-lle-var v. to bear
o-bre-na-tu-ral adj. supernatural
o-bre-nom-bre m. nickname
o-bren-ten-der v. to understand
o-bre-pa-sar v. to surpass
o-bre-pe-so m. overlaod
o-bre-pre-cio m. surcharge
o-bre-sa-lien-te adj. outstanding
o-bre-sa-lir v. to project
o-bre-sal-tar v. to startle
o-bre-sal-to m. fright
o-bres-cri-to m. address
o-bres-ti-mar v. to overestimate
o-bre-to-do m. coat; overcoat

so-bre-vi-vien-te adj. surviving
so-bre-vi-vir v. to survive
so-bri-na f. niece
so-bri-no m. nephew
so-ca-rrón, -na m., f. one who is sarcastic
so-ca-rro-ne-rí-a f. sarcasm
so-ca-var v. to excavate
so-cia-bi-li-dad f. friendliness
so-cia-ble adj. sociable
so-cial adj. social
so-cie-dad f. society
so-cio, -cia m., f. member
so-cio-e-co-no-mi-co, -ca adj. socioeconomic
so-cio-lo-gí-a f. sociology
so-cio-lo-gi-co, -ca adj. sociological
so-cio-lo-go, -ga m., f. sociologist
so-co-rrer v. to aid
so-co-rro m. aid
so-dio m. sodium
so-fá f. sofa
so-fis-ma m. sophism
so-fis-ta adj. sophistic
so-fis-ti-ca-cion f. sophistication
so-fis-ti-ca-do, -da adj. sophisticated
so-fo-ca-cion f. suffocation
so-fo-ca-dor, -ra adj. suffocating
so-fo-car v. to suffocate; to suppress
so-ga f. rope
so-ja f. soybean
so-juz-gar v. to subjugate
sol m. sun
so-la-men-te adv. only
so-la-no m. the east wind
so-lar adj. solar
so-la-rium m. solarium
so-laz m. relaxation
sol-da-do m. soldier
sol-da-dor m. solderer
sol-da-du-ra f. soldering
sol-dar v. to join
so-le-a-do adj. sunny
so-le-cis-mo m. solecism

so-le-dad f. loneliness
so-lem-ne adj. solemn
so-lem-ni-dad f. solemnity
so-le-van-tar v. to lift
so-li-ci-ta-cion f. request
so-li-ci-tan-te m., f. petitioner
so-li-ci-tar v. to ask for; to request
so-li-ci-to, -ta adj. solicitous
so-li-ci-tud f. request; solicitude
so-li-da-ri-dad f. solidarity
so-li-dez f. solidity
so-li-di-fi-ca-cion f. solidification
so-li-di-fi-car v. to solidify
só-li-do adj. solid
so-li-lo-quio m. soliloquy
so-lis-ta f. soloist
so-li-vian-tar v. to irritate
so-li-viar v. to lift something
so-lo adj. alone
sols-ti-cio m. solstice
sol-tar v. to let go; to loosen
sol-te-ro adj. single
sol-tu-ra f. confidence; looseness
so-lu-ble adj. soluable
so-lu-cion f. solution
so-lu-cio-nar v. to solve
sol-ven-cia f. solvency
sol-ven-tar v. to resolve
sol-ven-te adj. solvent
so-ma-ti-co, -ca adj. somatic
so-ma-ti-za-cion f. somatization
so-ma-ti-zar v. to somatize
som-bra f. shade
som-brar v. to shade
som-bre-ar v. to shade
som-bre-ro m. hat
som-brí-o, -a adj. sullen
so-me-ter v. to subordinate
so-me-ti-mien-to m. submission
som-no-len-cia f. somnolence
so-ña-do, -da adj. crazy
so-ñar v. to sound
soñ-da f. sounding
son-de-ar v. to sound
son-de-o m. sounding

so-ne-to m. sonnet
so-ni-do m. sound
so-no-ri-dad f. sonority
so-no-ro, -ra adj. sonority
so-no-ro, -ra adj. sound
son-re-ir v. to smile
son-rien-te adj. smiling
son-ri-sa f. smile
son-ro-jo m. blush
son-ro-sar v. to turn pink
son-sa-car v. to wheedle
so-ña-do, -da adj. dream
so-ña-dor, -ra m., f. dreamer
so-ñar v. to dream
so-ño-len-cia f. somnolence
so-ño-lien-to, -ta adj. sleepy
so-pa f. soup
so-pa-pe-ar v. to slap
so-pa-po m. slap
so-pe-sar v. to wiegh
so-pla-dor, -ra adj. blowing
so-plar v. to blow
so-por m. sleepiness
so-por-ta-ble adj. bearable
so-por-tar v. to support
so-por-te m. support
so-pra-no m. soprano
sor-ber v. to absorb
sor-be-te m. sherbet
sor-bo m. sip
sor-de-ra f. deafness
sor-di-dez f. squalor
sór-di-do, -da adj. squalid
sor-do, -da adj. deaf
sor-na f. sarcasm
sor-pren-den-te adj. surprising
sor-pren-der v. to surprise
sor-pre-sa f. surprise
sor-pre-si-vo, -va adj. unexpected
sor-ti-ja f. ring
so-se-ga-do, -da adj. peaceful
so-se-gar v. to calm one down
so-sie-go m. quiet
sos-la-yo, -ya adj. slanted
so-so, -sa adj. dull
sos-pe-cha f. suspicion
sos-pe-char v. to suspect
sos-pe-cho-so, -sa adj. suspicious

sos-tén *m.* support; sustenance

sos-te-ne-dor *m.* supporter

sos-te-ner *v.* to uphold; to support

sos-te-ni-do, -da *adj.* sustained

sos-te-ni-mien-to *m.* sustenance; support

so-ta-na *f.* soutane

so-ta-no *m.* basement

Sr. *abbr. Senor, m.* Mr.

Sra. *abbr. Senora, f.* Mrs.

stan-dard *adj.* standard

su, sus *adj.* her; his; its; your

sua-ve *adj.* sweet; soft

sua-vi-dad *f.* smoothness; sweetness

sua-vi-za-dor, -ra *adj.* softening

sua-vi-zar *v.* to smooth; to soften

su-bal-ter-no, -na *adj.* subordinate

su-ba-rren-dar *v.* to sublet

su-ba-rrien-do *m.* sublease

su-bas-ta *f.* auction

su-bas-tar *v.* to auction

sub-co-mi-sion *f.* subcommittee

sub-cons-cien-te *adj.* subconscious

sub-cu-ta-ne-o, -a *adj.* subcutaneous

sub-di-vi-sion *f.* subdivision

su-bes-ti-mar *v.* to underestimate

su-bi-ba-ja *m.* seesaw

su-bi-do, -da *adj.* deep

su-bir *v.* to raise; to go up; to come

su-bi-ta-men-te *adv.* suddenly

su-bi-to *adj.* hasty

sub-je-ti-vi-dad *f.* subjectivity

sub-je-ti-vo, -va *adj.* subjective

su-ble-var *v.* to annoy

su-bli-ma-ción *f.* sublimation

su-bli-mar *v.* to sublimate

su-bli-me *adj.* sublime

sub-ma-ri-no, -na *adj.* submarine

su-bor-di-na-ción *f.* subordination

su-bor-di-na-do, -da *adj.* subordinate

su-bor-di-nar *v.* to subordinate

sub-sa-nar *v.* to correct

subs-cri-bir *v.* to subscribe to; to sign

subs-crip-ción *f.* subscription

subs-crip-tor, -ra *m., f.* subscriber

sub-se-cuen-te *adj.* subsequent

sub-si-diar *v.* to subsidize

sub-si-dio *m.* subsidy

sub-sis-ten-cia *f.* subsistence

sub-sis-tir *v.* to subsist

subs-tan-cia *f.* substance

subs-tan-cial *adj.* substantial

subs-tan-ciar *v.* to substantiate

subs-tan-cio-so, -sa *adj.* substantial

subs-ti-tu-ción *f.* substitution

subs-ti-tuir *v.* to substitute

subs-ti-tu-ti-vo, -va *adj.* substitute

subs-trac-ción *f.* subtraction

subs-tra-er *v.* to subtract; to deduce

sub-sue-lo *m.* basement

sub-ter-fu-gio *m.* subterfuge

sub-te-rrá-ne-o, -a *adj.* underground

sub-tí-tu-lo *m.* subtitle

su-bur-ba-no, -na *adj.* suburban

su-bur-bio *m.* suburb

sub-ven-ción *f.* subsidy

sub-ven-cio-nar *v.* to subsidize

sub-yu-gar *v.* to subjugate

suc-ción *f.* suction

su-ce-da-ne-o, -a *adj.* substitute

su-ce-der *v.* to succeed

su-ce-sión *f.* succession

su-ce-si-va-men-te *adv.* successively

su-ce-si-vo, -va *adj.* consecutive

su-ce-so *m.* event

su-ce-sor, -ra *adj.* succeeding

su-cie-dad *f.* filth

su-cio, -cia *adj.* vile; dirty

su-cu-len-cia *f.* succulence

su-cu-len-to, -ta *adj.* succelent

su-cum-bir *v.* to succumb

sud *m.* south

su-dar *v.* to sweat

su-des-te *m.* southeast

su-do-es-te *m.* southwest

su-dor *m.* sweat

su-do-ri-fe-ro, -ra *adj.* sudoriferous

su-do-ro-so, -sa *adj.* sweaty

sue-gra *f.* mother-in-law

sue-gro *m.* father-in-law

sue-lo *m.* floor; soil; ground

suel-to, -ta *adj.* nimble; loose

sue-ño *m.* dream; sleep

sue-ro *m.* serum

suer-te *f.* luck

su-fi-cien-cia *f.* competence

su-fi-cien-te *adj.* sufficient

su-fi-jo *m.* suffix

su-fra-gio *m.* suffrage

su-fra-gis-ta *f., m.* suffragist

su-fri-do, -da *adj.* patient

su-frir *v.* to suffer; to endure something

su-ge-ren-cia *f.* suggestion

su-ge-rir *v.* to suggest

su-ges-tión *f.* suggestion

su-ges-ti-vo, -va *adj.* suggestive

sui-ci-da *adj.* suicidal

sui-ci-dio *m.* suicide

su-je-ción *f.* subjection

su-je-tar *v.* to subject; to fasten

su-je-to, -ta *adj.* subject

sul-fu-ro *m.* sulfide

su-ma-men-te *adv.* extremely

su-mar *v.* to add up

su-ma-ria-men-te *adv.* summarily

su-ma-rio, -ria *adj.* brief

su-mer-gir *v.* to submerge

su-mi-de-ro *m.* drain

su-mi-nis-trar *v.* to supply

su-mi-nis-tro *m.* supply

su-mir *v.* to submerge into something

su-mi-sión *f.* submission

su-mi-so, -sa *adj.* submissive

sun-tuo-si-dad *f.* sumptuousness

sun-tuo-so, -sa *adj.* sumptuous

su-pe-di-tar *v.* to subordinate

su-pe-ra-bun-dar *v.* to superabound

su-pe-rar *v.* to surpass; to beat

su-pe-res-truc-tu-ra *f.* superstructure

su-per-fi-cial *adj.* superficial

su-per-fi-cie *f.* surface

su-per-fi-no, -na *adj.* very fine

su-per-fluo, -a *adj.* superfluous

su-pe-rin-ten-den-te *m., f.* superintendent

su-pe-rior *adj.* superior; better

su-pe-rio-ri-dad *f.* superiority

su-per-mer-ca-do *m.* supermarket

su-per-po-bla-ción *f.* overpopulation

su-per-po-ten-cia *f.* superpower

su-per-pro-duc-ción *f.* overproduction

su-per-só-ni-co, -ca *adj.* supersonic

su-pers-ti-ción *f.* superstition

su-pers-ti-cio-so, -sa *adj.* superstitious

su-per-vi-sar *v.* to supervise

su-per-vi-sión *f.* supervision

su-per-vi-ven-cia *f.* survival

su-pi-no, -na *adj.* supine

su-plan-tar *v.* to supplant

su-ple-men-tal *adj.* supplemental

su-plen-te *adj.* substitute

su-pli-car *v.* to implore

su-po-ner *v.* to imagine

something; to suppose

su-po-si-ción f. supposition

su-po-si-to-rio m. suppository

su-pre-mo, -ma adj. supreme

su-pri-mir v. to eliminate

su-pues-to, -ta adj. supposed; assumed

su-pu-rar v. to suppurate

sur m. south

sur-car v. to plow

sur-gir v. to arise

su-rre-a-lis-to adj. surrealistic

sur-ti-do, -da m. selection adj. assorted

sur-ti-dor, -ra m. supplier

sur-tir v. to supply something

sus-cep-ti-bi-li-dad f. susceptibility

sus-cep-ti-ble adj. susceptible

sus-pen-der v. to interrupt

sus-pen-sión f. suspension

sus-pen-si-vo, -va adj. suspensive

sus-pen-so-rio, -ria f. suspensory

sus-pi-ca-cia f. distrust

sus-pi-caz adj. being distrustful

sus-pi-rar v. to sigh

sus-pi-ro m. sigh

sus-ten-ta-mien-to m. sustenance

sus-ten-tar v. to uphold; to sustain

sus-tne-to m. support; sustenance

sus-to m. scare

su-su-rran-te adj. rustling

su-su-rrar v. to murmur; to whisper

su-su-rro m. whisper

su-til adj. subtle

su-ti-le-za f. subtlety

su-tu-ra f. suture

su-tu-rar v. to suture a wound

su-yo, -ya adj. their; her; his; your

ta-ba f. bone of the ankle

ta-ba-cal m. field for tobacco

ta-ba-ca-le-ro, -ra m., f. tobacco dealer

ta-ba-co m. tobacco

ta-ba-no m. gadfly

ta-ba-que-rí-a f. tobacco shop

ta-ber-na f. tavern

ta-ber-ná-cu-lo m. tabernacle

ta-ber-ne-ro, -ra m., f. bartender

ta-bi-que m. partition

ta-bla f. table

ta-ble-a-do, -da m. pleats

ta-ble-ro m. board

ta-ble-ta f. tablet

ta-bu-la-dor m., f. tabulator

ta-bu-re-te m. stool

ta-co-no, -na adj. stingy

tá-ci-to, -ta adj. tacit

ta-ci-tur-no, -na adj. taciturn

ta-co m. pad; wedge

ta-cón m. heel

tác-ti-co, -ca adj. tactical

tac-til adj. tactile

tac-to m. touch; tact

ta-cha f. flaw

ta-char v. to cross something out

ta-cho m. can

ta-chue-la f. tack

ta-fe-tán m. taffeta

ta-hur m. cardsharp

tai-ma-do, -da adj. crafty

ta-ja-da f. profit

ta-jan-te adj. sharp

ta-jar v. to slice

ta-jo m. cut

tal adj. such

ta-la f. ruin

ta-la-dor, -ra adj. cutting

ta-la-drar v. to drill

ta-la-dro m. drill

ta-lar v. to cut something down

tal-co m. talc

ta-le-ga f. wealth

ta-len-to m. talent

ta-len-to-so, -sa adj. talented

ta-lis-man m. talisman

ta-lon *m.* talon; heel
ta-lo-na-rio *m.* checkbook
ta-lla *f.* size; height
ta-lla-do, -da *adj.* engraved; carved
ta-lla-dor *m.* engraver
ta-llar *v.* to carve
ta-lle *m.* figure; shape
ta-ller *m.* shop
ta-loo *m.* stem
ta-ma-no, -na *adj.* very big
tam-ba-le-an-te *adj.* staggering
tam-ba-le-ar *v.* to stagger
tam-bien *adv.* too; also
tam-bor *m.* drum
tam-bo-ra *f.* drum
tam-bo-ril *m.* little drum
tam-bo-ri-le-ar *v.* to beat
tam-bo-ri-le-o *m.* beating
ta-miz *m.* sieve
ta-mi-zar *v.* to filter
tam-po-co *adv.* nor; niether
tan *adv.* as; so
tan-da *f.* shift; turn
tan-gen-te *adj.* tangent
tan-gi-ble *adj.* tangible
tan-go *m.* tango
tan-gue-ar *v.* to tango
tan-que *m.* tanker
tan-te-ar *v.* to consider; to test
tan-to, -ta *adj.* so many
ta-ner *v.* to play
ta-pa *f.* cover; lid
ta-pa-do-m *v.* to block something
ta-par *v.* to block something
ta-pe-te *m.* carpet
ta-piar *v.* to wall something in
ta-pi-ce-ro, -ra *m., f.* upholsterer
ta-pio-ca *f.* tapioca
ta-piz *m.* tapestry
ta-pi-zar *v.* to upholster; to hang tapestries
ta-pon *m.* cork
ta-qui-gra-fi-a *f.* stenography
ta-qui-gra-fiar *v.* to write using shorthand
ta-qui-gra-fo, -fa *m., f.* stenographer
ta-ra *f.* defect

ta-rán-tu-la *f.* tarantula
ta-ras-car *v.* to bite
tar-dan-za *f.* delay
tar-dar *v.* to delay
tar-de *f.* afternoon
tar-dí-o, -a *adj.* late
ta-ra-a *f.* homework
ta-ri-fa *f.* tariff
ta-ri-far *v.* to give or apply a tariff to something
tar-je-ta *f.* card
ta-rro *m.* jar
tar-ta *f.* pie
tar-ta-mu-de-o *m.* stammering
tar-tán *m.* tartan
tár-to-ro, -ra *adj.* tartar
ta-sa *f.* rate
ta-sa-cion *f.* appraisal
ta-sa-dor, -ra *adj.* appraising
ta-sa-je-ar *v.* to jerk something
ta-sa-jo *m.* jerky
tas-ca *f.* joint
ta-ta-ra-bue-la *f.* great-great-grandmother
ta-ta-ra-bue-lo *m.* great-great-grandfather
ta-ta-ra-nie-ta *f.* great-great-granddaughter
ta-ta-ra-nie-to *m.* great-great-grandson
ta-tau-je *m.* tattoo
ta-tuar *v.* to tattoo
tau-ro-ma-quia *f.* bullfighting
ta-xi *m.* taxi
ta-xi-der-mia *f.* taxidermy
ta-xis-ta *m., f.* one who drives a taxie
ta-xo-no-mi-a *f.* taxonomy
ta-za *f.* bowl; cup
té *pron.* you
te-a *f.* torch
te-a-tral *adj.* theatrical
te-a-tra-li-dad *f.* theatricality
te-a-tro *m.* theater
te-cia *f.* key
te-cla-do *m.* keyboard
tec-ni-co, -ca *adj.* technical
tec-no-cra-cia *f.* technocracy
tec-no-lo-gí-a *f.* technology
tec-no-ló-gi-co, -ca *adj.* technological

te-char v. to roof a building

te-cho m. ceiling; roof

te-dio m. tedium

te-dio-so, -sa adj. tedious

te-ja f. tile

te-jar v. to tile

te-jer v. to knit

te-ji-do m. weave

te-jón m. badger

te-la f. fabric; film

te-la-ra-ña f. spider's web

te-le-co-mu-ni-ca-ción f. telecommunication

te-le-di-fun-dir v. to telecast

te-le-di-fu-sion f. to telecast

te-le-fo-na-zo m. telephone call

te-le-fo-ne-ar v. to phone someone

te-le-fo-ni-ca-men-te adv. by a phone

te-le-fo-nis-ta m., f. telephone operator

te-lé-fo-no m. telephone

te-le-fo-to m. telephoto

te-le-gra-fí-a f. telegraphy

te-le-gra-fiar v. to telegraph

te-le-grá-fi-co, -ca adj. telegraphic

te-le-gra-fis-ta m., f. telegrapher

te-lé-gra-fo m. telegraph

te-le-gra-ma f. telegram

te-le-man-do m. remote control

te-le-me-trí-a f. telemetry

te-le-pa-tí-a f. telepathy

te-le-pá-ti-co, -ca adj. telepathic

te-les-có-pi-co, -ca adj. telescopic

te-les-co-pio m. telescope

te-le-ti-po m. teletype

te-le-vi-sar v. to televise

te-le-vi-sión f. television

te-le-vi-sor m. television

te-lón m. curtain

te-lu-rio m. tellurium

te-ma f. subject; obsession

te-má-ti-co, -ca adj. thematic

tem-blar v. to tremble

tem-ble-que-ar v. to tremble

tem-blor m. earthquake; tremor

te-mer v. to be afraid of

te-me-ro-so, -sa adj. frightening

te-mor m. fear

tem-pe-ra-men-tal adj. temperamental

tem-pe-ra-men-to m. weather

tem-pe-ran-cia f. temperance

tem-pe-rar v. to calm

tem-pe-ra-tu-ra f. temperature

tem-pes-tad f. storm

tem-pes-tuo-so, -sa adj. stormy

tem-pla-do, -da adj. mild

tem-plan-za f. moderation

tem-plar v. to temper; to tune; to appease

tem-ple m. mood; temper

tem-plo m. temple

tem-po-ra-da f. season

tem-po-ral adj. temporal

tem-po-ra-ne-o, -a adj. temporary

tem-pra-ne-ro, -ra adj. early

tem-pra-no, -na adj. early

te-na-ci-dad f. tenacity

te-naz f. tenacious

ten-den-cia f. tendency

ten-der v. to stretch something out

ten-di-do, -da adj. spead out

ten-dón m. tendon

te-ne-bro-so, -sa adj. obscure; dark

te-ne-dor m. one who owns

te-nen-cia f. possession

te-ner v. to contain; to have; to keep

te-nia f. tapeworm

te-nien-te m. lieutenant

te-nis m. tennis

te-nis-ta m., f. one who plays tennis

ten-sar v. to stretch

ten-sión f. tension

ten-so, -sa adj. tense

ten-ta-ción f. temptation

ten-tá-cu-lo m. tentacle

ten-ta-dor, -ra adj. tempting

ten-ta-ti-vo, -va *adj.* tentative
te-ñir *v.* to make dark
te-o-cra-cia *f.* theocracy
te-o-lo-gi-a *f.* theology
te-o-lo-go, -ga *m., f.* theologian
te-o-re-ma *m.* theorem
te-o-re-ti-co, -ca *adj.* theoretical
te-ó-ri-a *f.* theory
te-o-re-ti-co, -ca *adj.* theoretical
te-o-ri-zar *v.* to theorize
te-ó-so-fo, -fa *m., f.* theosophist
te-qui-la *f.* tequila
te-ra-peu-ta *m., f.* therapist
te-ra-péu-ti-co, -ca *adj.* therapeutic
te-ra-pia *f.* therapy
ter-ce-ro, -ra *adj.* third
ter-cia-do, -da *adj.* brown
ter-cio, -cia *adj.* third
ter-cio-pe-lo *m.* velvet
ter-co, -ca *adj.* stubborn
ter-gi-ver-sar *v.* to distort
ter-mal *adj.* thermal
ter-mi-na-cion *f.* ending; termination
ter-mi-nal *adj.* terminal
ter-mi-nar *v.* to complete; to end something
tér-mi-no *m.* ending
ter-mi-no-lo-gi-a *f.* terminology
ter-mi-ta *m.* termite
ter-mo-di-ná-mi-ca *f.* thermodynamics
ter-mo-e-lec-tri-co, -ca *adj.* thermoelectric
ter-mó-me-tro *m.* thermometer
ter-mos-ta-to *m.* thermostat
ter-no *m.* a set of three things
ter-nu-ra *f.* tenderness
ter-ra-plen *m.* embankment
te-rra-que-o, -a *adj.* terrestrial
te-rra-za *f.* terrace
te-rre-mo-to *m.* earthquake
te-rre-nal *adj.* earthly
te-rre-no, -na *adj.* earthly

te-rres-tre *adj.* terrestrial
te-rri-ble *adj.* terrible
te-rri-to-rial *adj.* territorial
te-rri-to-rio *m.* territory
te-rror *m.* terror
te-rro-ri-fi-co, -ca *adj.* terrifying
te-rro-ris-ta *m., f.* terrorist
ter-so, -sa *adj.* smooth
te-sis *f.* thesis
te-son *m.* tenacity
te-so-ne-ro, -ra *adj.* tenacious
te-so-re-ri-a *f.* treasury
te-so-re-ro, -ra *m., f.* treasurer
te-so-ro *m.* treasure
tes-ti-cu-lo *m.* testicle
tes-ti-fi-car *v.* to testify
tes-ti-go *m.* one who sees something; witness
tes-ti-mo-niar *v.* to testify
tes-ti-mo-nio *m.* testimony
te-ta *f.* udder
té-ta-no *m.* tetanus
te-ti-lla *f.* teat
tex-til *adj.* textile
tex-to *m.* textbook
tex-tu-ra *f.* texture
tez *f.* complexion
ti *pron.* yourself
tí-a *f.* aunt
tia-ra *f.* tiara
ti-bia *f.* tibia
ti-bu-rón *m.* shark
tiem-po *m.* weather; time
tien-da *f.* store; shop
tien-to *m.* caution; touch
tier-no, -na *adj.* tender
tie-rra *f.* land; country
tie-so, -sa *adj.* arrogant
ties-to *m.* flowerpot
ti-foj-de-o, -a *adj.* typhoid
ti-fón *m.* typhoon
ti-fus *m.* typhus
ti-gre *m.* tiger
ti-gre-sa *f.* tigress
ti-je-re-te-ar *v.* to snip
ti-je-re-te-o *m.* snipping
ti-mar-dor, -ra *m., f.* cheat
ti-mar *v.* to cheat
tim-bra-do, -da *adj.* stamped
tim-brar *v.* to stamp

tim-bre *m.* ring
ti-mi-dez *f.* timidity
tí-mi-do, -da *adj.* timid
ti-mo *m.* thymus
ti-mo-ra-to, -ta *adj.* shy
tin-gla-do *m.* platform
ti-no *m.* good judgment
tin-ta *f.* dye
tin-te *m.* dye
tin-te-ro *m.* inkwell
tin-ti-nar *v.* to clink something
tin-tu-ra *f.* tincture
ti-ña *f.* ringworm
tí-o *m.* uncle
tí-pi-co, -ca *adj.* typical
ti-pi-fi-car *v.* to typify
ti-po *m.* type; kind
ti-po-gra-fí-a *f.* typofraphy
ti-ra-da *f.* distance
ti-ra-ní-a *f.* tyranny
ti-ra-ni-zar *v.* to tyrannize
ti-ra-no, -na *adj.* tyrannical
ti-ran-te *adj.* tight
ti-ran-tez *f.* tightness
ti-rar *v.* to throw
ti-ri-tar *v.* to shiver
ti-ro *m.* shot; throw
ti-ro-te-o *m.* shooting
ti-sis *f.* tuberculosis
ti-te-re *m.* puppet
ti-ti-le-o *m.* quivering
ti-ti-ri-tar *v.* to quiver
ti-tu-be-o *m.* staggering
ti-tu-la-do, -da *adj.* titled
tí-tu-lo *m.* title
ti-za *f.* chalk
tiz-nar *v.* to smudge
to-a-lla *f.* towel
to-bi-llo *m.* ankle
to-bo-gán *m.* sled
to-ca-dor *m.* dressing room
to-car *v.* to ring; to handle; to touch
to-da-ví-a *adj.* every; all
to-do, -da *adj.* all; every
to-le-ran-cia *f.* tolerance
to-le-ran-te *adj.* tolerant
to-le-rar *v.* to tolerate
to-lon-dron, -ona *m., f.* scatterbrain
to-ma *f.* intake; taking

to-ma-dor, -ra *adj.* drinking
to-mar *v.* to have; to take
to-ma-te *m.* tomato
to-na-da *f.* tune
to-na-li-dad *f.* tonality
to-nel *m.* barrel
to-ne-la-da *f.* ton
to-ne-la-je *m.* tonnage
to-ni-fi-car *v.* to tone
to-ni-na *f.* tuna
to-no *m.* tone
ton-te-rí-a *f.* foolishness
ton-to *m.* fool
tó-pi-co *m.* topic
to-po *m.* mole
to-po-gra-fí-a *f.* topography
to-pó-gra-fo *m.* topographer
to-que *m.* beat; touch
to-que-te-ar *v.* to handle
to-que-te-o *m.* handling
to-ra-ci-co, -ca *adj.* thoracic
tor-ce-du-ra *f.* twist
tor-cer *v.* to sprain; to bend
to-re-a-dor *m.* toreador
to-re-ar *v.* to fight
to-re-o *m.* bullfighting
tor-men-ta *f.* storm
tor-men-to *m.* torment
tor-men-to-so, -sa *adj.* stormy
tor-na-do *m.* tornado
tor-na-sol *m.* sunflower
tor-na-so-la-do, -da *adj.* iridescent
tor-ne-ar *v.* to turn
tor-ne-o *m.* tournament
tor-ni-llo *m.* screw
tor-ni-que-te *m.* tourniquet
to-ro *m.* bull
to-ron-ja *f.* grapefruit
tor-pe-de-ar *v.* to torpedo
tor-pe-za *f.* stupidity
tor-por *m.* torpor
to-rrar *v.* to roast
to-rre *f.* castle
to-rren-cial *adj.* torrential
to-rren-te *m.* torrent
tó-rri-do, -da *adj.* torrid
tor-sión *f.* torsion
tor-so *m.* torso
tor-ta *f.* cake
tor-to-la *f.* turtledove
tor-tu-ga *f.* turtle

tor-tuo-so, -sa *adj.* tortuous
tor-tu-ra *f.* torture
tor-tu-rar *v.* to torture
tos *f.* coughing
tos-co, -ca *adj.* crude
to-ser *v.* to cough
tos-que-dad *f.* coarseness
tos-ta-do, -da *adj.* roasted
tos-ta-dor, -ram., *f.* toaster
tos-tar *v.* to roast; to toast
to-tal *adj.* total
to-ta-li-dad *f.* totality
to-ta-li-ta-rio, -ria *adj.* totalitarian
to-ta-li-zar *v.* to total
to-xe-mia *f.* toxemia
to-xi-ci-dad *f.* toxicity
tó-xi-co, -ca *adj.* poison
to-xi-co-lo-go, -ga *m., f.* toxicologist
to-xi-na *f.* toxin
to-zu-do, -da *adj.* stubborn
tra-ba *f.* obstacle; bolt
tra-ba-ja-dor *m.* worker
tra-ba-jar *v.* to work
tra-ba-jo *m.* job; work
tra-ba-jo-so, -sa *adj.* demanding
tra-bar *v.* to fasten; to bolt
tra-bu-car *v.* to mix up
trac-ción *f.* traction
trac-tor *m.* tractor
tra-di-ción *f.* tradition
tra-di-cio-nal *f.* traditional
tra-duc-ción *f.* translation
tra-du-cir *v.* to express
tra-duc-tor, -ra *adj.* translating something
tra-er *v.* to wear; to carry; to bring
tra-fi-car *v.* to deal
trá-fi-co *m.* traffic
tra-gl-luz *v.* skylight
tra-gar *v.* to devour; swallow
tra-ge-dia *f.* tragedy
trá-gi-co, -ca *adj.* tragic
tra-gi-co-me-dia *f.* tragicomedy
tra-go *m.* gulp
trai-ción *f.* treason
trai-cio-nar *v.* to betray another
tra-je *m.* dress

tra-je-a-do, -da *adj.* dressed
tra-je-ar *v.* to dress
tra-ji-nar *v.* to carry
tra-ma *f.* plot
tra-ma-dor, -ra *m., f.* weaver
tra-mar *v.* to scheme
tra-mi-ta-ción *f.* transaction
tra-mi-tar *v.* to negotiate
tra-mo *m.* flight
tram-pa *f.* trap
tram-pe-ar *v.* to cheat
tram-po-lin *m.* trampoline
tram-po-so, -sa *adj.* cheating
tran-ce *m.* trance; crisis
tran-qui-li-dad *f.* tranquility
tran-qui-li-zan-te *adj.* tranquilizing
tran-qui-lo, -la *adj.* tranquil
tran-sac-ción *f.* transaction
tran-sat-lan-ti-co, -ca *adj.* transatlantic
trans-bor-dar *v.* to transfer
trans-bor-do *m.* transfer
trans-cen-den-cia *f.* transcendence
trans-cen-den-tal *adj.* transcendental
trans-cen-der *v.* to transcend
trans-con-ti-nen-tal *adj.* transcontinental
trans-cri-bir *v.* to transcribe
trans-crip-cion *f.* transcription
tran-se-un-te *adj.* transient
trans-fe-ren-cia *f.* transference
trans-fe-rir *v.* to transfer
trans-fi-gu-ra-ción *f.* transfiguration
trans-for-ma-cion *f.* transformation
trans-for-ma-dor, -ra *adj.* transforming
trans-for-mar *v.* to convert; to transform
trans-fun-dir *v.* to transfuse
trans-fu-sión *f.* transfusion
trans-gre-dir *v.* to transgress
trans-gre-sión *f.* transgression
tran-si-ción *f.* transition

tran-sis-tor *m.* transistor
tran-si-tar *v.* to travel
tran-si-ti-vo, -va *adj.* transitive
trán-si-to *m.* traffic
tran-si-to-rio, -ria *adj.* temporary
trans-la-ción *f.* translation
trans-lu-ci-do, -da *adj.* translucent
trans-mi-gra-ción *f.* tranmigration
trans-mi-grar *v.* to transmigrate
trans-mi-tir *v.* to transmit
trans-mu-tar *v.* to transmute
trans-pa-ren-te *adj.* transparent
trans-pi-ra-ción *f.* perspiration
trans-pi-rar *v.* to perspire
trans-plan-tar *v.* to transplant
trans-po-ner *v.* to transplant; to move
trans-por-ta-ción *f.* transportation
trans-por-tar *v.* to transport
trans-po-si-cion *f.* transposition
trans-ver-so, -sa *adj.* transverse
tran-vi-a *m.* streetcar
tra-pe-cio *m.* trapezoid
tra-pe-zoi-de *m.* trapezoid
trá-que-a *f.* trachea
tras *prep.* behind; after
tra-sat-lan-ti-co, -ca *adj.* transatlantic
tras-cen-den-te *adj.* transcendent
tras-cen-der *v.* to extend
tra-se-gar *v.* to decant
tras-fon-do *m.* background
tra-sie-go *m.* decanting
tras-la-ción *f.* translation
tras-la-dar *v.* to transcribe; to move
tras-la-do *m.* transfer
tras-no-cha-do, -da *adj.* trite
tras-pa-pe-lar *v.* to misplace something
tras-pa-pe-la-do, -da *adj.* misplaced
tras-pa-sar *v.* to break
tras-pa-so *m.* transfer
trans-plan-tar *v.* to transplant
tras-qui-lar *v.* to shear
tras-to-car *v.* to twist
tras-tor-nar *v.* to disrupt
tras-tro-car *v.* to twist
tra-sun-tar *v.* to summarize
tra-ta-mien-to *m.* treatment; process
tra-tar *v.* to process; to handle
tra-to *m.* treatment
trau-ma *m.* trauma
trau-ma-ti-co, -ca *adj.* traumatic
trau-ma-ti-zar *v.* to traumatize
tra-ve-si-a *f.* crosswind; crossroad
tra-ve-su-ra *f.* mischief
tra-vie-so, -sa *adj.* mischievous
tra-yec-to *m.* way
tra-yec-to-ria *f.* trajectory
tra-za *f.* plan
tra-zar *v.* to outline something
tra-zo *m.* line
tré-bol *m.* clover
tre-ce *adj.* thirteen
tre-cho *m.* in parts; stretch
tre-gua *f.* rest
trein-ta *adj.* thirty
trein-ta-vo *f.* thirtieth
trein-te-na *f.* thirty
tre-men-do, -da *adj.* terrible; horrible
tre-men-ti-na *f.* turpentine
tre-mo-lar *v.* to wave
tre-mo-li-na *f.* rustling
tre-mor *m.* tremor
tren *m.* train
tren-ci-lla *f.* braid
tren-za *f.* braid
tren-zar *v.* to braid
tre-pi-dar *v.* to vibrate
tres *adj.* three
tres-cien-tos *adj.* three hundred
tres-pies *m.* tripod

tre-za-vo, -va *adj.* thirteenth
tri-a-da *f.* triad
trian-gu-lar *adj.* triangular
trián-gu-lo *adj.* triangular
tri-bal *adj.* tribal
tri-bu *f.* tribe
tri-bu-la-ción *f.* tribulation
tri-bu-no *m.* tribune
tri-bu-tar *v.* to pay
tri-bu-ta-rio, -ria *adj.* tributary
tri-bu-to *m.* tribute
tri-cen-te-na-rio *m.* tricentennial
tri-ci-clo *m.* trcycle
tri-co-lor *adj.* tricolor
tri-cus-pi-de *adj.* tricuspid
tri-gal *m.* field of wheat
tri-ge-si-mo, -ma *adj.* thirtieth
tri-go *m.* wheat
tri-go-no-me-tri-a *f.* trigonometry
tri-lin-gue *adj.* trilingual
tri-lo-gi-a *f.* trilogy
tri-lla-dor, -ra *adj.* threshing
tri-lli-zo *m.* triplet
tri-mes-tral *adj.* quarterly
trin-cha-dor, -ra *adj.* carving
trin-char *v.* to carve
tri-no-mio *m.* trinomial
tri-o *m.* trio
tri-ple *adj.* triple
tri-pli-ca-ción *f.* triplication
tri-pli-ca-do *adj.* triplicate
tri-pli-car *v.* to triplicate
tri-plo, -pla *adj.* triple
tri-po-de *m., f.* tripod
tri-qui-no-sis *f.* trichinosis
tris-ca *f.* crack
tris-car *v.* to stamp
tris-te *adj.* miserable; sad
tris-te-za *f.* sorrow
tri-tu-rar *v.* to chew; to triturate
triun-fa-dor, -ra *adj.* triumphant
triun-fan-te *adj.* triumphant
triun-fo *m.* triumph
tri-vial *adj.* trivial
tri-via-li-dad *f.* triviality
tri-za *f.* piece
tro-car *v.* to barter

tro-fe-o *m.* trophy
tro-glo-di-ta *adj.* barbarous
tro-le *m.* trolley
trom-bon *m.* trombone
trom-bo-sis *f.* thrombosis
trom-pa *f.* horn
trom-pe-ar *v.* to punch
trom-pe-ta *f.* trumpet
trom-pe-tis-ta *m., f.* trumpeter
trom-pi-car *v.* to trip
trom-po *m.* top
tro-na-da *f.* thunderstorm
tro-na-dor, -ra *adj.* thundering
tro-nan-te *adj.* thundering
tro-nar *v.* to thunder
tron-co *m.* trunk
tron-cha *f.* slice
tro-pel *m.* confusion
tro-pe-li-a *f.* violence
tro-pe-zar *v.* to trip
tro-pi-cal *adj.* tropical
tro-pi-co *m.* tropic
tro-pie-zo *m.* stumble
tro-po *m.* trope
tro-que-lar *v.* to mint
tro-ta-da *f.* trot
tro-ta-dor, -ra *adj.* trotting
tro-va *f.* ballad
tro-zo *m.* chunk; part; piece
tru-co *m.* trick
true-no *m.* thunder
try-far *v.* to lie
tú *pron.* you
tu-ba *f.* tuba
tu-ber-cu-li-na *f.* tuberculin
tu-ber-cu-lo-sis *f.* tuberculosis
tu-be-ro-so, -sa *adj.* tuberous
tu-bo *m.* tube
tu-bu-la-do, -da *adj.* tubular
tu-bu-lar *adj.* tubular
tu-can *m.* toucan
tues-te *m.* toasting
tu-fo *m.* fume
tu-li-pan *m.* tulip
tu-llir *v.* to cripple
tum-ba *f.* tomb
tum-bar *v.* to knock out
tum-bo *m.* jolt
tu-mes-cen-cia *f.* tumes-

cence

tu-mes-cen-te *adj.* tumescent

tu-mor *m.* tumor

tu-mu-lo *m.* tomb

tu-mul-to *m.* tumult

tu-mul-tuo-so, -sa *adj.* tumultuous

tu-nan-ta *adj.* cunning

tun-da *f.* beating

tun-de-ar *v.* to beat

tun-di-dor, -ra *m., f.* one who shears

tun-di-du-ra *f.* shearing

tun-dir *v.* to shear

tun-dra *f.* tundra

tú-nel *m.* tunnel

tungs-te-no *m.* tungsten

tu-ni-ca *f.* tunic

tu-pé *m.* toupee

tu-pi-do, -da *adj.* dense; thick

tu-pir *v.* to weave close together

tur-ba *f.* mob

tur-ba-cion *f.* confusion

tur-ba-dor, -ra *adj.* disturbing

tur-ban-te *m.* turban

tur-bar *v.* to embarrass; to upset another

tur-bie-dad *f.* opaqueness

tur-bi-na *f.* turbine

tur-bio, -bia *adj.* turbulent; muddy

tur-bión *m.* shower

tur-bu-len-cia *f.* turbulence

tur-bu-len-to, -ta *adj.* turbulent

tu-ris-ta *f.* tourist

tu-rís-ti-co, -ca *adj.* tourist

tur-nar *v.* taking turns at something

tur-no *m.* turn

tur-que-sa *f.* turquoise

tu-ru-la-to, -ta *adj.* being stunned

tu-sa *f.* cornhusk

tu-sar *v.* to trim

tu-te-ar *v.* to address another as tu

tu-tor, -ra *m., f.* guardian

tu-yo, -ya *adj.* yours

u-be-rri-mo, -ma *adj.* luxuriant

u-bi-ca-cion *f.* placing

u-bi-car *v.* to locate

u-bre *f.* udder

u-fa-nar-se *v.* to boast about something

u-fa-no, -na *adj.* pleased

úl-ce-ra *f.* ulcer

ul-ce-ra-cion *f.* ulceration

ul-ce-rar *v.* to ulcerate

ul-ce-ro-so, -sa *adj.* ulcerous

ul-te-rior *adj.* subsequent

ul-te-rior-men-te *adv.* subsequently

ul-ti-ma-men-te *adv.* finally

ul-ti-mar *v.* to finish; to conclude

ul-ti-ma-tum *m.* ultimatum

úl-ti-mo, -ma *adj.* final; last

ul-tra *adv.* besides

ul-tra-de-re-cha *f.* the far right

ul-tra-jan-te *adj.* outrageous

ul-tra-jar *v.* to insult

ul-tra-je *m.* insult

ul-tra-ma-ri-no, -na *adj.* overseas

ul-tra-mo-der-no, -na *adj.* ultramodern

ul-tra-so-ni-co, -ca *adj.* ultrasonic

ul-tra-so-ni-do *m.* ultrasound

ul-tra-vio-le-ta *adj.* ultraviolet

um-bi-li-cal *adj.* umbilical

um-bral *m.* threshold

um-brí-o, -a *adj.* shady

um-bro-so, -sa *adj.* shady

un *indef. art.* an; a

u-ña *indef. art.* an; a

u-ná-ni-me *adj.* unanimous

u-na-ni-mi-dad *f.* unanimity

un-cir *v.* to yoke

un-de-ci-mo, -ma *adj.* eleventh

un-du-lan-te *adj.* undulating

un-du-lar *v.* to undulate

un-güen-to *m.* ointment

u-ni-ce-lu-lar *adj.* unicellular

u-ni-ci-dad *f.* uniqueness

ú-ni-co, -ca *adj.* single; sole

u-ni-cor-nio *m.* unicorn

u-ni-dad *f.* unity; each

u-ni-do, -da adj. united
u-ni-fi-ca-cion f. unification
u-ni-fi-car v. to unify
u-ni-for-mar v. to make something uniform
u-ni-for-me adj. even; uniform
u-ni-for-mi-dad f. uniformity
u-ni-la-te-ral adj. unilateral
u-nion f. joint; unity
u-nir(se) v. to unite together
u-ni-se-xo adj. unisex
u-ní-so-no, -na adj. to be in unison with
u-ni-ta-ria, -ria adj. unified
u-ni-ver-sal adj. world-wide; universal
u-ni-ver-sa-li-dad f. universality
u-ni-ver-sa-li-zar v. to universalize
u-ni-ver-si-dad f. university
u-ni-ver-si-ta-rio, -ria adj. university
u-ni-ver-so m. universe
u-no, -na adj. one
un-tar v. to spread; to grease
un-to m. grease
un-tuo-si-dad f. greasiness
un-tuo-so, -sa adj. greasy
un-tu-ra f. greasing
u-ña f. toenail; fingernail
u-ra-nio m. uranium
ur-ba-ni-dad f. urbanity
ur-ba-ni-za-cion f. urvanization
ur-ba-ni-zar v. to develop
ur-ba-no, -na adj. urban
u-re-a f. urea
u-re-ter m. ureter
u-re-tra f. urethra
ur-gen-cia f. urgency
ur-gen-te adj. urgent
u-ri-na-rio, -ria adj. urinary
u-san-za f. custom
u-sar v. to use
u-so m. use
us-ted pron. you
u-sual adj. usual
u-su-ra f. usury
u-sur-par v. to usurp
u-ten-si-lio m. utensil
ú-til adj. useful

va-ca f. cow
va-ca-ción f. vacation
va-can-te adj. vacant
va-cia-de-ro m. dump
va-cia-do m. cast
va-ciar v. to void; to empty; to drain
va-ci-la-ción f. vacillation; hesitation
va-ci-lan-te adj. hesitating
va-ci-lar v. to falter; to vacillate
va-cío, -cia adj. devoid; empty; void; hollow
va-cui-dad f. vacuity
va-cu-na-ción f. vaccination
va-cu-nar v. to vaccinate
va-cu-no, -na adj. bovine
va-cuo, -cua adj. vacuous
va-de-ar v. to overcome
va-ga-bun-do, -da adj. vagabond
va-ga-men-te adv. vaguely
va-gan-cia f. vagrancy
va-gar v. to roam; to stray; to wander
va-gi-do m. cry
va-go, -ga adj. hazy; wandering; vague
va-gón m. van
va-gue-ar v. to wander
va-gue-dad f. vagueness
va-ho m. vapor; steam
vai-ni-lla f. canilla
vai-vén m. fluctuation
va-le m. voucher
va-le-de-ro, -ra adj. valid
va-len-cia f. valence
va-len-tía f. courage; valor; bravery
va-len-tón, -ona adj. boastful
va-len-to-na f. boast
va-ler v. to be of value; to have authority over; to be of worth
va-le-ro-so, -sa adj. valorous; courageous
va-li-a f. worth
va-li-da-ción f. validation
va-li-dar v. to validate
va-li-dez f. validity
vá-li-do, -da adj. good
va-lien-te adj. brave; valiant

va·li·ja *f.* suitcase

va·lio·so, -sa *adj.* valuable

va·lor *m.* valor; worth; importance

va·lo·ra·ción *f.* appraisal

va·lo·rar *v.* to appraise something

va·lo·ri·za·ción *f.* appraisal

va·lo·ri·zar *v.* to appraise something

vals *m.* waltz

va·luar *v.* to value something

vál·vu·la *f.* valve

va·llar *v.* to put a fence around; to fence in

va·lle *m.* valley

vam·pi·ro *m.* vampire

va·na·glo·ria *f.* pride

va·na·glo·rio·so, -sa *adj.* boastful

va·na·men·te *adv.* foolishly; vainly

van·da·lis·mo *m.* vandalism

va·ni·dad *f.* vanity

va·ni·do·so, -sa *m., f.* one who is vain

va·no, -na *adj.* vain

va·por *m.* steam

va·po·ri·za·dor *m.* vaporizer

va·po·ri·zar *v.* to vaporize

va·po·ro·so, -sa *adj.* steamy; vaporous

va·que·ta *f.* hide of a cow

va·ra *f.* rod; stalk

va·rar *v.* to beach

va·re·a·dor, -ra *m., f.* cowhand

va·re·ar *v.* to cudgel

va·ria·ble *adj.* variable

va·ria·ción *f.* change; variation

va·ria·do, -da *adj.* varied

va·rien·te *adj.* varying

va·riar *v.* to change

va·rie·dad *f.* variety

va·rio, -ria *adj.* varied

va·ri·lla *f.* rob

va·rón *m.* man

va·ro·nil *adj.* virile

va·sa·llo, -lla *adj.* subordinate

vas·cu·lar *adj.* vascular

va·sec·to·mí·a *f.* vasectomy

va·si·ja *f.* container

va·so *m.* vessel; glass

vas·to, -ta *adj.* vast

va·ti·ci·nar *v.* to predict

va·ti·ci·nio *m.* prediction

va·tio *m.* watt

ve·ci·nal *adj.* local

ve·ci·na·men·te *adv.* next

ve·cin·dad *f.* vicinity

ve·ci·no, -na *adj.* near; next

vec·tor *m.* vector

ve·da *f.* prohibition

ve·da·do, -da *adj.* prohibited

ve·dar *v.* to suspend; to prohibit

ve·ge·ta·ción *f.* vegetation

ve·ge·tal *adj.* vegetable

ve·ge·tar *v.* to vegetate

ve·ge·ta·ria·no, -na *adj.* vegetarian

ve·ge·ta·ti·vo, -va *adj.* vegetative

ve·he·men·cia *f.* vehemence

ve·he·men·te *adj.* vehement

ve·hí·cu·lo *m.* vehicle

vein·te *adj.* twenty

ve·ja·ción *f.* vexation

ve·ja·men *m.* vexation

ve·jar *v.* to persecute; to vex

ve·jez *f.* old age

ve·li·ga *f.* bladder

ve·la *f.* sail

ve·la·da *f.* evening

ve·la·do, -da *adj.* veiled

ve·lar *v.* to veil

ve·lei·do·so, -sa *adj.* fickle

ve·lo *m.* viel

ve·lo·ci·dad *f.* velocity

ve·loz *adj.* swift

ve·llo *m.* fuzz

ve·llón *m.* sheepskin

ve·llu·do, -da *adj.* hairy

ve·na *f.* vein

ve·na·blo *m.* javelin

ve·na·do *m.* venison

ven·ce·dor, -ra *m., f.* conqueror

ven·cer *v.* to conquer; to beat another

ven·ci·do, -da *adj.* conquered; defeated

ven·ci·mien·to *m.* defeat; collapse

ven-da-je *m.* bandage

ven-dar *v.* to bandage

ven-de-dor, -ra *m., f.* seller

ven-der *v.* to sell

ven-di-mia-dor, -ar *m., f.* one who picks grapes

ve-ne-no *m.* poison

ve-ne-no-si-dad *f.* poisonousness

ve-ne-no-so, -sa *adj.* poisonous

ve-ne-ra-ble *adj.* venerable

ve-en-ra-ción *f.* veneration

ve-ne-rar *v.* to venerate

ven-gan-za *f.* revenge; vengeance

ven-gar *v.* to avenge

ve-nia *f.* forgiveness

ve-nial *adj.* venial

ve-ni-da *f.* return

ve-ni-de-ro, -ra *adj.* upcoming

ve-nir *v.* to come

ven-ta *f.* sale

ven-ta-ja *f.* benefit

ven-ta-jo-so, -sa *adj.* advantageous

ven-ta-na *f.* window

ven-ti-la-ción *f.* ventilation

ven-ti-la-dor *m.* fan

ven-ti-lar *v.* to air

ven-tis-ca *f.* blizzard

ven-tis-que-ro *m.* blizzard

ven-to-si-dad *f.* gas

ven-to-so, -sa *adj.* windy

ven-tri-cu-lar *adj.* ventricular

ven-trí-cu-lo *m.* ventricle

ven-tri-lo-cuo, -a *m., f.* ventriloquist

ven-tu-ra *f.* happiness

ven-tu-ro-so, -sa *adj.* fortunate

ver *v.* to sight; to see

ve-ra *f.* edge

ve-ra-ci-dad *f.* veracity

ve-ra-ne-o *m.* vacationing

ve-ra-no *m.* summer

ve-ras *f.* earnestness

ve-raz *adj.* truthful

ver-bal *adj.* verbal

ver-bal-men-te *adv.* verbally

ver-bo *m.* verb

ver-bo-rre-a *f.* verbosity

ver-bo-si-dad *f.* verbosity

ver-bo-so, -sa *adj.* verbose

ver-dad *f.* truth

ver-da-de-ro, -ra *adj.* truthful

ver-de *adj.* green

ver-dor *m.* verdancy

ver-do-so, -sa *adj.* greenish

ver-du-ra *f.* greenery

ve-re-dic-to *m.* verdict

ver-gel *m.* orchard

ver-gon-zo-so, -sa *adj.* shameful

ver-güen-za *f.* shyness

ve-rí-di-co, -ca *adj.* true

ve-ri-fi-ca-ción *f.* verification

ve-ri-fi-ca-dor, -ra *m., f.* checker

ve-ri-fi-car *v.* to check on; to verify something

ver-mi-ci-da *adj.* vermicidal

ver-nal *adj.* vernal

ve-ro-si-mi-li-tud *f.* probability

ver-sa-do, -da *adj.* versed

ver-sá-til *adj.* versatile

ver-sa-ti-li-dad *f.* versatility

ver-sí-cu-lo *m.* versicle

ver-si-fi-car *v.* to versify

ver-sión *f.* version

ver-so *m.* verse

ver-te-bra *f.* vertebra

ver-te-bra-do, -da *adj.* vertebrate

ver-te-bral *adj.* vertebral

ver-ter *v.* to shed

ver-ti-cal *adj.* vertical

ver-ti-ca-li-dad *f.* verticality

ver-tien-te *f.* spring

vér-ti-go *m.* vertigo

ve-sí-cu-la *f.* vesicle

ve-si-cu-lar *adj.* vesicular

ves-tí-bu-lo *m.* vestibule

ves-ti-do *m.* clothing; dress

ves-ti-du-ra *f.* garment

ves-ti-gio *m.* vestige

ves-ti-men-ta *f.* clothes

ves-tir *v.* to attire; to wear; to dress

ve-tar *v.* to veto

ve-te-ar *v.* to streak

ve-te-ra-no, -na *m., f., adj.* veteran

ve-te-ri-na-rio, -ria *m., f.* veterinarian

vez f. time

vía f. means; way

via-ble adj. viable

via-jar v. to journey; to travel

via-je m. journey; trip

vial adj. traffic

vian-da f. food

vi-bo-ra f. viper

vi-bra-ción f. vibration

vi-brar v. to shake; to vibrate

vi-ce-pre-si-den-cia f. vicepresidency

vi-ce-pre-si-den-te m. vicepresident

vi-ciar v. to corrupt; to falsify; to pollute

vi-cio m. vice

vi-cio-so, -sa adj. depraved

vi-ci-si-tud f. vicissitude

vic-ti-ma f., m. victim

vic-to-ra-ar v. to cheer

vic-to-ria f. victory

vic-to-rio-so, -sa adj. victorious

vid f. grapevine

vi-da f. life

vi-de-o m. video

vi-de-o-ca-se-te m. videocassette

vi-de-o-cin-ta f. videotape

vi-dria-do, -da adj. glazed

vi-drie-ro, -ra m., f. glazier

vi-drio m. glass

vi-drio-so, -sa adj. glassy

vie-jo, -ja adj. aged; old

vien-to m. wind

vier-nes m. Friday

vi-gen-cia f. force

vi-gi-lan-cia f. vigilance

vi-gi-lan-te adj. heedful; vigilant

vi-gi-lar v. to guard

vi-gi-lia f. vigil

vi-gor m. strength; vigor

vi-go-ro-so, -sa adj. forceful; vigorous

vi-hue-la f. guitar

vi-le-za f. vileness

vi-lla f. village

vi-lla-no, -na adj. peasant

vi-na-gre m. vinegar

vi-na-gre-ta f. vinaigrette

vin-cu-lar v. to link

vin-di-ca-ción f. cindication

vin-di-car v. to vindicate

vi-ni-lo m. vinyl

vi-no m. wine

vi-ne-do m. vineyard

vio-la f. viola

vio-la-ce-o, -a adj. violet

vio-la-ción f. violation.

vio-lar v. to violate

vio-len-cia f. violence; enbarrassment; rape

vio-len-tar tr. to force; to distort; to break into

vio-len-to, -ta adj. violent

vio-le-ta, f., adf violet

vio-lín f. violin

vio-li-nis-ta m., f. violinist

vio-lón m. double bass player; double bass

vi-pe-ri-no, adj. venomous

vi-ra-je m. turning point; veering turn

vi-rar tr. to turn; to tone; to swerve

vir-gen adf., f. virgin

vir-il adj. virile

vir-tual adj. virtual

vi-ru-len-to, -ta adj. virulent

vi-rus m., inv. virus

vi-ru-ta f. shavings

vi-sar tr. to sight; to endorse

vis-co-si-dad f. viscosity

vi-se-ra f. visor

vi-si-llo m. windo curtain

vi-sión f. vision

vi-si-tar v. to visit

vis-ta f. sight; view

vis-to-so, -a adj. colorful

vi-sual adj. visual

vi-tal adj. vital

vi-ta-mi-na f. vitamin

vi-to-re-ar tr. to cheer

vi-tral m. stained-glass window

viu-da f. widow

viu-do m. widower

vi-vaz adj. lively

vi-ven-cia f. experience

vi-ve-res m., pl. provisions

vi-ve-ro m. BOT. fish hatchery; nursery

vi-ve-za f. liveliness;

sharpness; quickness
vi-vi-do, -da adj. vivid
vi-vien-da f. dwelling; housing
vi-vien-te adj. living
vi-vi-fi-ca-dor, -ra adj. vivifying
vi-vir v. to reside; to live
vi-vo, -va adj. vivid; lively
vo-ca-blo m. term
vo-ca-bu-la-rio m. vocabulary
vo-ca-ción f. job; occupation; vocation
vo-cal adj. vocal
vo-ca-li-za-ción f. vocalization
vo-ce-ar intr., tr. to shout
vo-ce-o m. shouting
vo-ce-ro, -a m., f. spokesman; spokeswoman
vo-la-da f. short flight
vo-lan-do adv. in a flash
vo-lan-te adj. balance wheel; steering wheel
vo-lar v. to fly; to blow up; to disappear
vo-la-tín m. acrobatic stunt
vo-la-ti-ne-ro, -a m., f. tightrope walker
vol-cán m. volcano
vo-le-ar ARG. to scatter
vo-li-ción f. volition
vol-ta-je m. voltage
vol-tear v. to upset; to turn over
vol-te-re-ta f. somersault
vol-tí-me-tro m. voltmeter
vol-tio m. volt
vo-lu-ble adj. fickle; voluble
vo-lu-men m. volume
vo-lun-tad f. will; wish; intention
vo-lun-ta-rio, -ria adj. voluntary
vo-lun-ta-rio-so, -a adj. willing; willful
vo-lup-tuo-si-dad f. voluptuousness
vol-ver v. to turn; to return; to recur; to restore
vo-mi-tar tr. to spew; to vomit; to spill
vo-mi-ti-vo, -a adj., m. vomitive

tive
vo-ra-ci-dad f. voracity
vo-rá-gi-ne f. whirlpool
vo-ra-gi-no-so, -a adj. turbulent
vo-raz adj. voracious
vór-ti-ce m. center of a cyclone; vortex
vos pron., m., f. you
vo-se-ar tr. to address
vo-se-o m. used in addressing someone
vo-so-tras pron., f. you
vo-so-tros pron., m. you
vo-ta-ción f. voting; vote
vo-tan-te m., f. voter
vo-tar v. to vote
vo-ti-vo adj. votive
voz f. voice
vo-za-rrón m. booming voice
vuel-co m. to overturn; overturning
vue-lo m. flight
vuel-to, -a m., f. revolution
vues-tra adj. your
vul-ca-ni-zar tr. to vulcanize
vul-gar adj. vulgar; common
vul-ga-ri-dad f. vulgarity
vul-ga-ris-mo m. vulgarism
vul-ga-ri-zar tr. to popularize; to vulgarize
vul-go m. masses
vul-ne-ra-bi-li-dad f. vulnerability
vul-ne-rar tr. to violate; to wound
vul-va f. vulva

wat m. watt
wel-ter m. welterweight
whis-ky m. whiskey

xe-no-fo-bia f. xenophobia
xi-ló-fo-no m. xylophone
xi-lo-gra-fí-a f. xylography

ya-ca-fe *m.* alligator
ya-cer *intr.* to lie; to be
ya-guar *m.* jaguar
yam-bi-co *adj.* iambic
yan-qui *adj., m., f.* Yankee
yar-da *f.* yard
ya-te *m.* yacht
ye-gua *f.* mare
ye-gua-da *f.* herd of horses
yel-mo *m.* helmet
ye-ma *f.* yolk
yen *m., FIN.* yen
yer-ba *f.* grass
yer-bal *m. F.P.* field of mate
yer-mar *tr.* to strip
yer-mo, -a *adj.* barren
yer-no *m.* son-in-law
ye-rra *f.* cattle branding
ye-rro *m.* fault; sin
yer-to *adj.* frozen stiff
ye-se-ro *adj.* plaster
ye-so *m.* gypsum
yo *pron.* I; me
yo-da-do, -a *adj.* iodized
yo-da-to *m.* iodate
yo-do *m.* iodine
yo-du-ro *m.* iodide
yo-ga *m.* yoga
yo-g(h)i *m.* yogi
yo-gur(t) *m.* yogurt
yo-yo *m.* yo-yo
yu-ca *f.* manioc
yu-cal *m.* yucca field
yu-do *m.* judo
yuu-ga-da *f.* day's plowing; yoke
yu-gu-lar *adj., f.* jugular
yun-que *m.* anvil
yun-ta *f.* yoke
yu-te *m.* jute

yux-ta-po-ner *tr* to juxtapose
yux-ta-po-si-cion *f.* juxtaposition
yu-yal *m.* weed patch
yu-yo *m.* weed
yu-yu-ba *f.* jujube

za-far(se) *v.* loosen
za-gal *m.* boy; lad
za-ga-la *f.* lass
za-ma-rro *m.* sheepskin
zam-bu-lli-da *f.* dive
zam-bu-llir *v.* plunge into
za-na-ho-ria *f.* carrot
zan-ja *f.* trench; ditch
za-pa-te-ria *f.* shoestore
za-pa-te-ro *m.* shoemaker
za-pa-ti-lla *v.* slipper
za-pa-to *m.* shoe
zar *m.* czar
za-ri-na *f.* czarina
zar-za-mo-ra *f.* blackberry
zo-co *adj.* left-handed
zo-dia-co *m.* zodiac
zo-na *f.* zone
zoo-lo-gia *f.* zoology
zoo-lo-gi-co *adj.* zoological
zoo-ló-go *m.* zoologist
zo-rra *f.* fox
zo-rro *m.* fox
zo-zo-brar *v.* overturn
zum-bar *v.* whirr; buzz
zu-mo *m.* juice
zu-mo-so *adj.* juicy
zur-cir *v.* stitch

a *indef. article* una; un
a-back *adv.* atras
a-ba-cus *n.* ábaco
a-ban-don *v.* abandonar
a-base *v.* humillar; rebajar
a-bate *v.* disminuir; reducir
ab-bey *n.* monasterio
ab-bre-vi-a-tion *n.* abreviación
ab-di-cate *v.* abdicar
ab-do-men *n.* abdomen
ab-duct *v.* secuestrar
ab-er-ra-tion *n.* aberración
a-bet *v.* instigar; ayudar
ab-hor *v.* aborrecer
a-bide *v.* habitar; soportar
a-bil-i-ty *n.* habilidad
ab-ject *adj.* abyecto
ab-jure *v.* abjurar
a-ble *adj.* capaz; competente
ab-ne-gate *v.* renunciar; negar
ab-nor-mal *adj.* anormal
a-board *adv.,prep.* a bordo
a-bode *n.* domicilio
a-bol-ish *v.* abolir
a-bom-i-nate *v.* abominar
ab-o-rig-i-nes *n.* aborigenes
a-bor-tion *n.* aborto
a-bound *v.* abundar
a-bout *prep.* sobre; alrededor de
a-bove *prep.* sobre; encima de
a-bra-sion *n.* abrasión
a-breast *adv.* de frente; al lado
a-bridge *v.* abreviar; resumir
a-broad *adv.* fuera de casa; en el extranjero
ab-ro-gate *v.* abrogar
ab-rupt *adj.* brusco
ab-scess *n.* absceso
ab-scond *v.* fugarse
ab-sent *adj.* ausente
ab-so-lute *adj.* completo; absoluto
ab-solve *v.* absolver
ab-sorb *v.* absorber
ab-stain *v.* abstenerse
ab-ste-mi-ous *adj.* abstemio
ab-stract *v.* abstraer
ab-surd *adj.* absurdo

a-bun-dant *adj.* abundante
a-buse *v.* abstraer
a-but *v.* confinar
a-byss *n.* abismo
ac-a-dem-ic *adj.* academico
a-cad-e-my *n.* academia
ac-cede *v.* acceder; consentir; subir
ac-cel-er-ate *v.* acelerar
ac-cent *n.* acento
ac-cept *v.* recibir
ac-cess *n.* acceso
ac-ces-si-ble *adj.* accesible
ac-ces-so-ry *n.,pl.* accesorios; complice
ac-ci-dent *n.* accidente
ac-claim *v.* aclamar
ac-cli-mate *v.* aclimatar
ac-co-lade *n.* acolada
ac-com-mo-date *v.* acomodar
ac-com-pa-ny *v.* acompanar
ac-com-plice *n.* cómlice
ac-com-plish *v.* cumplir; acabar
ac-cord *n.* acuerdo
ac-cor-di-on *n.* acordeón
ac-count *v.* explicar
ac-count-a-ble *adj.* responsable
ac-cu-mu-late *v.* acumular
ac-cu-ra-cy *n.* exactitude
ac-cu-rate *adj.* exacto; fiel
ac-cuse *v.* acusar; culpar
ac-cus-tom *v.* acostumbrar
a-ce-tic *adj.* acetico
ac-e-tone *n.* acetone
ache *n.* dolor
a-chieve *v.* acabar
ac-id *adj.* ácido
ac-knowl-edge *v.* reconocer; confesar; agradecer
ac-me *n.* cima
ac-ne *n.* acne
ac-o-lyte *n.* acolito
a-corn *n.* bellota
a-cous-tics *n.* acustica
ac-quaint *v.* enterar
ac-quaint-ance *n.* conocido
ac-qui-esce *v.* consentir
ac-quire *v.* adquirir
ac-quit *v.* absolver
a-cre *n.* acre

ac-rid *adj.* acre
ac-ri-mo-ny *n.* acrimonia
ac-ro-bat *n.* acrobata
a-cross *prep.* a traves de
act *v.* fingir; hacer
ac-tion *n.* acción
ac-ti-vate *v.* activar
ac-tive *adj.* activo
ac-tor *n.* actor
ac-tress *n.* actriz
ac-tu-al *adj.* actual; real
a-cu-i-ty *n.* agudeza
a-cu-men *n.* agudeza
a-cute *adj.* agudo; fino
ad-age *n.* adagio
a-dapt *v.* adaptar
add *v.* sumar; añadir
ad-di-tion *n.* adición
ad-dress *v.* dirigir (se a)
a-dept *n., adj.* experto
ad-e-quate *adj.* adecuado; suficiente
ad-here *v.* adherirse; pegarse; cumplir
ad-he-sive *adj., n.* adhesivo
ad-ja-cent *adj.* adyacente
ad-jec-tive *n.* adjetivo
ad-join *v.* juntar; estar contiguo
ad-journ *v.* suspender
ad-judge *v.* juzgar; sentenciar
ad-just *v.* ajustar; adaptar
ad-ju-tant *n.* ayudante
ad-lib *v.* improvisar
admin-is-ter *v.* administrar
ad-min-is-tra-tion *n.* administración
ad-mire *v.* admirar
ad-mis-si-ble *adj.* admisible
ad-mis-sion *n.* entrada; confesión
ad-mit *v.* confesar; admitir
ad-mon-ish *v.* amonestar
a-do-be *n.* adobe
ad-o-les-cence *n.* adolescencia
a-dopt *v.* adoptar; aceptar
a-dore *v.* adorar
a-dorn *v.* adornar
a-dren-a-line *n.* adrenalina
a-droit *adj.* habil; diestro

ad-u-la-tion *n.* adulación
a-dult *adj.* mayor
a-dul-ter-y *n.* adulterio
ad-vance *v.* avanzar
ad-van-tage *n.* ventaja
ad-ven-ture *n.* aventura
ad-ven-ture-some *adj.* aventurado
ad-verb *n.* adverbio
ad-ver-sar-y *n.* adversario
ad-verse *adj.* adverso; contrario
ad-ver-si-ty *n.* adversidad
ad-ver-tise *v.* publicar
ad-vice *n.* consejo
ad-vise *v.* avisar
ad-vo-cate *v.* abogar
adz, adze *n.* azuela
ae-gis *n.* egido
aer-ate *v.* airear
aer-i-al *adj.* aereo
aer-o-naut-ics *n. pl.* aeronautica
aes-thete *n.* esteta
aes-thet-ic *adj.* estetico
a-far *adv.* lejos
af-fa-ble *adj.* afable; cortes
af-fair *n.* amorosa
af-fect *v.* afectar
af-fec-ta-tion *n.* afectación
af-fec-tion *n.* afeccion
af-fec-tion-ate *adj.* cariñoso
af-fi-ance *v.* desposarse
af-fi-da-vit *n.* declaración jurada
af-fil-i-ate *v.* afiliar
af-fin-i-ty *n.* afinidad
af-firm *v.* afirmar
af-firm-a-tive *n.* aserción
af-fix *v.* anadir; fijar
af-flic-tion *n.* aflicción
af-flu-ence *n.* afluencia
af-flu-ent *adj.* rico; opulento
af-ford *v.* tener medios para; dar
af-front *v.* afrentar
a-fire *adj., adv.* ardiendo
a-flame *adj., adv.* en llamas
a-float *adj., adv.* a flote
a-foul *adj., adv.* enredado
a-fraid *adj.* atemorizado
a-fresh *adv.* de nuevo; otra vez

aft *adj., adv.* en (a) popa
af-ter *prep.* detras de
af-ter-birth *n.* secundinas
af-ter-noon *n.* tarde
af-ter-ward *adv.* despues
a-gain *adv.* otra vez
a-gainst *prep.* contra
a-gape *adj., adv.* boqui-abierto
age *n.* edad
a-ged *adj.* viejo
a-gen-cy *n.* agencia; accion; medio
a-gen-da *n. pl.* orden del dia
a-gent *n.* agente; representante
ag-glom-er-ate *v.* aglomerar
ag-gran-dize *v.* engrandecer
ag-gra-vate *v.* agravar
ag-gre-gate *v.* agregar; juntar
ag-gres-sion *n.* agresión
ag-gres-sive *adj.* agresivo
a-ghast *adj.* horrorizado
a-gil *adj.* agil
a-gil-i-ty *n.* agilidad
ag-i-tate *v.* agitar; inquietar
a-glow *adj.* ardiente
ag-nos-tic *n.* agnostico
a-go *adj.* pasado
ag-o-ny *n.* agonia; angustia
a-grar-i-an *adj.* agrario
a-gree *v.* acordar
a-gree-a-ble *adj.* agradable; conforme
a-gree-ment *n.* acuerdo
ag-ri-cul-ture *n.* agricultura
a-gron-o-my *n.* agronomia
a-ground *adv.* encallado
a-head *adv.* al frente
aid *n.* ayuda
ail-ment *n.* enfermedad; dolencia
aim *v.* aspirar
air *n.* aire
air con-di-tion-er *n.* acondicionador de aire
air-plane *n.* avion
air-port *n.* aeropuerto
air-raid *n.* ataque aereo
air-y *adj.* ligero; alegre
aisle *n.* nave lateral; pasillo
a-jar *adj., adv.* entreabierto

a-kin *adj.* semejante; consanguineo
al-a-bas-ter *n.* alabastro
a-lac-ri-ty *n.* alacridad
a-larm *n.* alarma
a-larm-ist *n.* alarmista
al-ba-tross *n.* albatros
al-be-it *conj.* aunque
al-bi-no *n.* albino
al-bum *n.* album
al-bu-men *n.* albumen
al-bu-min *n.* albumina
al-che-my *n.* alquimia
al-co-hol *n.* alcohol
ale *n.* cerveza
a-lee *adv.* a sotavento
a-lert *adj.* alerte
al-fal-fa *n.* alfalfa
al-ga *n.* alga
al-ge-bra *n.* algebra
a-li-as *n.* alias
al-i-bi *n.* coartada; excusa
al-ien *n.* extranjero
al-ien-ate *v.* enajenar
a-light *v.* bajar; posarse
a-lign *v.* alinera; aliar
a-like *adj.* semejante
al-i-ment *n.* alimento
al-i-men-ta-ry *adj.* alimenticio
al-i-mo-ny *n.* alimentos
a-live *adj.* activo
al-ka-lize *v.* alcalizar
all *adj.* todo
al-lay *v.* aliviar; aquietar
al-le-ga-tion *n.* alegación
al-lege *v.* alegar; declarar
al-leged *adj.* supuesto; alegado
al-le-giance *n.* lealtad
al-le-go-ry *n.* alegoria
al-ler-gy *n.* alergia
al-le-vi-ate *v.* calmar
a-l-e-v-i-a-t-i-o-n *n.* aligeramiento
al-ley *n.* callejuela
al-li-ance *n.* alianza
al-li-ga-tor *n.* caiman
al-lo-cate *v.* asignar
al-lo-ca-tion *n.* reparto; cupo
al-lot *v.* asignar; distribuir; adjudicar
al-low *v.* dar; permitir

al-low-ance *n.* ración; permision
al-loy *n.* aleación
al-lude *v.* aludir
al-lure *v.* tentar
al-lu-sion *n.* alusion
al-lu-vi-um *n.* derrubio
al-ly *n.* aliado; confederado
al-ma-nac *n.* almanaque
al-might-y *adj.* omnipotente; todopoderoso
al-mond *n.* almendra; almendro
al-most *adv.* casi
alms *n.* limosna
a-loft *adv.* en alto
a-lone *adj.* solo
a-long *adv., con., prep.* a lo largo
a-loof *adv. lejos* reservado
a-loud *adv.* en voz alta; alto
al-pha-bet *n.* alfabeto
al-read-y *adv.* ya
al-so *adv.* también; ademas
al-tar *n.* altar
al-ter *v.* cambiar; alterar; modificar
al-ter-a-tion *n.* alteración
al-ter-ca-tion *n.* altercación
al-ter e-go *n.* alter ego
al-ter-nate *v.* alternar
al-ter-na-tive *n.* alternativa
al-though *conj.* aunque
al-tim-e-ter *n.* altímetro
al-ti-tude *n.* altura; altitude
al-to *n.* alto; contralto
al-to-geth-er *adv.* en total
a-lu-mi-num *n.* aluminio
a-lum-na *n., f.* graduada
a-lum-nus *n.* graduado
al-ways *adv.* siempre
a.m. antemeridiano
a-mal-gam *n.* amalgama
a-mal-gam-ate *v.* amalgamar
a-mass *v.* acumular; amontonar
am-a-teur *n.* aficionada
am-a-to-ry *adj.* amatorio
a-maze *v.* asombrar
a-maze-ment *n.* sorpresa
am-a-zon *n.* amazona
am-bas-sa-dor *n.* embajador

am-ber *n.* ambar
am-bi-dex-trous *adj.* ambidextro
am-bi-gu-i-ty *n.* ambiguedad; doble sentido
am-big-u-ous *adj.* ambiguo
am-bi-tion *n.* ambición
am-bi-tious *adj.* ambicioso
am-biv-a-lence *n.* ambivalencia
am-ble *v.* amblar; andar lentamente
am-bu-late *v.* andar
am-bu-la-to-ry *a.* ambulante
am-bus-cade *n.* emboscada
am-bush *n.* emboscada; docil; respinsable
a-me-ba *n.* amiba
a-mel-io-rate *v.* mejorar
a-mel-io-ra-tion *n.* mejora; mejoramiento
a-men *int.* amen
a-me-na-ble *adj.* docil
a-mend *v.* enmendar; corregir
a-mends *n., pl.* compensación
a-men-i-ty *n.* amenidad
A-mer-i-can *adj.* americano
am-e-thyst *n.* amatista
a-mi-a-ble *adj.* amable
am-i-ca-ble *adj.* amistoso
a-mid *prep.* en medio de; entre.
a-mid-ships *adv.* en medio del navio
a-miss *adv., adj.* impropiamente; mel
am-mo-nia *n.* municion
am-ne-sia *n.* amnesia
am-nes-ty *n.* amniastia
a-moe-ba *n.* amiba
a-mong *prep.* en medio de
a-mor-al *adj.* amoral
am-o-rous *adj.* amoroso
a-mor-phous *adj.* amoroso
am-or-tize *v.* amortizar
a-mount *n.* cantidad; suma
am-pere *n.* amperio
am-phib-i-an *adj., n.* anfibio
am-phib-i-ous *adj.* anfibio
am-phi-the-a-ter *n.* anfiteatro

am-ple *adj.* abundante
am-pli-fy *v.* amplificar
am-pli-tude *n.* amplitud; abundancia
am-pu-tate *v.* amputar
am-pu-ta-tion *n.* amputación
a-muck *adv.* furiosamente
am-u-let *n.* amuleto
a-muse-ment *n.* pasatiempo
an *indef. article* una; un; uno
a-nach-ro-nism *n.* anacronismo
a-na-con-da *n.* anaconda
a-nae-mi-a *n.* anemia
an-a-gram *n.* anagrama
a-nal *adj.* anal
an-al-ge-sic *adj.* analgesico
a-nal-o-gize *v.* analogizar
a-nal-o-gy *n.* analogía
a-nal-y-sis *n.* analisis
an-a-lyst *n.* analizador
an-a-lyze *v.* analizar
an-ar-chism *n.* anarquismo
an-ar-chist *n.* anarquista
an-ar-chy *n.* anarquía
a-nat-o-my *n.* anatomia
an-ces-tor *n.* antepasado
an-ces-try *n.* linaje; abolengo
an-chor *n.* ancla; áncora
an-cho-vy *n.* anchoa
an-cient *adj.* antiguo
and *conj.* y
an-ec-dote *n.* anecdota
a-ne-mi-a *n.* anemia
an-e-mon-e-ter *n.* anemometro
an-es-the-sia *n.* anestesia
an-es-thet-ic *n., adj.* anestesico
a-new *adv.* de nuevo; otra vez
an-gel *n.* angel
an-gel-ic *adj.* angelico
an-ger *n.* ira; colera
an-gle *n.* angulo
an-gle-worm *n.* lombriz
An-glo-Sax-on *v., adj.* anglosajon
an-gor-a *n.* angora
an-gry *adj.* enfadado
an-guish *n.* angustia; ansioa
an-gu-lar *adj.* angular; an-
guloso
an-hy-drous *adj.* anhidro
an-i-mad-ver-sion *n.* animadversion
an-i-mad-vert *v.* censurar
an-i-mal *n.* animal
an-i-mal-ize *v.* animalizar
an-i-mate *v.* dar vida
an-i-ma-tion *n.* animación
an-i-mos-i-ty *n.* animosidad
an-ise *n.* anis
an-kle *n.* tobillo
an-nals *n., pl.* anales
an-neal *v.* templar
an-nex *v.* anexar; adjuntar
an-nex-a-tion *n.* anexión
an-ni-hi-late *v.* aniquilar
an-ni-hi-la-tion *n.* aniquilación
an-ni-ver-sa-ry *n.* aniversario
an-no-tate *v.* anotar
an-nounce *v.* proclamar
an-nounce-ment *n.* anuncio
an-noy *v.* molestar
an-noy-ance *n.* fastidio
an-nu-al *adj.* anual
an-nu-i-ty *n.* renta vitalicia
an-nul *v.* anular
an-nul-ment *n.* anulación
an-nun-ci-ate *v.* anunciar
an-nun-ci-a-tion *n.* anunciación
an-ode *n.* anodo
a-noint *v.* untar; ungir
a-nom-a-lous *adj.* anomalo
a-nom-a-ly *n.* anomalia
a-non-y-mous *adj.* anonimo
an-oth-er *adj., pron.* otro
an-swer *v.* contestar; responder
ant *n.* hormiga
ant-ac-id *n.* antiacido
an-tag-o-nist *n.* antagonista
an-tag-o-nize *v.* contender
ant-arc-tic *adj.* antartico
ant-eat-er *n.* oso hormiguero
an-te-cede *v.* anteceder
an-te-ced-ent *n.* antecedente
an-te-date *v.* antedatar; preceder
an-te-di-lu-ve-an *adj.* antediluviano

an-te-lope n. antilope
an-ten-na n. antena
an-te-ri-or adj. anterior
an-te-room n. antecamara
an-them n. antifona. na-tion-al an-them himno nacional
an-ther n. antera
an-thol-o-gy n. antologia
an-thra-cite n. antracita
an-thrax n. antrax
an-thro-poid adj. antropoide
an-thro-pol-o-gist n. antropologo
an-thro-pol-o-gy n. antropologia
an-ti prefix anti; contra
an-ti-bi-ot-ic n. antibiotico
an-ti-bod-y n. anticuerpo
an-tic n. travesura; cabriola
an-tic-i-pate v. anticipar; esperar
an-tic-i-pa-tion n. anticipacion; expectacion
an-ti-cli-max n. anticlimax
an-ti-dote n. antidoto
an-tip-a-thy n. antipatia
an-tip-odes n. antipoda
an-ti-quate v. anticuar; antiquado
an-ti-quat-ed adj. viejo; anticuado
an-tique adj. antiguo
an-tiq-ui-ty n. antiguedad
an-ti-Sem-i-tism n. antisemitismo
an-ti-sep-tic adj., n. antiseptico
an-ti-so-cial adj. antisocial
an-tith-e-sis n. antitesis
an-ti-tox-in n. antitoxina
an-to-nym n. antonimo
-nus n. ano
an-vil n. yunque
anx-i-e-ty n. inquietud; ansia
anx-ious adj. impaciente
an-y adj., pron. alguno; algun
an-y-bod-y pron. alguien
an-y-how adv. de cualquier modo; de todas formas
an-y-one pron. alguien; alguno
an-y-thing pron. algo

an-y-way adv. de cualquier modo; de todas formas
an-y-where adv. en todas partes; dondequiera
a-or-ta n. aorta
a-part adv. aparte. a-part from aparte de
a-part-ment n. apartamento
ap-a-thet-ic adj. indiferente
ap-a-thy n. apatia
ape n. mono
ap-er-ture n. abertura
a-pex n. apice
aph-o-rism n. aforismo
aph-ro-dis-i-ac n. afrodisiaco
a-pi-a-rist n. colmenero
a-pi-ar-y n. colmenar
a-piece adv. cada uno; por persona
a-plomb n. aplomo
a-poc-a-lypse n. apocalipsis
a-pol-o-gize v. disculparse
a-pol-o-gy n. apologia; disculpa
ap-o-plec-tic adj. apopletico
ap-o-plex-y n. apoplejia
a-port adv. a babor
a-pos-tate n. apostata
a-pos-ta-tize v. apostatar
a-pos-tle n. apostol
ap-os-tol-ic adj. apostolico
a-pos-tro-phe n. apostrofo
a-poth-e-car-y n. boticario
ap-pall, ap-pal v. aterrar
ap-pa-rat-us n. aparato
ap-par-el n. ropa
ap-par-ent a. claro; aparente
ap-pa-ri-tion n. fantasma
ap-peal n. apelacion
ap-peal v. apelar
ap-pear v. parecer
ap-pear-ance n. apariencia
ap-pease v. apaciguar
ap-pel-lant n. apelante
ap-pel-la-tion n. nombre
ap-pend v. anexar
ap-pen-dage n. apendice
ap-pen-dec-to-my n. apendectomia
ap-pen-di-ci-tis n. apendicitis
ap-pen-dix n. apendice
ap-per-tain v. pertenecer

ap-pe-tite *n.* gana
ap-pe-tiz-ing *adj.* apetitoso; apetitivo
ap-plaud *v.* aplaudir
ap-plause *n.* aplauso
ap-ple *n.* manzana
ap-pli-cant *n.* suplicante
ap-pli-ca-tion *n.* aplicación
ap-ply *v.* aplicar
ap-point *v.* señalar; nombrar
ap-point-ment *n.* cita; nombramiento
ap-por-tion *v.* repartir
ap-po-si-tion *n.* aposición
ap-prais-al *n.* valoración
ap-praise *v.* valorar
ap-pre-ci-ate *v.* apreciar; volorar; agradecer
ap-pre-ci-a-tion *n.* aprecio; aumento en valor
ap-pre-hend *v.* entender
ap-pre-hen-sion *n.* aprenhension
ap-pren-tice *n.* aprendiz, *v.* poner de aprendize
ap-prixe, ap-prize *v.* informar
ap-proach *v.* aproximarse
ap-pro-ba-tion *n.* aporobación
ap-pro-pri-ate *v.* apropiarse; destinar; *adj.* apropiado
ap-prov-al *n.* aprobación
ap-prove *v.* aprobar
ap-prox-i-mate *v.* aproximar
ap-ri-cot *adj.* albaricoque
A-pril *n.* abril
a-pron *n.* delantal, *m.*
ap-ro-pos of *prep.* a proposito de
apt *adj.* apto; listo
ap-ti-tude *n.* aptitud
a-quar-i-um *n.* acuario
a-quat-ic *adj.* acuatico
aq-ue-duct *n.* acueducto
a-que-ous *adj.* acueo
aq-ui-line *adj.* aguileño
Ar-ab *n., adj.* arabe, *m., f.*
Ar-a-bic nu-me-rals *n.* numeros arabigos
ar-a-ble *adj.* labrantio; cultivable
ar-bi-ter *n.* arbitro

ar-bi-trar-y *adj.* arbitrario
ar-bi-trate *v.* arbitrar
ar-bi-tra-tion *n.* arbitraje
ar-bo-re-al *adj.* arboreo
ar-bo-re-tum *n.* jardin botanico
arc *n.* arce. *v.* formar un arco voltaico
ar-cade *n.* arcada; galeria
arch *n.* arco. *v.* arquear
arch- *prefix* principal
ar-chae-ol-o-gy, ar-che-ol-o-gy *n.* arqueología
ar-cha-ic *adj.* arcaico
arch-an-gel *n.* arcangel
arch-bish-op *n.* arzobispo
arch-duch-ess *n.* archiduquest
arch-duke *n.* archiduque
arch-er *n.* arquero
arch-er-y *n.* ballesteria
arch-e-type *n.* arquetipo
ar-chi-pel-a-go *n.* archipielago
ar-chi-tect *n.* arquitecto
ar-chi-tec-tur-al *adj.* arquitectonico
ar-chi-tec-ture *n.* arquitectura
ar-chive *n.* archivo
arch-priest *n.* arcipreste
arc-tic *adj.* artico
ar-dent *adj.* ardiente; fervoroso
ar-dor *n.* ardor
ar-du-ous *adj.* arduo; dificil
a-re-na *n.* areña
ar-gon *n.* argo
ar-got *n.* jerga
ar-gue *v.* razonar
ar-gu-ment *n.* disputa
ar-gu-men-ta-tive *adj.* argumentador
a-ri-a *n.* aria
ar-id *adj.* arido
a-rid-i-ty *n.* aridez
a-rise *v.* alzarse; surgir
a-ris-toc-ra-cy *n.* aristocracía
a-ris-to-crat *n.* aristocrata
a-ris-to-crat-ic *adj.* aristocratico
a-rith-me-tic *n.* aritmetica
a-rith-me-ti-cian *n.* arit-

netico
k n. arca
m n. brazo
ma-da n. armada
ma-dil-lo n. armadillo
ma-ment n. armamento
n-ful n. brazado
mi-stice n. armisticio
moire n. armario
mor n. armadura
mored adj. blindado
mor-y n. armeria
n-pit n. sobaco
my n. ejercito
o-ma n. aroma
o-mat-ic adj. aromatico
ound adv. alrededor
ouse v. despertar; excitar
range v. arreglar; prevenir
range-ment n. orden
rant adj. consumado
ray n. orden; formación;
dorno. v. colocar; ataviar
rest v. detener
ri-val n. llegada
rive v. llegar
ro-gance n. arrogancia
ro-gant adj. arrogante
row n. flecha
row-head n. punta de
echa
sen-al n. arsenal
sen-ic n. arsenico
- son n. incendio
remeditado
n. arte
ke-ri-al adj. arterial
ter-y n. arteria
ful adj. ingenioso; astuto
thrit-ic adj. artrico
thri-tis n. artritis, f.
ti-cle n. articulo; objeto
ti-cu-late v. articular
tic-u-la-tion n. articulación
ti-fi-cial adj. artificial
til-ler-y n. artillería
ist n. artista
tis-tic adj. artistic
conj., adv. como
bes-tos, as-bes-tus n.
sbesto
cend v. subir; ascender

as-cen-sion n. ascensión
as-cent n. subida; cuesta
as-cer-tain v. averiguar
as-ce-tic adj. ascetico. n. asceta m., f.
as-cet-i-cism n. ascetismo
as-cribe v. atribuir
a-sex-u-al adj. asexual
ash n. ceniza; fresno
a-shamed adj. avergonzado
a-side adv. a un lado n. aparte
as-i-nine adj. asnal
ask v. rogar; preguntar
a-skance adv. con recelo
a-slant adv. al sesgo. prep. a traves de
a-sleep adv., adj. dormido
asp n. aspid
as-par-a-gus n. esparrago
as-pect n. aspecto; aire
as-per-i-ty n. aspereze
as-per-sion n. calumnia
as-phalt n. asfalto
as-phyx-i-ate v. asfixiar
as-phyx-i-a-tion n. asfixia
as-pi-ra-tion n. aspiración; anhelo
as-pire v. aspirar
as-pi-rin n. aspirina
ass n. burro; tonto
as-sail v. acometer
as-sail-ant n. asaltador
as-sas-in n. asesino
as-sas-si-na-tion n. asesinato
as-sault v. atacar
as-sem-ble v. juntar
as-sem-bly n. asamblea
as-sent n. asentimiento
as-sert v. afirmar
as-sess v. fijar; tasar
as-set n. haber
as-sev-er-ate v. aseverar
as-sid-u-ous adj. asiduo
as-sign v. asignar
as-sign-ment n. asignación
as-sim-i-late v. asimilar
as-sist v. ayudar
as-sist-ance n. ayuda
asth-ma n. asma
asth-mat-ic adj. asmatico
as-ton-ish v. asombrar

as-ton-ish-ment n. asombro
as-trol-o-gy n. astrología
as-tron-o-my n. astronomía
at prep. a; en
ath-lete n. atleta
ath-let-ic adj. atletico
at-om n. átomo
a-tom-ic adj. atomico
a-top prep. sobre
at-tach v. pegar; sujetar
at-tack v. atacar
at-tempt v. intentar
at-tend v. asistir
at-ten-tion n. atención
at-tract v. atraer
at-trac-tion n. atracción
a-typ-i-cal adj. atipico
au-di-ence n. publico
au-di-tion n. audición
au-di-to-ry adj. auditivo
Au-gust n. agosto
aunt n. tia
au-then-tic-i-ty n. autenticidad
au-thor n. autor
au-thor-i-ty n. autoridad
au-thor-ize v. autorizar
au-to-bi-og-ra-pher n. autobiografo
au-to-bi-og-ra-phy n. autobiografía
au-to-mat-ic adj. automatico
au-to-ma-tion n. automatización
au-to-mo-bile n. automovil; coche
au-ton-o-mous a. autonomo
a-venge v. vengar
av-e-nue n. avenida
a-ver v. afirmar
av-er-age adj. medio
a-vert v. apartar
a-wait v. esperar
a-wake v. despertar(se)
a-way adv. lejos
aw-ful adj. horrible
awk-ward adj. embarazoso
ax-i-om n. axioma
ax-i-o-mat-ic adj. axiomatico
ax-is n. axis; eje
ax-le n. eje
aye, ay int., n. si
az-ure adj., n. azul celeste

bab-ble v. murmurar; barbotar; susurrar
ba-boon n. mandril
ba-bush-ka n. pañuelo
ba-by n. nino
ba-by-hood n. infancia
ba-by-ish adj. infantil
bac-cha-nal n. bacanal
bach-e-lor n. soltero
bach-e-lor-hood n. soltería
ba-cil-lus n. bacilo
back n. espalda
back-ache n. dolor de espalda
back-bit-ing n. murmuración
back-bone n. espinazo
back-break-ing adj. agobiador
back-date v. antedatar
back-er n. promotor
back-gam-mon n. chaquete
back-ground n. fondo
back-hand-ed adj. ambiguo
back-lash n. sacudida
back-pack n. mochila
back-side n. trasero
back-stairs adj. furtivo
back-track v. desandar
back-up n. suplente; reserva
back-ward adv. atras
back-ward-ness n. retraso
ba-con n. tocino
bac-te-ri-al adj. bacteriaño
bac-te-ri-cide n. bactericida
bac-ter-i-um n. bacteria
bad adj. malo
badge n. insignia
bad-ger n. tejon
bad-ly adv. mal
bad-min-ton n. volante
baf-fle v. desconcertar; confundir
baf-fle-ment n. confusion
baf-fling adj. desconcertante
bag n. bolso; saco
bag-gage n. equipaje
bag-pipe n. gaita
bail v. afianzar
bail-iff n. alguacil
bail-or n. fiador
bait n. carnada
bake v. cocer en horno
bak-er n. panadero

ak-er-y n. panaderia
ak-ing n. cocción
al-ance n. equilibrio
al-anced adj. balanceado
al-co-ny n. balcon
ald adj. calvo
ald-ness n. calcicie
ale n. bala
ale-ful adj. funesto
alk v. oponerse
all n. pelota
al-lad n. balada
al-le-ri-na n. bailarina
al-let n. ballet
al-lis-tic adj. balistico
al-loon n. globo
al-lot n. votación
alm n. balsamo
al-sa n. balsa
am-boo n. bambú
an v. prohibir
a-nal adj. banal
a-nan-a n. platano
and n. banda
and-age v. vendar
an-dit n. bandido
an-do-leer n. bandolera
ane-ful adj. nocivo
ang v. golpear
angs n. flequillo
an-gle n. esclava
an-ish v. desterrar
an-ish-ment n. proscripción; exilio
an-is-ter n. baranda
an-jo n. banjo
ank n. banco
ank-er n. banquero
ank-ing n. banca
ank-rupt adj. arruinado
an-ner n. bandera
an-quet n. banquete
an-ter f. broma
ap-tism n. bautismo
ap-tist n. bautista
ap-tis-ter-y n. baptisterio
ap-tize v. bautizar
ar v. excluir
ar-br-i-an adj. barbaro
ar-bar-ic adj. barbaro
ar-bar-i-ty n. barbaridad
ar-ba-rous adj. barbaro
ar-ber n. peluquero

bar-ber-shop n. peluqueria
bar-bi-tu-rate n. barbiturico
bare adj. desnudo; v. desnudar
bare-faced adj. descarado
bare-ly adv. simplemente; apenas
bar-gain n. ganga; convenio
bar-gain-ing n. negociación
barge n. gabarra
bar-i-tone n. baritono
bar-i-um n. bario
bark v. ladrar; n. ladrido
bar-ley n. cebada
bar-maid n. cantinera
barn n. granero
bar-na-cle n. percebe
ba-rom-et-er n. barometro
bar-o-met-ric adj. barométrico
bar-on n. baron
bar-on-ess n. baronesa
ba-roque adj. barroco
bar-racks n. barraca
bar-rel n. barril
bar-ren adj. infecundo; infructuoso; yermo
bar-ri-cade n. barricada
bar-ri-er n. barrear
bar-tend-er n. camarero
bar-ter v. trocar
bas-al adj. basico
ba-salt n. basalto
base n. base
base-ball n. béisbol
base-board n. zocalo
base-less adj. infundado
base-ment n. sotáno
bash v. golpear
bash-ful adj. timido
ba-sic adj. basico
ba-sic-i-ty n. basicidad
bas-il n. albahaca
ba-sil-i-ca n. basilica
ba-sin n. jofaina
ba-sis n. base
bask v. complacerse
bas-ket n. cesta
bas-ket-ball n. baloncesto
bas-ket-ry n. cesteria
baste v. hilvanar
bat v. golpear; n. maza
batch n. hornada

bate *v.* disminuir
bath *n.* baño
bathe *v.* bañar(se)
bath-ing suit *n.* traje de baño
bath-tub *n.* bañera
ba-ton *n.* batuta
bat-tal-ion *n.* batallon
bat-ter *v.* estropear; golpear
bat-ter-y *n.* bateria
bat-tle *v.* luchar, *n.* lucha
bat-tle-ground *n.* campo de batalla
bat-tle-ship *n.* acorazado
bau-ble *n.* baratija
baud *n.* baudio
bawl *v.* llorar
bay *n.* bahia
bay-o-net *n.* bayoneta
ba-zaar *n.* bazar
ba-zoo-ka *n.* bazuca
be *v.* estar; ser
beach *n.* playa
bea-con *n.* almenara; faro
bead *n.* abalorio
beak *n.* pico
beam *n.* rayo
bean *n.* frijol; habichuela
bear *n.* oso; *v.* llevar
bear-a-ble *adj.* soportable
beard *n.* barba
beard-ed *adj.* barbudo
bear-er *n.* portador
bear-ing *n.* porte
beast *n.* bestia
beast-ly *adj.* bestial
beat *v.* vencer; golpear
beat-en *adj.* derrotado
beat-er *n.* batidor
be-a-tif-ic *adj.* beatifico
be-at-i-fy *v.* beatificar
beat-ing *n.* latido; paliza
be-at-i-tude *n.* beatitud
beau-ti-ful *adj.* hermoso
beau-ti-ful-ly *adj.* ballamente
beau-ty *n.* belleza
bea-ver *n.* castor
be-cause *conj.* porque
beck-on *v.* llamar
be-come *v.* hacer(se)
be-com-ing *adj.* apropiado
bed *n.* cama

be-daz-zle *v.* deslumbrar
bed-cham-ber *n.* alcoba
bed-lam *n.* alboroto
bed-room *n.* alcoba
bed-side *adj.* (de) cabecera
bee *n.* abeja
beech *n.* haya
beef-y *adj.* musculoso
bee-hive *n.* colmena
beer *n.* cerveza
bees-wax *n.* cera
beet *n.* remolacha
bee-tle *n.* escarabajo
be-fit *v.* convenir
be-fit-ting *adj.* conveniente
be-fore *prep.* antes de, *adv.* delante
be-fore-hand *adv.* antes
be-fud-dle *v.* confundir
beg *v.* pedir
beg-gar *n.* pobre
beg-gar-ly *adj.* misero
be-gin *v.* comenzar
be-gin-ner *n.* novato
be-gin-ning *n.* comienzo
be-grudge *v.* envidiar
be-guile *v.* seducir
be-have *v.* funcionar; comportarse
be-hav-ior *n.* comportamiento
be-head *v.* descabezar
be-hind *adv.* atras; detras; *prep.* detras de
be-hold *v.* contemplar
be-hold-en *adj.* obligado
be-hoove *v.* convenir
beige *adj.* beige
be-ing *n.* ser
be-la-bor *v.* machacar
be-lat-ed *adj.* tardio
be-lief *n.* fe
be-liev-a-ble *adj.* creible
be-lieve *v.* creer
be-liev-er *n.* creyente
bell *n.* cascabel
bellflower *n.* campanilla
bel-li-cose *adj.* belicoso
bel-lig-er-ence *n.* beligerancia
bel-lig-er-ent *adj.* beligerante
bel-low *v.* rugir

bel-ly n. estomago
be-long v. estar
be-long-ings n. pertenencias
be-lov-ed adj. querido
be-low adv. abajo, prep. debajo de
belt n. cinturon
be-moan v. lamentar
bench n. banco
bend v. doblar; inclinar
bend-er n. juerga
be-neath prep. debajo de
ben-e-dic-tion n. bendición
ben-e-fac-tor n. benefactor
ben-e-fice n. beneficio
be-nef-i-cent adj. benefico
ben-e-fi-cial adj. beneficioso
ben-e-fi-ci-ar-y n. beneficiario
ben-e-fit n. beneficio
be-nev-o-lence n. benevolencia
be-nev-o-lent adj. benevolo
be-nign adj. benigno
bent adj. empenado; torcido
be-numb v. entorpecer
be-queath v. legar
be-quest n. legado
be-rate v. reprender
be-reave-ment n. duelo
be-reft adj. privado
ber-ryn. baya
berth n. camarote
be-ryl-li-um n. berilio
be-seech v. implorar
be-set v. acosar
be-side prep. cerca
be-sides prep. ademas de
be-siege v. asediar
be-smirch v. manchar
best adj. mejor
bes-tial adj. bestial
bes-ti-al-i-ty n. bestialidad
be-stow v. conceder
bet n. apuesta
be-to-ken v. presagiar
be-tray v. revelar
be-tray-al n. traición
be-trothed n. novio
bet-ter adv., adj. mejor
bet-ter-ment n. mejoramiento
bet-tor n. apostador

be-tween adv. en medio; prep. entre
bev-eled adj. biselado
bev-er-age n. bebida
bev-y n. grupo
be-wail v. lamentar
be-wil-der v. aturdir
be-wil-der-ment n. aturdimiento
be-witch v. hechizar
be-witch-ment n. hechizo
be-yond prep. despues de
bi-an-nu-al adj. semestral
bi-as n. prejuicio
bib n. babero
Bi-ble n. Biblia
Bib-li-cal adj. biblico
bib-li-og-ra-pher n. bibliografo
bib-li-og-ra-phy n. bibliografia
bib-li-o-phile n. bibliofilo
bi-car-bon-ate n. bicarbonato
bi-cen-ten-ni-al adj. bicentario
bi-ceps n. biceps
bi-cy-cle n. bicicleta
bi-cy-clist n. biciclista
bid n. oferta; v. mandar
bid-ding n. oferta
bi-en-ni-al adj. bienal
bi-fo-cal adj. bifocal
bi-fur-cate v. bifurcarse
bi-fur-ca-tion n. bifurcación
big adj. grande
big-a-mist n. bigamo
big-a-my n. bigamia
big-ness n. grandeza
bike n. bicicleta
bik-er n. motociclista
bi-lat-er-al adj. bilateral
bile n. bilis
bi-lin-gual adj. bilingue
bil-ious adj. bilioso
bilk v. defraudar
bill n. pico; cuenta
bill-board n. cartelera
bil-let v. alojar
bill-fold n. cartera
bil-liards n. billar
bil-lion n. billon
bil-lion-aire n. billonario

bil-low *n.* oleada
bil-low-y *adj.* ondulante
bi-month-ly *adj.* bimestram
bin *n.* cajon
bi-na-ry *adj.* binario
bind *v.* encuadernar; atar
bind-er *n.* atadura; encuadernador
bind-ing *n.* encuadernación
bin-oc-u-lar *n.* gemelos
bi-no-mi-al *adj.* binomio
bi-o-chem-i-cal *adj.* bioquimico
bi-o-chem-ist *n.* bioquimico
bi-o-chem-is-try *n.* bioquimica
bi-og-ra-pher *n.* biografo
bi-o-graph-ic *adj.* biografico
bi-og-ra-phy *n.* biografia
bi-o-log-ic *adj.* biologico
bi-ol-o-gist *n.* biologo
bi-ol-o-gy *n.* biologia
bi-on-ics *n.* bionica
bi-o-phys-ics *n.* biofisica
bi-op-sy *n.* biopsia
bi-par-tite *adj.* bipartito
bi-ped *n.* bipedo
bi-plane *n.* biplaño
birch *n.* abedul
bird *n.* pajaro
bird-cage *n.* jaula
bird-seed *n.* alpiste
birth *n.* nacimiento
birth-day *n.* cumpleanos
bis-cuit *n.* bizcocho
bi-sect *v.* bisecar
bi-sec-tion *n.* bisección
bish-op *n.* obispo
bis-muth *n.* bismuto
bi-son *n.* bisonte
bit *n.* pedazo
bite *v.* picar
bit-ing *adj.* mordaz; cortante
bit-ter *adj.* cortante; implacable; amargo
bit-ter-ness *n.* rencor; encarnizamiento
bit-ter-sweet *adj.* agridulce
bi-tu-mi-nous *adj.* bituminoso
bi-va-lent *adj.* bivalente
bi-valve *adj.* bivalvo
bi-week-ly *adj.* quincenal

bi-zarre *adj.* raro
blab-ber *v.* cotorrear
black *adj.* negro
black-and-blue *adj.* amoratado
black-ber-ry *n.* zarzamora
black-bird *n.* mirlo
black-board *n.* pizarra
black-en *v.* difamar
black-head *n.* grano
black-mail *v.* chantajear
black-mail-er *n.* chantajista
black-smith *n.* herrero
black-top *n.* asfalto
blad-der *n.* vejiga
blade *n.* pala; hoja
blame *v.* culpar
bland *adj.* insulso
blank *n., adj.* blanco
blan-ket *n.* manta
blare *v.* resonar
blas-pheme *v.* blasfemar
blas-phe-mous *adj.* blasfemo
blas-phe-my *n.* blasfemia
blast *v.* destruir; *n.* explosion
blast-ed *adj.* maldito
bla-tant *adj.* patente
blaze *n.* joguera; llamarada; *v.* arder
bleach *n.* lejia; *v.* blanquear
bleach-ers *n.* gradas
blear *adj.* sombrio; frio
bleat *v.* balar
bleed *v.* sangrar
blem-ish *n.* manchar
blend *n.* mezcla; *v.* mezclar
blend-er *n.* licuadora
bless *v.* bandecir
bless-ed *adj.* santo
bless-ing *n.* bendición
blind *v.* cegar; *adj.* ciego
blind-ers *n.* anteojeras
blind-ing *adj.* cegador
blind-ly *adv.* ciegamente
blind-ness *n.* ceguera
blink *v.* pestanear; ceder
blink-ing *adj.* parpadeante
bliss *n.* felicidad
bliss-ful *adj.* feliz
blis-ter *v.* ampollar(se)
blis-ter-ing *adj.* forzado;

abrasador
bliz-zard n. ventisca
block n. manzana
block-ade adj. bloqueo
block-age n. obstrucción
blond adj. rubio
blonde adj. rubia
blood n. sangre
blood-less adj. exangüe
blood-thrist-y adj. sanguinario
blood-y adj. sangriento
bloom v. florecer
blos-som n. flor
blot n. mancha
blotch n. mancha
blouse n. blusa
blow v. inflar; soplar
blow-gun n. cerbatana
blow-torch n. soplete
blow-up n. explosión
bludg-eon v. aporrear
blue adj. azul
blue-bell n. campanilla
blue-print n. cianotipo
blunt adj. abrupto
blur v. nublar
blur-ry adj. confuso
blush n. sonrojo
blus-ter v. bramar
boar n. verraco
board n. consejo
board-er n. pensionista
board-ing-house n. pensión
boast v. alardear
boast-ful adj. jactancioso
boast-ing n. jactancia
boat n. barco
boat-man n. lanchero
bob-ber n. flotador
bob-bin n. bobina
bod-ice n. cuerpo
bod-i-ly adj. corporal
bod-y n. cuerpo
bod-y-guard n. guardaespaldas
bog n. cienaga
bo-gus adj. falso
boil v. cocer; hervir
boil-er n. caldera
boil-ing adj. hirviente
bois-ter-ous adj. ruidoso; bullicioso

bold adj. descarado; intrepido
bod-ster v. apoyar
bolt n. perno; pestillo
bomb n. bomba
bom-bard v. acosar; bombardear
bom-bard-ment n. bombardeo
bomb-er n. bombardero
bomb-ing n. bombardeo
bomb-shell n. bomba
bo-nan-za n. bonanza
bond n. atadura; bono
bone n. hueso
bon-fire n. hoguera
bon-net n. cofia
bo-nus n. sobresueldo
bon-y adj. huesudo
book n. libro
book-bind-ing n. encuadernación
book-end n. sujetalibros
book-ing n. reservación
book-sell-er n. librero
book-store n. libreria
boom n. prosperidad
boo-mer-ang n. bumerang
boor n. patan
boor-ish adj. tosco
boost v. levantar
boot n. bota
booth n. puesto; cabina
boot-leg v. contrabandear
boo-ty n. botin
bor-der n. borde; frontera
bor-der-line n. frontera
bore v. aburrir
bore-dom n. aburrimiento
bor-ing adj. aburrido
born adj. nacido
bor-ough n. municipio
bor-row v. apropiarse
bor-row-er n. prestatario
bos-om n. pecho
boss n. jefe
bo-tan-ic adj. botanico
bot-a-nist n. botanico
bot-a-ny n. botanica
botch v. chapucear
both adj. los dos
both-er v. molestar(se)
both-er-some adj. molesto

bot-tle n. botella
bot-tom n. base; fondo
bot-tom-less adj. sin fondo
bot-u-lism n. botulismo
bough n. rama
bouil-lon n. caldo
boul-e-vard n. avenida
bounce v. rebotar
bounc-ing adj. fuerte
bound v. saltar
bound-a-ry n. limite
bound-less adj. ilimitado
boun-te-ous adj. abundante
boun-ti-ful adj. generoso
boun-ty n. generosidad
bou-quet n. ramo
bour-geois n. burgues
bour-geoi-sie n. burguesia
bout n. ataque
bo-vine adj. bovino
bow v. inclinarse; doblegarse
bow-el n. intestino
bowl n. tazon; fuente
bowl-ing n. bolos
box n. caja
box-er n. boxeador
box-ing n. boxeo
boy n. chico; niño
boy-cott v. boicotear
boy-friend n. novio
bra n. sosten
brace n. puntal
brace-let n. brazalete
brac-ing adj. fortificante
brack-et n. corchete
brack-ish adj. salino
brag v. jactarse
brain n. cerebro
brain-y adj. listo
brake v. frenar
bran n. salvado
branch n. rama
brand n. modo; marca
brand-ing n. hierra
bran-dish v. blandir
bran-dy n. conac
brash adj. insolente; impetuoso
brass n. laton
bras-siere n. sosten
bracs-y adj. descarado
brave adj. valiente
brav-er-y n. valor

brawn-y adj. musculoso
bra-zen adj. descarado
bra-zier n. brasero
breach n. rupture; violación
bread n. pan
bread-bas-ket n. panera
breadth n. extension
break v. quebrar; romper
break-a-ble adj. rompible
break-age n. rotura
break-down n. depresión; desglose
break-fast n. desayuno
break-through n. adelanto
break-up n. desintegración; separacion
breast n. pecho
breast-bone n. esternon
breath n. respiración
breathe v. respirar
breath-ing n. respiración
breath-tak-ing adj. impresionante
breed v. criar; reproducirse
breed-er n. criador
breed-ing n. crianza
breeze n. brisa
breez-y adj. ventoso
brev-i-ty n. brevedad
brew-er n. cervecero
brew-er-y n. cerveceria
bribe v. cohechar
brick n. ladrillo
brick-lay-er n. albanil
bri-dal n. boda
bride n. novia
bridge n. puente
bri-dle n. brida
brief adj. breve
brief-case n. cartera
brief-ing n. reunion
bri-gade n. brigada
bright adj. brillante
bright-en v. iluminar(se)
bright-ness n. lustre
bril-liance n. brillo
bril-liant adj. brillante
brim n. borde
bring v. traer
bri-quet n. briqueta
brisk adj. vigoroso
bris-tle n. cerda
brit-tle adj. fragil

broach n. broche
broad adj. extenso; ancho
broad-cast v. transmitir; emitir
broad-cast-ing n. transmision
broad-en v. ensanchar(se)
broad-mind-ed adj. comprensivo
bro-cade n. brocado
broc-co-li n. brecol
bro-chure n. folleto
bro-ken adj. roto; quebrado
bro-ken-down adj. decrepito
bro-ker-age n. corretaje
bro-mide n. bromuro
bro-mine n. bromo
bron-chi-al adj. bronquial
bron-chi-tis n. bronquitis
bronze n. bronce
brook n. arroyo
broom n. escoba
broth n. caldo
broth-el n. burdel
broth-er n. hermano
broth-er-hood n. fraternidad
broth-er-in-law n. cuando
broth-er-ly adj. fraterno
brow n. ceja
brown adj. moreno
brown-out n. parcial
browse v. pacer; curiosear
bruise n. contusión
brunt n. impacto
brush n. cepillo
bru-tal adj. brutal
bru-tal-i-ty n. brutalidad
bru-tal-ize v. brutalizar
brute n. bruto
buc-ca-neer n. bucanero
buck-et n. balde
buck-le n. jebilla
bud n. yema
bud-dy n. compadre
budge v. ceder
budg-et v. presupuestar
buf-fa-lo n. bufalo
buff-er n. intercesor
buf-fet n. bofetada
buf-foon n. bufon
bug n. bicho
bu-gle n. clarin
build v. construir

build-er n. constructor
build-ing n. construcción
bulb n. bulbo
bulge n. bulto
bulk-y adj. pesado
bull n. toro
bull-dog n. buldog
bull-doz-er n. excavadora
bul-let n. bala
bul-le-tin n. boletin
bull-fight-er n. torero
bul-rush n. espadana
bul-wark n. baluarte
bum-ble-bee n. abejorro
bump n. choque
bump-y adj. agitado
bun n. bollo
bunch n. racimo
bun-dle n. fajo; bulto
bun-ny n. conejito
buoy n. boya
buoy-ant adj. boyante
bur n. erizo
bur-den n. carga
bu-reauc-ra-cy n. burocracía
bu-reau-crat n. burocrata
burg-er n. hamburguesa
bur-glar n. ladron
bur-glar-ize v. robar
bur-i-al n. entierro
bur-lap n. arpillera
bur-ly adj. robusto
burn v. incendiar
burn-er n. quemador
burn-ing adj. ardiente
burn-out n. extinción
burnt adj. quemado
burp n. eructo
bur-ro n. burro
burst v. romper
bur-y v. enterrar
bus n. autobus
bus-boy n. ayudante
bush n. arbusto
bushed adj. agotado
busi-ness n. oficio
but conj. pero
but-ter n. mantequilla
but-ter-fly n. mariposa
buy v. comprar
buy-er n. comprador
by adv. cerca, prep. cerca de; por

cab *n.* taxi
ca-bal *n.* cabala
cab-a-la *n.* cabala
cab-a-ret *n.* cabaret
cab-bage *n.* col
cab-driv-er *n.* taxista
cab-in *n.* cabana
cab-i-net *n.* gabinete
cab-i-net-mak-er *n.* ebanista
cab-i-net-work *n.* ebanisteria
ca-ble *n.* cable
ca-ble-gram *n.* cablegrama
ca-ca-o *n.* cacao
ca-chet *n.* cacareo
cac-tus *n.* cacto
ca-dav-er *n.* cadaver
ca-dav-er-ous *adj.* cadav-
erico
cad-die *n.* caddy
ca-dence *n.* cadencia
ca-det *n.* cadete
cad-mi-um *n.* cadmio
ca-du-ce-us *n.* caduceo
ca-fe *n.* cafe
caf-e-te-ri-a *n.* cafeteria
caf-feine *n.* cafeina
caf-tan *n.* tunica
cage *n.* jaula
ca-jole *v.* engatusar
cake *n.* pastel
cal-a-bash *n.* calabaza
cal-a-mine *n.* calamina
cal-am-i-ty *n.* calamidad
cal-ci-fi-ca-tion *n.* cal-
cificación
cal-ci-fy *v.* calcificar
cal-ci-um *n.* calcio
cal-cu-late *v.* calcular
cal-cu-lat-ed *adj.* intencional
cal-cu-lat-ing *adj.* calculador
cal-cu-la-tion *n.* calculo
cal-cu-la-tor *n.* calculadora
cal-dron *n.* caldera
cal-en-dar *n.* calendario
cal-i-ber *n.* calibre
cal-i-brate *v.* calibrar
cal-i-bra-tion *n.* calibración
cal-i-co *n.* calico
cal-i-per *n.* calibrador
ca-liph *n.* califa
cal-is-then-ics *n.* calistenia
ca-lix *n.* caliz
call *v.* llamar

call-er *n.* cisitante
cal-lig-ra-pher *n.* caligrafo
cal-lig-ra-phy *n.* caligrafia
call-ing *n.* vocación
cal-lous *v.* encallecerse
cal-low *adj.* inmaturo
cal-lus *n.* callo
calm *v.* calmar(se); *n.* calma
calm-ness *n.* tranquilidad
cal-or-ic *adj.* calorico
cal-o-rie *n.* caloria
ca-lum-ni-ate *v.* calumniar
cal-va-ry *n.* calvario
ca-lyx *n.* caliz
ca-ma-ra-der-ie *n.* cama-
raderia
cam-bi-um *n.* cambium
cam-el *n.* camello
ca-mel-lia *n.* camelia
cam-e-o *n.* camafeo
cam-er-a *n.* camara
cam-ou-flage *n.* camuflaje
camp *v.* acampar
cam-paign *n.* campana
camp-er *n.* campista
cam-phor *n.* alcanfor
can *v.* poder
ca-nar-y *n.* canario
can-cel *v.* cancelar; matar;
anular
can-cel-la-tion *n.* can-
celacion
can-cer *n.* cancer
can-cer-ous *adj.* canceroso
can-des-cent *adj.* candente
can-did *adj.* franco
can-di-da-cy *n.* candidatura
can-di-date *n.* candidato
can-died *adj.* escarchado
can-dle *n.* cirio; vela
can-dle-hold-er *n.* candelero
can-dle-stick *n.* candelero
can-dor *n.* franqueza
can-dy *n.* azucar
cane *n.* cana; baston
ca-nine *adj.* canino
can-is-ter *n.* lata
canned *adj.* enlatado
can-ni-bal *n.* canibal
can-ni-bal-ism *n.* cani-
balismo
can-ni-bal-is-tic *adj.* canibal
can-non *n.* conon

ca-noe *n.* canoa
ca-non-i-za-tion *n.* canonización
can-on-ize *v.* canonizar
can-ta-loupe *n.* cantalupo
can-teen *n.* cantina
can-vas *n.* lona
can-yon *n.* canon
cap *n.* tapa
ca-pa-bil-i-ty *n.* capacidad
ca-pa-ble *adj.* capaz
ca-pa-cious *adj.* espacioso
ca-pac-i-ty *n.* capacidad
ca-per *n.* cabriola
cap-il-lar-y *n.* capilar
cap-i-tal *n., adj.* capital
cap-i-tal-ism *n.* capitalismo
cap-i-tal-ist *n.* capitalista
cap-i-tal-is-tic *adj.* capitalista
cap-i-tal-i-za-tion *n.* capitalización
cap-i-tal-ize *v.* capitalizar
cap-i-tal-ly *adv.* admirablemente
cap-i-tol *n.* capitolio
ca-pit-u-late *v.* capitular
ca-price *n.* capricho
ca-pri-cious *adj.* caprichoso
cap-sule *n.* capsula
cap-tain *n.* capitan
cap-tion *n.* subtitulo
cap-tious *adj.* capcioso
cap-ti-vate *v.* cautivar
cap-tive *adj.* cautivo
cap-tiv-i-ty *n.* cautividad
cap-tor *n.* capturador
cap-ture *v.* capturar
car *n.* coche
car-a-mel *n.* caramelo
car-at *n.* quilate
car-a-van *n.* caravana
car-bide *n.* carburo
car-bine *n.* carabina
car-bo-hy-drate *n.* carbohifrato
car-bon *n.* carbono
car-bon-ate *v.* carbonatar
car-bun-cle *n.* carbunco
car-bu-re-tor *n.* carburador
car-cin-o-gen-ic *adj.* cancerigeno
card *n.* tarjeta

car-di-ac *adj.* cardiaco
car-di-nal *adj.* cardinal
car-di-o-gram *n.* cardiograma
car-di-ol-o-gy *n.* cardiología
care *v.* cuidar
ca-reer *n.* carrera
care-free *adj.* despreocupado
care-ful *adj.* cuidadoso
care-less *adj.* espontaneo; descuidado
ca-ress *n.* caricia
care-tak-er *n.* portero
car-go *n.* carga
car-i-ca-ture *n.* caricatura
car-nage *n.* carniceria
car-nal *adj.* carnal
car-ni-val *n.* carnaval
car-ni-vore *n.* carnivoro
car-niv-o-rous *adj.* carnivoro
ca-rous-al *n.* jarana
car-ou-sel *n.* carrusel
car-pen-try *n.* carpinteria
car-pet *n.* alfombra
car-riage *n.* carruaje
car-ri-er *n.* carrero
car-rot *n.* zanahoria
car-ry *v.* lograr; llevar
car-sick *adj.* mareado
cart *n.* carro
cart-age *n.* acarreo
car-tel *n.* cartel
car-ti-lage *n.* cartilago
cart-load *n.* carretada
car-toon *n.* tira
car-toon-ist *n.* caricaturista
car-tridge *n.* cartucho
carve *v.* esculpir
carv-ing *n.* escultura
case *n.* caja
cahs *n.* efectivo
cash-ew *n.* anacardo
cash-ier *n.* cajero
cash-mere *n.* cachemira
ca-si-no *n.* casino
cask *n.* barril
cas-se-role *n.* cacerola
cas-sette *n.* casete
cast *v.* dar; fundir; echar
cas-ta-nets *n.* castanuelas
caste *n.* casta
cas-ti-gate *v.* castigar

cas-tle n. castillo
cas-trate v. castrar
cas-tra-tion n. castración
ca-su-al adj. casual
cas-u-al-ly adv. casualmente
ca-su-ist-ry n. casuistica
cat n. gato
ca-tab-o-lism n. catabolismo
cat-a-log n. catalogo
cat-a-lyst n. catalizador
cat-a-lyt-ic adj. catalitico
cat-a-lyze v. catalizar
cat-a-pult n. catapulta
cat-a-ract n. catarata
cat-as-tro-phe n. catastrofe
cat-a-stroph-ic adj. cata-
strofico
cat-a-ton-ic adj. catatonico
catch v. prender; coger
catch-er n. receptor
catch-ing adj. contagioso
catch-y adj. capcioso
cat-e-chism n. catecismo
cat-e-gor-ic adj. categorico
cat-e-gor-i-cal-ly adv. cate-
goricamente
cat-e-go-rize v. clasificar
cat-e-go-ry n. categoria
cat-er-pil-lar n. oruga
cat-er-waul v. chillar
ca-thar-sis n. catarsis
ca-the-dral n. catedral
cath-ode n. catodo
cath-o-lic adj. catolico
ca-thol-i-cism n. catolicismo
cat-nip n. nebeda
cat-tail n. espadaña
cat-tle n. ganado
cat-tle-man n. ganadero
cau-li-flow-er n. coliflor
cau-sa-tion n. causalidad
caus-a-tive adj. causativo
cause n. razon; causa
cause-way n. elevada
caus-tic adj. caustico
cau-ter-ize v. cauterizar
cau-tion v. amonestar
cau-tion-ar-y adj. preventivo
cau-tious adj. cauteloso
cav-al-ry n. caballeria
cave n. cueva
cav-ern n. caverna
cav-ern-ous adj. cavernoso

cav-i-ty n. cavidad
ca-vort v. cabriolar
cay n. cayo
cesse v. suspender
cease-less adj. continuo
ce-dar n. cedro
cede v. ceder
ceil-ing n. techo
cel-e-brant n. celebrante
cel-e-brate v. celebrar
cel-e-brat-ed adj. celebre
cel-e-bra-tion n. celebración
ce-leb-ri-ty n. celebridad
cel-er-y n. apio
ce-les-tial adj. celestial
cel-i-ba-cy n. celibato
cel-i-bate adj. celibe
cell n. celda
cel-lar n. sotano
cel-lo-phane n. celofan
cel-lu-lar adj. celular
cel-lu-loid n. celuloide
cel-lu-lose n. celulosa
ce-ment n. cemento
cem-e-ter-y n. cementerio
cen-ser n. insensario
cen-sor n. censor
cen-so-ri-ous adj. cen-
surador
cen-sor-ship n. censura
cen-sure v. censurar
cen-sus n. censo
cent n. centavo
cen-taur n. centauro
cen-ten-ni-al adj. centenario
cen-ter n. centro
cen-ti-grade adj. centigrado
cen-ti-gram n. centiframo
cen-ti-li-ter n. centilitro
cen-ti-me-ter n. centimetro
cen-tral adj. central
cen-tral-ize v. centralizar(se)
cen-tric adj. centrico
cen-trif-u-gal adj. centrifugo
cen-tu-ry n. siglo
ce-phal-ic adj. cefalico
ce-ram-ic adj. ceramico
ce-re-al n. cereal
cer-e-bral adj. cerebral
cer-e-brum n. cerebro
cer-e-mo-ni-al adj. cere-
monial
cer-e-mo-ni-ous adj. cere-

monioso

cer-e-mo-ny n. ceremonia
cer-tain adj. seguro; cierto
cer-tain-ly adv. ciertamente
cer-tain-ty n. certeza
cer-ti-fi-a-ble adj. certificable
cer-tif-i-cate n. certificado
cer-ti-fi-ca-tion n. certificación
cer-ti-fied adj. certificado
cer-ti-fy v. certificar
cer-ti-tude n. certidumbre
cer-vix n. cerviz
ces-sa-tion n. cesación
ces-sion n. cesion
chafe v. frotar; rozar
cha-grin v. desilusionar
chain n. cadena
chair n. silla
chair-man n. presidente
chair-man-ship n. presidencia
chair-wo-man n. presidenta
cha-let n. chalet
chal-ice n. caliz
chalk n. tiza
chalk-board n. pizarra
chal-lenge v. desafiar
chal-leng-er n. desafiador
cham-ber-lain n. chambelan
cha-me-leon n. camaleon
champ n. campeon
cham-pagne n. champana
cham-pi-on n. campeon
cham-pi-on-ship n. campeonato
chance n. oportunidad; casualidad
chan-cel-ler-y n. cancilleria
chan-cel-lor n. canciller
change v. transformar; cambiar
change-a-ble adj. cambiable
change-o-ver n. cambio
chang-er n. cambiador
chan-nel n. canal
chant n. canto
cha-os n. caos
cha-ot-ic adj. caotico
chap-el n. capilla
chap-er-one n. carabina
chap-lain n. capellan
chap-ter n. capitulo

char-ac-ter n. caracter
char-ac-ter-is-tic n. caracteristica
char-ac-ter-ize v. caracterizar
char-coal n. carboncillo
charge v. pedir; cargar
cha-ris-ma n. carisma
char-i-ta-ble adj. caritativo
char-i-ty n. caridad
charm n. encanto
charm-er n. encantador
charm-ing adj. encantador
chart v. trazar
char-ter n. carta
chase v. perseguir
chaste adj. casto
chas-ten v. castigar
chas-tise v. castigar
chas-ti-ty n. castidad
chat v. charlar
chat-ter v. charlar
chau-vin-ist n. chauvinista
chau-vin-is-tic adj. chauvinista
cheap adj. barato
cheap-en v. degradar(se)
cheap-ly adv. barato
cheap-ness n. tacaneria
cheat v. engañar
cheat-er n. tramposo
cheat-ing adj. tramposo
check n. cheque; parada; cuenta
check-book n. chequera
check-ered adj. a cuadros
cheek n. mejilla
cheep adj. piada
cheer v. alegrar; alentar
cheer-ful adj. alegre
cheer-i-ly adv. alegremente
cheer-less adj. triste
cheese n. queso
cheese-cake n. quesadilla
chef n. cocinero
chem-i-cal n. quimico
chem-ist n. quimico
chem-is-try n. quimica
che-mo-ther-a-py n. quimioterapia
cher-ish v. abrigar; querer
cher-ry n. cerezo
cher-ub n. querubin

che-ru-bic *adj.* querubico
chess *n.* ajedrez
chest *n.* pecho
chest-nut *n.* castaña
chew *v.* masticar
chew-ing *n.* masticación
chick-en *n.* pollo
chick-pea *n.* garbanzo
chief *n.* jefe
chif-fon *n.* chifon
child *n.* hijo; niño
child-birth *m.* parto
child-ish *adj.* aninado
child-like *adj.* infantil
chil-i *n.* chile
chill *n.* frio
chill-ing *adj.* frio
chime *n.* carillon
chim-ney *n.* chimenea
chim-pan-zee *n.* chimpance
chin *n.* barba
chi-na *n.* china
chip *n.* astilla; *v.* astillar
chip-per *adj.* jovial
chi-ro-prac-tor *n.* quiropractico
chirp *v.* gorjear
chis-el *n.* cincel
chis-el-er *n.* cincelador
chiv-al-rous *adj.* caballeresco
chiv-al-ry *n.* caballerosidad
chive *n.* cebollino
chlo-ride *n.* cloruro
chlo-rine *n.* cloro
chlo-ro-phyll *n.* clorofila
choc-o-late *n.* chocolate
choice *adj.* selecto; *n.* preferencia
choir *n.* coro
choke *v.* ahogar; atorar; estrangular
chol-er-a *n.* colera
chol-er-ic *adj.* colerico
cho-les-ter-ol *n.* colesterol
chomp *v.* ronzar
choose *v.* escoger
choos-ing *n.* selección
chop *v.* cortar
cho-ral *n.* coral
cho-re-og-ra-pher *n.* coreografo
cho-re-og-ra-phy *n.* coreografia

cho-sen *adj.* escogido
chow *n.* comida
Christ *n.* Cristo
chris-ten *v.* bautizar
chris-ten-ing *n.* bautismo
Chris-tian *n.* cristiano
Chris-ti-an-i-ty *n.* cristianismo
Christ-mas *n.* Navidad
chro-mat-ic *adj.* cromatico
chrome *m.* cromo
chro-mi-um *n.* cromo
chro-mo-some *n.* cromosoma
chron-ic *adj.* cronico
chron-i-cle *n.* cronica
chron-o-log-ic *adj.* cronologico
chro-nol-o-gy *n.* cronologia
chrys-a-lis *n.* crisalida
chry-san-the-mum *n.* crisantemo
chum *n.* compañero
chunk *n.* trozo
church *n.* iglesia
church-man *n.* clerigo
churn *n.* mantequera
chute *n.* conducto; rampa
ci-ca-da *n.* cigarra
ci-der *n.* sidra
ci-gar *n.* puro
cig-a-rette *n.* cigarrillo
cinch *n.* cincha
cin-der *n.* carbonilla
cin-e-ma *n.* cine
cin-e-mat-ic *adj.* filmico
cin-e-ma-tog-ra-phy *n.* cinematografia
cin-na-mon *n.* canela
ci-pher *v.* cifrar
cir-cle *n.* ciclo
cir-cuit *n.* circuito
cir-cu-lar *adj.* circular
cir-cu-late *v.* circular
cir-cu-lat-ing *adj.* circulante
cir-cu-la-tion *n.* circulación
cir-cum-cise *v.* circuncidar
cir-cum-cised *adj.* circunciso
cir-cum-ci-sion *n.* circuncision
cir-cum-fer-ence *n.* circunferencia

cir-cum-nav-i-gate v. circunnavegar
cir-cum-scribe v. circunscribir
cir-cum-spect adj. circunspecto
cir-cum-stance n. circunstancia
cir-cum-stan-tial adj. circunstancial
cir-cus n. circo
cir-rho-sis n. cirrosis
cir-rus n. cirro
cis-tern n. cisterna
cit-a-del n. ciudadela
ci-ta-tion n. citación
cite v. citar
cit-i-zen n. ciudadano
cit-i-zen-ship n. ciudadania
cit-rus adj. citrico
cit-y n. ciudad
civ-et n. civeta
civ-ic adj. civico
civ-il adj. civil
ci-vil-ian n. civil
ci-vil-i-ty n. civilidad
civ-i-li-za-tion n. civilización
civ-i-lize v. civilizar
claim v. merecer; reclamar
clair-voy-ance n. clarividencia
clair-voy-ant adj. clarividente
clam n. almeja
clam-or n. clamor
clam-or-ous adj. clamoroso
clamp n. abrazadera
clan n. clan
clan-gor n. estruendo
clap v. aplaudir
clap-per n. badajo
clap-ping n. aplausos
clar-et n. clarete
clar-i-fi-ca-tion n. clarificación
clar-i-fy v. clarificar
clar-i-net n. clarinete
clar-i-on adj. sonoro
clar-i-ty n. claridad
clash v. entrechocarse
class n. clase
clas-sic adj. clasico
clas-si-cal adj. clasico
clas-si-cism n. clasicismo

clas-si-cist n. clasicista
clas-si-fi-ca-tion n. clasificación
clas-si-fied adj. clasificado
clas-si-fy v. clasificar
class-y adj. elegante
clause n. clausula
claus-tro-pho-bi-a n. claustrofobia
clav-i-chord n. clavicordio
clav-i-cle n. clavicula
claw n. garra
clay n. arcilla
clean v. limpiar
clean-cut adj. definido
clean-er n. limpiador
clean-ing n. limpieza
clean-li-ness n. limpieza
cleanse v. limpiar
cleans-er n. limpiador
clear adj. despejado; transparente
clear-cut adj. claro
clear-ing n. claro
clear-ly adv. claramente
cleav-age n. division
cleave v. adherir; partir
cleav-er n. cuchillo
clem-en-cy n. clemencia
cler-gy n. clero
cler-gy-man n. clerigo
cler-ic adj. clerigo
cler-i-cal adj. clerical
clerk n. oficinista
clev-er adj. listo
clev-er-ness n. inteligencia
cli-ent n. cliente
cli-mac-tic adj. culminante
cli-mate n. clima
cli-mat-ic adj. climatico
cli-max n. climax
climb v. trepar
climb-er n. alpinista
climb-ing adj. trepador
clin-ic n. clinica
clin-i-cal adj. clinico
cli-ni-cian n. clinico
clip v. cortar
cloak n. manto
clock n. reloj
clog n. atasco
clois-ter n. claustro
clone n. clon

close v. cerrar
closed adj. cerrado; vedado
close-down n. cierre
close-ly adv. atentamente; de cerca
close-ness n. proximidad
close-out n. liquidacion
clos-et n. armario
clos-ing n. cierre
clot n. coagulo
cloth n. tela
clothe v. arropar
clothes n. ropa
cloth-ing n. ropa
cloud n. nube
cloud-burst n. aguacero
cloud-y adj. nuboso
clout n. bofetada
clo-ver n. trebol
clown n. payaso
club n. palo; trebol
clue n. pista
clump n. grupo
clum-sy adj. pesado
coach n. vagon; coche
coach-man n. cochero
co-ag-u-late v. coagular(se)
co-ag-u-la-tion n. coagulacion
coal n. carbon
co-a-lesce v. unirse
co-a-li-tion n. coalición
coarse adj. tosco
coars-en v. vulgarizar
coarse-ness n. aspereza
coast n. costa
coast-al adj. costero
coast-er n. trineo
coat n. pelo
coat-ed adj. banado
coat-ing n. capa; bano
coat-tail n. faldon
coax v. engatusar
coax-ing n. engatusamiento
cob n. elote
co-balt n. cobalto
cob-bler n. zapatero
co-bra n. cobra
cob-web n. telarana
co-caine n. cocaina
coc-cyx n. coccix
cock n. gallo
cock-ade n. escarapela

cock-a-too n. cacatua
cock-i-ness n. presunción
cock-le n. berberecho
cock-pit n. cancha
cock-roach n. cucaracha
cock-tail n. coctel
co-coa n. cacao
co-coa-nut n. coco
co-coon n. capullo
code n. codigo
co-de-fend-ant n. coacusado
co-deine n. codeina
cod-fish n. bacalao
cod-i-fy v. codificar
co-di-rec-tion n. codireccion
co-ed adj. coeducacional
co-ed-u-ca-tion n. coeducación
co-ed-u-ca-tion-al adj. coeducacional
co-ef-fi-cient n. coeficiente
co-erce v. coercer
co-er-cion n. coercion
co-ex-ist v. coexistir
co-ex-is-tence n. coexistencia
co-ex-ten-sive adj. coextenso
cof-fee n. cafe
cof-fer n. cofre
cof-fin n. ataud
cog n. diente
cog-i-tate v. meditar
cog-nac n. conac
cog-ni-tion n. cognición
cog-ni-zance n. conocimiento
cog-ni-zant adj. enterado
co-hab-it v. cohabitar
co-here v. adherirse
co-her-ence n. coherencia
co-her-ent adj. coherente
co-he-sion n. cohesion
co-he-sive adj. cohesivo
co-hort n. compañero
coil n. rollo
coin v. acunar; n. moneda
co-in-cide v. coincidir
co-in-ci-dence n. coincidencia
co-in-ci-den-tal adj. coincidente

co-la *n.* cola
col-an-der *n.* colador
cold *n., adj.* frio
cold-blood-ed *adj.* impasible
cold-heart-ed *adj.* insensible
cold-ness *n.* frialdad
col-ic *n.* colico
col-i-se-um *n.* coliseo
co-li-tis *n.* colitis
col-lab-o-rate *v.* colaborar
col-lab-o-ra-tion *n.* colaboración
col-lab-o-ra-tion-ist *n.* colaboracionista
col-lab-o-ra-tive *adj.* cooperativo
col-lab-o-ra-tor *n.* colaborador
col-lage *n.* collage
col-laspe *v.* desplomarse; caerse
col-laps-i-ble *adj.* plegable
col-lar *n.* cuello
col-lar-bone *n.* clavicula
col-late *v.* colacionar
col-lat-er-al *adj.* colateral
col-league *n.* colega
col-lect *v.* recoger; reunir; coleccionar
col-lect-ed *adj.* sosegado
col-lec-tion *n.* coleccion
col-lec-tive *adj.* colectivo
col-lec-tiv-ist *n.* colectivista
col-lec-tiv-ize *v.* colectivizar
col-lec-tor *n.* colector
col-lege *n.* colegio
col-le-gian *n.* estudiante
col-le-giate *adj.* universitario
col-lide *v.* chocar
col-li-sion *n.* choque
col-loid *n.* coloide
col-lo-qui-al *adj.* familiar
col-lo-qui-um *n.* cologuio
col-lo-quy *n.* coloquio
col-lude *v.* confabularse
col-lu-sion *n.* confabulación
co-logne *n.* colonia
co-lon *n.* colon
colo-nel *n.* coronel
co-lo-ni-al *adj.* colonial
co-lo-ni-al-ist *n.* colonialista
col-o-nist *n.* colonizador
col-o-ni-za-tion *n.* colonización
col-o-nize *v.* colonizar
col-o-niz-er *n.* colonizador
col-on-nade *n.* columnata
col-o-ny *n.* colonia
col-or *v.* colorear; *n.* color
col-or-a-tion *n.* coloración
col-ored *adj.* coloreado
col-or-ful *adj.* pintoresco
col-or-ing *n.* coloración
col-or-less *adj.* incoloro
co-los-sal *adj.* colosal
co-los-sus *n.* coloso
co-los-to-my *n.* colostomia
col-umn *n.* columna
col-umn-ist *n.* columnista
co-ma *n.* coma
co-ma-tose *adj.* comatoso
comb *v.* peinar; *n.* peine
com-bat *v.* conbatir
com-bat-ant *n.* combatiente
com-bat-ive *adj.* combativo
com-bi-na-tion *n.* combinación
com-bine *v.* combinar
com-bo *n.* conjunto
com-bus-ti-ble *adj.* conbustible
com-bus-tion *n.* combustion
come *v.* llegar; venir
come-back *n.* replica
co-me-di-an *n.* comediante
co-me-di-enne *n.* comedianta
com-e-dy *n.* comedia
come-on *n.* incentivo
com-et *n.* cometa
com-fort *v.* consolar
com-fort-a-ble *adj.* confortable
com-fort-er *n.* consolador
com-ic *adj.* comico
com-i-cal *adj.* comico
com-ing *adj.* venidero
com-ma *n.* coma
com-mand *n.* mando; *v.* mandar
com-man-dant *n.* comandante
com-mand-er *n.* comandante
com-mand-ing *adj.* imponente

com-man-do *n.* comando

com-mem-o-rate *v.* conmemorar

com-mem-o-ra-tion *n.* conmemoración

com-mence *v.* comenzar

com-mence-ment *n.* comienzo

com-mend *v.* encomendar

com-men-da-tion *n.* recomendación

com-men-su-rate *adj.* proporcionado

com-ment *n.* observación

com-men-tar-y *n.* comentario

com-men-tate *v.* comentar

com-merce *n.* comercio

com-mer-cial *adj.* comercial

com-mer-cial-ism *n.* comercialismo

com-mer-cial-ize *v.* comercializar

com-mis-er-ate *v.* compadecerse

com-mis-sar *n.* comisario

com-mis-sar-y *n.* economato

com-mis-sion *v.* encargar; *n.* comision

com-mis-sion-er *n.* comisario

com-mit *v.* entregar

com-mit-ment *n.* compromiso

com-mit-tal *n.* obligación

com-mit-tee *n.* comite

com-mode *n.* comoda

com-mo-dore *n.* comodoro

com-mon *adj.* comun

com-mon-place *adj.* ordinario

com-mon-wealth *n.* comunidad

com-mo-tion *n.* tumulto

com-mu-nal *adj.* comunal

com-mune *v.* comulgar

com-mu-ni-ca-ble *adj.* comunicable

com-mu-ni-cate *v.* comunicar(se)

com-mu-ni-ca-tion *n.* comunicación

com-mu-ni-ca-tive *adj.* comunicativo

com-nu-ca-tor *n.* comunicante

com-mun-ion *n.* comunion

com-mu-nism *n.* comunismo

com-mun-ist *n.* comunista

com-mu-nis-tic *adj.* comunista

com-mu-ni-ty *n.* comunidad

com-mu-ta-tion *n.* conmutación

com-mu-ta-tive *adj.* conmutativo

com-mute *v.* conmutar

com-pact *adj.* compacto

com-pan-ion *n.* compañero

com-pan-ion-ship *n.* companerismo

com-pa-ny *n.* compañia

com-pa-ra-ble *adj.* comparable

com-par-a-tive *adj.* comparativo

com-pare *v.* comparar

com-par-i-son *n.* comparacion

com-part-ment *n.* compartimiento

com-pass *n.* compas

com-pas-sion *n.* compasión

com-pas-sion-ate *adj.* compasivo

com-pat-i-ble *adj.* compatible

com-pa-tri-ot *n.* compatriota

com-pel *v.* compeler

com-pel-ling *adj.* incontestable

com-pen-sate *v.* compensar

com-pen-sa-tion *n.* conpensación

com-pete *v.* competir

com-pe-tence *n.* competencia

com-pe-tent *adj.* competente

com-pe-ti-tion *n.* competencia

com-pet-i-tive *adj.* competitivo

com-pet-i-tor *n.* competidor

com-pi-la-tion *n.* com-

pilacion
com-plie v. compilar
com-plain v. quejarse
com-plain-ant n. demandante
com-plaint n. queja
com-plai-sant adj. complaciente
com-ple-ment n. complemento
com-ple-men-ta-ry adj. complementario
com-plete adj. completo
com-ple-tion n. terminación
com-plex adj. complejo
com-plex-ion n. caracter
com-plex-i-ty n. complejidad
com-pli-nance n. conformidad
com-pli-ant adj. obediente
com-pli-cate v. complicar
com-pli-cat-ed adj. complicado
com-pli-ca-tion n. complicación
com-plic-i-ty n. complicidad
com-pli-ment n. honor; elogio
com-pli-men-ta-ry adj. elogioso
com-ply v. obedecer
com-po-nent n. componente
com-port-ment n. comportamiento
com-pose v. redactar
com-posed adj. tranquilo
com-pos-er n. compositor
com-pos-ite adj. compuesto
com-po-si-tion n. composición
com-po-sure n. serenidad
com-pound adj. compuesto
com-pre-hend v. comprender
com-pre-hen-si-ble adj. comprensible
com-pre-hen-sion n. comprensión
com-pre-hen-sive adj. comprensivo; general
com-press n. compresa
com-pressed adj. comprimido

com-pres-sion n. compresión
com-prise v. constar de; comprender
com-pro-mise n. compromiso; v. componer
com-pro-mis-ing adj. comprometedor
com-pul-sion n. compulsión
com-pul-sive adj. obsesivo
com-pul-so-ry adj. compulsorio
com-pu-ta-tion n. calculo
com-pute v. computar
com-put-er n. computador
com-put-er-ize v. computarizae
com-rade n. camarada
con adv. contra
con-cave adj. concavo
con-ceal v. ocultar
con-ceal-ment n. encubrimiento
con-cede v. conceder
con-ceit-ed adj. vanidoso
con-ceiv-a-ble adj. concebible
con-ceive v. concebir
con-cen-trate v. concentrar(se)
con-cen-tra-tion n. concentración
con-cen-tric adj. concentrico
con-cept n. concepto
con-cep-tion n. concepción
con-cep-tu-al adj. conceptual
con-cern v. concernir
con-cerned adj. preocupado
con-cern-ing prep. acerca de
con-cert n. concierto
con-cet-ed adj. conjunto
con-cer-to n. concierto
con-ces-sion n. concesión
con-cil-i-ate v. conciliar
con-cil-i-a-tion n. conciliacion
con-cise adj. conciso
con-clude v. concluir
con-clu-sion n. conclusión
con-clu-sive adj. concluyente

con-coc-tion *n.* confección
con-cord *n.* concordia
con-crete *adj.* concreto
con-cur *v.* concurrir
con-cur-rence *n.* concurrencia
con-cur-rent *adj.* concurrente
con-cus-sion *n.* concusión
con-dem-na-ble *adj.* condenable
con-den-sa-tion *n.* condensación
con-dence *v.* condensar(se)
con-dens-er *n.* condensador
con-de-scend-ing *adj.* condescendiente
con-di-ment *n.* condimento
con-di-tion *v.* condicionar
con-done *v.* condonar
con-duc-tor *n.* cobrador
con-fed-er-a-cy *n.* confederación
con-fed-er-a-tion *n.* confederacion
con-fer *v.* oferenciar
con-fess *v.* confesar
con-fide *v.* confiar
con-fi-dence *n.* confianza
con-fi-den-tial *adj.* confidencial
con-firm *v.* confirmar
con-flict *v.* chocar
con-form-i-ty *n.* conformidad
con-fron-ta-tion *n.* confrontación
con-fuse *v.* confundir
con-fu-sion *n.* confusión
con-gest *v.* acumular
con-ges-tion *n.* congestión
con-glom-er-a-tion *n.* conglomeración
con-grat-u-la-tion *n.* felicitación
con-gre-gate *v.* congregar(se)
con-junc-tion *n.* conjunción
con-jure *v.* conjurar
con-nect *v.* conectar
con-no-ta-tion *n.* connotación
con-note *v.* connotar

con-sec-u-tive *adj.* consecutivo
con-serv-a-to-ry *n.* conservatorio
con-serve *v.* conservar
con-sid-er *v.* considerar
con-sid-er-a-tion *n.* consideración
con-sist *v.* consistir
con-sol-i-date *v.* consolidar
con-sol-i-da-tion *n.* consolidación
con-stan-cy *n.* constancia
con-stant *adj.* continuo
con-sti-tu-tion *n.* constitución
con-struc-tion *n.* construcción
con-sult *v.* consultar
con-sume *v.* consumir
con-sump-tion *n.* consunción
con-tain *v.* contener
con-tam-i-na-tion *n.* contaminación
con-tem-plate *v.* proyectar
con-tem-po-rar-y *n.* contemplación
con-tend *v.* afirmar; contender
con-ti-nen-tal *adj.* continental
con-tin-gen-cy *n.* contingencia
con-tin-ue *v.* seguir; continuar
con-trac-tion *n.* contracción
con-tra-dict *v.* contradecir
con-trast *v.* contrastar
con-tri-bu-tion *n.* contribucion
con-trol *v.* dirigir; controlar
con-va-lesce *v.* convalecer
con-ven-tion *n.* convención
con-verge *v.* convergir
con-ver-sa-tion *n.* conversacion
con-verse *v.* conversar
con-ver-sion *n.* conversión
con-vey *v.* llevar
con-vic-tion *n.* convicción
con-vince *v.* convencer
con-vul-sion *n.* convulsion

cook n. cocinero; v. cocinar
cook-ie n. galleta
cool adj. fresco
co-or-di-nate v. coordinar
co-or-di-na-tion n. coordinación
cop-per n. cobre
cop-y v. copiar
cor-dial-i-ty n. cordialidad
corn n. maiz
cor-po-ral adj. corporal
cor-po-ra-tion n. corporación
cor-pu-lent adj. gordo
cor-pus-cu-lar adj. corpuscular
cor-ral v. acorralar
cor-rect v. corregir
cor-rec-tion n. corrección
cor-re-spond v. escribir
cor-re-spond-ence n. correspondencia
cor-rode v. corroer
cor-ro-sion n. corrosion
cor-rup-tion n. corrupción
cos-met-ic n. cosmetico
cos-mic adj. cosmico
cost v. costar; n. precio
couch n. sofa
count n. cuenta; v. contar
coun-try n. campo; país
cou-ple n. pareja
cou-ra-geous adj. valiente
course n. plato; dirección
cous-in n. prima; primo
cov-er n. cubierta, v. cubrir
cow n. vaca
cow-boy n. vaquero
coy-o-te n. coyote
crab n. cangrejo
crack-er n. galleta
crash n. choque; estallido
crate n. cajon
cra-ter n. crater
crave v. ansiar
crav-ing n. anhelo
crawl v. gatear; arrastrarse
cray-on n. pastel
craze v. enloquecer
crazed adj. loco
cra-zy adj. loco
cream n. crema

cream-y adj. cremoso
crease v. doblar
cre-ate v. producir; crear
cre-a-tion n. creación
cre-a-tive adj. creador
cre-a-tiv-i-ty n. originalidad
cre-a-tor n. creador
crea-ture n. criatura
cre-dence n. credito
cre-den-tial n. credencial
cred-i-ble adj. creible
cred-it n. credito; reconocimiento
cred-it-a-ble adj. loable
cred-u-lous adj. credulo
creed n. credo
creep-y adj. espeluznante
cre-mate v. incinerar
cre-ma-tion n. incineración
crepe n. crespon
cres-cent n. medialuna
crest n. cresta
cre-tin n. cretiño
crew n. equipo
crib n. pesebre
crick-et n. grillo
crime n. crimen
crim-i-nal n., adj. criminal
crin-kle v. arrugar(se)
crip-ple v. mutilar
cri-sis n. crisis
crisp adj. crespo
crisp-y adj. crujiente
crit-ic n. critico
crit-i-cal adj. critico
crit-i-cism n. critica
crit-i-cize v. criticar
cri-tique n. critica
croc-o-dile n. cocodrilo
cro-cus n. azafran
crook n. angulo; baculo
crook-ed adj. corvo
crop n. fusta; cultivo
cross-beam n. traviesa
cross-bow n. ballesta
cross-cur-rent n. contracorriente
cross-ex-am-ine v. interrogar
cross-ing n. crucé
cross-word puz-zle n. crucigrama
crouch v. acuclillarse

cross v. cruzar, n. cruz
crow v. cacarear
crowd n. gentio; multitud
crowd-ed adj. concurrido
crown n. corona
crown-ing n. coronación
cru-ci-ble n. crisol
cru-ci-fix n. crucifijo
cru-ci-fix-ion n. crucifixión
cru-ci-fy v. crucificar
crude adj. tosco; ordinario; crudo
crude-ness n. tosquedad
cru-el adj. cruel
cru-el-ty n. crueldad
cruise v. navegar
crumb n. migaja
crum-ble v. desmigajar(se)
crum-ple v. estrujar(se)
crunch-y adj. crujiente
cru-sade n. cruzada
cru-sad-er n. cruzado
crush v. aplastar
crust n. costra; corteza
crus-ta-cean n. crustaceo
crust-y adj. costroso
cry v. llorar
crypt n. cripta
crys-tal n. cristal
crys-tal-line adj. cristaliño
crys-tal-lize v. cristalizar(se)
crys-tal-log-ra-phy n. cristalografia
cube n. cubo
cu-bic adj. cubico
cu-bi-cle n. compartimiento
cub-ist n. cubista
cu-cum-ber n. pepiño
cud-dle v. abrazar(se)
cue n. taco
cu-li-nar-y adj. culinario
cul-mi-nate v. culminar
cul-pa-ble adj. culpable
cul-prit n. culpable
cult n. culto
cul-ti-vate v. cultivar
cul-ti-va-tion n. cultivo
cul-ti-va-tor n. cultivador
cul-tur-al adj. cultural
cul-ture n. cultura
cul-tured adj. culto
cum-ber v. embarazar
cum-ber-some adj. em-

barazoso
cu-mu-late v. acumular
cu-mu-la-tive adj. acumulativo
cun-ning adj. habil; astuto
cup n. taza
cup-ful n. taza
cur-a-ble adj. curable
curb n. bordillo
curd n. cuajada
cure n. cura
cu-ri-os-i-ty n. curiosidad
cu-ri-ous adj. curioso
curl v. enrollar(se); rizar(se)
cur-ren-cy n. moneda
cur-rent n., adj. corriente
cur-rent-ly adj. actualmente
curse n. desgracia; maldición
curs-ed adj. maldito
cur-sor n. cursor
cur-tain n. telon
cur-va-ture n. curvatura
curve n. curva
curved adj. curvo
cus-to-di-an n. custodio
cus-to-dy n. custodia
cus-tom n. costumbre
cus-tom-ar-i-ly adv. acostumbrada
cut adj. cortado; n. cortadura; v. cortar
cu-ta-ne-ous adj. cutaneo
cute adj. mono
cu-ti-cle n. cuticula
cut-ler-y n. cubiertos
cy-a-nide n. cianuro
cy-cle n. ciclo
cy-clic adj. ciclico
cy-clist n. ciclista
cy-clone n. ciclón
cyl-in-der n. cilindro
cy-lin-dri-cal adj. cilindrico
cym-bal n. cimbalo
cyn-i-cal adj. cinico
cyn-i-cism n. cinismo
cy-press n. cipres
cyst n. quiste
cys-tic adj. enquistado
cys-ti-tis n. cistitis
cy-to-plasm n. citoplasma
czar n. zar
cza-ri-na n. zariña

dab v. tocar ligeramente
dab-ble v. salpicar
dad n. papa
daft adj. loco
dag-ger n. punal
dai-ly adj. diario
dain-ti-ness n. delicadeze
dain-ty adj. delicado
dair-y n. lecheria; queseria
dair-y-man n. lechero
da-is n. estrado
dale n. valle
dal-li-ance n. diversión
dal-ly v. perder tiempo; entretenerse
dam v. represar, n. presa
dam-age v. danar; perjudicar
damn v. condenar
dam-na-ble adj. detestable
damned adj. condenado
damp adj. humedo
damp-en v. mojar
dance n. baile, v. bailar
dan-cer n. bailador
dan-druff n. caspa
dan-ger n. peligro
dan-ger-ous adj. peligroso
dan-gle v. colgar
dank adj. liento
dap-pled adj. rodado
dare v. arriesgarse
dar-ing n. atrevimiento
dark n. oscuridad, adj. oscuro
dark-en v. oscurecer
dark-ness n. oscuridad
darl-ing n. querido
darn v. zurcir
dash v. precipitarse; romper
dash-board n. tablere de instrumentos
date n. cita; fecha
daub v. pintarrajar
daugh-ter n. hija
daugh-ter-in-law n. nuera
daunt-less adj. impavido
daw-dle v. perder el tiempo
dawn v. amanecer
day n. dia
day-break n. amanecer
day-dream n. ensueño
day-light n. luz del dia
day-time n. dia

daze v. aturdir
daz-zle v. deslumbrar
dea-con n. diacono
dea-con-ry n. diaconía
dead adj. muerto
dead-en v. amortiguar
dead-end n. calle sin salida
dead-ly adj. mortal
deaf adj. sordo
deaf-en v. ensordecer
deaf-ness n. sordera
deal n. cantidad; trato; reparto
deal-er n. tratante
dean n. decaño; dean
dear adj. querido; caro
dear-ness n. carestia
death n. muerte
death-less adj. inmortal
death-ly adj. mortal
de-ba-cle n. fracaso
de-bar v. prohibir
de-bate v. debatir
de-bauch v. corromper
de-bauch-er-y n. libertinaje
de-bil-i-tate v. debilitar
de-bil-i-ta-tion n. debilitación
de-bil-i-ty n. debilidad
deb-it n. debe
deb-o-nair adj. cortes; elegante
de-bris n. escombros
debt n. deuda
debt-or n. deudor
de-but, de-but n. presentación; estreno
deb-u-tant, deb-u-tante n. debutante
de-cade n. deceñio
dec-a-dence n. decadencía
dec-a-dent adj. decadente
de-can-ter n. garrafa
de-cay v. decaer; cariarse; deteriorar
de-cease v. morir
de-ceased adj. muerto
de-ceit n. engano
de-ceit-ful adj. enganoso
de-ceive v. enganar
De-cem-ber n. diciembre
de-cen-cy n. decencía
de-cent adj. decente

de-cep-tion *n.* fraude

de-cide *v.* decidir

de-cid-ed *adj.* decidido

de-cid-ed-ly *adv.* decididamente

dec-i-mal *n.* decimal

de-ci-pher *v.* descifrar

de-ci-sion *n.* decision; firmeze

de-ci-sive *adj.* decisivo

de-ci-sive-ly *adv.* con resolución

deck *v.* adornar

dec-la-ra-tion *n.* declaración

de-clare *v.* declarar

de-cline *v.* rehusar

de-com-pose *v.* descomponer(se)

de-com-po-si-tion *n.* descomposición

de-cor-ate *v.* adornar; condecorar

dec-o-ra-tion *n.* decoración; ornato

dec-o-ra-tor *n.* decorador

de-coy *n.* senuelo

de-crease *v.* disminuir(se)

de-creas-ing-ly *adv.* en disminucion

de-cree *n.* decreto

de-crep-it *adj.* decrepito

de-cry *v.* rebajar

de-duce *v.* deducir

de-duct *v.* restar

de-duc-tion *n.* descuento

deed *n.* hecho

deem *v.* juzgar

deep *adj.* profundo

deep-en *v.* intensificar

de-face *v.* desfigurar

def-a-ma-tion *n.* difamación

de-fame *v.* difamar

de-fault *n.* a falta de

de-feat *n.* derrota *v.* vencer; frustrar

de-fect *n.* defecto

de-fec-tion *n.* defección

de-fec-tive *adj.* defectuoso

de-fend *v.* defender

de-fend-ant *n.* demandado

de-fense, de-fence *n.* defensa

de-fen-sive *adj.* defensivo

de-fer *v.* diferir; aplazar

def-er-ence *n.* deferencia

de-fer-ment *n.* apazamiento

de-fi-ance *n.* desafio

de-fi-ant *adj.* provocativo

de-fi-cien-cy *n.* deficiencia

de-fi-cient *adj.* insuficiente

def-i-cit *n.* deficit

de-file *v.* manchar

de-fine *v.* definir

def-i-nite *adj.* concreto; definido

de-fi-ni-tion *n.* definición

de-fin-i-tive *adj.* definitivo

de-flate *v.* desinflar

de-fla-tion *n.* desinflación

de-flect *v.* desviar

de-form *v.* desfigurar; deformar

de-form-i-ty *n.* deformidad

de-fraud *v.* defraudar; estafar

de-fray *v.* pagar

deft *adj.* diestro

deft-ness *n.* habilidad

de-funct *adj.* difunto

de-fy *v.* desafiar; contravenir

de-gen-er-ate *v.* degenerar

deg-ra-da-tion *n.* degradación

de-grade *v.* degradar

de-gree *n.* rango

de-hy-drate *v.* deshidratar

de-hy-dra-tion *n.* deshidratación

de-i-fy *v.* deificar

deign *v.* dignarse

de-i-ty *n.* deidad

de-ject-ed *adj.* abatido

de-jec-tion *n.* melancolia; abatimiento

de-lay *v.* aplazar; demorar

de-lec-ta-ble *adj.* deleitable

de-le-gate *v.* delegar

de-le-ga-tion *n.* diputación

de-lete *v.* tachar

de-le-tion *n.* supresión; borradura

de-lib-er-ate *v.* deliberar

del-i-ca-cy *n.* delicadeze

del-i-cate *adj.* delicado; fino

de-li-cious *adj.* delicioso

de-light *v.* deleitar

de-light-ful *adj.* encantador

de-lin-e-ate *v.* delinear

de-lin-e-a-tion *n.* bosquejo

de-lin-quen-cy *n.* delincuencia

de-lin-quent *adj., n.* delincuente

de-lir-i-ous *adj.* delirante

de-lir-i-um *n.* delirio

de-liv-er *v.* entregar

de-liv-er-y *n.* entrega

del-ta *n.* delta

de-lude *v.* inganar

del-uge *n.* diluvio

de-lu-sion *n.* engano; ilusión

de-luxe *adj.* de lujo

delve *v.* cavar

de-mand *v.* demandar; exigir

de-moc-ra-cy *n.* democracia

dem-o-crat *n.* democrata

dem-o-crat-ic *adj.* democratico

dem-on-strate *v.* demostrar

dem-on-stra-tion *n.* demostración

de-mor-al-ize *v.* desmoralizar

dn *n.* estudio

de-nom-i-na-tion *n.* denominación

de-nom-i-na-tor *n.* denominador

de-note *v.* denotar

de-nounce *v.* denunciar

dense *adj.* denso

den-si-ty *n.* densidad

den-tist *n.* dentista

de-nun-ci-ate *v.* denunciar

de-nun-ci-a-tion *n.* denuncia

de-par-ture *n.* salida

de-pend-en-cy *n.* dependencia

de-port *v.* deportar

de-por-ta-tion *n.* deportación

de-prave *v.* depravar

de-praved *adj.* depravado

de-pres-sion *n.* desaliento

depth *n.* fondo

de-ride *v.* mofar

de-ri-sion *n.* irrision

der-i-va-tion *n.* derivación

de-rive *v.* derivar(se)

der-rick *n.* grua

de-scend *v.* bajar; descender

de-scend-ant *n.* descendiente

de-scribe *v.* describir

de-scrip-tion *n.* descripción

de-scrip-tive *adj.* descriptivo

des-ert *n.* desierto

de-sert-er *n.* desertor

de-serve *v.* merecer

de-sign *v.* idear; disenar

des-ig-nate *v.* senalar; nombrar

des-ig-na-tion *n.* nombramiento

de-sing-er *n.* disenador; dibujante

de-sire *v.* desear

de-sist *v.* desistir

desk *n.* pupitre

des-o-la-tion *n.* desolación

de-spair *v.* desesperar

des-per-ate *adj.* desesperado; arriesgado

des-per-a-tion *n.* desesperación

des-pi-ca-ble *adj.* despreciable

de-spise *v.* despreciar

de-spite *prep.* a pesar de

des-sert *n.* postre

de-stroy *v.* destruir

de-struct-i-ble *adj.* destructible

de-struc-tion *n.* destrucción

de-tain *v.* retener

de-ter *v.* disuadir

de-ter-mi-na-tion *n.* determinación

de-ter-mine *v.* resolver; determinar

de-test-a-ble *adj.* detestable

de-val-u-a-tion *n.* devaluación

dev-as-tate *v.* devastar

dev-as-ta-tion *n.* devastación

de-vel-op *v.* desenvolver

de-vice *n.* ingenio; estratagema

dev-il *n.* diablo

de-vi-ous *adj.* tortuoso

de-vise *v.* inventar
de-void *adj.* desprovisto
de-vote *v.* dedicar
dev-o-tee *n.* devoto
dev-o-tion *n.* devoción; lealtad
de-vour *v.* devorar
di-a-be-tes *n.* diabetes
di-a-bet-ic *adj.* diabetico
di-ag-nose *v.* diagnosticar
di-a-bol-ic *adj.* diabolico
di-a-dem *n.* diadema
di-ag-nose *v.* diagnosticar
di-ag-no-sis *n.* diagnostico
di-ag-o-na. *adj., n.* diagonal
di-a-gram *n.* diagrama
di-al *v.* marcar
di-a-lect *n.* dialecto
di-a-logue *n.* dialogo
di-am-e-ter *n.* diametro
di-a-met-ric *adj.* diametral
dia-mond *n.* diamante; oros
dia-per *n.* panal
di-a-phragm *n.* diafragma
di-ar-rhe-a *n.* diarrea
di-a-ry *n.* diario
dice *n.* dados
dick-er *v.* regatear
dic-tate *v.* mandar; dictar
dic-ta-tion *n.* dictado
dic-ta-tor *n.* dictador
dic-tion-ar-y *n.* diccionaio
die *v.* morir
dif-fer-ence *n.* diferencia
dif-fer-ent *adj.* diferente
dif-fi-cult *adj.* dificil
dif-fi-cul-ty *n.* dificultad
dif-fu-sion *n.* difusion
dig *n.* excavacion; *v.* extraer
di-ges-tion *n.* digestion
dig-it *n.* dedo
dig-ni-fy *v.* dignificar
di-lem-ma *n.* dilema
dil-i-gence *n.* diligencia
dil-i-gent *adj.* diligente
di-lute *v.* diluir
di-lu-tion *n.* dilución
dim *adj.* oscuro
di-min-ish *v.* disminuir(se)
dine *v.* cenar
din-ner *n.* cena
di-plo-ma-cy *n.* diplomacia
dip-lo-mat *n.* diplomatico

dip-lo-mat-ic *adj.* diplomatico
di-rect *v.* dirigir, *adj.* directo
di-rec-tion *n.* dirección
di-rec-tor *n.* director
dis-a-ble *v.* inutilizar
dis-ap-pear *v.* desaparecer
dis-ap-pear-ance *n.* desaparición
dis-as-trous *adj.* desastroso
dis-a-vow *v.* desconocer
dis-charge *v.* despedir
dis-ci-pli-nar-y *adj.* disciplinario
dis-ci-pline *v.* disciplinar, *n.* castigo
dis-con-nect *v.* desconectar
dis-con-tin-u-ous *adj.* discontinuo
dis-cov-er *v.* descubrir
dis-crep-an-cy *n.* discrepancia
dis-cus-sion *n.* discusión
dis-ease *n.* enfermedad
dis-guise *n.* disfraz, *v.* disfrazar
dish *n.* plato
dis-hon-or *v.* deshonrar
dis-hon-or-a-ble *adj.* deshonroso
dis-in-fect-ant *n.* desinfectante
dis-in-ter-est *n.* desinteres
disk *n.* disco
dis-lo-cate *v.* dislocar
dis-lo-ca-tion *n.* dislocación
dis-o-bey *v.* desobedecer
dis-or-der *n.* desorden
dis-pense *v.* dispensar
dis-play *n.* demostrar
dis-pute *n.* disputa, *v.* disputar
dis-qual-i-fy *v.* descalificar
dis-solve *v.* disolver(se)
dis-suade *v.* disuadir
dis-sua-sion *n.* disuasion
dis-tance *n.* distancia
dis-tant *adj.* distante
dis-till *v.* destilar
dis-till-er-y-n *n.* destileria
dis-tinc-tion *n.* distinción
dis-tin-guish *v.* distinguir
dis-tract *v.* distraer

dis-trac-tion n. distracción
dis-tri-bu-tion n. distribución
dis-turb v. perturbar
dis-turb-ance n. disturbio
di-verge v. divergir
di-ver-gence n. divergencia
di-ver-sion n. diversion
di-ver-si-ty n. diversidad
di-vert v. divertir
di-vide v. dividir(se)
di-vin-i-ty n. divinidad
diz-zy adj. mareado
do v. cumplir; hacer
doc-tor n. medico
doc-u-ment n. documentar
dog n. perro
dog-mat-ic adj. dogmatico
doll n. muneca
dol-lar n. dolar
do-mes-tic adj. domestico
do-mes-ti-cate v. domesticar
dom-i-nant v. dominar
dom-i-na-tion n. dominación
dom-i-neer v. tiranizar
dom-i-neer-ing a. dominante
do-min-ion n. dominio
don v. ponerse
do-nate v. donar
done adj. hecho
do-nor n. donante
doom n. juicio; suerte
door n. puerta
dope n. narcotico
dor-mi-to-ry n. dormitorio
dor-sal adj. dorsal
dos-age n. dosificación
dose n. dosis
dot n. punto
dot-age n. chochez
dou-ble v. doblar(se)
doubt n. duda, v. dudar
dough n. maxa
dough-nut n. buñuelo
dour adj. austero
douse v. mojar; zambullir
dow-a-ger n. vuida de un titulado
dow-dy adj. desalinado; poso elegante
down prep., adv. abajo
down-cast adj. abatido
down-fall n. caida
down-heart-ed adj. desa-

nimado
down-ward adv. hacia abajo
doze v. dormitar
doz-en n. doceña
drab adj. monotono
draft n. destacamento; giro; borrador
drag v. arrastar
drag-on n. dragon
drain v. agotar; desaguar
drain-age n. desague; drenaje
dra-ma n. drama
dra-mat-ic adj. dramatico
dram-a-tist n. dramaturgo
dram-a-tize v. dramatizar
drape v. poner colgaduras
dra-per-y n. paneria
dras-tic a. drastico; energico
draw v. sacar; dibujar; arrastrar
draw-back n. desventaja
draw-bridge n. puente levadizo
draw-er n. cajon
dread v. temer
dread-ful adj. terrible
dream v. sonar, n. sueño
dream-er n. sonador
dredge v. dragar
dreg n. heces
drench v. empapar
dress n. vestido, v. vestir(se)
dress-er n. aparador
drib-ble v. caer gota a gota
drift n. impulso de la corriente; monton
drift-wood n. madera lievada por el agua
drill v. taladrar
drink n. bebida, v. beber
drip v. gotear
drive v. manejar; empujar; conducir
driz-zle v. llovliznar
droll adj. gracioso
drone n. zangano
drool v. babear
droop v. inclinar
drop n. gota; declive
drop-sy n. hidropesia
dross n. escoria
drought n. sequia

drown v. ahogar; engar

drowse v. adormecer(se)

drow-sy adj. soñoliento

drudg-er-y n. faena penosa

drug n. droga

drug-gist n. farmaceutico; boticario

drum n. tambor

drum-stick n. baqueta

drunk adj. borracho

drunk-ard n. borracho

drunk-en adj. borracho

du-al-i-ty n. dualidad

dub v. armar caballero

du-bi-ous adj. dudoso

duch-ess n. duquesa

duck n. pato

duct n. conducto

dude n. petimetre

due adj. debido; oportuno

duel n. duelo

du-et n. duo

duke n. duque

dull adj. embotado; torpe

dumb adj. mudo

dum-found v. pasmar

dum-my n. maniqui

dump v. descargar

dump-ling n. bola de masa

dunce n. zopenco

dune n. duna

dung n. estiercol

dun-geon n. mazmorra

du-pli-cate adj. duplicado, v. duplicar

du-pli-ca-tion n. duplicación

du-ra-tion n. duración

dur-ing prep. durante

dusk n. crepusculo

dusk-y adj. oscuro

dust n. polvo

du-ti-ful adj. obediente

du-ty n. derechos

dwell v. habitar

dwell-ing n. morada

dwin-dle v. disminuir

dye n. tinte

dy-nam-ic adj. dinamico

y-na-mite n. dinamita

y-na-mo n. dinamo

dinamo

nas-ty n. dinastia

-en-ter-y n. disenteria

each adv. para cada uño

ea-ger adj. impaciente

ea-ger-ness n. ansia

ea-gle n. aguila

ea-glet n. aguilucho

ear n. oido; oreja

ear-drum n. timpaño del oido

earl n. conde

ear-li-ness n. precocidad

ear-ly adj. primitivo adv., adj. temprano

earn v. merecer

ear-nest a. fervoroso; serio

ear-nest-ly adv. con seriedad

earn-ings n. sueldo

ear-ring n. pendiente

ear-shot n. alcance del oido

earth n. mundo; tierra

earth-en-ware n. loza de barro

earth-ly adj. mundaño

earth-quake n. terremoto

earth-y a. terroso

ease v. facilitar, n. facilidad

ea=sel n. caballete

eas-i-ly adv. facilmente

eas-i-ness n. facilidad

east n. este

east-ern adj. del este

east-ward adv. hacia el este

eas-y adj. facil

eas-y-go-ing a. acomodadizo; de manga ancha

eat v. gastar; comer

eat-a-ble a. comestible

eaves n. alero

eaves-drop v. escuchar a escondidas; espiar

ebb v. menguar.; decaer

eb-on-y n. ebaño

ec-cen-tric adj. excentrico

ec-cen-tric-i-ty n. excentricidad

ec-cle-si-as-tic a., n. eclesiastico

ech-o n. eco

e-clipse v. eclipsar

e-clip-tic adj. ecliptico

ec-o-lo-gic a. ecologiso

e-col-o-gist n. ecologo

e-col-o-gy n. ecologia
e-co-nom-ic adj. economico
e-co-nom-ic-al a. economico
e-co-nom-ics n. economia
e-con-o-mist n. economista
e-con-o-mize v. economizar
e-con-o-my n. economia
ec-sta-sy n. extasis
ec-stat-ic a. extatico
ec-u-men-i-cal n. ecumenico
ec-ze-ma n. eczema; ec-cema
ed-dy n. remolino
e-den-tate a. desdentado
edge n. filo; agudeza; borde
ed-i-ble a. comestible
e-dict n. edicto
ed-i-fi-ca-tion n. edificación
de-i-fice n. edificio
ed-i-fy v. edificar
ed-it v. editar
e-di-tion n. edición
ed-i-tor n. editor
ed-i-to-ri-al a. editorial
ed-i-to-ri-al-ist n. editorialista
ed-u-cate v. educar
ed-u-ca-tion n. educación
eel n. anguila
ee-rie a. espantoso; fantastico
ef-face v. borrar
ef-fect v. efectuar, n. resultado
ef-fec-tive a. efectivo; eficaz
ef-fec-tu-al a. eficaz
ef-fem-i-nate a. afeminado
ef-fer-vesce v. estar en efervescencia
ef-fer-ves-cence n. efervescencia
ef-fer-ves-cent adj. efervescente
ef-fe-ca-cious a. eficaz
ef-fi-cien-cy n. eficiencia
ef-fi-cient adj. eficiente
ef-fi-gy n. efigie
ef-fort n. esfuerzo
ef-fort-less a. sin esfuerzo
ef-fuse v. derramar
ef-fu-sion n. efusion

ef-fu-sive a.j exspansivo; efusivo
egg n. huevo
e-go n. el yo
e-go-tist n. egotista
e-gress n. salida
eight adj. ocho
eight-een adj. dieciocho
eighth adj. octavo
eight-y adj. ochenta
ei-ther adv. tampoco; tambien, adj. cualquier
e-ject v. echar; expulsar
e-jec-tion n. expusion
eke v. aumentar
e-lab-o-rate v. elaborar
e-lab-ra-tion n. elaboración
e-lapse v. pasar
e-last-ic a. elastico
e-las-tic-i-ty n. elasticidad
e-late v. alegrar
e-la-tion n. regocijo
el-bow n. codo
eld-er a. mayor
el-der-ly a. de edad
eld-est a. el major
e-lect v. elegir
e-lec-tion n. elección
e-lec-tive adj. electivo
e-lec-tor n. elector
e-lec-tor-ate n. electorado
e-lec-tric a. electrico; vivo
e-lec-tri-cian n. electricista
e-lec-tric-i-ty n. electricidad
e-lec-tro-cute v. electrocutar
e-lec-trode n. electrodo
e-lec-tron n. electron
e-lec-tron-ic a. electronico
el-e-gance n. elegancia
el-e-gant adj. elegante
el-e-gize v. hacer una elegia
el-e-gy n. elegia
el-e-ment n. elemento
el-e-men-ta-ry adj. elemental
el-e-phant n. elefante
el-e-vate v. elevar
el-e-va-tion n. elevación
el-e-va-tor n. ascensor
e-lev-en adj. once
e-lev-enth a.,n. undecimo

elf-in *a.* e elfo

e-lic-it *v.* sacar

el-i-gi-bil-i-ty *n.* elegibilidad

el-i-gi-ble *a.* elegible; deseable

e-lim-i-nate *v.* eliminar

e-lim-i-na-tion *n.* eliminación

e-lite *n.* lo mejor

e-lix-ir *n.* elixir

elk *n.* alce

el-lipse *n.* elipse

el-lip-ti-cal *a.* eliptico

elm *n.* olmo

e-lo-cu-tion *n.* elocución

e-lon-gate *v.* alargar

e-lope *v.* fugarse con su amante para casarse

e-lope-ment *n.* fuga

e-lo-quence *n.* elocuencia

e-lo-quent *a.* elocuente

else *a.* otro; mas

e-lu-ci-date *v.* elucidar

e-lude *v.* eludir; escapar de

e-lu-sive *a.* esquivo

e-ma-ci-ate *v.* enflaquecer(se)

e-man-ci-pate *v.* emancipar

e-man-ci-pa-tion *n.* emancipación

em-balm *v.* embalsamar

em-bar-go *n.* embargo

em-bark *v.* embarcar(se)

em-bar-rass *v.* desconcertar

em-bas-sy *n.* embajada

em-ber *n.* ascua

em-bez-zle *v.* desfalcar

em-blem *n.* emblema

em-boss *v.* realzar

em-brace *v.* abrazar; aceptar; abarcar

em-broi-der *v.* recamar

em-bry-o *n.* embrion

em-er-ald *n.* esmeralda

e-merge *v.* salir

e-mer-gence *n.* salida

e-mer-gen-cy *n.* crisis

em-er-y *n.* esmeril

em-i-grant *n.* emigrante

em-i-grate *v.* emigrar

em-i-gra-tion *n.* emigración

em-i-nence *n.* eminencia

em-i-nent *adj.* eminente

em-is-sar-y *n.* emisario

e-mis-sion *n.* emision

e-mit *v.* emitir

e-mo-tion *n.* emoción

em-per-or *n.* emperador

em-pha-sis *n.* enfasis

em-pha-size *v.* acentuar; recalcar

em-phat-ic *a.* enfatico

em-pire *n.* imperio

em-ploy *v.* emplear

em-ploy-ee *n.* empleado

em-ploy-er *n.* amo; patron

em-ploy-ment *n.* empleo; colocacion

em-pow-er *v.* autorizar

em-press *n.* emperatriz

emp-ti-ness *n.* vacuidad; vacio

emp-ty *v.* vaciar, *adj.* desocupado

em-u-late *v.* emular

e-mul-sion *n.* emulsion

e-mul-sive *a.* emulsivo

en-a-ble *v.* hacer que; permitir

en-act *v.* decretar; hacer el papel de

e-nam-el *n.* esmalte

en-am-or *v.* enamorar

en-case *v.* encerrar; encajar

en-chant *v.* encantar

en-chant-ing *adj.* encantador

en-chant-ment *n.* encanto

en-cir-cle *v.* cenir; rodear

en-close *v.* cercar; encerrar; incluir

en-clo-sure *n.* cercamiento; carta adjunta

en-com-pass *v.* cercar; abarcar

en-core *n.* repeticion

en-coun-ter *n.* encuentro

en-cour-age *v.* animar; fomentar

en-croach *v.* usurpar; pasar los limites

en-cum-ber *v.* estorbor; gravar

en-cy-clo-pe-dia *n.* enciclopedia

end *n.* final; fin

en-dan-ger v. poner en peligro
en-dear v. hacer querer
en-deav-or n. esfuerzo
end-ing n. fin
en-dorse v. endosar
en-dorse-ment n. endoso
en-dow v. dotar
en-dur-ance n. resistencia
en-dure v. durar
en-e-my n. enemigo
en-er-get-ic adj. energico
en-er-gy n. energia
en-force v. hacer cumplir; exigir
en-gage v. engranar; apalabrar
en-gage-ment n. obligación
en-gine n. motor; locomotora
en-gi-neer n. ingeniero
en-gi-neer-ing n. ingenieria
Eng-lish n. ingles
en-grave v. grabar
en-gross v. absorber; monopolizar
en-hance v. aumentar
e-nig-ma n. enigma
en-join v. imponer
en-joy v. disfrutar
en-joy-ment n. disfrute
en-large v. extender(se)
en-large-ment n. aumento; ampliación
en-light-en v. iluminar; instruir
en-list v. alistar(se)
en-liv-en v. avivar
en-mi-ty n. enemistad
e-nor-mous adj. enorme
e-nough adv. bastante
en-slave v. entrar
en-ter-tain-ment n. espectaculo
en-thu-si-asm n. entusiasmo
en-thu-si-ast n. entusiasta
en-tire adj. entero
en-tire-ly adv. totalmente
en-trance n. entrada
en-trust v. entregar
en-try n. partida; entrada
en-vel-op v. envolver
en-zyme n. enzima

ep-i-dem-ic n. epidemia
ep-i-sode n. episodio
ep-och n. epoca
e-qua-bil-i-ty n. uniformidad
e-qua-ble a. uniforme
e-qual v. igualar, n. igual
e-qual-i-ty adj. igualdad
e-qual-ly adv. igualmente
e-qual-ize v. igualar
e-qual-ly adv. igualmente
e-qua-nim-i-ty n. ecuanimidad
e-quate v. comparar
e-qua-tion n. ecuación
e-qua-tor n. ecuador
e-ques-tri-enne n. jineta
e-qui-lib-ri-um n. equilibrio
e-quip v. proveer; equipar
e-quip-ment n. equipo
eq-ui-ta-ble a. equitat
e-qui-ty n. equidad
e-quiv-a-lent adj. equivalente
e-ra n. era
e-rad-i-cate v. desarraigar
e-rase v. borrar
e-ras-er n. borrador
ere conj. antes de que
e-rect v. erigir
e-rec-tion n. erección
er-mine n. armiño
e-rode v. corroer
e-ro-sion n. erosion
e-rot-ic a. erotico
err v. vagar; errar
er-rand n. recado
er-rant a. errante
er-ror n. error
er-u-dite a. erudito
er-u-di-tion n. erudicion
e-rupt v. estar en erupción
e-rup-tion n. erupción
es-ca-la-tor n. escalera movil
es-ca-pade n. aventura
es-cape v. escapar; huir
es-chew v. evitar
es-cort v. acompanar, n. acompanante
e-soph-a-gus, oe-soph-a-gus n. esofago
es-o-ter-ic a. esoterico
es-pe-cial adj. especial

es-pe-cial-ly *adv.* especialmente

es-pi-o-nage *n.* espionaje

es-pouse *v.* adherirse a; casarse

es-py *v.* divisar; percibir

es-say *n.* ensayo

es-sence *n.* esencia; perfume

es-sen-tial *adj.* esencial

es-tab-lish *v.* establecer; probar; fundar

es-tab-lish-ment *n.* establecimiento

es-tate *n.* finca; propiedad

es-teem *v.* estimar

es-thet-ic *a.* estetico

es-ti-ma-ble *a.* estimable

es-ti-mate *v.* calcular; estimar

es-ti-ma-tion *n.* juicio; aprecio

es-thet-ic *adj.* estetico

es-ti-mate *v.* estimar

es-ti-ma-tion *n.* juicio; aprecio

as-trange *v.* apartar

es-tu-ar-y *n.* estuario

et cet-er-a *n.* etcetera

etch *v.* grabar al agua fuerte

etch-ing *n.* aguafuerte

e-ter-nal *adj.* eterno

e-ter-nal-ly *adv.* eternamente

e-ter-ni-ty *n.* eternidad

e-ther *n.* eter

e-the-re-al *a.* etereo

eth-i-cal *adj.* etico

eth-ics *n.* etica

eth-nic *a.* etnico

eth-nol-o-gy *n.* etnologia

et-i-quette *n.* etiqueta

e-tude *n.* estudio

eu-lo-gize *v.* elogiar

eu-lo-gy *n.* elogio

eu-pho-ri-a *n.* euforia

eu-phor-ic *adj.* euforico

e-vac-u-ate *v.* evacuar

e-vac-u-a-tion *n.* evacuación

e-vade *v.* evadir

e-val-u-ate *v.* evaluar

e-val-u-a-tion *n.* evaluación

e-van-gel-i-cal *a.* evangelico

e-van-ge-list *n.* evangelista

e-vap-o-rate *v.* evaporar(se)

e-vap-o-ra-tion *n.* evaporación

e-va-sion *n.* evasion

e-va-sive *a.* evasivo

eve *n.* vispera

e-ven *adj.* igualar

eve-ning *n.* tarde

e-vent *n.* suceso

e-vent-ful *a.* memorable

e-ven-tu-al-i-ty *n.* eventualidad

ev-er *adv.* siempre; junca; jamas

eve-ry *adj.* todo

e-vict *v.* expulsar

e-vic-tion *n.* desahucio

ev-i-dence *n.* evidencia

ev-i-dent *a.* evidente

e-vil *n.* mal

e-vil-do-er *n.* malhechor

e-voke *v.* evocar

ev-o-lu-tion *n.* desarrollo; evolución

e-volve *v.* desarrollar

ewe *n.* oveja

ew-er *n.* aguamanil

ex-act *adj.* exacto

ex-act-ing *a.* exigente

ex-ag-ger-ate *v.* exagerar

ex-ag-ger-a-tion *n.* exageración

ex-alt *v.* exaltar; honrar

ex-al-ta-tion *n.* exaltacion

ex-am-in-a-tion *n.* examen

ex-am-ine *v.* examinar

ex-am-in-er *n.* examinador

ex-am-ple *n.* ejemplo

ex-as-per-ate *v.* exasperar

ex-as-per-a-tion *n.* exasperación

ex-ca-vate *v.* excavar

ex-ca-va-tion *n.* excavación

ex-ceed *v.* superar; exceder

ex-ceed-ing-ly *adv.* sumamente

ex-cel *v.* sobresalir; aventajar

ex-cel-lence *n.* excelencia

ex-cel-lent *a.* excelente

ex-cept *v.* exceptuar

ex-cep-tion *n.* excepción

ex-cep-tion-al *a.* excepcional

ex-cerpt v. citar un texto
ex-cess n. exceso
ex-ces-sive a. excesivo
ex-change v. cambiar
ex-cise n. impuestos sobre ciertos articulos
ex-cit-a-ble a. excitable
ex-cite v. excitar
ex-cite-ment n. agitacion; emocion
ex-cit-ing a. emocionante
ex-claim v. exclamar
ex-cla-ma-tion n. exclamacion
ex-clude v. excluir
ex-clu-sion n. exclusion
ex-clu-sive a. exclusivo
ex-com-mu-ni-cate v. excomulgar
ex-com-mu-ni-ca-tion n. excomunion
ex-cre-ment n. excremento
ex-cur-sion n. viaje; excursion
ex-cuse v. excusar; perdonar
ex-e-cute v. ejecutar; llevar a cabo
ex-e-cu-tion n. ejecución
ex-ec-u-tive a. ejecutivo
ex-ec-u-tor n. albacea
ex-em-pla-ry a. ejemplar
ex-er-cise n. ejercicio
ex-hale v. exhalar; espirar
ex-haust v. agotar
ex-hib-it v. mostrar; presentar
ex-hi-bi-tion n. exposición
ex-hil-a-rate v. vigorizar; alegrar
ex-hort v. exhortar
ex-i-gent a. exigente
ex-ile n. exilado; destierro
ex-ist v. existir
ex-ist-ence n. existencia
ex-it n. salida
ex-o-dus n. exxo
ex-or-bi-tant a. excesivo
ex-ot-ic adj. exotico
ex-pand v. extendeer; ensanchar
ex-panse n. extension
ex-pan-sion n. expansion
ex-pan-sive a. expansivo

ex-pect v. experar; contar con
ex-pect-an-cy n. expectacion
ex-pect-ant a. expectante
ex-pec-ta-tion n. expectacion
ex-pe-di-en-cy n. conveniencia
ex-pe-di-ent a. conveniente
ex-pe-dite v. facilitar; acelerar
ex-pe-di-tion n. expedición
ex-pel v. expulsar
ex-pend v. expender
ex-pend-i-ture n. gasto
ex-pe-ri-ence v. experimentar
ex-per-i-ment n. experimento
ex-pire v. terminar
ex-pla-na-tion n. explicación
ex-pli-cit a. explicito
ex-plode v. estallar; volar
ex-ploit n. hazaña
ex-plo-ra-tion n. exploracion
ex-plor-e v. explorar; examinar
ex-plor-er n. explorador
ex-plo-sion n. explosion
ex-po-nent n. exponente
ex-port v. exportar
ex-por-ta-tion n. exportacion
ex-pose v. exponer; desenmascarar
ex-press v. expresar
ex-pres-sion n. expresion
ex-pres-sive adj. expresion
ex-tend v. extender
ex-ten-sion n. extension
ex-te-ri-or adj. exterior
ex-tinct adj. extinto
ex-tinc-tion n. extinción
ex-tra n. extra
ex-tra-or-di-nar-y adj. extraordinario
ex-treme adj. extremo
ex-ul-ta-tion n. exultación
eye n. ojo
eye-let n. ojete
eye-sight n. vista
eye-tooth n. colmillo
eye-wit-ness n. testigo ocular

fa-ble *n.* fabula
fab-ric *n.* tela
fab-ri-cate *v.* inventar
fab-u-lous *adj.* fabuloso
fa-cade *n.* fachada
face *n.* cara
fa-cial *adj.* facial
fa-cile *adj.* facil
fa-cil-i-tate *v.* facilitar
fa-cil-i-ty *n.* facilida
fac-sim-i-le *n.* facsimile
fact *n.* hecho
fac-tion *n.* facción
fac-tor *n.* factor
fac-to-ry *n.* fabrica
fac-tu-al *a.* basado en datos
fac-ul-ty *n.* facultad
fad *n.* novedad
fade *v.* descolorar(se)
fag *v.* fatigar
fag-ot *n.* haz de lena
Fahr-en-heit *adj.* de Fahrenheit
fail *v.* acabar; faltar
fail-ure *n.* fracaso
faint *v.* desmayarse
faint-ness *n.* debilidad
fair *adj.* justo; rubio
fair-ly *adv.* justamente
fair-y *n.* hada
faith *n.* fe
faith-ful *adj.* fiel
faith-less *adj.* desleal
fake *n.* impostura
fal-con *n.* halcon
fall *v.* caer(se)
fal-la-cious *adj.* enganoso
fal-la-cy *n.* error; falacia
fal-li-ble *adj.* falible
fal-low *adj.* en barbecho
false *adj.* falso
false-hood *n.* mentira
false-ly *adv.* falsamente
fal-si-fy *v.* falsificar
fal-si-ty *n.* falsedad
fal-ter *v.* vacilar; titubear
fame *n.* fama
fa-mil-iar *adj.* familiar
fa-mil-i-ar-i-ty *n.* familiaridad
fam-i-ly *n.* familia
fam-ine *n.* hambre
fam-ish *v.* morirse de hambre

fa-mous *adj.* famoso
fan *n.* aficionado
fa-nat-ic *n.*, *adj.* fanatico
fa-nat-i-cism *n.* fanatismo
fan-ci-er *n.* aficionado
fan-ci-ful *adj.* fantastico
fan-cy *n.* fantasia
fan-fare *n.* toque de trompetas
fang *n.* colmillo
fan-tas-tic *adj.* fan
fan-ta-sy *n.* fantasia
far *adv.* lejos
far-a-way *adj.* remoto
farce *n.* farsa
far-ci-cal *adj.* ridiculo
fare *v.* pasarlo
fare-well *ent.* adiós
far-fetched *adj.* improbable
farm *n.* granja
farm-house *n.* alquería
far-off *adj.* lejano
fas-ci-nate *v.* fascinar
fas-cism *n.* fascismo
fas-cist *n.* facista
fash-ion *n.* estilo; moda; uso
fash-ion-a-ble *adj.* de moda
fast *adj.* rapidamente; rapido
fas-ten *v.* abrochar; asegurar
fas-tid-i-ous *adj.* fino; esquilimoso
fat *adj.* gordo
fa-tal *adj.* fatal
fa-tal-ism *n.* fatalismo
fa-tal-ist *n.* fatalista
fa-tal-i-ty *n.* fatalidad
fate *n.* suerte
fate-ful *adj.* fatal
fa-ther *n.* padre
fa-ther-hood *n.* paternidad
fa-ther-in-law *n.* suegro
fath-om *n.* braza, *v.* penetrar
fa-tigue *n.* fatiga
fat-ten *v.* engordar
fau-cet *n.* grifo
fault *n.* culpa; falta
fault-y *adj.* defectuoso
fa-vor *n.* favor
fa-vor-a-ble *adj.* favorable
fa-vored *adj.* favorecido
fa-vor-ite *adj.*, *n.* favorito
fa-vor-it-ism *n.* favoritismo

fawn n. cervato
faze v. perturbar
fear n. miedo
fear-ful adj. temeroso
fear-less adj. intrepido
fear-some adj. temible
fea-si-bil-i-ty n. viabilidad
fea-si-ble adj. factible
feast n. banquete; fiesta
feat n. proeza
feath-er n. pluma
feath-er-y adj. plumoso
fea-ture n. facción; rasgo
Feb-ru-ar-y n. febrero
fe-ces n. excrementos
fe-cund adj. fecundo
fed-er-al adj. federal
fed-er-a-tion n. federación
fee n. honorario
fee-ble adj. debil
fee-bly adv. flojamente
feed v. alimentar
feel v. sentir(se)
feel-er n. antena
feel-ing n. emoción
feign v. fingir
feint n. treta
fe-lic-i-tate v. flicitar
fe-lic-i-tous a. oportuno; feliz
fe-lic-i-ty n. felicidad
fe-line adj. felino
fell v. talar
fel-low n. compañero
fel-low-ship n. companerismo
fel-on n. criminal
fel-o-ny n. crimen
felt n. fieltro
fe-male n. hembra
fem-i-nine adj. femenino
fe-mur n. femur
fence v. esgrimir
fenc-ing n. esgrima
fend v. rechazar
fen-der n. guardafango
fer-ment v. fermentar
fer-men-ta-tion n. fermentacion
fern n. helecho
fe-ro-cious adj. feroz
fe-ro-ci-ty n. ferocidad
fer-ret n. huron
fer-ry n. transbordador

fer-tile adj. fecundo; fertil
fer-til-i-ty n. fecundidad
fer-ti-lize v. fertilizar
fer-ti-liz-er n. abono
fer-vid adj. fervido
fer-vor n. fervor
fes-ter v. enconarse
fes-ti-val n. fiesta
fes-tive adj. festivo
fes-tiv-i-ty n. regocijo; fiesta
fes-toon n. feston
fetch v. ir por
fetch-ing adj. atractivo
fete, fete n. fiesta
fet-id adj. fetido
fet-ish n. fetiche
fet-it adj. fetido
fet-ter n. grillos
fet-tle n. condición
fe-tus n. feto
feud n. enemistad
feu-dal adj. feudal
feu-dal-ism n. feudalismo
fe-ver n. fiebre
fe-ver-ish adj. febril
few adj. pocos
fi-an-ce n. novio
fi-an-cee n. novia
fi-as-co n. fiasco
fi-at n. fiat
fib v. mentir
fi-ber, fi-bre n. fibra
fi-brous adj. fibroso
fick-le adj. inconstante
fic-tion n. ficcion
fic-tion-al adj. novelesco
fic-ti-tious adj. ficticio
fid-dle n. violin
fi-del-i-ty n. fidelidad
fidg-et v. inquietar
fidg-et-y adj. inquieto; azogado
field n. prado; campo
fiend n. demonio
fiend-ish adj. diabolico
fierce adj. feroz
fier-y a. ardiente; apaionado
fif-teen adj. quince
fif-teenth adj. decimoquinto
fifth adj. quinto
fif-ti-eth adj. quincuagesimo
fif-ty adj. cincuenta
fig n. higo

fight v. pelear; luchar, n. pelea; lucha

fight-er n. guerrero

fig-ment n. invención

fig-ur-a-tive adj. figurado

fig-ure n. tipo; figura

fig-ure-head n. mascaron de proa

fig-ur-ine n. figurin

fil-a-ment n. filamento

filch v. ratear

file n. lima; archivo; fila

fi-let n. filete. Also fil-let

fil-i-bus-ter n. obstruccionist

fil-i-gree n. filigraña

fil-ings n. limaduras

fill v. llenar

fill-ing n. empaste; relleno

fil-ly n. potra

film n. película

fil-ter n. filtro

filth n. inmundicia

filth-y adj. sucio

fin n. aleta

fi-nal adj. final

fi-na-le n. final

fi-nal-ist n. finalista

fi-nal-i-ty n. finalidad

fi-nal-ly adv. finalmente; por fin

fi-nance n. finanzas

fi-nan-cial adj. financiero

fin-an-cier n. financiero

finch n. pinzón

find v. hallar; encontrar

fine adj. fino; admirable; multa, v. multar

fin-er-y n. adornos

fi-nesse n. sutileza; diplomacia

fin-ger n. dedo

fin-ger-nail n. uña

fin-ger-print n. huella dactilar

fin-ish v. terminar; acabar

fi-nite adj. finito

fir n. abeto

fire n. fuego

fire-arm n. arma de fuego

fire-crack-er n. petardo

fire en-gine n. bomba de incendios

fire-fly n. luciérnaga

fire-man n. bombero

fire-place n. hogar

firm adj. firme

fir-ma-ment n. firmamento

firm-ly adv. firmemente

firm-ness n. firmeza

first adj. primero

first-class adj. de primera clase

first-hand adj. de primera mano

first-rate a. de primera clase

fis-cal adj. fiscal

fish n. pez

fish-er-man n. pescador

fish-ery n. pesquera

fish-y adj. sospechoso

fis-sion n. fisión

fis-sure n. grieta

fist n. puño

fist-i-cuffs n. punetazor

fit v. probar; acomodar, adj. adecuado

fit-ful adj. espasmodico

fit-ting n. ajuste; adj. propio; conveniente

five adj. cinco

fix v. arreglar

fix-a-tion n. fijación

fix-ed adj. fijo

fix-ture n. cosa o instalación fija

fla-by adj. flojo; debil

flag n. bandera

flag-on n. jarro; frasco

fla-grant adj. notorio

flag-stone n. losa

flail n. mayal

flair n. instinto

flake n. escama, v. formar hojuelas

flak-y adj. escamoso

flam-boy-ant adj. llamativo

flame n. llama; v. flamear

flam-ma-ble adj. inflamable

flank n. ijada; lado, v. lindar; flanquear

flap v. ondear

flare v. brillar; fulgurar, n. bengala

flash n. relampago; rafaga, v. lanzar

flash-light n. linterna

electrica
flash-y *adj.* charro
flask *n.* frasco
flat *adj.* plano; llano
flat-ter-y *n.* adulacion
flaunt *v.* lucir
fla-vor *n.* sabor
fla-vor-ing *n.* condimento
flaw *n.* imperfeccion
flax *n.* lino
flay *v.* desollar
flea *n.* pulga
fleck *n.* mancha
flee *v.* fugarse; huir
fleece *n.* vellon
fleec-y *adj.* lanudo
fleet *adj.* veloz
fleet-ing *adj.* fugaz
flesh *n.* carne
flex *v.* doblar
flex-i-ble *adj.* flexible
flick *n.* golpecito
fli-er *n.* aviador
flight *n.* vuelo
flim-sy *adj.* endeble
flinch *v.* acobardarse
fling *v.* arrojar
flint *n.* pedernal
flip *v.* mover de un tiron
flip-pant *adj.* ligero
flirt *v.* flirtear; coquetear
flit *v.* revolotear
float *v.* flotar; hacer flotar
flock *n.* rebano
floe *n.* tempano
flog *v.* azotar
flood *n.* diluvio
floor *n.* suelo; piso
flop *v.* caer pesadamente; fracasar
flo-ra *n.* flora
flo-ral *adj.* floral
flor-id *adj.* florido
flo-rist *n.* florista
floss *n.* seda floja
flo-til-la *n.* flotilla
flounce *v.* moverse airadamente
floun-der *v.* tropezar
flour *n.* harina
flour-ish *v.* florecer; blandir
flout *v.* mofarse
flow *v.* fluir

flow-er *n.* flor
flu *n.* gripe
fluc-tu-ate *v.* fluctuar
flue *n.* canon de chimenea
flu-en-cy *n.* fluidez
flu-ent *adj.* facundo
fluff-y *adj.* plumosa
flu-id *adj.* fluido
flude *n.* chirpia
flunk *v.* no aprobar
flu-o-res-cent *adj.* fluores-cente
flur-ry *n.* rafaga; agitacion
flush *adj.* nivelado
flus-ter *v.* aturdir
flute *n.* flauta
flut-ter *n.* aleteo, *v.* revolotear
flux *n.* mudanza; flujo
fly *v.* volar, *n.* mosca
fly-er *n.* aviador
fly-wheel *n.* rueda volante
foal *n.* potro
foam *n.* espuma
fo-cus *v.* enfocar
fod-der *n.* forraje
foe *n.* enemigo
fog *n.* niebla
fo-gy *n.* sona de ideas anticuadas
foi-ble *n.* flaco
foil *n.* hoja; florete
foist *v.* encajar
fold *v.* plegar; doblar
fold-er *n.* carpeta
fo-li-age *n.* follaje
folk *n.* gente
folk-lore *n.* folklore
fol-li-cle *n.* foliculo
fol-low *v.* perseguir; seguir
fol-low-er *n.* seguidor
fol-ly *n.* locura; tonteria
fo-ment *v.* fomentar
fond *adj.* carinoso
fon-dle *v.* acariciar
fond-ly *adv.* afectuosamente
food *n.* alimento
fool *n.* tonto
fool-har-dy *adj.* temerario
fool-ish *adj.* necio
fool-proof *adj.* infalible
foot *n.* pata; pie
foot-ball *n.* futbol

foot-note n. nota
foot-print n. huella
foot-step n. paso
fop n. petimetre
for conj. pues, prep. para; por
for-age n. forraje
for-ay n. correria
for-bear v. contenerse
for-bid v. prohibir
for-bid-den adj. prohibido
for-ceps n. forceps
for-ci-ble a. energico; eficaz
ford n. vado
fore adj. anterior
fore-arm n. antebrazo
fore-bode v. presagiar
fore-cast v. pronosticar
fore-fa-ther n. antepasado
fore-fin-ger n. dede indice
fore-go v. preceder; renunciar
fore-gone a. predeterminado
fore-ground n. primer plano
fore-head n. frente
for-eign adj. extranjero
for-eign-er n. extranjero
fore-man n. capatiz
fore-most adj. primero
fore-run-ner n. precursor
fore-see v. prever
foresight n. prevision; perspicacia
fore-skin n. prepucio
for-est n. bosque
fore-tell v. predecir
for-ev-er adv. siempre
fore-word n. prefacio
for-feit v. perder
forge n. fragua
for-ger-y n. falsificación
for-get v. olvidar(se)
for-get-ful adj. olvidadizo
for-give v. perdonar
fork n. tenedor
for-lorn adj. abandonado
form n. forma
for-mal adj. ceremonioso
for-mal-i-ty n. formalidad
for-mat n. formato
for-ma-tion n. formación
for-mer adj. anterior
for-mer-ly adv. an-

tiguamente
for-mi-da-ble adj. formidable
for-mu-la n. formula
for-ni-cate v. fornicar
for-ni-ca-tion n. fornicación
for-sake v. abandonar
fort n. fuerte
forth adv. en adelante
forth-com-ing adj. próximo
forth-right adj. directo
for-ti-fi-ca-tion n. fortificacion
for-tune n. fortuna
for-ty adj. cuarenta
for-ward adv. adelante
fos-sil n. fosil
foul adj. sucio
foun-da-tion n. fundación
foun-tain n. fuente
four n. cuarto
four-teen adj. catorce
fourth adj. cuarto
fox n. zorra
fra-cas n. rina
frac-tion n. fracción
frac-ture v. quebrar, n. fractura
frag-ile adj. frágil
frag-ment n. fragmento
fra-grence n. fragancia
fra-grant adj. oloroso
frail adj. debil; fragil
frail-ty n. fragilidad
frame n. estructura; marco
fframe-work n. esqueleto
franc n. franco
fran-chise n. derecho de sufragio
frank adj. franco
frank-in-cense n. incienso
frank-ly adv. francamente
frank-ness n. franqueza
fran-tic adj. frenetico
fra-ter-ni-ty n. fraternidad
fraud n. fraude
fraught adj. lleno de
fray v. deshilacharse
freak n. monstruosidad; finomeno
freck-le n. peca
free v. libertar, adj. libre
free-dom n. libertad
free-way n. autopista

freeze v. helar(se); congelar
freight n. flete
freight-er n. buque de carga
French n., adj. frances
fre-net-ic adj. frenetico
fren-zy n. frenesi
fre-quen-cy n. frecuencia
fre-quent adj. frecuente
fres-co n. fresco
fresh adj. fresco
fresh-en v. refrescar
fret v. apararse
fret-ful adj. displicente
fri-ar n. fraile
fric-tion n. friccion
Friday n. viernes
friend n. amigo, amiga
friend-ly adj. amistoso
frieze n. friso
fright n. susto
fright-en v. asustar
frig-id adj. frio
frill n. lechuga
fringe n. orla; margen
frisk v. retoar
frit-ter v. desperdiciar
fro adv. atras
frock n. vestido
from prep. desde; de
fron-tal adj. frontal
frown n. ceno
fru-gal adj. frugal
fruit n. fruta
frus-trate v. frustrar
frus-tra-tion n. frustracion
fry v. freir
fu-gi-tive n., adj. fugitivo
full adj. completo; lleno
ful-ly adv. completamente
func-tion n. funcionar
func-tion-al adj. funcional
fun-da-men-tal adj. fundamental
fun-ny adj. comico
fu-ri-ous adj. furioso
fur-ni-ture n. mueblaje
fur-ther adj., adv. mas lejos
fuse n. fusible; espoleta
u-tile adj. inutil
uzz n. pelusa

gab-ar-dine n. gabardina
ga-ble n. aguilon; faldon
gad v. andorrear
gad-fly n. tabaon
gad-get n. aparato
gaff n. arpon
gag v. amordazar
gai-e-ty n. alegria
gai-ly adv. alegremente
gain v. ganar
gain-say v. contradecir
gait n. modo de andar
ga-la n. fiesta
gal-ax-y n. galaxia
gale n. ventarron
gall n. bilis
gal-lant adj. valeroso
gal-lant-ry n. galanteria
gal-ler-y n. galeria
gal-ley n. galera; fogon
gal-lon n. galon
gal-lop n. galope
gal-lows n. horca
gal-va-nize v. galvanizar
gam-bit n. gambito
gam-ble v. jugar
gam-bol v. brincar
game n. partido; juego
gam-ut n. gama
gan-der n. ganso
gang n. pandilla
gan-grene n. gangrena
gang-ster n. gangster; pistolero
gang-way n. pasillo
gap n. hueco
ga-rage n. garaje
garb n. vestido
gar-bage n. basura
gar-ble v. mutilar
gar-den n. jardin
gar-gan-tu-an a. colosal
gar-gle v. gargarizar
gar-ish n. llamativo
gar-land n. guirnalda
gar-ment n. prenda de vestir
gar-ner n. granero
gar-net n. granate
gar-nish v. adornar
gar-ret n. guardilla
gar-ri-son n. guarnicion
gar-ru-lous adj. garrulo
gar-ter n. liga

gas *n.* gasolina

gas-e-ous *adj.* gaseous

gash *n.* cuchillada

gas-o-line *n.* gasolina

gasp *v.* boquear

gas-tric *adj.* gastrico

gas-tron-o-my *n.* gastronomia

gate *n.* puerta

gate-way *n.* paso

gath-er *v.* fruncir; reunir

gauche *adj.* torpe

gaud-y *adj.* chillon

gauge *n.* norma de medida; indicador

gaunt *adj.* flaco

gaunt-let *n.* guantelete

gauze *n.* gasa

gawk-y *adj.* desgarbado

gay *adj.* alegre; vistoso

gaze *v.* mirar

ga-zelle *n.* gacela

ga-zette *n.* gaceta

gaz-et-teer *n.* diccionario geografico

gear *v.* engranar

gel-a-tin *n.* gelatina

ge-lat-i-nous *adj.* gelatinoso

geld *v.* castrar

gem *n.* joya; gema

gen-der *n.* genero

gene *n.* gen

ge-ne-al-o-gy *n.* genealogia

gen-er-al *adj.* general

gen-er-al-i-ty *n.* generalidad

gen-er-al-ize *v.* generalizar

gen-er-ate *v.* generar

gen-er-tion *n.* generador

gen-er-a-tor *n.* generador

ge-ner-ic *adj.* generico

gen-er-os-i-ty *n.* generosidad

gen-er-ous *adj.* generoso

gen-e-sis *n.* genesis

ge-net-ic *adj.* genesico

gen-ial *adj.* afable

gen-i-tal *adj.* genital

gen-ius *n.* genio

gen-o-cide *n.* genocidio

gen-teel *adj.* elegante; bien criado

gen-til-i-ty *n.* gentilize

gen-tle *adj.* suave; apacible

gen-tle-man *n.* caballero

gen-tly *adv.* suavemente

gen-u-ine *adj.* genuino; sincero

ge-nus *n.* género

ge-o-gra-pher *n.* geógrafo

ge-o-gra-phic, ge-o-graph-i-cal *adj.* geografico

ge-o-gra-phy *n.* geografia

ge-o-log-ic *adj.* geologico

ge-ol-o-gist *n.* geologo

ge-ol-o-gy *n.* geologia

ge-o-met-ric *adj.* geométrico

ge-om-e-try *n.* geometria

ge-o-phys-i-cal *a.* geofisico

ge-o-phys-ics *n.* geofisica

ger-i-at-rics *n.* geriatria

germ *n.* germen

ger-mane *adj.* relativo

ger-mi-nate *v.* germinar

ger-mi-na-tion *n.* germinación

ger-und *n.* gerundio

ges-tic-u-late *v.* gesticular

ges-ture *n.* gesto

get *v.* lograr; obtener

gey-ser *n.* geiser

ghast-ly *adj.* horrible

gher-king *n.* pepinillo

ghost *n.* fantasma

ghost-ly *adj.* espectral

ghoul *n.* demonio

GI *n.* soldado

giant *adj.* gigantesco

gib-ber-ish *n.* galimatias; jerga

gib-bon *n.* gibón

gibe, jibe *v.* mofarse; burlarse

gib-let *n.* menudillos

gid-di-ness *n.* vertigo

gid-dy *adj.* mareado; ligero

gift *n.* regalo; don

gi-gan-tic *adj.* gigantesco

gig-gle *n.* risa sofocada

gild *v.* dorar

gill *n.* agalla

gilt *adj.* dorado

gim-mick *n.* truco

gin *n.* desmotadera de algodon; ginebra

gin-ger *n.* jengibre

gin-ger ale *n.* cerveza de

jengibre
gin-ger-bread *n.* pan de jengibre
gin-ger-ly *adj.* cauteloso
gip-sy *n.* gitano
gi-raffe *n.* jirafa
gird *v.* cenir
gird-er *n.* viga
gir-dle *n.* cinto; faja
girl *n.* chica; niña
girl-ish *adj.* de niña
girth *n.* cincha
gist *n.* esencial; clave
give *v.* entregar; dar
giv-en *adj.* citado
giz-zard *n.* molleja
gla-cial *adj.* glacial
gla-cier *n.* glaciar
glad *adj.* alegre
glad-den *v.* regocijar
glade *n.* claro
glad-ly *adv.* con mucho gusto
glad-ness *n.* alegria
glad-i-o-lus *n.* gladiolo
glam-our, glam-or *n.* encanto
glam-our-ous *a.* encantador
glance *v.* rebotar; mirar
gland *n.* glandula
glan-du-lar *adj.* glandular
glar-ing *adj.* evidente
glare *v.* relumbrar
glass *n.* vidrio; vaso
glass-y *adj.* vitreo
glau-co-ma *n.* glaucoma
glaze *v.* vidriar
gleam *n.* espigar
glee *n.* jubilo
glen *n.* jubilo
glide *v.* deslizarse
glim-mer *v.* brillar debilmente
glimpse *n.* vislumbre
glint *v.* destellar
glis-ten *v.* relucir
glit-ter *v.* relucir
gloat *v.* manifestar saticfacion maligna
globe *n.* globo; esfera
glob-ule *n.* globulo
gloom *n.* tristeza
gloom-y *adj.* lobrego;

melancolico
glo-ri-fy *v.* glorificar
glo-ri-ous *adj.* glorioso
glo-ry *n.* gloria
gloss *n.* lustre
glos-sa-ry *n.* glosario
gloss-y *adj.* lustroso
glot-tis *n.* glotis
glove *n.* guante
glow *v.* brillar
glow-er *v.* mirar con ceño
glow-worm *n.* luciernaga
glue *v.* encolar
glum *adj.* abatido
glut *v.* hartar
glut-ton *n.* glotón
glut-ton-y *n.* gula
gnarl *v.* torcer
gnash *v.* rechinar
gnat *n.* jejen
gnaw *v.* roer
gnome *n.* gnomo
go *v.* ir
goad *n.* aguijada; incitar
goal *n.* meta; gol
goat *n.* cabra
gob-ble *v.* engullir
gob-let *n.* copa
gob-lin *n.* trasgo
God *n.* Dios
god-child *n.* ahijado
god-daugh-ter *n.* ahijada
god-dess *n.* diosa
god-fa-ther *n.* padrino
god-ly *adj.* piadoso
god-moth-er *n.* madrina
god-par-ent *n.* padrino; madrina
god-send *n.* buena suerte
god-son *n.* ahijado
gog-gles *n.* anteojos
go-ing *n.* ida; estado del camino
gold *n.* oro
golf *n.* golf
gon-do-la *n.* gondola
gon-do-lier *n.* goldolero
gong *n.* gong
gon-or-rhe-a *n.* gonorrea
good *n.* bien
good-by; good-bye *int.* adiós
good-heart-ed *adj.* amable

good-look-ing adj. guapo

good-ly adj. agradable; considerable

good-ness n. bondad

good-y n. golosina

goose n. ganso

goose-ber-ry n. uva espina

gore n. sangre

gorge n. barranco

gor-geous adj. magnifico; vistoso

gos-pel n. evangelio

gos-sa-mer n. gasa sutil

gos-sip n. chisme; comadre

gouge n. gubia

gourd n. calabaza

gour-met n. gastronomo

gout n. gota

gov-ern v. gobernar

gov-ern-ess n. institutriz

gov-ern-ment n. gobierno

gov-er-nor n. gobernador

gown n. vestido

grab v. asir; arrebatar

grace n. gracia

grace-ful adj. gracioso

gra-cious adj. agradable

gra-da-tion n. gradación

grade n. grado; clase

grad-u-al adj. gradual

grad-u-al-ly adv. poco a poco

grad-u-ate v. graduar(se)

grad-u-a-tion n. graduación

graft n. injerto; soborno

grain n. graño; bifra

gram n. grámo

gram-mar n. gramatica

gram-mat-i-cal adj. gramatical

gra-na-ry n. granero

grand adj. magnifico; grandioso

grand-child n. nieto

grand-daugh-ter n. nieta

grand-fa-ther n. abuelo

grand-moth-er n. abuela

grand-par-ent n. abuelo

grand-son n. nieto

grange n. cortijo

gran-ite n. granito

grant v. conferir; otorgar

gran-u-late v. granular

gran-ule n. grañulo

grape n. uva

grape-fruit n. toronja

graph n. grafica

graph-ic adj. grafico

graph-ite n. grafito

grap-nel n. arpeo

grap-ple n. arpeo

grasp v. agarrar; comprender

grasp-ing adj. codicioso

grass n. hierba

grass-hop-per n. saltamontes

grass-y adj. herboso

grate n. parrilla de hogar

grate-ful adj. agradecido

grat-i-fi-ca-tion n. gratificación; placer

grat-i-fy v. complacer; satisfacer

grat-ing n. reja

gra-tis adj., adv. gratis

grat-i-tude n. reconocimiento

gra-tu-i-tous adj. gratuito; injustificado

gra-tu-i-ty n. propina

grave n. sepultura

grav-el n. cascajo

grav-en adj. grabado

grave-yard n. cementerio

grav-i-tate v. gravitar

grav-i-ta-tion n. gravitación

grav-i-ty n. seriedad; gravedad

gra-vy n. salsa

gray, grey adj., n. gris

graze v. pacer; rozar

grease n. grasa

greas-y adj. grasiento

great adj. grande; gran

greed n. avaricia; codicia

greed-y adj. avaro; codicioso; goloso

green adj., n. verde

green-er-y n. verdura

greet v. saludar

greet-ing n. saludo

gre-gar-i-ous a. gregario

gre-nade n. granada de mano

grid n. reja; parrilla

grid-dle *n.* tortera

grid-i-ron *n.* campo de fútbol; parrilla

grief *n.* pesar

griev-ance *n.* agravio

grieve *v.* afligirse

griev-ous *adj.* grave; penoso

grif-fin, grif-fon *n.* grifo

grill *v.* asar a la parrilla

grille, grill *n.* verja

grim *adj.* inflexible; severo

grim-ace *n.* visaje

grime *n.* mugre

grim-y *adj.* mugriento

grin *v.* sonreir

grind *v.* moler; pulverizar

grind-stone *n.* muela

grip *n.* agarro; apreton; saco de mano

grippe *n.* gripe

gris-ly *adj.* horroroso

gris-tle *n.* cartilago

grit *n.* arena; firmeza

grit-ty *adj.* arenoso

griz-zled, griz-zly *adj.* gris

groan *v.* gemir

gro-cer *n.* abacero

gro-cer-y *n.* abaceria

groin *n.* ingle

groom *n.* novio; mozo de caballos

groove *n.* estria

grope *v.* buscar a tientas

gross *adj.* bruto; grosero; grueso

gro-tesque *adj.* grotesco

grot-to *n.* gruta

grouch *v.* refunfuñar

ground *n.* tierra; terreno; razon; poso

ground-work *n.* fundamento

group *n.* grupo

grouse *v.* quejarse

grove *n.* abboleda

grov-el *v.* arrastrarse

gym *n.* gimnasio

gym-nast *n.* gimnasta

gym-nas-tic *adj.* gimnastico

gy-ne-col-o-gy *n.* ginecologia

gyp *v.* estafar

gyp-sum *n.* jeso

hab-it *n.* costumbre

hab-it-a-ble *adj.* habitable

hab-i-tat *n.* habitación

hab-i-ta-tion *n.* habitación

ha-bít-u-al *adj.* habitual

ha-bit-u-ate *v.* acostumbrarse

hack *v.* acuchillar

hack-neyed *adj.* trillado

had *v. pt. and pp. of* have

hag *n.* bruja

hag-gard *adj.* ojeroso

hag-gle *v.* regatear

hail *n.* granizo, *v.* granizar

hail-stone *n.* piedra de granizo

hair *n.* pelo; cabello

hair-breadth *n.* ancho de un pelo

hair-dress-er *n.* peluquero

hair-pin *n.* horquilla

hale *adj.* robusto

half *n.* mitad

half-way *n.* pasillo

hall *n.* sala

hal-le-lu-jah *int.* aleluya

hal-low *v.* consagrar

hal-lu-cin-a-tion *n.* alucinación

hall-way *n.* pasillo

hal-o-n *n.* halo; aureola

halt *v.* parar

hal-ter *n.* cabestro

halve *v.* partir por mitad

ham *n.* jamón

ham-burg-er *n.* hamburguesa

ham-let *n.* aldehuela

ham-mer *v.* martillar, *n.* martillo

ham-mock *n.* hamaca

ham-per *v.* impedir

hand *n.* mano

hand-bag *n.* bolso

hand-book *n.* manual

hand-cuff *n.* esposas

hand-ful *n.* puñado

hand-i-cap *n.* desventaja

hand-ker-chief *n.* panuelo

han-dle *n.* mango; manubrio

hand-some *adj.* hermoso

hand-y *adj.* conveniente; prozimo; habil

hang v. pegar; colgar
hang-er-on n. pegote
hank-er v. anhelar
hap-haz-zard adj. fortuito
hap-pen v. pasar
hap-pen-ing n. acontecimiento
hap-pi-ly adv. alegremente
hap-pi-ness n. alegria
hap-py adj. feliz
har-bor n. puerto
hard adj. firme
har-dy adj. robusto
harm v. dañar
harm-ful adj. dañino
har-mo-ni-ous adj. armonioso
har-mo-ny n. armonia
harsh adj. severo
harsh-ness n. severidad
har-vest v. cosechar
hat n. sombrero
hatch v. empollar, n. portezuela
hatch-et n. machado
hate n. odio, v. odiar
hate-ful adj. odioso
have v. tener
hawk n. halcon
haz-ard v. arriesgar, n. azar
he pron. el
head n. cabeza
head-ache n. dolor de cabeza
head-ing n. título
head-land n. promontorio
head-light n. faro
head-quar-ters n. cuartel general
head-way n. progreso
heal v. sanar; curar
health n. salud
health-ful adj. sano
heap n. monton
hear v. oir
hear-ing n. oido
hear-say n. rumor
hearse n. coche funebre
heart n. corazón
heart-ache n. angustia
heart-break n. angustia
hearten v. alentar
heart-felt adj. sincero

hearth n. hogar
heat v. calentar, n. calor
heat-er n. calentador
heath n. brezal
heave v. levantar
heav-en n. cielo
heav-y adj. fuerte
heck-le v. interrumpor
hec-tic adj. febril
hedge n. seto
heed v. escuchar
heel n. talon
heft n. bulto
heif-er n. vaquilla
height n. altura
height-en v. elevar
hei-nous adj. atroz
heir n. heredero
heir-ess n. heredera
heir-loom n. herencia; reliquia de familia
hel-i-cop-ter n. helicoptero
he-li-um n. helio
he-lix n. hélice
hell n. infierno
hell-ish adj. infernal
hel-lo int. hola
helm n. timon
hel-met n. casco
help n. ayuda, v. ayudar
help-ful adj. util
help-ing n. ración
help-less adj. incapaz
hem n. dobladillo
hem-i-sphere n. hemisferio
hem-i-spher-ic adj. hemisferico
hem-or-rhage n. hemorragia
hem-or-rhoid n. hemorroides
hemp n. cañamo
hen n. gallina
hence adv. de aquí; por lo tanto
her pron. obj. and poss. she
her-ald n. heraldo; precursor
he-ral-dic adj. heraldico
her-ald-ry n. heraldica
herb n. hierba
her-ba-ceous adj. herbáceo
her-cu-le-an adj. hercúleo
herds-man n. pastor

ere *adv.* aquí	**hiss** *v.* silbar
ere-af-ter *adv.* en el futuro	**his-to-ri-an** *n.* historiador
e-red-i-tar-y *adj.* hereditario	**his-tor-ic** *adj.* historico
e-red-i-ty *n.* herencia	**his-to-ry** *n.* historia
ere-in *adv.* incluso	**hit** *n.* golpe, *v.* golpear
er-e-sy *n.* herejía	**hitch** *v.* atar
er-e-tic *n.* hereje	**hitch-hike** *v.* hace autostop
ere-to-fore *adv.* hasta ahora	**hith-er** *adv.* aca
er-it-age *n.* herencia	**hive** *n.* colmena
er-mit *n.* ermitaño	**hoard** *n.* provision
er-mit-age *n.* ermita	**hoarse** *adj.* ronco
er-ni-a *n.* hernia	**hoax** *n.* engaño
e-ro *n.* heroe	**hob-ble** *v.* cojear
e-ro-ic *adj.* heroico	**hob-by** *n.* pasatiempo
er-o-ine *n.* heroína	**ho-bo** *n.* vagabundo
er-o-ism *n.* heroísmo	**hod** *n.* azadon
er-on *n.* garszo	**hog** *n.* puerco
ers *pron. poss of.* she	**hoist** *v.* alzar
er-self *pron.* ella misma; si misma	**hold** *v.* contener; tener
es-i-tant *adj.* vacilante	**hold-ing** *n.* tenencia
es-i-tate *v.* vacilar	**hole** *n.* hoyo
et-er-o-ge-ne-ous *adj.* heterogénio	**hol-i-day** *n.* día de fiesta
ew *v.* tajar	**hol-low** *adj.* vacío
ax-a-gon *n.* hexágono	**hol-ly** *n.* acebo
ex-ag-o-nal *adj.* hexagonal	**hol-o-caust** *n.* holocausto
-ber-nate *v.* invernar	**hol-ster** *n.* pistolera
c-cup *n.* hipo	**hom-age** *n.* homenaje
de *v.* ocultar(se)	**home** *n.* casa
d-e-ous *adj.* horrible; feo	**home-ly** *adj.* feo
-er-ar-chy *n.* jerarquía	**home-sick** *adj.* nostálgico
-er-ogylphic *adj.* jeroglífico	**home-ward** *adv.* hacia casa
gh *adj.* alto	**home-y** *adj.* comodo
ke *n.* caminata	**hom-i-cide** *n.* homicidio
lar-i-ous *adj.* alegre	**hom-i-ly** *n.* homilia
lar-i-ty *n.* alegría	**ho-mo-gen-e-ous** *adj.* homogéneo
l *n.* colina	**hone** *n.* piedra de afilar
t *n.* puño	**hon-est** *adj.* honrado
m *pron. obj. of* he	**hon-es-ty** *n.* honradez
m-self *pron.* el mismo	**hon-ey** *n.* miel
nd *adj.* trasero	**hon-ey-comb** *n.* panal
nd-er *v.* impedir	**hon-ey-moon** *n.* luna de miel
nd-most *adj.* postrero	**hon-ey-suck-le** *n.* madreselva
nge *n.* gozne	**hon-or** *v.* honrar, *n.* honor
nt *n.* indirecta	**hon-or-a-ble** *adj.* honorable
p *n.* cadera	**hon-or-ar-y** *adj.* honorario
p-po-pot-a-mus *n.* hipopótamo	**hood** *n.* capucha
re *v.* alquilar	**hood-lum** *n.* matón
re-ling *n.* mercenario	**hood-wink** *v.* enganar
s *pron.* suyo	**hoof** *n.* casco
	hook *n.* gancho, *v.*

enganchar; encorvar
hoop *n.* aro
hoot *v.* ulular, *n.* grito
hop *n.* salto, *v.* saltar
hope *v.* desear, *n.* esperanza
hope-less *adj.* desesperado
horde *n.* horda
ho-ri-zon *n.* horizonte
hor-i-zon-tal *adj.* horizontal
hor-mone *n.* hormona
horn *n.* cuerno
hor-o-scope *n.* horoscopo
hor-ri-ble *adj.* horrible
hor-ri-fy *v.* horrorizar
hor-ror *n.* horror
horse *n.* caballo
horse-man *n.* jinete
horse-pow-er *n.* caballo de fuerza
horse-rad-ish *n.* rabaño picante
horse-shoe *n.* herradura
hor-ti-cul-ture *n.* horticultura
hose *n.* medias
hose *n.* manga
ho-sier-y *n.* calceteria
hos-pi-ta-ble *a.* hospitalario
hos-pi-tal *n.* hospital
hos-pi-tal-i-ty *n.* hospitalidad
host *n.* anfitrion; patron; multitud
hos-tage *n.* rehén
host-ess *n.* huéspeda
hos-tile *adj.* hostil
hos-til-i-ty *n.* hostilidad
hot *adj.* caliente
ho-tel *n.* hotel
hot-house *n.* invernáculo
hound *n.* podenco, *v.* perseguir
hour *n.* hora
house *n.* casa
house-keep-er *n.* ama e llaves
hous-ing *n.* alojamiento
how *adv.* cómo
how-ev-er *adv.* en todo caso, *conj.* sin embargo
howl *v.* aullar
hub *n.* cubo
hud-dle *v.* amontonar(se)
hue *n.* color; matiz

hug *v.* abrazar
huge *adj.* enorme
hulk *n.* casco
hull *n.* cascara; casco
hum *v.* zumbar; canturrear
hu-man *n.* humano
hu-man-i-ty *n.* humanidad
hum-ble *adj.* humilde
hu-mid *adj.* humedo
hu-mid-i-fy *v.* humdedecer
hu-mid-i-ty *n.* humedad
hu-mil-i-ate *v.* humillar
hu-mil-i-a-tion *n.* humillación
hu-mil-i-ty *n.* humildad
hum-ming-bird *n.* colibrí
hu-mor *n.* complacer
hump *n.* giba; joroba
hunch *v.* corazonada
hunch-back *n.* jorobado
hun-dred *adj.* ciento
hun-dredth *adj.* centesimo
hun-ger *n.* hambre
hun-gry *adj.* hambriento
hunt *v.* cazar
hunt-er *n.* cazador
hur-dle *n.* valla; zarzo
hurl *v.* lanzar
hur-ri-cane *n.* huracan
hur-ry *v.* apresurar; darse prisa
hurt *v.* hacer daño; doler; danar
hus-band *n.* esposo
hush *n.* cascara
husk-y *adj.* ronco
hus-sy *n.* picara
hus-tle *v.* empujar
hy-brid *n.* híbrido
hy-drant *n.* boca de reigo
hy-dro-gen *n.* hidrogeno
hy-e-na *n.* hiena
hy-giene *n.* higiene
hymn *n.* himno
hyp-no-sis *n.* hipnosis
hyp-no-tize *v.* hipnotizar
hyp-o-crite *n.* hipocrita
hy-po-der-mic *adj.* hipodérmico
hy-pot-e-nuse *n.* hipotenusa
hy-poth-e-sis *n.* hipotesis
hy-po-thet-i-cal *a.* hipotetico
hys-te-ri-a *n.* histerismo
hys-ter-ic *adj.* histérico

pron. yo
bis n. ibis
e n. hielo
e-berg n. iceberg
e cream n. helado
ci-cle n. carambano
e-ing n. garapiña
con n. icono
con-o-clast n. iconoclasta
cy adj. helado
de-a n. idea
de-al adj. ideal
de-al-ize v. idealizar
den-ti-cal adj. idéntico
den-ti-fi-ca-tion n. identificación
den-ti-fy v. identificar
den-ti-ty n. identidad
de-ol-o-gy n. ideología
i-om n. idiotismo
i-o-mat-ic adj. idiomático
i-i-o-syn-cra-sy n. idiosincrasia
i-ot n. idiota
dle adj. ocioso
dol n. idolo
dol-a-trous adj. idolatra
dol-a-try n. idolatria
dol-ize v. idolatrar
conj. si
-nite v. encender(se)
-no-ble adj. innoble
-le-git-i-ma-cy n. ilegitimidad
le-git-i-mate adj. ilegítimo
lic-it adj. ilicito
-lit-er-ate adj., m. analfabeto
-ness n. enfermedad
lu-mi-nate v. iluminar
lu-sion n. ilusión
lus-trate v. ilustrar
lus-tra-tion n. ilustración; ejemplo
-age n. imagen
-ag-i-nar-y adj. imaginario

im-ag-i-na-tion n. imaginación
im-ag-ine v. imaginar
im-be-cile n., adj. imbécil
im-i-tate v. imitar
im-i-ta-tion n. imitación; copia
im-ma-ture adj. inmaturo
im-meas-ur-a-ble a. inmensurable
im-me-di-ate adj. inmediato
im-mense adj. inmenso
im-mer-sion n. inmersion
im-mi-grant n. inmigrante
im-mi-grate v. inmigrar
im-mi-gra-tion n. inmigración
im-mi-nent adj. inminente
im-mo-bile adj. inmovil
im-mo-dest adj. impudico
im-mor-al adj. inmoral
im-mor-tal adj. inmortal
im-mune adj. inmune
im-mu-ni-ty n. inmunidad
imp n. diablillo
im-pact n. impacto
im-pair v. deteriorar
im-part v. comunicar; relatar; dar
im-par-tial adj. imparcial
im-pa-tient a. impaciente
im-peach v. acusar
im-pec-ca-ble adj. impecable
im-pede v. impedir; estorbr
im-ped-i-ment n. impedimento; estorbo
im-pel v. impulsar
im-pe-ri-al a. imperial
im-pe-ri-ous adj. imperioso
im-per-son-al adj. impersonal
im-per-ti-nent a. impertinente
im-per-vi-ous a. impenetrable
im-pe-tus n. impetu
im-pi-e-ty n. impiedad
im-ple-ment n. herramienta
im-pli-cate v. enredar
im-plore v. implorar
im-ply v. dar a entender; significar

im-po-lite adj. descortes
im-port v. importar
im-por-tance n. importancia
im-por-tant adj. importante
im-pose v. imponer
im-pos-si-ble adj. imposible
im-pos-ter n. impostor
im-pos-tor n. impostor
im-po-tence n. impotencia
im-pov-er-ish v. empobrecer
im-prac-ti-cal adj. impracticable
im-press v. estampar;
 imprimir; impresionar
im-pres-sion n. impresión
im-print v. imprimir
im-prove v. mejorar
im-prove-ment n. mejora
im-pro-vise nl improvisar
im-pulse n. impulso
in adv. dentro, prep.
 durante, en
in-a-bil-i-ty n. inhabilidad
in-ca-pac-i-tate v. incapacitar
inch n. pulgada
in-ci-den-tal adj. incidental
in-cin-er-ate v. incinerar
in-ci-sion n. incisión
in-cite v. incitar
in-cli-na-tion n. inclinación
in-clu-sion n. inclusión
in-com-pa-ra-ble adj. incomparable
in-com-pe-tent adj. incompetente
in-com-plete adj. incompleto
in-cor-rect adj. incorrecto
in-crease v. crecer; acrecentar
in-crim-i-nate v. incriminar
in-de-cen-cy n. indecencia
in-de-cent adj. indecente
in-deed adv. de veras
in-def-i-nite adj. indefinido
in-dem-ni-ty n. ondemnización
in-dent v. mellar
in-den-ta-tion n. mella
in-de-pend-ence n. independencia
in-de-pend-ent adj. independiente

in-de-struct-i-ble a. indestructible
in-dex n. índice
in-di-cate v. indicar
in-di-ca-tion n. indicación
in-dict v. acusar
in-dif-fer-ent adj. indiferente
in-dig-e-nous a. indígena
in-di-gent a. indigente
in-di-ges-tion n. indigestión
in-dig-nant a. indignado
in-dig-ni-ty n. indignidad
in-di-go n. añil
in-dir-ect adj. indirecto
in-dis-creet a. indiscreto
in-dis-cre-tion n. indiscreción
in-dis-pen-sa-ble a. imprescindible
in-di-vid-u-al n. individuo
in-di-vid-u-al-i-ty n. individualidad
in-doc-tri-nate v. doctrinar
in-do-lent a. indolente
in-door a. interior; de puertas adentro
in-doors adv. dentro
in-duce v. inducir
in-duct v. iniciar
in-dulge v. satisfacer; consentir
in-dus-tri-al adj. industrial
in-er-tia n. inercia
in-ev-i-ta-ble adj. inevitable
in-fa-my n. infamia
in-fan-cy n. infancia
in-fect v. infectar
in-fec-tion n. infección
in-fe-ri-or adj. inferior
in-fi-del-i-ty n. infidelidad
in-fil-trate v. infiltrarse
in-fi-nite adj. infinito
in-fin-i-tive n. infinitivo
in-fin-i-ty n. infinidad
in-fir-ma-ry n. enfermería
in-flame v. inflamar;
 provocar
in-flam-ma-ble adj. inflamable
in-flate v. inflar
in-fla-tion n. inflación
in-flec-tion n. inflexión
in-flict v. infligir; imponer

in-flu-ence n. influencia
in-flu-en-za n. gripe
in-form v. informar
in-for-mal adj. sin ceremonia
in-for-ma-tion n. informacion
in-for-ma-tive adj. informativo
in-fre-quent adj. infrecuente
in-fu-ri-ate v. enfurecer
in-fu-sion n. infusion
in-gen-ious adj. ingenioso
in-ge-nu-i-ty n. ingeniosidad
in-got n. lingote
in-gre-di-ent n. ingrediente
in-hab-it v. habitar
in-hab-i-tant n. habitante
in-hale v. inhalar; aspirar
in-her-ent a. inmanente; inherente
in-her-it v. heredar
in-her-it-ance n. herencia
in-hib-it v. inhibir
in-hi-bi-tion n. inhibición
in-hu-man a. inhumano; cruel
in-iq-ui-ty n. iniquidad
in-i-tial adj. inicial
in-i-ti-ate v. iniciar
in-i-ti-a-tion n. iniciación
in-i-ti-a-tive n. iniciativa
in-ject v. inyectar
in-jec-tion n. inyección
in-jure v. hacer daño a; ofender
in-ju-ry n. daño; injuria
in-jus-tice n. injusticia
ink n. tinta
ink-ling n. sospecha
in-let n. entrada; ensenada
in-mate n. inquilino
inn n. posada
in-nate adj. innato
in-ner adj. interior
in-no-cence n. inocencia
in-no-cent adj. inocente
in-no-va-tion n. innovación
in-nu-en-do n. indirecta
in-nu-mer-a-ble a. innumerable
in-oc-u-late v. inocular
in-oc-u-la-tion n. inoculación
in-quest n. pesquisa judicial

in-quire v. preguntar
in-quir-y n. indagación; pregunta
in-qui-si-tion n. inquisición
in-sane adj. insensato; loco
in-san-i-ty n. locura
in-scribe v. inscribir
in-scrip-tion n. inscripción
in-sect n. insecto
in-se-cure a. inseguro; precario
in-sert v. insertar; meter
in-ser-tion n. inserción
in-side n. interior
in-sight n. perspicacia
in-sig-ni-a-n. insignias
in-sig-nif-i-cance n. insignificancia
in-sin-u-ate v. insinuar
in-sin-u-a-tion n. insinuación; indirecta
in-sip-id adj. insipido
in-sist v. insistir
in-sist-ent a. insistente; porfiado
in-so-lence n. insolencia
in-so-lent adj. insolente
in-som-ni-a n. insomnio
in-spect v. examinar; inspeccionar
in-spec-tion n. inspección
in-spi-ra-tion n. inspiración
in-spire v. inspirar; estimular
in-stall v. instalar
in-stall-ment n. plazo; entrega
in-stance n. ejemplo
in-stant n. instante
in-stan-ta-ne-ous a. instantaneo
in-stead adv. en lugar de; en vez de
in-step n. empeine
in-sti-gate v. instigar
in-stinct n. instinto
in-stinc-tive adj. instintivo
in-sti-tute v. instituir; empezar
in-sti-tu-tion n. institución
in-struct v. instruir; ensenar
in-struc-tion n. instrucción
in-stru-ment n. instrumento
in-suf-fi-cient adj. in-

suficiente

in-su-late v. sislar
in-su-la-tion n. aislamiento
in-su-lin n. insulina
in-sult n. insulto; ultraje
in-sur-ance n. seguro
in-sure v. asegurar
in-sur-rec-tion n. insurección
in-tact adj. intacto
in-te-ger n. numero entero
in-te-grate v. integrar
in-te-gra-tion n. integración
in-teg-ri-ty n. integridad
in-tel-lect n. intelecto
in-tel-li-gence n. inteligencia
in-tel-li-gent adj. inteligente
in-tend v. proponerse; querer decir
in-tense adj. intenso
in-ten-si-ty n. intensidad
in-tent adj. atento; absorto
in-ter v. enterrar
in-ter-cede v. interceder
in-ter-cept v. interceptar
in-ter-ces-sion n. intercesión
in-ter-change v. intercambiar
in-ter-course n. comercio; trato; coito
in-ter-est n. interes
in-ter-fere v. intervenir; meterse
in-ter-im n. interin
in-te-ri-or adj. interior
in-ter-jec-tion n. interjección
in-ter-lude n. intemedio
in-ter-me-di-ate adj. intermedio
in-ter-mis-sion n. intermisión
in-tern n. interno
in-ter-nal adj. interior
in-ter-na-tion-al adj. internacional
in-ter-play n. interacción
in-ter-[pose v. interponer
in-ter-pret v. explicar; interpretar; entender
in-ter-pre-ta-tion n. interpretación
in-ter-ro-gate v. interrogar
in-ter-ro-ga-tion n. interrogación

in-ter-rupt v. interrumpir
in-ter-rup-tion n. interrupcion
in-ter-sec-tion n. intersección
in-ter-twine n. entretejer(se)
in-ter-val n. intervalo
in-ter-vene v. intervenir
in-ter-view n. entrevista
in-tes-tine n. intestino
in-ti-mate v. intimar
in-tim-i-date v. intimidar
in-to prep. en
in-tol-er-ant adj. intolerante
in-to-na-tion n. entonación
in-tox-i-cate v. emriagar; encitar
in-tran-si-tive adj. intransitivo
in-tra-ve-nous adj. intravenoso
in-trep-id adj. intrepido
in-tri-ca-cy n. complejidad; enredo
in-tri-cate adj. intrincado
in-trigue v. intrigar; fascinar
in-trin-sic adj. intrinseco
in-tro-duce v. introducir
in-tro-duc-tion n. introducción
in-trude v. entremeterse
in-tu-i-tion n. intuición
in-ure v. habituar
in-vade v. invadir
in-va-lid adj. invalido
in-var-i-a-ble adj. invariable
in-va-sion n. invasion
in-vent v. inventar
in-ven-tion n. invención
in-ven-to-ry n. inventario
in-ver-sion n. inversión
in-vert v. invertir
in-ver-te-brate a., n. invertebrado
in-vest v. investir
in-ves-ti-gate v. investigar
in-ves-ti-ga-tion n. investigacion
in-vig-or-ate v. vigorizar
in-vin-ci-ble adj. invencible
in-vis-i-ble adj. invisible
in-vi-ta-tion n. invitación

n-vite v. invitar
n-vo-ca-tion n. invocación
n-voice n. factura
n-voke v. invocar; implorar
n-vol-un-tar-y adj. involun-
tario
n-volve v. complicar;
comprometer; enredar
n-ward adv. hacia dentro
o-dine n. yodo
on n. ion
ron v. planchar, n. plancha
ron-ic adj. ironica
ro-ny n. ironia
r-ra-di-ate v. irradiar
r-ra-tion-al adj. irracional
r-rec-on-cil-a-ble adj. ir-
reconciliable
r-ref-u-ta-ble adj. irrefutable
r-reg-u-lar adj. irregular
r-rel-e-vant adj. inaplicable
r-re-sist-i-ble adj. irresistible
r-re-spon-si-ble adj. ir-
responsable
r-ri-gate v. regar
r-ri-tate v. irritar; provocar;
molestar
s v. third person pres. sing
of be
s-land n. isla
sle n. isla
so-late v. aislar
sos-ce-les adj. isosceles
s-sue v. publicar; salir, n.
resultado; emision
th-mus n. pl. istmo
pron. le; la; lo; ello; ella; el
tal-ic n. usu. pl. letra bas-
tardilla
tal-i-cize tr. imprimir en
cursiva
ch v. picar
ch-y adj. que da picazon;
impaciente
tem n. articulo; partida
tem-ize v. detallar
er-ate tr. iterar; repetir
tin-er-ar-y n. itinerario
s pron., adj. poss. case of it
self pron. el, ella, ello, o,
so, mismo
vo-ry n. pl. marfil
vy n. hiedra

jab v. golpear
jab-ber v. farfullar
jack n. mozo; marinero;
gato; sota
jack-al n. chacal
jack-ass n. burro
jack-et n. chaqueta
jack-nife n. navaja
jack-pot n. bote
jade n. jade
jag-uar n. jaguar
jail v. encarcelar, n. carcel
jam v. apinar; atascar
jamb n. jamba
jam-bo-ree n. francachela
jangle n. sonido discordante
jan-i-tor n. portero
Jan-u-ar-y n. enero
jar n. jarra
jar-gon n. jerga
jas-mine n. jazmín
jaun-dice n. ictericia
jaunt n. excursión
jave-lin n. jabalina
jaw n. quijada
jay n. arrendajo
jazz n. jazz
jeal-ous adj. celoso
Jeep n. trademark. jeep
jeer v. mofarse; befar
jell v. cuajar(se)
jel-ly n. jalea
jel-ly-fish n. medusa
jeop-ar-dize v. arriesgar
jeop-ar-dy n. pelogro
jerk v. arrojar; sacudir
jer-kin n. justillo
jer-sey n. jersey
jest n. chanza
jet n. chorro; surtidor; avion;
a reaccion; azabache
jet-same n. echazón
jet-ti-son v. echazón
jet-ty n. malecon; muelle
jew-el n. joya
jew-el-er n. joyero
jew-el-ry n. joyas
jif-fy n. instante
jib n. jiga
jig-saw n. sierra de vaiven
jig-saw puzzle n. rom-
pecabezaw
jilt v. dar calcbazar

jim-my n. palanqueta
jin-gle v. retinir; tintinear
jinx n. gafe
jit-ters n. inquietud
job n. trabajo
jock-ey n. jockey
jo-cose a. jocoso
joc-u-lar a. jocoso
joc-und a. alegre
jog v. empujar; correr despacio
join v. unir(se)
joint n. juntura; union
joist n. viga
joke n. chiste; broma
jok-er n. bromista
jol-ly adj. alegre
jolt v. sacudir
jon-quil n. junquillo
jour-nal n. periodico
jour-nal-ism n. periodismo
jour-nal-ist n. periodista
jour-ney v. viajar, n. viaje
joy-ous adj. alegre
judge n. juez; v. juzgar
ju-di-cial adj. judicial
jug-gle v. hacer juegos malabares
jug-u-lar adj. yugular
juice n. jugo
July n. julio
jum-ble v. mezclar
jump n. salto, v. saltar
jump-er n. saltador
junc-tion n. juntura; empalme
junc-ture n. juntura; coyuntura
June n. junio
jun-gle n. selva
jun-ior adj. mas joven; menor
ju-ni-per n. enebro
junk n. trastos viejos; junco
ju-ris-dic-tion n. jurisdiccion
ju-ris-pur-dene n. jurisprudencia
ju-rist n. jurista
ju-ror n. jurado
ju-ry n. jurado
just adj. justo; imparcial
jus-ti-fy v. justificar
ju-ve-nile adj. joven

kale n. col rizada
ka-lei-do-scope n. calidoscopio
kan-ga-roo n. canguro
kar-at n. uilate
keel n. quilla
keen adj. agudo; perspicaz; entusiasta; afilado
keep v. detener; tener; cumplir
keep-ing n. custodia
keg n. cuñete
ken v. saver
ken-nel n. perrera
ker-chief n. pañuelo
ker-nel n. almendra; mucleo
ker-o-sene n. ueroseno
ketch n. queche
ketch-up n. salsa picante de tomate
ket-tle n. tetera
key n. llave
key-board n. teclado
key-stone n. piedra clave
khak-i n. caqui
kick v. dar patadas; dar un puntapie
kid n. cabrito
kid-nap v. secuestrar
kid-ney n. riñon
kill v. matar
kiln n. horno
kil-o-c-cle n. kilociclo
kil-o-gram n. kilogramo
kil-o-me-ter n. kilometro
kil-o-watt n. kilovation
kin n. parientes
kind adj. bueno; n. genero
kin-der-gar-ten n. jardín de la infancia
kind-heart-ed a. bondadoso
kin-dle v. encender
kind-ly adj. bondadoso
kind-ness n. benevolencia
kin-dred n. parientes
king n. rey
king-dom n. reino
kink n. coca; peculiaridad
kin-ship n. parentesco
kins-man n. pariente
kiss n. beso; v. besar
kit n. equipo; avios
kitch-en n. cocina

kite *n.* equipo; avios

kith *n.* amigos

kit-ten *n.* gatito

knack *n.* mana

knap-sack *n.* mochila

knave *n.* bribón

knav-er-y *n.* bellaquería

knav-ish *adj.* bellaco

knead *v.* amasar

knee *n.* rodilla

knee-cap *n.* rotula

kneel *n.* arrodillarse

knee-pad *n.* rodillera

knell *n.* doble

knick-ers *n.* bombachos

knick-knack *n.* chuchería

knife *v.* acuchillar, *n.* cuchillo

knight *n.* caballero

knight-hood *n.* caballerosidad

knit *v.* hacer punto; juntar

knit-ting *n.* tejido

knob *n.* tirador; buto

knock *v.* golpear

knock-down *adj.* que derriba

knock-er *adj.* picaporte

knock-ing *n.* llamada

knoll *n.* otero

knot *v.* anudar

knot-hole *n.* agujero

knot-ted *adj.* anudado; nudoso

knot-ty *adj.* enredado; nudoso

know *v.* saber; conocer

know-a-ble *adj.* conocible

know-how *n.* pericia

know-ing *a.* astuto; habil

know-ing-ly *adv.* a sabiendas

knowl-edge *n.* saber

knowl-edge-a-ble *adj.* erudito

known *adj.* concido

know-noth-ing *n.* ighorante

knuck-le *n.* nudillo

ko-a-la *n.* koala

ook *n.* excentrico

o-ran *n.* Alcorán; Coran

o-sher *adj.* legitimo; conforme a las reglas

ow-tow *v.* postarse

lab *n.* laboratorio

la-bel *v.* marcar; *n.* etiqueta; rotulo

la-bi-al *adj.* labial

la-bor *v.* trabajar, *n.* trabajo

lab-o-ra-to-ry *n.* laboratorio

la-bored *adj.* peon; trabajador; jornalero

la-bo-ri-ous *adj.* laborioso

lab-y-rinth *n.* laberinto

lac *n.* laca

lace *v.* encordonar; *n.* encaje

lac-er-ate *v.* lacerar

lac-er-ation *n.* laceración

lach-ry-mal *adj.* lagrimal

lack *v.* faltar; hacer falta; *n.* falta

lack-ey *n.* lacayo

lack-ing *adj.* deficiente; *prep.* sin

lack-lus-ter *adj.* deslucido

la-con-ic *adj.* laconico

lac-quer *n.* laca

lac-tase *n.* lactasa

lac-tate *v.* lactar

lac-ta-tion *n.* lactancia

lac-tic *adj.* lactico

lac-tose *n.* lactoxa

la-cu-na *n.* laguna

lac-y *adj.* de encaje

lad *n.* chico

lad-der *n.* escalera

lad-die *n.* chico

lade *v.* agobiar

lad-en *adj.* agobiado; cargado

la-dle *n.* cucharón

la-dy *n.* dama

la-dy-bug *n.* mariquita

lag *v.* trasarse; rezagarse

lag-gard *adj.* rezagado

la-goon *n.* laguna

la-ic *adj.* laico

lair *n.* madriguera

la-i-ty *n.* laicos

lake *n.* lago

lamb *n.* cordero

lame *v.* baldar; *adj.* renco; cojo

la-me *n.* lame

la-ment *v.* deplorar; lamentar

la-men-ta-ble *adj.* lamentable

lam-en-ta-tion n. lamentacion

la-ment-ed adj. lamentado

lam-i-na n. lamina

lam-i-nate v. laminar

lam-i-nat-ed adj. laminado

lam-i-na-tion n. laminación

lamp n. lampara

lam-poon v. satirizar; n. satira

lam-prey n. lamprea

lance n. lanza

lan-cet n. lanceta

land v. pais; tierra

land-ed adj. hacendado

land-fall n. recalada

land-hold-er n. terrateniente

land-ing n. amaraje; desembarco

land-lord n. arrendador

land-mark n. mojón

land-own-er n. terrateniente

land-scape n. panorama

lane n. ruta; vereda; camino

lan-guage n. lenguaje

lan-guid adj. lánguido

lan-guish v. decaer; languidecer

lan-guish-ing adj. lánguido

lan-guor n. languidez

lan-guor-ous adj. lánguido

lan-o-lin n. lanolina

lan-tern n. linterna

lap n. falda; v. plegar; doblar

la-pel n. solapa

lap-i-dar-y n. lapidario

lapse v. faltar; caer; decaer; deslizarse

lapsed adj. caduco

lar-ce-ny adj. robo

lard n. lardo

large adj. grande

lar-gess n. donativo; generosidad

lar-va n. larva

lar-val adj. larval

lar-yn-gi-tis n. laringitis

lar-y-nx n. laringe

la-ser n. laser

lash n. latigo; ázote; latigazo

lash-ing n. fustigación; azotaina

lass n. muchacha

las-si-tude n. lasitude

las-so n. lazo

last adv. finalmente; adj. final

last-ing adj. duradero

last-ly adv. finalmente

latch n. aldabilla

late adv. tarde

late-ly adv. ultimamente

la-ten-cy n. latencia

late-enss n. tardanza

la-tent adj. latente

la-ter adj. posterior

lat-er-al adj. lateral

lat-est adj. último

la-tex n. latex

lath-er n. espuma

lat-i-tude n. latitud

la-trine n. letrina

lat-ter adj. ultimo

lat-ter-day adj. reciente

lat-tice n. celosia; v. enrejar

lat-tice-work n. enrejado

laud v. alabar; elogiar

laud-a-ble adj. laudable

laud-a-to-ry adj. laudatorio

laugh n. risa; v. reir(se)

laugh-a-ble adj. absurdo; comico

laugh-ing adj. risueño

laugh-ter n. risa

launch v. lanzar; iniciar; botar

launch-er n. lanzador

launch-ing n. lanzamiento

laun-der v. lavar(se)

laun-dered adj. lavado

laun-der-er n. lavandero

laun-dry n. lavanderia

lau-rel n. laurel

la-va n. lava

lav-en-der n. lavanda

lav-ish adj. espendido; generoso

law n. derecho; ley

law-ful adj. legitimo

law-less adj. sin leyes

law-mak-er n. legislador

lawn n. césped

law-yer n. abogado

lax adj. laxo

lax-a-tive n. laxante

lax-i-ty n. laxitud
lay v. acostar; poner
lay-er n. estrato
lay-out n. distribución
la-zi-ness n. pereza
la-zy adj. perezoso
lead v. mandar; conducir
lead-en adj. plombeo
lead-er n. lider
lead-er-ship n. mando
lead-ing n. emplomado
leaf n. hoja
leaf-let n. panfleto
leaf-y adj. hojoso
league n. liga
leak v. gotear; salirse; n. gotera; agujero
lean adj. magro
lean-ing n. inclinación
leap v. saltar
learn v. aprender
learn-ed adj. erudito
learn-er n. principiante
learn-ing n. aprendizaje
lease-hold n. arrendamiento
lease-hold-er n. arrendatario
leash n. traílla
leas-ing n. arrendamiento
least adv. menos, adj. menor
leath-er n. cuero
leath-er-y adj. curtido
leave v. salir; dejar; irse
leav-en v. leudar
leav-ing n. salida
lech-er-ous adj. lujurioso
lech-er-y n. lujuria
lec-ture v. sermonear; reprender; n. reprimenda; conferencia
lec-tur-er n. conferenciante
leech n. sanguijuela
leek n. puerro
left adj. izquierdo
left-o-ver adj. sobrante
left-y n. zirdo
leg n. pierna
leg-a-cy n. herencia
le-gal adj. legal
le-gal-ist n. legalista
le-gal-is-tic adj. legalista
le-gal-i-ty n. legalidad

le-gal-ize v. legalizar
leg-ate n. legado
le-ga-tion n. legación
leg-end n. leyenda
leg-end-ar-y adj. legendario
leg-gings n. polainas
leg-i-bil-i-ty n. legibilidad
leg-i-ble adj. legible
le-gion n. legion
le-gion-ar-y n. legionario
le-gion-naire n. legionario
leg-is-late v. legislar
leg-is-la-tion n. legislación
leg-is-la-tor n. legislador
le-git-i-ma-cy n. legitimidad
le-git-i-mate adj. legitimo
le-git-i-mize v. legitimar
lei-sure n. ocio
lem-on n. limon
lem-on-ade n. limonada
lend v. impartir; prestar
lend-er n. prestador
length n. extensión; longitud; tramo; largo
length-en v. prolongar(se); alargar(se)
length-y adj. prolongado
le-nient adj. indulgente
lens n. lente
len-til n. lenteja
le-o-nine adj. leonino
leop-ard n. leopardo
lep-er n. leproso
lep-ro-sy n. lepra
lep-rous adj. leproso
le-sion n. lesión
less adv., adj. menos
less-en v. disminuir
less-er adj. menor
les-son n. lección
let v. dejar; permitir
let-down n. desilusión
le-thal adj. letal
le-thar-gic adj. letargico
leth-ar-gy n. letargo
let-ter n. carta
let-tered adj. letrado
let-ter-ing n. rotulo
let-tuce n. lechuga
leu-ke-mi-a n. leucemia
lev-el n. llano; nivel
lev-i-ta-tion n. levitación
lev-y v. recaudar; exigir

lewd adj. lujurioso
lewd-ness n. lujuria
lex-i-cog-ra-phy n. lexicografía
lex-i-con n. lexicon
li-a-bil-i-ty n. obligación
li-a-ble adj. sujeto; responsable
li-ar n. mentiroso
li-ba-tion n. libación
lib-er-al adj. liberal
lib-er-ate v. libertar
lib-er-ty n. libertad
li-brar-y n. biblioteca
lie v. mentir; acostarse
life n. vida
lift v. levantar(se); elevar
light n. lampara; luz
light-ly adv. ligeramente
like n. gusto, v. gustar
like-ness n. semejanza
li-lac n. lila
lil-y n. lirio
lim-bo n. limbo
lime n. lima
lim-it v. limitar
lim-ou-sine n. limusina
line v. alinear; rayar, n. raya; linea
li-on n. león
lip n. labio
liq-uid n. liquido
liq-ui-date v. liquidar
liq-uor n. licor
list n. lista
lit-er-al adj. literal
lit-er-ar-y adj. literario
lit-er-a-ture n. literatura
lit-tle n., adj., adv. poco, adj. pequeno
live v. vivir
liz-ard n. lagarto
lob-ster n. langosta
lo-cal adj. local
lo-cal-i-ty n. localidad
lo-cate v. encontrar
lone adj. solitario
lone-ly adj. solo
lone-ly adj. solo
long adj. largo
look n. mirada, v. buscar; mirar
loose v. soltar, adj. disoluto;

suelto
lost adj. perdido
lo-tion n. loción
lot-ter-y n. loteria
loud adj. alto
love v. amar; querer, n. amor
love-ly adj. hermoso
low adv., adj. bajo, adv. abajo
low-er v. bajar
loy-al adj. fiel
loy-al-ty n. fidelidad
lu-bri-cant n. lubricante
lu-bri-cate v. lubricar
lu-bri-cious adj. lúbrico
lu-cent adj. luminoso
lu-cid adj. cuerdo; lucido
lu-cid-i-ty n. lucidez
luck n. suerte
luck-less adj. desafortunado
luck-y adj. fortuito
lu-cra-tive adj. lucrativo
lu-di-crous adj. ridiculo
lug v. halar
lug-gage n. equipaje
luke-warm adj. tibio
lull v. sosegar; embaucar
lum-bar adj. lumbar
lum-ber n. leno
lum-ber-ing adj. torpe; pesado
lu-mi-nance n. luminancia
lu-mi-nar-y n. luminar
lu-mi-nes-cence n. luminiscente
lu-mi-nous adj. luminoso
lump n. masa; terron
lu-na-cy n. locura
lu-nar adj. lunar
lunch v. almorzar, n. almuerz
lus-ter n. lustre
lus-ty a. robusto
lute n. laud
lux-u-ri-ant a. lozano
lux-u-ry n. lujo
lye n. lejia
lymph n. linfa
lynch n. linchar
lynx n. lince
lyre n. lira
lyr-ic adj. lírico

ma-ca-bre adj. macabro
mac-a-ro-ni n. macarrones
mac-a-roon n. mostachon
ma-chaw n. guacamayo
mac-er-ate v. macerar(se)
ma-chet-e n. machete
mach-i-nate v. maquinar
mach-i-na-tion n. maquinacion
ma-chine n. maquina
ma-chine-gun n. ametrallar
ma-chin-er-y n. maquinaria
ma-chin-ist n. maquinista
mack-er-el n. caballa
mac-ra-me n. macrame
mac-ro-bi-ot-ics n. macrobiotica
mac-ro-cosm n. macrocosmo
mac-ro-scop-ic adj. macroscopico
mad adj. furioso
mad-cap adj. alocado
mad-den v. enloquecer
mad-den-ing adj. enloquecedor
made-up adj. incentado
mad-ness n. locura
mag-a-zine n. revista
mag-got n. gusano
mag-ic n. magia
mag-i-cal adj. mágico
ma-gi-cian n. mago
mag-is-te-ri-al adj. magistral
mag-is-trate n. magistrado
mag-nate n. magnate
mag-ne-si-um n. magnesio
mag-net-ic adj. magnetico
mag-net-ism n. magnetismo
mag-net-ize v. magnetizar
mag-ni-fi-ca-tion n. ampliación
mag-nif-i-cence n. magnificencia
mag-nif-i-cent adj. magnifico
mag-ni-fi-er n. amplificador
mag-ni-fy v. aumentar
mag-ni-tude n. magnitud
mag-num v. magnum
ma-hog-a-ny n. caoba
maid n. soltera
mail n. correo

mail-box n. buzón
mail-man n. cartero
main-tain v. mantener
main-te-nance n. mantenimiento
ma-jes-tic adj. majestuoso
maj-es-ty n. majestad
ma-jor adj. mayor
ma-jor-i-ty n. mayoria
make v. ganar; crear; hacer
mak-er n. fabricante
mak-ing n. fabricación
mal-a-dy n. dolencia
ma-lar-i-a n. malaria
mal-con-tent adj. malcontento
male adj. masculino; macho
mal-e-dic-tion n. maldición
ma-lev-o-lence n. malevolencia
ma-lev-o-lent adj. malévolo
mal-func-tion v. funcionar mal
mal-ice n. malicia
ma-li-cious adj. malicioso
ma-lig-nan-cy n. malignidad
ma-lig-nant adj. maligno
mall n. alameda
mal-le-a-ble adj. maleable
mal-nour-ished adj. desnutrido
mal-nu-tri-tion n. desnutrición
malt n. malta
mal-treat v. maltratar
mal-treat-ment n. maltratamiento
mam-mal n. mamifero
mam-ma-li-an adj. mamifero
mam-ma-ry adj. mamario
man n. hombre
man-age v. manejar
man-age-a-ble adj. manejable
man-age-ment n. gerencia
man-da-rin n. mandarin
man-date n. mandato
man-da-to-ry adj. mandante
man-do-lin n. mandolina
ma-neu-ver v. maniobrar
ma-neu-ner-a-ble adj. maniobrable
man-ga-nese n. manganeso

man-gle v. mutilar
man-go n. mango
man-hood n. madurez
ma-ni-a n. manía
ma-ni-ac adj. maniaco
ma-ni-a-cal adj. maniaco
man-ic adj. maniaco
man-i-cure n. manicura
man-i-cur-ist n. manicuro
man-i-fest adj. manifiesto
man-i-fes-ta-tion n. manifestación
man-i-fes-to n. manifiesto
ma-ni-kin n. maniquí
ma-nip-u-late v. manipular
ma-nip-u-la-tion n. manipulación
ma-nip-u-la-tive adj. de manipuleo
ma-nip-u-la-tor n. manipulador
man-li-ness n. hombría
man-ly adj. masculino
man-ne-quin n. maniquí
man-ner n. manera
man-nered adj. amanerado
man-ner-ism n. amaneramiento
man-nish adj. hombruno
man-tel n. manto
man-tle n. manto
man-u-al adj. manual
man-u-fac-ture n. manufactura
man-u-fac-tured adj. manufacturado
man-u-fac-tur-ing adj. manufacturero
man-u-script n. manuscrito
man-y adj. muchos
map n. mapa
ma-ple n. arce
map-mak-er n. cartografía
mar v. desfigurar
mar-a-thon n. maraton
ma-raud-er n. merodeador
mar-ble n. marmol
mar-bled adj. jaspeado
mar-bling n. marmoración
march v. marchar
March n. marzo
mar-ga-rine n. margarina
mar-gin s. margen

mar-gin-al adj. marginal
mar-i-gold n. maravilla
ma-ri-na n. marina
mar-i-nate v. marinar
ma-rine adj. marino
mar-i-ner n. marinero
mar-i-tal adj. marital
mar-i-time adj. marítimo
mark n. marca
marked adj. marcado
mark-er n. marcador
mar-ket v. vender; n. mercado
mar-ket-a-ble adj. vendible
mar-ket-er n. vendedor
mark-ing n. marca
mar-ma-lade n. mermelada
ma-roon v. abandonar
mar-quis n. marques
mar-riage n. matrimonio
mar-ried adj. casado
mar-row n. medula
mar-ry v. casar(se)
marsh n. pantano
mar-shal n. mariscal
marsh-y adj. pantanoso
mar-su-pi-al adj. marsupial
mart n. mercado
mar-tial adj. marcial
mar-tyr n. martir
mar-tyr-dom n. martirio
mar-vel s. maravilla
mar-vel-lous adj. maravilloso
mas-cot n. mascota
mas-cu-line adj. masculion
mas-cu-lin-i-ty n. masculinidad
mash v. majar
mash-er n. majador
mask n. mascara
mas-och-ism n. masoquismo
mas-o-chist n. masoquista
mas-o-chis-tic adj. masoquista
ma-son-ary n. albanileria
mas-quer-ade n. mascarada
mass n. masa
mas-sa-cre n. masacre
mas-sage v. masajear
mas-sive adj. masivo
mast n. mastil
mas-tec-to-my n. mastec-

tomia

mas-ter *n.* maestro

mas-ter-ful *adj.* habil

mas-ter-ly *adj.* magistral

mas-ter-y *n.* maestria

mas-tic *adj.* mastique

mas-ti-cate *v.* masticar

mas-toid *n.* mastoides

mat *n.* estera

mate *n.* hembra; compañero

ma-te-ri-al *adj., n.* material

ma-te-ri-al-ist *n.* materialista

ma-te-ri-al-is-tic *adj.* materialista

ma-te-ri-al-i-ty *n.* materialidad

math *n.* matematicas

math-e-mat-i-cal *adj.* matematico

math-e-ma-ti-cian *n.* matematico

math-e-mat-ics *n.* matematicas

mat-i-nee *n.* matinee

ma-tri-arch *n.* matriarca

ma-tri-ar-chal *adj.* matriarcal

ma-tri-ar-chy *n.* matriarcado

ma-tric-u-late *v.* matricular(se)

ma-tric-u-la-tion *n.* matriculación

mat-ri-mo-ni-al *adj.* matrimonial

mat-ri-mo-ny *n.* matrimonio

ma-trix *n.* matriz

ma-tron *n.* matrona

ma-tron-ly *adj.* matronal

mat-ted *adj.* esterado

mat-ter *n.* materia

mat-ting *n.* estera

mat-tress *n.* colchon

mat-u-ra-tion *n.* maduración

ma-ture *v.* madurar, *adj.* maduro

ma-tur-i-ty *n.* madurez

maul *v.* maltratar

mauve *n.* malva

max-im *n.* máxima

max-i-mal *adj.* máximo

max-i-mum *adj.* máximo

May *n.* mayo

may *v.* poder

may-be *adj.* tal vez

may-on-naise *n.* mayonesa

may-or *n.* alcalde

may-or-al-ty *n.* alcadia

me *pron.* mi; me

mead-ow *n.* pradera

mea-ger *adj.* pobre; magro

meal *n.* comida

mean *v.* intentar

me-an-der *v.* vagar

mean-ing *n.* significado

mean-ing-ful *adj.* significativo

mean-ing-less *adj.* insignificante

mea-sles *n.* rubeola

meas-ure *v.* medir

meas-ured *adj.* mesurado

meas-ure-ment *n.* medición

meat *n.* carne

meat-y *adj.* carnoso

me-chan-ic *n.* mecánico

me-chan-i-cal *adj.* mecánico

mech-a-nism *n.* mecánismo

mech-a-nize *v.* mecanizar

med-al *n.* medalla

me-dal-lion *n.* medallon

med-dle *v.* entremeterse

med-dler *n.* entremetido

me-di-an *adj.* mediano

me-di-ate *v.* mediar

me-di-a-tion *n.* mediación

me-di-a-tor *n.* mediador

med-ic *n.* medico

med-i-cal *adj.* medico

med-i-cate *v.* medicinar

med-i-ca-tion *n.* medicación

med-i-cine *n.* medicina

me-di-e-val *adj.* midieval

me-di-o-cre *adj.* mediocre

me-di-oc-ri-ty *n.* mediocridad

med-i-tate *v.* meditar

med-i-ta-tion *n.* meditación

meet *v.* reunirse; encontras(se)

mel-o-dy *n.* melodia

mel-on *n.* melon

mem-ber *n.* miembro

mem-o-ra-ble *adj.* memorable

men-tal *adj.* mental

men-tion *v.* mencionar; *n.* mencion

mer-cu-ry n. mercurio
mer-it v. merecer
mer-ry adj. festivo
mes-sage n. comunicación
mes-sen-ger n. mensajero
met-al n. metal
me-te-or-ol-o-gy n. meteorologia
meth-od n. metodo
mi-crobe n. microbio
mi-cro-phone n. microfono
mi-cro-scope n. microscopio
mid-dle n., adj. medio
mid-night n. medianoche
mi-grate v. emigrar
mil-i-tary adj. militar
mi-li-tia n. milicia
milk n. leche
mil-lion n. millón
mil-lion-aire n. millonario
mind v. obedecer, n. mente
min-er-al n. mineral
min-is-ter n. ministro
mi-nor adj. menor
mi-nor-i-ty n. minoria
mi-nus prep. menos
mir-a-cle n. milagro
mir-ror n. espejo
mis-chie-vous adj. malicioso
miss v. perder
mis-sion n. misión
mis-sion-ar-y n. misionero
mis-ter n. senor
mis-treat v. maltratar
mit-i-gate v. mitigar
mit-ten n. mitón
mix n. mezcla, v. mezclar(se)
mix-ture n. mezcla
mod-el v. modelar, n. modelo
mod-er-ate v. moderar, adj. moderno
mod-ern n. moderno
mod-est adj. modesto
mod-i-fi-ca-tion n. modificación
mod-i-fy v. modificar
mod-u-late v. modular
moist adj. humedo
mois-ten v. humedecer(se)
moist-ness n. humedad

mois-ture n. humedad
mois-tur-iz-er v. humedecer
mo-lar n. molar
mo-las-ses n. melaza
mold v. moldear, n. molde
mold-er v. desmoronar(se)
mold-ing n. mohoso
mo-lec-u-lar adj. molecular
mol-e-cule n. molecula
mole-hill n. topera
mol-li-fy v. molificar
mol-lusk n. molusco
mol-ten adj. fundido
mom n. mama
mo-ment n. momento
mo-men-tar-i-ly adv. momentáneamente
mo-men-tar-y adj. momentaneo
mo-men-tum n. momento
mon-arch n. monarca
mo-nar-chic adj. monarquico
mon-ar-chist n. monarquico
mon-ar-chy n. monarquia
mon-as-ter-y n. monasterio
mo-nas-tic adj. monastico
Mon-day n. lunes
mon-e-tar-y adj. monetario
mon-ey n. dinero
mon-eyed adj. adinerado
mon-goose n. mangosta
mo-ni-tion n. admonición
mon-i-tor n. monitor
mon-i-to-ry adj. admonitorio
monk n. monje
mon-key n. mono
monk-hood n. monacato
monk-ish adj. monacal
mon-o-chro-mat-ic adj. monocromatico
mo-noc-u-lar adj. monocular
mo-nog-a-my n. monogamia
mon-o-gram n. monograma
mon-o-graph n. monografía
mon-o-lith n. monolito
mon-o-lith-ic adj. monolitico
mon-o-plane n. monoplano
mo-nop-o-lize v. monopolizar
mo-nop-o-ly n. monopolio
mon-o-rail n. monocarril
mo-no-tone n. monotonia

mo-not-o-nous *adj.* monotono

mo-not-o-ny *n.* monotonía

mon-ox-ide *n.* monoxido

mon-soon *n.* monzon

mon-ster *n.* monstruo

mon-stros-i-ty *n.* monstruosidad

mon-strous *adj.* monstruoso

mon-tage *n.* montaje

month *n.* mes

month-ly *adj.* mensual

mon-u-ment *n.* monumento

mon-u-men-tal *adj.* monumental

moo *v.* mugir

mood *n.* humor

moon *n.* luna

moor *v.* amarrar

moor-age *n.* amarradero

moor-ing *n.n* amarradero

moose *n.* anta

mop *n.* estropajo

mo-ped *n.* ciclomotor

mor-al *adj.* moral

mo-rale *n.* moral

mor-al-ist *n.* moralista

mor-al-is-tic *adj.* moralizador

mo-ral-i-ty *n.* moralidad

mor-al-ize *v.* moralizar

mor-bid *adj.* morboso

mor-bid-i-ty *n.* morbosidad

more *n., adv., adj.* mas

more-o-ver *adv.* ademas

morn-ing *n.* manana

mor-phine *n.* morfina

mor-phol-o-gy *n.* morfología

mor-tal *n., adj.* mortal

mor-tal-i-ty *n.* mortalidad

mor-tu-ar-y *n.* mortuorio

mos-qui-to *n.* mosquito

most *adj.* muy; mas

moth *n.* polilla

moth-er *n.* madre

moth-er-hood *n.* maternidad

moth-er-in-law *n.* suegra

mo-tor-cy-cle *n.* motocicleta

moun-tain *n.* montaña

mouse *n.* ratón

mouth *n.* boca

move *v.* mundar; mover

mov-ie *n.* pelicula

Mr. *n.* señor

Mrs. *n.* señora

Ms. *n.* señora

much *adj.* muy, *n., adv., adj.* mucho

mul-ti-ple *adj.* multiple

mul-ti-pli-ca-tion *n.* multiplicación

mul-ti-ply *v.* multiplicar

mul-ti-pur-pose *adj.* multiuso

mul-ti-tude *n.* multitud

mum-ble *v.* mascular

mum-my *n.* momia

munch *v.* ronzar

mun-dane *adj.* mundaño

mu-nic-i-pal *adj.* municipal

mu-nic-i-pal-i-ty *n.* municipalidad

mu-nif-i-cence *n.* munificencia

mu-nif-i-cent *adj.* munifico

mur-der *v.* matanza

mur-der-er *n.* asesino

mur-der-ous *adj* asesiño

mur-mur *v.* murmurar

mus-cle *n.* musculo

mus-cu-lar *adj.* musculoso

muse *v.* meditar

mu-se-um *n.* museo

mu-sic *n.* musica

mu-si-cal *adj.* musical

mu-si-cal-i-ty *n.* musicalidad

mu-si-cian *n.* musico

mus-ing *n.* contemplación

mus-ket *n.* mosquete

mus-ket-eer *n.* mosquetero

mus-lin *n.* muselina

mus-sel *n.* mejillon

must *v.* deber

mus-tache *n.* bigote

mu-ti-late *v.* mutilar

muz-zle *n.* hocico; boca

my *adj.* mi

myr-i-ad *n.* miriada

my-self *pron.* yo mismo

mys-te-ri-ous *a.* misterioso

mys-ter-y *n.* misterio

mys-tic *a.* mistico

mys-ti-cism *n.* misticismo; mistica

myth *n.* mito

myth-ic *a.* mitico

my-thol-o-gy *n.* mitología

nab v. prender
na-dir n. nadir
nag n. jaca
nail v. clavar, n. clavo
na-ive adj. ingenuo
na-ive-te n. ingenuidad
naked adj. desnudo
name v. apellido; nombre
name-less adj. anonimo
name-ly adv. a saber
name-sake n. tocayo
nap n. siesta
nape n. nuca
nap-kin n. servilleta
nar-cis-sism n. narcisismo
nar-cis-sus n. narciso
nar-cot-ic n. narcotico
nar-rate v. narrar
nar-ra-tion n. narración
nar-ra-tive adj. narrativo
nar-ra-tor n. narrador
nar-row adj. estrecho; limitado; angosto
nar-row-ing n. limitación
na-sal adj. nasal
na-sal-i-ty n. nasalidad
nas-ty adj. antipatico; sucio; obsceno
na-tal adj. natal
na-tal-i-ty n. natalidad
na-tion n. nation
na-tion-al n., adj. nacional
na-tion-al-ist n. nacionalista
na-tion-al-is-tic adj. nacionalista
na-tion-al-i-ty n. nacionalidad
na-tion-al-ize v. nacionalizar
na-tive adj. natal; innato; nativo
na-tiv-i-ty n. natividad
nat-u-ral adj. natural
nat-u-ral-ist n. naturalista
nat-u-ral-is-tic adj. naturalista
nat-u-ral-ize v. naturalizar(se)
nat-u-ral-ly adv. naturalmente
na-ture n. genero; naturaleza
naught n. nada
naugh-ty adj. verde; travieso

nau-se-a n. nausea
nau-se-ate v. dar nauseas a
nau-se-at-ing adj. nauseabundo
nau-se-ous adj. nauseabundo
nau-ti-cal adj. nautico
na-val adj. naval
nav-i-ga-ble adj. navegable
nav-i-gate v. navegar
nav-i-ga-tion n. navegación
nav-i-ga-tor n. navegante
nay adv. no
near prep. cerca de, adv. cerca, adj. próximo
near-by adj. próximo
near-ly adj. caso
neat adj. claro; limpio; fantastico
neb-u-la n. nebulosa
neb-u-lar adj. nebuloso
nec-es-sar-y adj. necesario
ne-ces-si-tate v. necesitar
ne-ces-si-ty n. necesidad
neck n. cuello
neck-lace n. collar
neck-line n. escote
ne-crol-o-gy n. necrología
ne-cro-sis n. necrosis
nec-tar n. nactar
nec-tar-ine n. pelon
need v. necesitar
need-ful adj. necessario
nee-dle n. aguja
need-less adj. superfluo
need-y adj. necesitado
ne-far-i-ous adj. nefario
ne-gate v. negar
ne-ga-tion n. negación
neg-a-tive n. negativa
ne-glect v. descuidar
ne-glect-ful adj. negligente
neg-li-gence n. negligencia
neg-li-gent adj. negligente
neg-li-gi-ble adj. insignificante
ne-go-tia-ble adj. negociable
ne-go-ti-ate v. negociar
ne-go-ti-a-tion n. negociación
ne-go-ti-a-tor n. negociador
neigh-bor n. projimo; vecino
neigh-bor-hood n. barrio

neigh-bor-ing adj. vecino
neigh-bor-ly adj. amable
nei-ther pron. ninguno, conj. tampoco; ni
ne-ol-o-gism n. neologismo
ne-ol-o-gist n. neologo
ne-on n. neon
ne-o-phyte n. neofito
neph-ew n. sobrino
nep-o-tism n. nepotismo
nerve n. nervio
nerve-less adj. sin nervios
nerv-ous adj. nervioso
nerv-ous-ness n. nerviosidad
nest n. nido
net n. red
net-ting n. red
net-tle n. ortiga
net-work n. red
neu-ral-gia n. neuralgia
neu-ral-gic adj. neuralgico
neu-ri-tis n. neuritis
neu-ro-sis n. nervioso
neu-rol-o-gist n. neurologo
neu-rol-o-gy n. neurología
neu-rot-ic adj. neurótico
neu-tral n., adj. neutral
neu-tral-i-ty n. neutralidad
neu-tral-ize v. neutralizar
neu-tral-iz-er n. neutralizador
neu-tron n. neutron
nev-er adv. jamás; nunca
nev-er-more adv. nunca mas
nev-er-the-less adv. sin embargo
new adj. nuevo
new-found adj. nuevo
new-ly adv. nuevamente
news n. nuevas
news-cast n. noticiario
news-cast-er n. locutor
news-pa-per n. diario
news-y adj. informativo
newt n. tritón
new-ton n. neutonio
next adj. próximo
nib-ble v. mordiscar
nice adj. agradable; amable
ni-ce-ty n. delicadeza; precisión
niche n. nicho

nick n. neusca; mella
nick-el n. niquel
nick-name n. apodo
nic-o-tine n. nicotina
niece n. sobrina
nigh adv. cerca
night n. noche
night-fall n. anochecer
night-gown n. camison
night-in-gale n. ruiseñor
night-light n. lamparilla
night-ly adj. nocturno
night-mare n. pesadilla
night-time n. noche
nine adj. nueve
nine-teen adj. diecinueve
nine-ty adj. noventa
ninth adj. noveno
no n., adj. no
no-bod-y n., pron. nadie
noise n. ruido
nois-y adj. ruidoso
none pron. nadie; nada
noon n. mediodia
nor conj. ni
nor-mal adj. normal
nor-mal-ly adv. normalmente
north n. norte
north-east n. nordeste
north-west n. noroeste
nose n. nariz
not adv. no
no-ta-ble adj. notable
no-ta-tion n. notación
note v. notar, n. nota
no-ti-fy v. notificar
no-tion n. nocion
no-to-ri-ous adj. notorio
No-vem-ber n. noviembre
now adv. ahora
nu-cle-ar adj. nuclear
nude n., adj. desnudo
num-ber v. numerar, n. numero
nu-mer-i-cal adj. numerico
nu-mer-ous adj. numeroso
nut n. nuez
nu-tri-tion n. nutrición
nu-tri-tion-al adj. nutritivo
nu-tri-tious adj. nutritivo
nu-tri-tive adj. nutritivo
nuz-zle v. hocicar
ny-lon n. nailon

oak *n.* roble
oak-en *adj.* de roble
oar *n.* remo
o-a-sis *n.* oasis
oat *n.* avena
oath *n.* juramento
oat-meal *n.* gachas de avena
ob-du-ra-cy *n.* obstinación
ob-du-rate *adj.* obstinado; insensible
o-be-di-ence *n.* obediencia
o-be-di-ent *adj.* obediente
o-bese *adj.* obeso
o-be-si-ty *n.* obesidad
o-bey *v.* obedecer
ob-fus-cate *v.* ofuscar
ob-fus-ca-tion *n.* ofuscación
o-bit-u-ar-y *n.* obituario
ob-ject *v.* desaprobar; *n.* objeto
ob-jec-tion *n.* objeción
ob-jec-tion-a-ble *adj.* ofensivo
ob-jec-tive *n., adj.* objetivo
ob-li-gate *v.* obligar
ob-li-ga-tion *n.* obligación
o-blig-a-to-ry *adj.* obligatorio
o-blige *v.* obligar
o-blig-ing *adj.* complaciente
o-blique *adj.* oblicuo
o-blit-er-ate *v.* aniquilar; arrasar
o-bliv-i-on *n.* olvido
o-bliv-i-ous *adj.* olvidadizo
ob-long *adj.* oblongo
ob-nox-ious *adj.* insoportable; desagradable
o-boe *n.* oboe
ob-scene *adj.* obsceno
ob-scen-i-ty *n.* obscenidad
ob-scure *adj.* imperceptible; oscuro
ob-scu-ri-ty *n.* oscuridad
ob-e-qui-ous *adj.* servil
ob-ser-vance *n.* observacion; cumplimiento
ob-ser-vant *adj.* observador
ob-ser-va-tion *n.* observación
ob-ser-va-to-ry *n.* observatorio
ob-serve *v.* cumplir; observar
ob-serv-er *n.* observador
ob-sess *v.* obsesionar
ob-ses-sion *n.* obsesión
ob-ses-sive *adj.* obsesivo
ob-so-les-cence *n.* obsolencia
ob-so-lete *adj.* obsoleto
ob-sta-cle *n.* obstaculo
ob-stet-ric *adj.* obstetrico
ob-sti-na-cy *n.* obstinación
ob-sti-nate *adj.* obstinado
ob-struct *v.* obstruir
ob-struc-tion *n.* obstrucción
ob-struc-tion-ist *n.* obstruccionista
ob-tain *v.* obtener
ob-trude *v.* introducir
ob-tru-sion *n.* intrusión
ob-tuse *adj.* obtuso
ob-vi-ate *v.* obviar
ob-vi-ous *adj.* obvio
ob-vi-ous-ly *adj.* claro
oc-ca-sion *n.* ocasión
oc-ca-sion-al *adj.* ocasional
oc-clude *v.* ocluir
oc-cu-pan-cy *n.* ocupación
oc-cu-pant *n.* pasajero; inquilino
oc-cu-pa-tion *n.* ocupación
oc-cu-pa-tion-al *adj.* ocupacional
oc-cu-pied *adj.* ocupado
oc-cu-py *v.* ocupar
oc-cur *v.* ocurrir
oc-cur-rence *n.* presencia; suceso
o-cean *v.* oceáno
o-ce-an-ic *adj.* oceánico
oc-ta-gon *n.* octagono
oc-tag-o-nal *adj.* octogonal
oc-tane *n.* octano
oc-tave *n.* octavo
Oc-to-ber *n.* octubre
oc-to-ge-nar-i-an *adj.* octogenario
oc-to-pus *n.* pulpo
oc-u-lar *adj.* ocular
oc-u-lis *n.* oculista
odd *adj.* raro
odd-i-ty *n.* rareza
odds *n.* probabilidades
o-di-ous *adj.* odioso

o-di-um n. odio

o-dom-e-ter n. odometro

o-dor n. olor

o-dor-less adj. inoforo

o-dor-ous adj. fragante

od-ys-sey n. odisea

of prep. de

off adv. fuera

of-fend v. ofender

of-fend-er n. infractor

of-fense n. ofense

of-fen-sive adj. ofensivo

of-fer n. ofrecimiento, v. ofrecer

of-fer-ing n. ofrecimiento

of-fice n. oficina

of-fi-cer n. oficial

of-fi-cial n., adj. oficial

of-fi-ci-ate v. oficiar

of-fi-cious adj. oficioso

off-set v. compensar

oil n. aceite

oil-can n. alcuzq

oiled adj. aceitado

oil-y adj. aceitoso

oint-ment n. pomada

o-kra n. quingombo

old adj. anciano; viejo

old-en adj. pasado

old-fash-ioned adj. anticuado

ol-fac-to-ry adj. olfativo

ol-ive n. oliva

om-i-nous adj. ominoso

o-mis-sion n. omisión

o-mit v. omitir

om-ni-bus n. omnibus

om-nip-o-tence n. omnipotencia

om-nip-o-ten adj. omnipotente

on prep. sobre

once n., adv. una vez

on-col-o-gy n. oncologia

on-com-ing adj. que viene

one adj. uno; un

one-di-men-sion-al adj. unidimensional

on-er-ous adj. oneroso

one-self pron. uno

one-sid-ed adj. desigual

on-ion n. cebolla

on-look-er n. espectador

on-ly adj., adv. solo

on-rush n. embestida

on-to prep. sobre; en

on-ward adj. hacia adelante

on-yx n. onix

o-pac-i-ty n. opacidad

o-pal n. opalo

o-pal-es-cence n. opalescencia

o-paque adj. opaco

o-pen v. abrir, adj. abierto

o-pen-er n. abridor

o-pen-ing n. abertura

o-pen-mind-ed adj. receptivo

o-per-a n. opera

op-er-a-ble adj. operable

op-er-ate v. operar; actuar; manejar

op-er-at-ing adj. de mantenimiento

op-er-a-tion n. operación

op-er-a-tion-al adj. deoperacion

op-er-a-tive adj. operante

oph-thal-mol-o-gist n. oftalmolgo

oph-thal-mol-ogy n. oftalmologia

o-pi-ate n. opiato

o-pine v. opinar

o-pin-ion n. opinion

o-pi-um n. opio

op-po-nent n. adversario

op-por-tune adj. oportuno

op-por-tun-ist n. oportunista

op-por-tu-ni-ty n. oportunidad

op-pose v. oponerse

op-po-site adj. opuesto

op-po-si-tion n. oposición

op-press v. oprimir

op-pres-sion n. opresión

op-pres-sive adj. opresivo

op-pres-sor n. opresor

opt v. optar

op-yic adj. optico

op-ti-cal adj. optico

op-ti-cian n. optico

op-ti-mal adj. optimo

op-ti-mism n. optmismo

op-ti-mist n. optimista

op-ti-mis-tic adj. optimista

op-tion n. opción
op-tion-al adj. opcional
op-tom-e-try n. optometria
op-u-lent adj. opulento
or conj. u; o
o-ral adj. oral
or-ange adj. anaranjado, n. naranja
o-ra-tion n. oración
or-ches-tra n. orquesta
or-der n. orden
or-di-nar-y adj. ordinario
or-gan-ism n. organismo
or-gan-i-za-tion n. organización
or-gan-ize v. organizar
o-rig-i-nal adj. original
o-rig-i-nate v. originar
os-ten-ta-tion n. ostentación
oth-er prep. el otro, adj. otro
ounce n. onza
our adj. nuestro
our-selves pron. nosotros
out prep. fuera de, adv. fuera
out-er adj. externo
out-fit n. traje
out-line v. bosquejar, n. bosquejo
out-side adv. fuera, n. exterior
out-ward adj. exterior
o-va-ry n. ovario
o-va-tion n. ovación
ov-en n. horno
o-ver adj. otra vez, prep. sobre; encima de
o-ver-lap v. solapar
o-ver-night adj. de noche
o-ver-sight n. olvido
o-vert a. publico
o-ver-turn v. volcar
o-ver-weight adj. gordo
o-vum n. ovulo
owe v. tener deudas
owl n. buho
own v. reconocer
ox-ide n. oxido
ox-i-dize v. oxidar(se)
ox-y-gen n. oxigeno
ox-y-gen-ate v. oxigenar
oys-ter n. ostra
o-zone n. ozono

pa n. papá
pace n. paso
pa-cif-ic adj. pacifico
pac-i-fism n. pacifismo
pac-i-fy v. pacificar
pack n. fardo
pack-age n. paquete
pact n. pacto
pad n. almohadilla
pad-dle n. canalete
pad-lock n. candado
pa-gan n. pagano
page n. pagina
pag-eant n. espectaculo
pa-go-da n. pagoda
pail n. cubo
pain v. doler; n. dolor
pain-ful adj. doloroso
pains-tak-ing a. laborioso; esmerado
paint n. pintura, v. pintar
paint-ing n. pintura
pair n. pareja; par
pa-jam-as n. pijama
pal-ace n. palacio
pal-ate n. paladar
pale a. palido; claro
pa-le-on-tol-o-gy n. paleontologia
pal-ette n. paleta
pal-i-sade n. palizada
pall v. perder su sabor
pal-lid palido
pal-lor n. palidez
palm n. palma
palm-is-try n. quiromancia
pal-pa-ble adj. palpable
pal-pi-ta-tion n. palpitación
pal-try a. miserable
pam-per v. mimar
pam-phlet n. folleto
pan n. cazuela
pan-a-ce-a n. panacea
pan-cake n. hojuela
pan-cre-as n. pancreas
pan-de-mo-ni-um n. pandemonium
pane n. hoja de vidrio
pan-el n. panel
pang n. punzada; dolor
pan-han-dle v. mendigar
pan-ic n. terror
pan-o-ram-a n. panorama

pan-sy n. pensamiento
pant n., pl. pantalones
pan-the-ism n. panteismo
pan-ther n. pantera
pan-to-mime n. pantomima
pan-try n. despensa
pa-pa n. papa
pa-pa-cy n. papado; pontificado
pa-per n. papel
pa-pier-ma-che n. cartón piedra
pa-poose n. crio
pa-py-rus n. papiro
par n. par
par-a-ble n. parábola
par-a-chute n. paracaídas
pa-rade n. parada
par-a-dise n. paraíso
par-a-dox n. paradoja
par-af-fin n. paraffin
par-a-graph n. parrafo
par-al-lel a. paralelo
pa-ral-y-sis n. parálisis
par-a-lyze v. paralizar
par-am-e-ter n. parametro; limite
par-a-noi-a n. paranoia
par-a-pher-na-ia n. arreos
par-a-phrase n. parafrasis
par-a-site n. parásito
par-a-troop-er n. paracaidista
parcel n. paquete; bulto
parch v. secar
parch-ment n. pergamino
par-don n. perdón, v. perdonar
pare v. cortar
par-ent n. madre; padre
par-ren-the-sis n. parentesis
pa-ri-ah n. paria
par-ish n. parroquia
park v. aparcar, n. parque
par-ley v. parlamentar
par-lia-ment n. parlamento
par-lor n. sala de recibo
pa-ro-chi-al a. parroquial; estrecho
par-o-dy n. parodia
pa-role n. libertad bajo palabra
par-ox-ysm n. paroxismo

par-rot n. loro
par-ry v. parar
par-sley n. perejil
par-son n. clérigo
part v. separar(se); partir(se), n. parte
par-take v. tomar parte
par-tial adj. parcial
par-tial-i-ty n. parcialidad
par-tic-i-pant a. participe
par-tic-i-pate v. participar
par-tic-i-pa-tion n. participación
par-ti-ci-ple n. participio
par-ti-cle n. partículo
par-tic-u-lar adj. particular
par-tic-u-lar-i-ty n. particion; tabique
part-ing a. despendida
par-ti-san n. partidario
par-ti-tion n. partición; tabique
part-ner n. socio
par-tridge n. perdiz
par-ty n. fiesta
pass v. aprobar; pasar
pas-sage n. pasaje; travesia; pasadizo
pas-sen-ger n. pasajero; viajero
pas-sion n. pasión
pas-sion-ate a. apasionado
pas-sive adj. pasivo
pass-port n. pasaporte
pass-word n. santo y sena
past n., adj. pasado
paste n. enguido; pasta
paste-board n. carton
pas-teur-i-za-tion n. pasteurización
pas-teur-ize v. pasteurizar
pas-time n. pasatiempo
pas-tor n. pastor
pas-try n. pasteles
pas-ture n. pasto
pat v. golpecito; pastelillo
patch n. pedazo
pat-ent n. patente
pa-ter-nal adj. paterno
pa-ter-ni-ty n. paternidad
path n. senda
pa-thet-ic a. patético
pa-thol-o-gy n. patología

pa-tience n. paciencia
pa-tient a. paciente
pa-ti-o n. patio
pa-tri-ar-chy n. patriarcado
pat-ri-mo-ny n. patrimonio
pa-tri-ot n. patriota
pa-trol v. patrullar
pa-tron n. cliente
pat-tern n. patrón
pau-per n. pobre
pause n. pausa
pave v. empedrar; pavimentar
pave-ment n. pavimento
pa-vil-ion n. pabellon
paw v. manosear, n. pata
pawn v. empenar
pay v. pagar; ser provechoso
pay-roll n. nomina
pea n. guisante
peace n. paz
peace-ful a. tranquilo
peach n. melocoton
pea-cock n. pavo real; pavon
peak n. pico; cumbre
peal v. repicar
pea-nut n. cachuete
pear n. pera
pearl n. perla
peas-ant n. campesino
pab-ble n. guijarro
pec-ca-dil-lo n. pecadillo
pe-cu-liar adj. peculir
pe-cu-li-ar-i-ty n. peculiaridad
ped-al n. pedal
ped-dle v. vender por las calles
ped-dler n. buhonero
ped-es-tal n. pedestal
pe-des-tri-an n. peaton
ped-i-gree n. genealogia
peel v. pelar
peer n. par
peg n. clavija; estaca
pel-let n. bolita; pella
pelt n. piel
pel-vis n. pelvis
pen n. pluma
pe-nal a. penal
pen-al-ty n. pena; castigo
pen-cil n. lápiz

pend-ant n. pendiente
pend-ing adj. pendiente
pen-du-lum n. péndulo
pen-e-trate v. penetrar
pen-i-cil-in n. penicilina
pen-in-su-la n. península
pen-i-tent n. penitente
pen-i-ten-tia-ry n. presidio
pen-ny n. centavo
pen-sion n. pensión
pen-sive adj. pensativo
pen-ta-gon n. pentágono
pe-on n. peón
pe-o-ny n. peonía
peo-ple n. gente; pueblo
pep-per n. pimienta; pimiento
pep-per-mint n. menta
per prep. por
per-ceive v. percibir
per-cent n. por ciento
per-cent-age n. porcentaje
per-cep-tion n. percepción
perch n. percha; perca
per-di-tion n. perdición
per-en-ni-al a. perenne
per-fect adj. perfecto
per-fec-tion n. perfección
per-fo-rate v. perforar
per-form v. efectuar; hacer; representar
per-for-mance n. representación; función
per-fume n. perfume
per-il n. peligro
pe-rim-e-ter n. perimetro
pe-ri-od n. periodo
pe-ri-od-i-cal n. publicación periodica
pe-riph-er-y n. periferia
per-i-scope n. periscopia
per-ish v. perecer
per-jure v. perjurar(se)
per-ju-ry n. perjurio
per-ma-nent a. permanente
per-mis-sion n. permiso
per-mit v. permitir; tolerar
per-pen-dic-u-lar adj. perpendicular
per-pet-u-al a. perpetuo; continuo
per-plex v. confundir
per-se-cute v. perseguir

per-se-cu--tion n. persecución
per-sist v. persistir
per-son n. persona
per-son-al-i-ty n. personalidad
per-son-nel n. personal
per-spec-tive n. perspectiva
per-suade v. persuadi
per-ver-sion n. perversión
pe-ti-tion n. petición
phar-ma-cy n. farmacia
phi-los-o-phy n. filosofía
pho-bi-a n. fobia
pho-to-cop-y n. fotocopia
pho-to-graph n. foto
pho-tog-ra-phy n. fotografía
phrase n. frase
phys-i-cal adj. físico
phy-si-cian n. medico
pi-an-o n. piano
pick v. picar; elegir
pic-ture n. foto; cuadro; película
pie n. pastel
piece n. pedazo
pig n. cerdo
pi-geon n. paloma
pil-lar n. pilar
pine n. piño
pink adj. rosado
pipe n. pipa
pis-tol n. pistola
pit-y n. lástima
place v. poner, n. posición; sitio
plac-id adj. placido
plague n. plaga
plain adj., n. llano
plan v. planear, n. plano
plane n. avion; plano
plan-et n. planeta
plant v. plantar, n. planta
plas-ma n. plasma
plas-tic n., adj. plastico
plate n. plato
play v. tocar; jugar, n. juego
plea n. defensa
plead v. suplicar; defender
pleas-ure n. placer
plen-ti-ful adj. abundante

plen-ty n. abundancia
plum n. ciruela
plum-age n. plumaje
plu-ral n., adj. plural
pock-et n. bolsillo
po-em n. poema
po-et n. poeta
po-et-ic adj. poético
point n. punto
po-lice n. policía
po-lit-i-cal adj. politico
pol-i-ti-cian n. politico
pol-i-tics n. politicia
pol-lu-tion n. polución
pomp-ous adj. pomposo
pond n. estanque
po-ny n. jaca
pool n. piscina
poor adj. pobre
pop-u-lar adj. popular
pop-u-late v. poblar
pop-u-la-tion n. población
port n. puerto
por-tion n. parte
pose v. plantear
po-si-tion n. posición
pos-i-tive adj. positivo
pos-sess v. poseer
pos-ses-sion n. posesión
pos-si-bil-i-ty n. posibilidad
pos-si-ble adj. posible
post n. poste; puesto; correo
post-age n. porte; franqueo
post-card n. tarjeta
post-er n. cartel
pos-te-ri-or adj. posterior
post-man n. cartero
post-mark n. matasellos
post me-rid-i-em a. postmeridiano
post-mor-tem n. autopsia
post-pone v. alazar
post-script v. posdata
pos-ture n. postura
pot n. olla; tiesto
po-tas-si-um n. potasio
po-ta-to n. patata
po-tent a. potente; fuerte
po-ten-tial n. potencial
po-tion n. posion
pot-ter-y n. alfareria
pouch n. bolsa
poul-try n. aves de corral

pound n. libra
pour v. diluviar
pout v. hace puncheros
pov-er-ty n. pobreza
pow-der n. polvo
pow-er n. fuerza; poder
pow-er-ful a. potente; poderoso
prac-ti-cal adj. práctico
practice v. practicar; ejercer
prag-mat-ic a. pragmatico
pari-rie n. pradera
praise v. alabar
prank n. travesura
pray v. rezar
prayer n. oración
preach v. predicar
pre-am-ble n. preambulo
pre-cau-tion n. precaución
pre-dede v. preceder
prec-e-dent n. precedente
pre-cint n. recinto; distrito electoral
pre-cious adj. precioso
prec-i-pice n. precipicio
pre-cip-i-ta-tion n. precipitación
pre-cise a. preciso; exacto
pre-co-cious a. precoz
pre-cur-sor n. precursor
pred-e-ces-sor n. predecesor
pre-des-ti-na-tion n. predestinación
pre-dic-a-ment n. apuro
pre-dict v. pronosticar
pre-dic-tion n. pronostico
pre-dom-i-nant a. predominante
pref-ace n. prologo; prefacio
pre-fer v. preferir
pref-er-ence n. preferencia
pre-fix n. prefijo
preg-nan-cy n. embarazo
preg-nant adj. embarazada
pre-his-tor-ic adj. prehistorico
prej-u-dice n. prejuicio
pre-lim-i-nar-y n. preliminar
pre-lude n. preludio
pre-med-i-tate v. premeditar
pre-miere n. estreno
pre-mi-um n. prima

pre-mo-ni-tion n. presentimiento
pre-oc-cu-pied adj. preocupado
prep-a-ra-tion n. preparación
pre-pare v. preparar(se)
prep-o-si-tion n. preposición
pre-pos-ter-ous a. absurdo
pre-req-ui-site a. requisito previo
pre-rog-a-tive n. prerrogativa
pre-scribe v. prescribir
pre-scrip-tion n. recenta
pres-ence n. presencia
pre-sent adj. presente, v. presentar, n. regalo
pres-en-ta-tion n. presentación
pre-serv-a-tive a. preservativo
pre-serve v. preservar; conservar
pre-side v. presidir
pres-i-dent n. presidente
press n. prensa; imprenta
pres-sure n. presión; urgencia
pres-ti-gid-i-ta-tion n. prestidigitación
pres-tige n. prestigio
pre0sume v. presumir; suponer
pre-tend v. pretender
pre-tense n. pretexto
pret-ty a. guapo; bonito; mono
pre-vail v. prevalecer; predominar
pre-vent v. impedir
pre-vi-ous a. previo
prey n. presa
price n. precio
price-less a. inapreciable
prick v. punzar
pride n. orgullo
priest n. sacerdote
prim a. estirado
pri-ma-ry adj. primario
prime adj. primero
prim-i-tive adj. primitivo
pri-mo-gen-i-ture n.

primogeniture
prince n. príncipe
prin-cess n. princesa
prin-ci-pal n., adj. principal
prin-ci-pal-i-ty n. principado
prin-ci-ple n. principio
print v. imprimir
print-ing n. imprenta
pri-or a. anterior
pri-or-i-ty n. prioridad
pri-or-y n. priorato
prism n. prism
pris-on n. carcel
pri-va-cy n. soledad
pri-vate adj. privado
priv-i-lege n. privilegio
prize n. premio
prob-a-bil-i-ty n. probabilidad
prob-a-ble a. probable
probe n. sonda
prob-lem n. problema
pro-ce-dure n. procedimiento
pro-ceed v. proceder
proc-ess n. proceso
pro-claim v. proclamar
pro-cliv-i-ty n. proclividad; inclinación
pro-cras-ti-nate v. dilatar; aplazar
pro-cure v. obtener; alcahuetear
prod v. ponzar
prod-i-gal a. prodigo
pro-d-i-gy n. prodigio
pro-duce v. producir
prod-uct n. producto
pro-fane a. profano
pro-fan-i-ty n. profanidad
pro-fes-sion n. profesion
pro-fes-sor n. profesora; profesor
pro-fi-cien-cy n. pericia
pro-file n. perfil
prof-it n. ganancia; beneficio
pro-found a. profundo
pro-fuse a. profuso
pro-fu-sion n. profusion
prog-e-ny n. progenie
prog-no-sis n. pronostico
pro-gram n. programa
prog-ress n. progreso;

desarrollo
pro-gres-sive a. progresivo
pro-hib-it v. prohibir
pro-hi-bi-tion n. prohibición
pro-ject n. proyecto, v. proyectar
pro-jec-tile n. proyectile
pro-lif-ic adj. prolifico
pro-logue n. prolongar
pro-long v. prolongar
prom-i-nent a. prominente
pro-mis-cu-ous a. promiscuo; libertino
prom-ise v. prometer, n. promesa
prom-on-to-ry n. promontorio
pro-mote v. promover; fomentar; ascender
pro-mo-tion n. promoción
prompt a. puntual; pronto
pro-noun n. pronombre
pro-nounce v. pronunciar(se)
pro-nounced a. marcado
pro-nun-ci-a-tion n. pronunciación
proof n. prueba
proof-read-er n. corrector de pruebas
prop n. apoyo
prop-a-gan-da n. propaganda
pro-pel v. propulsar
pro-pel-ler n. helice
pro-pen-si-ty n. propensión; inclinación
prop-er a. propio; apropiado; decente
prop-er-ty n. propiedad
proph-e-cy n. profeciz
proph-e-sy v. profetizar
proph-et n. profeta
pro-phy-lac-tic a. profilatico
pro-pi-tious a. propicio
pro-por-tion n. proporción
pro-pose v. proponer(se); declararse
prop-o-si-tion n. proposición; propuesta
pro-pri-e-tor n. propietario
pro-pri-e-ty n. corrección; decoro

pro-scribe v. proscribir
prose n. prosa
pros-e-cute v. proseguir
pros-pect n. perspectiva
pros-per v. prosperar
pros-per-i-ty n. prosperidad
pros-ti-tute n. prostituta; ramera
pros-trate v. postrar(se); derribar
pro-tag-o-nist n. protagonista
pro-tect v. proteger
pro-tein n. proteina
pro-test n. protesta, v. protestar
pro-to-col n. protocolo
pro-ton n. proton
pro-to-plasm n. protoplasma
pro-trude v. salir fuera
proud a. orgulloso; arrogante
prove v. probar
pro-verb n. proverbio
pro-vide v. proveer
prov-ince n. provincia
pro-vi-sion n. provision
pro-voc-a-tive a. provocativa; provocador
pro-voke v. provocar
prow n. proa
prox-y n. poder; apoderado
prude n. gasmona
prune n. ciruela pasa
pry v. meterse; fisgonear
psalm n. salmo
pseu-do-nym n. seudonimo
psych-e-del-ic a. psiquedelico
psy-chi-a-trist n. psiquiatra
psy-chi-a-try n. psiquiatria
psy-cho-a-nal-y-sis n. psicoanalisis
psy-cho-an-a-lyze v. psicoanalizar
psy-cho-log-i-cal adj. psicológico
psy-chol-o-gy n. psicología
psy-cho-sis n. psicosis
pto-maine n. ptomaina
pub n. taberna
pu-ber-ty n. pubertad
pub-lic n., adj. público

pub-li-ca-tion n. publicación
pub-lish v. publicar
pub-lish-er n. editor
puck-er v. arrugar
pud-ding n. pudin
pud-dle n. charco
puff v. soplar; inflar
pug-na-cious a. pugnaz
puke v. vomitar
pull v. tirar; arrastrar
pul-ley n. polea
pul-mo-nar-y a. pulmonar
pulp n. pulpa
pul-pit n. púlpito
pulse n. pulso
pul-ver-ize v. pulverizar
pum-ice n. piedra pómez
pump n. bomba
pump-kin n. calabaza
pun n. juego de palabras o vocablos
punch v. punzar
punc-tu-al adj. puntual
punc-tu-a-tion n. puntuación
punc-ture n. pinchazo
pun-ish v. castigar
pu-ny a. encanijado
pu-pa n. crisalida
pu-pil n. estudiante; pupila
pup-pet n. titere
pur-chase v. comprar
pure adj. puro
pur-ga-to-ry n. purgatorio
pu-ri-fy v. purificar
pu-ri-tan n. puritano
pur-ple adj. purpureo
pur-pose n. fin; proposito; resolucion
purr n. ronroneo
purse n. bolsa
pur-sue v. perseguir
pur-suit n. perseguimiento; busca; ocupación
pus n. pus
push v. empujar; apretar
puss-y n. gatito
put v. meter; poner(se)
pu-tre-fy v. pudrir
pu-trid a. odrido
put-ty n. masilla
pyr-a-mid n. piramide
pyre n. pira
py-thon n. pitón

quack v. graznar; n. graznido

quad-ran-gle n. cuadrangulo

quad-rant n. cuadrante

quad-rate adj. cuadrante

quad-rat-ic adj. cuadratico

quad-ri-ceps n. cuadriceps

quad-ri-jat-er-al n., adj. cuadrilátero

quad-ri-ple-gi-a n. cuadriplejia

quad-ri-ple-gic adj. cuadriplejico

quad-ru-ple v. cuadruplicar(se)

quag-mire n. pantano

quail n. codorniz

quake v. temblar

qual-i-fi-ca-tion n. calificacion

qual-i-fied adj. acreditado; capacitado

qual-i-fi-er n. calificativo

qual-i-fy v. habilitar

qual-i-fy-ing adj. eliminatoria

qual-i-ta-tive adj. cualitativo

qual-i-ty n. calidad

qualm n. duda

quan-ti-ta-tive adj. cuantitativo

quan-ti-ty n. cantidad

quar-an-tine n. cuarentena

quar-rel n. riña

quar-rel-er n. pendenciero

quar-rel-some adj. pendeciero

quar-ry n. cantera

quart n. cuarto

quar-ter n. cuarto

qua-ter-deck n. alcazar

quar-ter-ly adj. trimestral

quar-tet n. cuarteto

quartz n. cuarzo

qua-ver v. temblar

queen n. reina

quench v. matar; apagar

quench-a-ble adj. apagar

ques-tion n. pregunta

quick adj. listo; rapido

qui-et adj. silencioso

quit v. dejar; irse

quo-ta-tion n. cita

quote v. citar

rab-bi n. rabino

rab-bit n. conejo

rab-ble n. chusma

rab-id adj. rabioso

ra-bies n. rabia

rac-coon n. mapache

race v. correr de prisa, n. raza

rac-er n. corredor

race-track n. pista

ra-cial adj. racial

rac-ism n. racismo

ra-cist n. racista

rack n. potro

rack-et n. raqueta

rac-y adj. picante

ra-dar n. radar

ra-di-al adj. radial

ra-di-ance n. resplandor

ra-di-ant adj. radiante

ra-di-ate v. radiar; emitir; brillar

ra-di-a-tion n. radiación

ra-di-a-tor n. radiador

rad-i-cal n., adj. radical

rad-i-cle n. radícula

ra-di-o n. radio

ra-di-o-ac-tive adj. radiactivo

ra-di-o-ac-tiv-i-ty n. radiactividad

ra-di-o-broad-cast v. radiar

ra-di-o-gram n. radiograma

ra-di-o-graph n. radiografia

ra-di-ol-o-gist n. radiologo

ra-di-ol-o-gy n. radiologia

rad-ish n. rábano

ra-di-um n. radio

ra-di-us n. radio

ra-don n. radon

raff-ish adj. ostentoso

raf-fle n. rifa

raft n. balsa

raft-er n. cabrio

rag n. trapo

rage v. enfurecerse

rag-ged adj. desigual

raid v. atacar

rail n. carril

rail-ing n. baranda

rail-road n. ferrocarril

rail-way n. ferrocarril

rain v. llover, n. lluvia

rain-bow n. arco iris

rain-coat *n.* impereable
rain-drop *n.* gota de lluvia
rain-fall *n.* precipitación
rain-wear *n.* ropa impermeable
rain-y *adj.* lluvioso
raise *v.* criar; ;evantar
raised *adj.* repujado
rai-sin *n.* pasa
rake *v.* restrillar, *n.* rastro
ral-ly *n.* reunión, *v.* reunir(se)
ram *n.* carnero
ram-ble *v.* divagar
ram-bler *n.* vagabundo
ram-bunc-tious *adj.* alborotador
ram-i-fi-ca-tion *n.* ramificación
ramp *n.* rampa
ram-page *n.* alboroto
ramp-ant *adj.* destartalado
ranch *n.* hacienda
ranch-er *n.* hacendado
ran-cid *adj.* rancio
ran-cor *n.* rencor
ran-cor-ous *adj.* rencoroso
ran-dom *adj.* fortuito
range *v.* colocar; alinear
rang-er *n.* guardabosques
rank *n.* rango; fila
rank-ing *adj.* superior
ran-kle *v.* enconarse
ran-sack *v.* saquear
ran-som *v.* rescatar, *n.* rescate
rant *v.* vociferar
rap *v.* golpear
ra-pa-cious *adj.* rapaz
ra-pac-i-ty *n.* rapacidad
rape *v.* violar, *n.* violación
rap-id *adj.* rapido
ra-pid-i-ty *n.* rapidez
rap-ine *n.* rapiña
rap-ist *n.* violador
rap-port *n.* relación
rapt *adj.* absorto
rap-ture *n.* rapto
rap-tur-ous *adj.* extasiado
rare *adj.* poco; raro
rar-e-fied *adj.* refinado
rar-e-fy *v.* enrarecer(se)
rar-ing *adj.* impaciente

rar-i-ty *n.* rareza
ras-cal *n.* bribón
rash *n.* erupción
rash-er *n.* tocino
rasp-ber-ry *n.* frambuesa
rasp-y *adj.* aspero
rat *n.* rata
rate *v.* tasar, *n.* razón
rath-er *adv.* un poco
rat-i-fy *v.* ratificar
rat-ing *n.* popularidad; clasificación
ra-tio *n.* proporción
ra-ti-oc-i-nate *v.* raciocinar
ra-tion *n.* ración
ra-tion-al *adj.* racional
ra-tion-ale *n.* explicación; raxon
ra-tion-al-i-ty *n.* racionalidad
ra-tion-al-i-za-tion *n.* racionalización
ra-tion-al-ize *v.* racionalizar
ra-tion-ing *n.* racionamiento
rat-tle *n.* ruido
rat-trap *n.* ratonera
raun-chy *adj.* sucio
rav-age *v.* destruir, *n.* estrago
rave *v.* delirar
rav-el *v.* deshilar(se)
ra-ven *n.* cuervo
ra-ven-ous *adj.* coraz
ra-vine *n.* barranco
rav-ing *adj.* extraordinario
rav-ish *v.* raptar
rav-ish-ing *adj.* encantador
raw *adj.* novato; crudo
ray *n.* rayo
ray-on *n.* rayón
reach *n.* alcance, *v.* extenderse; alargar
re-act *v.* reaccionar
re-ac-tion *n.* reacción
re-ac-tion-ar-y *n.* reaccionario
re-ac-tor *n.* reactor
read *v.* decir; leer
read-ing *n.* lección
re-ad-just *v.* reajustar
read-y *adj.* pront; listo
re-al *adj.* real
re-al-i-ty *n.* realidad
re-al-ize *v.* realizar

re-al-ly adv. realmente

realm n. reino

ream n. resma

rea-son v. razonar, n. razon

rea-son-a-ble adj. razonable

reb-el adj., n. rebelde

re-bel-lion n. rebelión

re-buke n. reprimenda

re-call v. retirar; hacer

re-cant v. retractar(se)

re-cede v. retroceder

re-ceipt n. ingresos

re-ceive v. acoger; recibir

re-cent adj. reciente

re-cep-ta-cle n. receptaculo

re-cep-tion n. recepción

re-cess n. nicho

re-ces-sion n. retroceso

rec-i-pe n. receta

re-cip-ro-cal adj. reciproco

rec-it-al n. recital

rec-i-ta-tion n. recitación

re-cite v. recitar

reck-on v. considerar

re-claim v. reclamar

re-cline v. recostar(se)

rec-luse n. recluso

rec-og-ni-tion n. reconocimiento

rec-om-pense n. recompensa

rec-on-cile v. reconciliar

re-con-struct v. reconstruir

re-cord n. disco, v. registrar

re-course n. recurso

re-cov-er v. recobrar

re-cruit n. recluta

rec-tan-gle n. rectangulo

rec-ti-fy v. rectificar

re-cu-per-ate v. recuperar

re-cu-per-a-tion n. recuperación

red adj. rojo

red-dish adj. rojizo

re-deem v. redimir

re-demp-tion n. redención

re-do v. rehacer

re-duce v. disminuir; reducir

re-duc-tion n. reducción

reef n. escollo

reek n. olor

re-fer v. referir(se)

ref-er-ee n. arbitro

ref-er-ence n. referencia

re-fill v. rellenar

re-fine v. refinar

re-fin-er-y n. refinería

re-flect v. reflejar

re-flec-tion n. reflejo

re-flex adj. reflejo

re-flex-ive adj. reflexive

re-form n. reforma, v. reformarse

re-form-a-to-ry n. reformatorio

re-fract v. refractar

re-frain v. refrenar

re-fresh v. refrescar

re-fresh-ment n. refresco

re-frig-er-ate v. refrigerar

ref-uge n. refugio

ref-u-gee n. refugiado

re-fund n. reembolso

re-fuse v. rehusar

re-gain v. recobrar

re-gard v. considerar

re-gen-er-ate v. regenerar

re-gent n. regente

re-gime n. regimen

reg-i-men n. regimen

reg-i-ment n. regimiento

re-gion n. región

reg-is-ter v. registrar, n. registro

re-gret n. sentimiento

reg-u-lar adj. regular

reg-u-la-tion n. regulación

re-ha-bil-i-tate v. rehabilitar

re-ha-bil-i-ta-tion n. rehabilitacion

re-hearse v. ensayar

reign v. reinar, n. reinado

re-im-burse v. reembolsar

rein n. rienda

re-in-car-na-tion n. reencarnacion

re-in-force v. reforzar

re-it-er-ate v. reiterar

re-ject v. rechazar

re-lapse n. recaida, v. reincidir

re-late v. relatar

re-lat-ed adj. afin

re-la-tion n. relación

re-lax v. relajar

re-lease n. descargo

re-lent v. ceder
re-li-a-ble adj. confiable
rel-ic n. reliquia
re-lief n. alivio
re-lieve v. aliviar
re-li-gion n. religión
re-li-gious adj. religioso
rel-ish n. apetencia, v. gustar
re-ly v. contar; confiar
re-main v. quedar(se)
rem-e-dy n. remedio
re-mem-ber v. acordarse de
re-mem-brance n. recuerdo
re-mind v. recordar
rem-i-nis-cence n. reminiscencia
re-miss adj. descuidado
re-mit v. remitir
re-mit-tance n. remesa
re-morse n. remordimiento
re-mote adj. remoto
re-move v. apartar(se); quitar(se)
ren-ais-sance n. renacimiento
rend v. hender
ren-der v. volver
ren-dez-vous n. reunirse
ren-e-gade n. renegado
re-new v. renovar(se)
re-nounce v. renunciar
re-nown n. renombre
rent v. alquilar, n. alquiler
re-pair v. remendar; reparar
re-pay v. pagar; recompensar
re-peat v. repetir(se)
re-pel v. repeler
re-per-cus-sion n. repercusión
rep-er-toire n. repertorio
re-place v. reponer
re-ply n. respuesta
re-port v. informar
rep-re-hen-si-ble adj. reprensible
rep-re-sen-ta-tion n. representación
re-press v. reprimir
rep-ri-mand v. reprender
re-proach n. reproche
re-pro-duce v. reproducir

rep-tile n. reptil
re-pub-lic n. república
re-pulse n. repulsa
rep-u-ta-tion n. reputación
re-quest v. rogar
re-quire v. necesitar; exigir
res-cue v. rescate
re-search v. investigar
re-sent v. resentirse de
res-er-va-tion n. reservación
re-serve v. reservar
re-side v. vivir; residir
res-i-dent n., adj. residente
re-sign v. resignarse
res-ig-na-tion n. resignación
res-in n. resina
re-sist v. resistir
re-sist-ance n. resistencia
res-o-lu-tion n. resolución
re-solve v. resolver(se)
re-sort n. recurso
re-source n. recurso
re-spect n. respeto
re-spect-a-ble adj. respetable
re-spect-ful adj. respetuoso
re-spect-ing prep. respecto
re-spec-tive adj. respectivo
res-pi-ra-tion n. respiración
res-pi-ra-tor n. respirador
res-pi-ra-to-ry adj. respiratorio
re-spire v. respirar
res-pite n. respiro
re-splen-dent adj. resplandeciente
re-spond v. responder
re-spon-dent adj. resplandeciente
re-sponse n. respuesta
re-spon-si-bil-i-ty n. responsabilidad
re-spon-si-ble adj. responsable
rest n. descansar
res-tau-rant n. restaurante
rest-ful adj. sosegado
res-ti-tute v. restituir
res-ti-tu-tion n. restitución
rest-less adj. inquieto
res-to-ra-tion n. restauración
re-store v. restaurar
re-strain v. refrenar

re-strict v. restringir
re-stric-tion n. restricción
re-sult n. resultado, v. resultar
re-sus-ci-tate v. resucitar
re-tain v. retener
re-tard v. retardar
ret-i-na n. retina
re-tire v. retirarse
re-tract v. retractar(se)
re-trieve v. recobrar
ret-ro-ac-tive adj. retroactivo
re-turn v. volver
re-un-ion n. reunión
re-veal v. revelar
rev-e-la-tion n. revelación
re-venge v. vengar(se)
re-verse adj. inverso
re-view n. resena
re-vise v. repasar; revisar
re-vi-sion n. revision
re-vive v. revivir
re-voke v. revocar
rev-o-lu-tion n. revolución
rev-o-lu-tion-ary n. adj. revolucionario
re-volve v. revolverse
re-volv-er n. revolver
re-ward n. recompensa
rhap-so-dy n. rapsodia
rhe-tor-i-cal adj. retorico
rheu-mat-ic adj. reumatico
rheu-ma-tism n. reumatismo
rhyme v. rimar, n. rima
rhythm n. ritmo
rib n. costilla
rib-bon n. cinta
rice n. arroz
rich adj. fertil; rico
rid v. librar(se)
rid-dle n. acertijo
ride v. montar
rid-i-cule v. ridiculizar
ri-dic-u-lous adj. ridiculo
ri-fle n. rifle
right adj. exacto; derecho
rig-id adj. rigido
rig-or-ous adj. riguroso
rind n. piel
ring v. sonar, n. anillo
rink n. pista
rip v. arrancar; rasgar
ripe adj. maduro

rise v. subir; levantarse
risk n. riesgo
rite n. rito
rit-u-al n., adj. ritual
ri-val-ry n. rivalidad
riv-er n. rio
roach n. cucaracha
road n. camino
roar v. rugir
rob v. robar
robe n. bata
ro-bust adj. robusto
rock n. roca
ro-dent n. roedor
roll n. rollo; lista
ro-mance n. amorio
ro-man-tic adj. romántico
ro-man-ti-cism n. romanticismo
roof n. tejado
room n. sitio; cuarto
roost-er n. gallo
root n. raiz
rope n. cuerda
rose n. rosa
ros-y adj. rosado
ro-tate v. girar
rough adj. tosco; aspero
rou-lette n. ruleta
round prep. alrededor de, adj. redondo
route n. ruta
rou-tine n. rutina
roy-al-ty n. realeza
rub v. rozar; fregar
rub-bish n. basura
ru-by n. rubi
rud-der n. timón
rude adj. tosco; rudo
ru-di-ment n. rudimento
rug n. alfombra
ru-in v. arruinar, n. ruina
rule v. gobernar, n. regla
rul-er n. regla
rum n. ron
ru-mor n. rumor
run v. correr
run-ning adj. corriente
ru-ral adj. rural
rust n. orin
rus-tic adj. rustico
ruth-less adj. despiadado
rye n. centeno

Sab-bath *n.* domingo
sa-ber *n.* sable
sa-ble *n.* cabellina
sab-o-tage *v.* sabotear, *n.* sabotaje
sac-cha-rin *n.* sacrina
sack *n.* saco
sac-ra-ment *n.* sacramento
sacred *adj.* sagrado
sac-ri-fice *v.* sacrificar, *n.* sacrificio
sac-ri-lege *n.* sacrilegio
sad *adj.* triste
sad-den *v.* entristecer
sad-dle *v.* ensillar
sad-ism *n.* sadismo
sa-fa-ri *n.* safari
safe *adj.* seguro
safe-ty *n.* seguridad
sag *v.* combar(se)
sa-ga *n.* saga
sage *n., adj.* sabio
sail *v.* nevegar, *n.* vela
sail-or *n.* marinero
saint *n., adj.* santo
sake *n.* consideración; motivo
sal-ad *n.* ensalada
sal-a-man-der *n.* salamandra
sal-a-ry *n.* salario
sale *n.* venta
sa-line *n.* salino
sa-li-va *n.* saliva
sal-low *n.* cetrino
sal-ly *n.* salida
salm-on *n.* salmón
sa-lon *n.* salón
sa-loon *n.* salón
salt *n.* sal
sal-u-tar-y *adj.* saludable
sal-u-ta-tion *n.* saludo
sa-lute *v.* sakudar
sal-vage *n.* salvamento
sal-va-tion *n.* salvación
salve *n.* unguento
sal-vo *n.* salva
same *adj.* mismo
sam-ple *v.* probar
san-a-to-ri-um *n.* sanatorio
sanc-ti-fy *v.* santificar
sanc-tion *n.* sanción
sanc-ti-ty *n.* santidad

sanc-tu-ar-y *n.* santuario
sand *n.* arena
san-dal *n.* sandalia
sand-stone *n.* arenisca
sand-wich *n.* bocadillo
sand-y *adj.* arenoso
sane *adj.* sano
san-gui-nar-y *a.* sanguinario
san-i-tar-i-um *n.* sanatorio
san-i-tar-y *adj.* sanitario
san-i-ta-tion *n.* instalación sanitaria
san-i-ty *n.* juicio sano
sap *n.* savia
sa-pi-ent *a.* sabio
sap-phire *n.* zafiro
sar-casm *n.* sarcasmo
sar-cas-tic *adj.* sarcastico
sar-coph-a-gus *n.* sarcofago
sar-dine *n.* sardina
sa-ri, sa-ree *n.* sari
sash *n.* faja
sas-sy *adj.* descarado
sa-tan *n.* Satanas
sa-tan-ic *a.* satanico
sate *v.* saciar; dsatisfacer
sat-el-lite *n.* satelite
sa-ti-ate *v.* saciar
sat-in *n.* raso
sa-tire *n.* satira
sat-is-fac-tion *n.* satisfaccion
sat-is-fy *v.* satisfacer
sat-u-rate *v.* saturar
Sat-ur-day *n.* sabado
sa-tyr *n.* satiro
sauce *n.* salsa
sau-cer *n.* platillo
sau-sage *n.* salchicha
sav-age *n., adj.* salvaje
save *v.* ahorrar; salvar
sav-ing *n.* economia
sav-ior *n.* salvador
sa-vor *n.* sabor
saw *n.* sierra
sax-o-phone *n.* saxofón
say *v.* decir
say-ing *n.* dicho
scab *n.* costra
scaf-fold *n.* andamio
scald *v.* escaldar
scale *n.* escala
scal-lop *n.* venera; feston
scalp *n.* pericraneo

scal-pel *n.* escalpelo
scan *v.* escudriñar
scan-dal *n.* escandalo
scan-dal-ize *v.* escandalizar
scant *adj.* escaso
scant-y *adj.* escaso
scape-goat *n.* cabeza de turco
scar *n.* cicatriz
scarce *adj.* escaso
scare *v.* asustar
scare-crow *n.* espantajo; espantapajaros
scarf *n.* bufanda
scar-let *n.* escarlata
scat-ter *v.* esparcir
scav-en-ger *n.* basurero
scene *n.* vista; escena
scen-er-y *n.* paisaje
scent *n.* pista; olor
sched-ule *n.* horario
scheme *v.* intrigar
schism *n.* cisma
schiz-o-phre-ni-a *n.* esquizofrenia
schol-ar *n.* erudito; alumno
schol-ar-ship *n.* erudición; beca
scho-las-tic *adj.* escolar
school *n.* escuela
sci-ence *n.* ciencia
sci-en-tist *n.* cientifico
scim-i-tar *n.* cimitarra
scis-sors *n.* tijeras
scoff *v.* mofarse
scold *v.* regañar
scoop *n.* paleta
scoot-er *n.* patinete
scope *n.* alcance
scorch *v.* chamuscar
score *n.* cuenta
scorn *n.* desden
scor-pi-on *n.* escorpión
scotch *v.* frustrar
scour *v.* fregar; recorrer
scout *n.* explorador
scowl *v.* poner mal gesto
scrag-gy *a.* escaranado
scram-ble *v.* revolver
scrap *n.* fragmento; sobras
scrape *v.* raer
scratch *v.* rayar; rasgunar;

rascar
scrawl *n.* garrabatos; garrapatos
scream *n.* grito
screen *n.* biombo; pantalla
screw *v.* atornillar, *n.* tornillo
scrib-ble *v.* garrapatear
scrim-mage *n.* arrebatina
script *n.* letra cursiva; guion
scrip-ture *n.* Sagrada Escritura
scroll *n.* rollo de pergamino
scrub *v.* fregar
scru-ple *n.* escrupulo
scru-ti-nize *v.* escudriñar
scru-ti-ny *n.* escrutinio
scuf-fle *v.* pelear
sculp-tor *n.* escultor
sculp-ture *v.* esculpir, *n.* escultura
scum *n.* espuma
scur-ry *v.* darse prisa
scur-vy *n.* escorbuto
scut-tle *v.* echar a pique
scythe *n.* guadana
sea *n.* mar
seal *n.* foca
seal *n.* sello *v.* cerrar
seam *n.* costura
sea-man *n.* marinero
seam-stress *n.* costurera
seam-y *a.* asqueroso
se-ance *n.* sesión de espiritistas
sea-port *n.* puerto de mar
sear *v.* marchitar; chamuscar
search *v.* buscar
sea-shore *n.* orilla del mar
sea-sick-ness *n.* mareo
sea-son *n.* estación
sea-son-ing *n.* condimento
seat *n.* sentar, *n.* asiento
sea-weed *n.* alga marina
se-clude *v.* aislar
se-clu-sion *n.* retiro
sec-ond *n., adj.* segundo
sec-ond-ar-y *adj.* secundario
sec-ond-hand *a.* de segunda mano
sec-ond-rate *a.* inferior
se-cre-cy *n.* secreto
se-cret *n., adj.* secreto
sec-re-tar-y *n.* secretario

se-crete v. secretar; ovultar

se-cre-tion n. secreción

sect n. secta

sec-tion n. sección

sec-tor n. sector

sec-u-lar adj. secular

se-cure adj. seguro

se-cu-ri-ty n. seguridad

se-date adj. sosegado

sed-a-tive n. sedativo

sed-en-tar-y a. sedentario

sed-i-ment n. sedimento

se-di-tion n. sedición

se-duce v. seducir

se-duc-tion n. seducción

see v. percibir; ver

seed n. semilla; simiente

seed-y a. desharrapado

seek v. buscar; solicitar

seem v. parecer

seem-ly a. decoroso; correcto

seep v. rezumarse

se-er n. profeta

seg-ment n. segmento

seg-re-gate v. segregar

seg-re-ga-tion n. segregación

seis-mo-graph n. sismógrafo

seize v. apoderarse de; asir

sei-zure n. asimiento

sel-dom adv. rarmente

se-lect adj. selecto, v. elegir

se-lec-tion n. selección

self n. See my-self, yourself

self-cen-tered a. egocentrico

self-com-mand n. dominio de si mismo

self-con-fi-dence n. confianza en si mismo

self con-scious a. timido

self-control n. dominio de si mismo

self-ev-i-dent a. patente

self-ex-plan-a-to-ry a. evidente; obvio

self-gov-ern-ment n. autonomia

self-im-por-tance n. presunción

self-ish a. egoista; interesado

self-less a. desinteresado

self-re-li-ance n. confianza en si mismo

self-same a. mismo

self-suf-fi-cient adj. independiente

self-will n. terquedad

sell v. vender

se-man-tics n. semantica

sem-blance n. parecido; apariencia

se-men n. semen

se-mes-ter n. semestre

sem-i-cir-cle n. semicirculo

sem-i-co-lon n. punto y coma

sem-i-fi-nal adj. semifinal

sem-i-nar n. seminario

sem-i-nar-y n. seminario

sem-i-of-fi-cial adj. semioficial

sem-i-pre-cious adj. semiprecioso

sem-i-week-ly a. bisemanal

sen-ate n. senado

sen-a-tor n. senador

send v. mandar; enviar

se-nile adj. senil

sen-ior adj. superior

sen-ior-i-ty n. antiguedad

sen-sa-tion n. sensación

sense v. percibir, n. sentido

sense-less a. sin sentido; insensato

sen-si-bil-i-ty n. sensibilidad

sen-si-ble adj. razonable

sen-si-tive adj. delicado

sen-si-tiv-i-ty n. delicadeza

sen-so-ry adj. sensorio

sen-su-al adj. sensual

sen-su-ous adj. sensorio

sen-tence n. frase

sen-ti-ment n. sentimiento

sen-ti-nel n. centinela

sen-try n. centinela

se-pal n. sepalo

sep-a-rate v. separar(se)

sep-a-ra-tion n. separación

Sep-tem-ber n. septiembre

sep-tic adj. septico

sep-ul-cher n. sepulcro

se-quel n. resultado

se-quence n. sucesión
se-questered a. aislado
se-ques-ter v. separar; aislar
se-quin n. lentejuela
ser-aph n. serafín
ser-e-nade n. serenata
se-rene n. sereno
se-ren-i-ty n. serenidad
serf n. siervo
ser-geant n. sargento
se-ri-al a. en serie
se-ries n. serie
se-ri-ous adj. serio
ser-mon n. sermon
ser-pent n. serpiente
se-rum n. suero
serv-ant n. serviente; servidor
serve v. servir
serv-ice n. servicio
serv-ice-man n. militar
ser-vile a. servil
ses-sion n. sesion
set v. fijar; poner(se)
set-back n. reves
set-ting n. engaste
set-tle v. arreglar; resolver
set-tle-ment n. colonizacion
set-tler n. colono
seven adj., n. siete
sev-en-teen adj. diecisiete
sev-enth n., adj. séptimo
sev-en-ty n., adj. setenta
sev-er v. cortar
sev-er-al a. varios; diversos
se-vere adj. severo
se-ver-i-ty n. severidad
sew v. coser
sew-er n. albañal
sex n. sexo
sex-tet n. sexteto
sex-u-al adj. sexual
sex-y a. provocativo
shab-by a. raído; en mal estado
shack n. choza
shack-le n. grillete
shade n. sombrear, n. sombra
shad-ing n. degradación
shad-ow n. sombra
shadowy a. umbroso; vago
shad-y adj. sombreado

shaft n. eje; pozo
shag-gy adj. velludo
shake v. estrechar; temblar
shak-y a. poso profundo
sham v. fingir(se), adj. fingido
sham-bles n. desorden
shame n. verguenza
shame-less al desvergonzado
sham-poo n. champú
shan-ty n. choza
shape v. formar, n. forma
shape-ly a. bien formado
share n. parte
shark n. tiburón
sharp adj. vivo; cortante
sharp-en v. afilar; sacar punta
shat-ter v. hacer(se) pedazos
shave v. afeitar(se)
shav-er n. maquina de afeitar
shawl n. chal
she pron. ella
shears n. tijeras grandes
shed v. quitarse; verter
sheen n. lustre
sheep n. oveja
sheep-ish a. timido
sheer adj. escarpado
sheet n. sábana; hoja; lamina
sheik, sheikh n. jeque
shelf n. estante
shell n. cascara
shel-lac, shel-lack n. goma laca
shell-fish n. marisco
shel-ter n. refugio
shep-herd n. pastor
sher-bet n. sorbete
sher-iff n. sheriff
sher-ry n. jerez
shield n. escudo
shift v. mover(se); cambiar
shil-ly-shal-ly v. vacilar
shim-mer v. rielar
shin n. espinilla
shine v. pulir; brillar
shin-gle n. ripia; tejamanil
shin-y adj. brillante

ship *n.* barco
ship-ment *n.* embarque; envio
ship-shape *a.* en buen orden
ship-wreck *n.* naufragio
shirk *v.* evitar; esquivar
shirt *n.* camisa
shiv-er *v.* temblar
shock *n.* susto; choque; postracion nerviosa
shod-dy *a.* de pacotilla; falso
shoe *n.* zapato
shoe-horn *n.* calzador
shoe-lace *n.* cordon
shoot *v.* espigar; disparar
shoot-ing *n.* tiro; caza con escopeta
shoot-ing star *n.* estrella fugaz
shop *n.* taller; tienda
shop-keep-er *n.* tendero
shore *n.* playa
short *adj.* breve; corto
short-age *n.* deficienca; escasez
short cir-cuit *n.* corto circuito
short-com-ing *n.* defecto
short-cut *n.* atajo
short-en *v.* acortar(se)
short-hand *n.* taquigrafía
short-lived *a.* de breve duración
short-tem-pered *a.* de mal genio
shot *n.* tiro; tirador
shot-gun *n.* escopeta
should *aux. v. past form of* shall
shoul-der *n.* hombro
shout *v.* gritar, *n.* grito
shov-el *n.* pala
show *v.* mostrar(se)
show-er *v.* ducharse, *n.* ducha
show-man *n.* director de espectaculos
shred *v.* hacer tiras
shrew *n.* arpia
shrewd *a.* sagaz; prudente
shriek *n.* chillar
shrill *a.* estridente

shrimp *n.* camarón
shrine *n.* relicario
shrink *v.* encoger(se)
shriv-el *v.* encoger(se); secar(se)
shroud *n.* mortaja
shrub *n.* arbusto
shrub-ber-y *n.* arbustos
shrug *v.* encogerse de hombros
shud-der *v.* extremecerse
shuf-fle *v.* arrastrar los pies; *(cards)* barajar
shun *v.* evitar; apartarse de
shut *v.* cerrar(se)
shut-ter *n.* contraventana
shut-tle *n.* lanzadera
shy *adj.* timido
sic *v.* atacar
sick *adj.* enfermo
sick-en *v.* enfermar(se)
sick-le *n.* hoz
sick-ness *n.* enfermedad
side *n.* partido; lado
side-burns *n.* patillas
side-long *a.* lateral
side-track *v.* desviar
side-walk *n.* acera
side-ways *adv.* obliquamente
siege *n.* sitio; cerco
sieve *n.* coladera; tamiz
sift *v.* tamizar
sigh *n.* suspiro, *v.* suspirar
sight *n.* visión; vista
sight-less *adj.* ciego
sight-see-ing *n.* visita de puntos de interes
sign *n.* signo; senal
sig-nal *n.* senal
sig-na-ture *n.* firma
sig-nif-i-cance *n.* significación
sig-ni-fy *v.* significar
si-lence *n.* silencio
si-lent *adj.* silencioso
sil-hou-ette *n.* silueta
sil-ic-a *n.* silice
sil-i-con *n.* silicio
silk *n.* seda
silk-y *adj.* sedoso
sil-ly *adj.* bobo
si-lo *n.* silo

silt *n.* sedimento

sil-ver *n.* plata

sil-ver-smith *n.* platero

sil-ver-ware *n.* vajilla de plata

sim-i-an *a.* simico

sim-i-lar *adj.* similar

sim-i-lar-i-ty *n.* semejanza

sim-mer *v.* hervir a fuego lento

sim-per *v.* sonreirse afectadamente

sim-ple *adj.* simple; facil

sim-pli-fy *v.* simplificar

sim-ply *adv.* sencillamente

sim-u-late *v.* simular

si-mul-ta-ne-ous *a.* simultaneo

sin *n.* pecado; transgresion

since *conj.* puesto que, *prep.* despues; desde

sin-cere *adj.* sincero

sin-cer-i-ty *n.* sinceridad

si-ne-cure *n.* sinecura

sin-ew *n.* tendón

sing *v.* cantar

sing-er *n.* cantante

sin-gle *adj.* único; soltero

sin-gle-hand-ed *a.* sin ayuda

sin-gu-lar *adj.* singular

sin-is-ter *adj.* siniestro

sink *v.* hundir(se)

sin-ner *n.* pecador

si-nus *n.* seno

sip *n.* sorbo, *v.* sorber

sir *n.* señor

sire *n.* padre

si-ren *n.* sirena

sir-loin *n.* solomillo

sis-ter *n.* hermana

sis-ter-in-law *n.* cuñada

sit *v.* sentar(se)

site *n.* sitio

sit-u-a-tion *n.* situacion

six *adj., n.* seis

six-teen *adj., n.* dieciséis

sixth *n., adj.* sexto

six-ty *adj., n.* sesenta

size *n.* talla

siz-zle *v.* chisporrotear

skate *v.* patinar

skel-e-ton *n.* esqueleto

skep-tic *n.* esceptico

skep-ti-cal *adj.* esceptico

sketch *n.* esbozo; bosquejo

skew-er *n.* broqueta

ski *v.* esquiar

skid *n.* patinazo

skill *n.* destreza; habilidad

skil-let *n.* sarten

skim *v.* expumar; desnatar; hojear

skin *n.* piel

skin-ny *adj.* flaco

skip *v.* saltar; pasar por alto

skir-mish *n.* escaramuza

skirt *n.* falda

skit *n.* parodia

skull *n.* cráneo

skunk *n.* mofeta

sky *n.* cielo

sky-rock-et *n.* cohete

sky-scrap-er *n.* rascacielos

slab *n.* table; plancha

slack *a.* flojo; negligente

slack-en *v.* aflojar

slacks *n.* pantalones

slagn *n.* excoria

slam *v.* cerrarse de golpe

slan-der *v.* calumniar, *n.* calumnia

slang *n.* argot

slant *v.* inclinar(se); sesgar(se)

slap *v.* pegar

slash *v.* acuchillar

slat *n.* tabilla

slate *n.* pizarra; lista de candidatos

slaugh-ter *v.* matar

slave *n.* esclavo

slav-er-y *n.* esclavitud

slay *v.* matar

sled *n.* trineo

sleek *a.* liso; pulcro

sleep *v.* dormir

sleep-y *a.* sonoliento

sleet *n.* aguanieve

sleeve *n.* manga

sleigh *n.* trineo

slen-der *adj.* delgado

sleuth *n. inf.* detective

slice *v.* tajar, *n.* tajada

slide *v.* deslizarse

slight *a.* pequeño; de poco importancia

slim *adj.* delgado
slime *n.* legamo
sling *v.* tirar; suspender
s l i p *v.* introducir; deslizar(se); resbalar; escaparse
slip-knot *n.* nudo corredizo
slip-per *n.* zapatilla
slip-per-y *adj.* resbaladizo
slip-up *n. inf.* equivocación
slit *v.* cortar
sliv-er *n.* astilla
slob-ber *v.* babear; babosear
slo-gan *n.* mote
slop *v.* verter
slope *v.* inclinar(se), *n.* inclinación
slot *n.* ranura
slov-en-ly *a.* descuidado; desaseado
slow *adj.* torpe; lento
slow-ly *adv.* despacio
slung *n.* posta
slug-gish *a.* perezoso; lento
slum *n.* barrio bajo
slump *v.* hundirse
slur *v.* comerse palabras; calumniar
slut *n.* pazpuerca; perra
sly *a.* astuto; disimulado
smack *v.* pegar
small *adj.* pequeño
small-pox *n.* viruelas
smart *adj.* listo; fresco
smash *v.* romper(se)
smear *v.* manchar; untar
smell *v.* oler
s m i l e *n.* sonrisa, *v.* sonreir(se)
smirk *n.* sonrisa afectada
smith *n.* herrero
smock *n.* blusa de labrador
smog *n.* niebla y humo mezclados
smoke *v.* fumar, *n.* humo
smol-der *v.* arder sin llamas
smooch *v. inf.* besar
smooth *adj.* suave
smooth-er *v.* ahogar(se); sofocar(se)
smudge *n.* mancha
smug *a.* papado de si mismo

smug-gle *v.* pasar de (o hacer) contrabando
snack *n.* merienda
snag *n.* obstaculo; rasgon
snail *n.* caracol
snake *n.* culebra
snap-shot *n.* foto
snare *n.* trampa
snatch *n.* fragmento; trocito
sneak *v.* moverse a hurtadillas
sneer *v.* mofarse
sneeze *n.* estornudo, *v.* estornudar
sniff *v.* husmear; oler
snip *v.* tijeretear
snob *n.* esnob
snooze *v. inf.* dormitar
snore *n.* ronquido, *v.* roncar
snow *v.* nevar, *n.* nieve
snow-ball *n.* bola de nieve
snow-flake *n.* copo de nieve
snow-man *n.* figura de nieve
snub *v.* desairar
snug-gle *v.* arrimarse
so *conj.* por tanto, *adv.* así; tan
soak *v.* remojar
soap *n.* jabón
soar *v.* remontarse
sob *v.* sollozar
so-ber *adj.* sobrio
so-bri-quet, sou-bri-quet *n.* apodo
so-called *a.* llamado; supuesto
soc-cer *n.* fútbol
so-cia-ble *adj.* sociable
so-cial *adj.* social
so-cial-ism *n.* socialismo
so-cial-ize *v.* socializar
so-ci-e-ty *n.* sociedad
so-di-um *n.* sodio
so-fa *n.* sofa
soil *v.* manchar, *n.* tierra
so-lar *adj.* solar
sol-dier *n.* soldado
sole-ly *adv.* solamente
sol-emn *adj.* solemne
so-lic-it *v.* solicitar
sol-id *n., adj.* solido
sol-i-dar-i-ty *n.* solidaridad
sol-i-tar-y *adj.* solitario

sol-u-ble adj. soluble
so-lu-tion n. solución
solve v. resolver
sol-vent adj. solvente
som-ber adj. sombrio
some pron. algunos, adj. alguno
some-bo-dy pron. alguien
some-day adv. algun dia
some-one pron. alguién
some-thing n. algo
some-times adv. a veces
son n. hijo
song n. canción
son-in-law n. yerno
soon adv. pronto
soothe v. calmar
so-pran-o n. soprano
sor-did adj. vil
sor-ry adj. triste
so-so adv. asi asi
soul n. alma
sound n. ruido
soup n. sopa
sour adj. agrio
south n. sur
south-east n. sudeste
south-ern adj. del sur
south-west n. sudoeste
sov-er-eign n., adj. soberano
space v. espaciar, n. espacio
spa-cious adj. espacioso
spa-ghet-ti n. espagueti
spasm n. espasmo
spas-mod-ic adj. espasmodico
spas-tic adj. espastico
spat-u-la n. espatula
speak v. decir; hablar
spear n. lanza
spe-cial adj. especial
spe-cial-ist n. especialista
spe-cial-ize v. especializar(se)
spe-cial-ty n. especialidad
spe-cies n. especie
spe-cif-ic adj. especifico
spec-i-fy v. especificar
spec-ta-cle n. espectaculo
spec-tac-u-lar adj. espectacular
speech-less adj. mudo

speed v. apresurarse; acelerar
spell v. deletrear
spell-bind v. encantar
spell-ing n. ortografia
spend v. gastar
sperm n. esperma
sperm-whale n. cachalote
sphere n. esfera
spher-i-cal adj. esferico
spice n. especia
spic-y adj. picante
spi-der n. arana
spill v. verter(se)
spin-ach n. espinaca
spi-nal adj. espinal
spine n. espinazo
spi-ral adj., n. espiral
spir-it n. espiritu
spir-it-u-al adj. espiritual
spir-it-u-al-ism n. espiritismo
spit v. escupir
spite n. rencor
splin-ter n. astilla
split v. dividir; separarse
spoil v. echar(se); estropear(se)
spo-ken adj. hablado
sponge n. esponja
spon-gy adj. esponjoso
spon-ta-ne-i-ty n. espontaneidad
spon-ta-ne-ous adj. espontaneo
spoon n. cuchara
spoon-ful n. cucharada
spo-rad-ic adj. esporadico
spore n. espora
sport n. deporte
sports-man n. deportista
spot n. mancha
spot-ty adj. manchado
spouse n. esposa; esposo
spread v. diseminar
spring n. primavera, v. saltar
spring-time n. primavera
spruce n. picea
spu-ri-ous adj. espurio
spy v. espiar
squad-ron n. escuadron
squal-id adj. desalinado
square adj., n. cuadrado

squeak n. chirrido, v. chillar
sta-bil-i-ty n. estabilidad
sta-ble adj. estable
sta-di-um n. estadio
stage n. etapa
stain n. mancha
stair n. escalón
stair-way n. escalera
stamp n. sello
stam-pede n. estampida
stand v. colocar
stand-ing adj. derecho
sta-ple n. grapa
sta-pler n. grabadora
star n. estrella
star-less adj. sin estrellas
star-ry adj. estrellado
start v. comenzar; empezar
state n. estado
stat-ic adj. estatico
sta-tion n. estación
sta-tis-tic n. estadistico
stat-ue n. estatua
stay v. quedar(se)
steal v. robar
steam v. empanar, n. vapor
steam-y adj. vaporoso
stem n. tallo
step n. escalera
step-broth-er n. hermanastro
step-daugh-ter n. hijastra
step-fa-ther n. padrastro
step-moth-er n. madrastra
step-sis-ter n. hermanastra
step-son n. hijastro
ste-ril-i-ty n. esterilidad
stick n. palo
stick-y adj. viscoso
stiff adj. rigido
still adj. tranquilo
stim-u-lant n. estimulante
stim-u-late v. estimular
stink v. hedor
stip-u-late v. estipular
stip-u-la-tion n. estipulación
stock-ing n. media
sto-i-cal adj. estoico
stom-ach n. estomago
stone n. piedra
stop v. terminar
stop-light n. semaforo
store n. almacen; tienda

stork n. cigüeña
storm n. tempestad
sto-ry n. piso; historia
stove n. estufa
straight adj. directo
strange adj. extraño; raro
stra-te-gic adj. estrategico
strat-e-gy n. estrategia
straw n. pajilla
straw-ber-ry n. fresa
stream n. arroyo
street n. calle
strength n. vigor; fuerza
strict adj. estricto
strike v. atacar; golpear
string n. cordel
stripe n. raya
striped adj. rayado
strong adj. robusto; fuerte
struc-tur-al adj. estructural
stu-dent n. estudiante
stu-di-o n. estudio
stud-y v. estudiar
stu-pen-dous adj. estupendo
stu-pid adj. estupido
style n. modo; estilo
sub-di-vide v. subdividir
sub-ject adj., n. sujeto
sub-jec-tive adj. subjetivo
sub-lease v. subarrendar
sub-let v. subarrendar
sub-li-mate v. sublimar
sub-li-ma-tion n. sublimacion
sub-lime a. sublime
sub-lim-i-ty n. sublimidad
sub-ma-rine n. submarino
sub-merge v. sumergir(se)
sub-mer-gence n. sumersión
sub-merse v. sumergir(se)
sub-mer-sion n. sumersión
sub-mis-sion n. sumisión
sub-mis-sive a. sumiso
sub-mit v. someter(se); presentar
sub-nor-mal adj. anormal
sub-or-di-nate a. subordinado; secundario; dependiente
sub-or-di-na-tion n. subordinacion

sub-poe-na, sub-pe-na n. citación; compareando

sub-scribe v. subscribir(se)

sub-scrip-tion n. subscripción

sub-se-quent a. subsiguiente

sub-ser-vi-ent a. servil

sub-side v. bajar; calmarse

sub-sid-i-ar-y a. ubsidiario

sub-si-dize v. subvencional

sub-si-dy n. subvención; subsidio

sub-sist v. subsistir; existir

sub-sis-tence n. subsistencia

sub-stance n. esencia; substancia

sub-stan-tial adj. substancial

sub-stan-ti-a-tion n. comprobación; justificación

sub-stan-tive n. substantivo

sub-sti-tute n. substituto, v. substituir

sub-sti-tu-tion n. substitución; reemplazo

sub-ter-fuge n. subterfugio

sub-ter-ra-ne-an a. subterraneo

sub-ti-tle n. subtítulo

sub-tle a. sutil; ingenioso; delicado; astuto

sub-tle-ty n. sutileza

sub-tract v. substraer

sub-trac-tion n. substracción; resta

sub-urb n. suburbio

sub-ur-ban a. suburbano

sub-ver-sion n. subversión

sub-ver-sive a. sobversivo

sub-vert v. subvertir

sub-way n. metro

suc-ceed v. suceder

suc-cess n. exito

suc-cess-ful a. prospero; afortunado

suc-ces-sion n. sucesión

suc-ces-sor n. sucesor

suc-cinct a. sucinto

suc-cor n. soccorro; auxilio

suc-cu-lent adj. suculento

suc-cumb v. sucumbir

such adv. tan, pron., adj. tal

suck v. chupar; mamar

suck-er n. piruli

suck-le v. lactar; amamantar

suc-tion n. succión

suf-fer v. sufrir

suf-fer-ance n. tolerancia

suf-fice v. bastar

suf-fi-cien-cy n. suficiencia

suf-fix n. sufijo

suf-fo-cate v. sofocar; as-fixiar

suf-frage n. sufragio

suf-fuse v. extender; banar

suf-fu-sion n. difusión

sug-ar n. azucar

sug-ar-y adj. azucarado

sug-gest v. sugerir

sug-ges-tion n. sugestión

sug-ges-tive a. sugestivo

su-i-cide n. suicida

suit n. traje

suit-a-ble a. apropiado

suit-case n. maleta

suite n. juego; serie

sul-fur, sul-phur n. azufre

sul-fu-ric ac-id n. acido sulfurico

sulk v. estar de mal humor

sul-len a. hosco

sul-ly v. manchar

sul-tan n. sultan

sul-tan-ate n. sultanato

sul-try a. bochornoso

sum v. sumar, n. suma

sum-ma-ry adj. sumario

sum-mer n. verano

sun n. sol

Sun-day n. domingo

sun-down n. puesta del sol

sun-flow-er n. girasol

sun-glass-es n. gafas de sol

sun-light n. luz del sol

sun-rise n. salida del sol

su-per-fi-cial adj. superficial

su-per-in-tend v. superentender

su-pe-ri-or n., adj. superior

su-pe-ri-or-i-ty n. superioridad

su-per-mar-ket n. supermercado

su-per-sti-tion n. superstición

su-per-sti-tious *adj.* supersticioso

su-pine *adj.* supino

sup-per *n.* cena

sup-ple-ment *n.* suplemento

sup-pli-cate *v.* suplicar

sup-pose *v.* suponer

sup-pres-sion *n.* supresión

su-prem-a-cy *n.* supremacía

su-preme *adj.* supremo

sure *adj.* seguro

sure-ly *adv.* seguramente

sur-face *n.* superficie

sur-geon *n.* cirujano

sur-ger-y *n.* cirugía

sur-name *n.* apellido

sur-prise *v.* sorprender, *n.* sorpresa

sur-vive *v.* sobrevivir

sus-cep-ti-ble *adj.* susceptible

sus-pend *v.* suspender

sus-pense *n.* incertidumbre

sus-pen-sion *adj.* suspensión

sus-pi-cion *n.* sospecha; sombra

sus-pi-cious *adj.* sospechoso

sus-tain *v.* sustentar

sus-te-nance *n.* sustento

svelte *a.* esbelto

swab *n.* torunda

swan *n.* cisne

swap *v.* cambiar

swarm *n.* enjambre

swash-buck-ler *n.* espadachín

swat *v.* matar

sway *v.* bambolearse; inclinar

swear *v.* jurar

swear-word *n.* palabrota

sweat *n.* sudor, *v.* sudar

sweat-y *adj.* sudoroso

sweet *adj.* dulce

sweet-en *v.* azucarar; endulzar

sweet-heart *n.* querida; novia

sweet-meat *n.* dulce

swell *v.* hinchar(se)

swerve *v.* torcer(se); desviar(se)

swift *a.* veloz

swig *v.* beber a grandes tragos

swill *n.* bazofia

swim *n.* natación, *v.* nadar

swim-mer *n.* nadador

switch *v.* cambiar

swiv-el *n.* alacrán, torniquete; girar

swoon *n.* desmayo

sword *n.* espada

sword-belt *n.* talabarte

sword-fish *n.* pez espada

sword-play *n.* esgrima

swordsman *n.* espadachín

syc-a-more *n.* sicómoro

syc-o-phant *n.* adulador

syl-lab-i-cate *v.* silabear

syl-lab-i-ca-tion *n.* silabeo

syl-la-bi-fy *v.* silabear

syl-la-ble *n.* sílaba

syl-la-bus *n.* resumen; programa

syl-van *a.* silvestre

sym-bol *n.* símbolo

sym-bol-ic *adj.* simbólico

sym-bol-ism *n.* simbolismo

sym-bol-ize *v.* simbolizar

sym-me-try *n.* simetría

sym-pa-thet-ic *a.* compasivo; sompático

sym-pa-thy *n.* simpatía

sym-pho-ny *n.* sinfonía

symp-ton *n.* síntoma

syn-a-gogue *n.* sinagoga

syn-chro-nize *v.* sincronizar(se)

syn-di-cate *v.* sindicar

syn-od *n.* sínodo

syn-o-nym *n.* sinónimo

syn-on-y-mous *adj.* sinónimo

syn-op-sis *n.* sinopsis

syn-the-sis *n.* síntesis

syn-thet-ic *adj.* sintético

syph-i-lis *n.* sífilis

sy-ringe *n.* jeringa

sy-rup *n.* jarabe; almíbar

sys-tem *n.* sistema

sys-tem-at-ic *a.* sistemático

sys-tem-a-tize *v.* sistematizar

tab   211   teamwork

tab n. cuenta
tab-er-nac-le n. tabernáculo
ta-ble n. mesa
ta-ble-spoon-ful n. cucharada
tab-let n. tableta
ta-boo, ta-bu a. tabú
tab-u-lar adj. tabular
tab-u-late v. tabular
tac-it a. tácito
tac-i-turn adj. taciturno
tack n. tachuela; virada
tack-le n. equipo; carga
tact n. tacto
tac-tics n. táctica
tad-pole n. renacuajo
taf-fe-ta n. tafetán
taf-fy n. caramelo
tag n. etiqueta; marbete
tail n. cola; rabo
tai-lor n. sastre
taint v. inficionar(se); corromper(se)
take v. coger; tomar; sacar
take-off n. despegue
tal-cum pow-der n. polvo de talco
tale n. cuenta
tal-ent n. talento
tal-ent-ed adj. talentoso
tal-is-man n. talismán
talk v. decir; hablar
talk-a-tive adj. hablador
tall a. alto
tal-low n. sebo
tal-ly n. cuenta
tal-on n. garra
tam-bou-rine n. pandereta
tame a. domesticado; manso; soso
tam-per v. estropear; falsificar
tan v. curtir; tostar
tan-dem adv. en tandem
tang n. sabor fuerte
tan-gent n., adj. alto
tan-ge-rine n. naranja mandarina o tangerina
tan-gi-ble adj. tangente
tan-gle v. enredar(se)
tan-go n. tango
tank n. tangible
tan-ta-lize v. atormentar

tan-ta-mount a. equivalente
tan-trum n. rabieta; berrinche
tap n. grifo; golpecito
tape n. tanque
ta-per v. afilar
tap-es-try n. tapiz
tape-worm n. cinta
tap-i-o-ca n. tenia
ta-pir n. tapir
tar v. alquitranar; embrear
ta-ran-tu-la n. tapioca
tar-dy adj. tarantula
tar-get n. blanco
tar-iff n. tardío
tar-nish v. deslustrar(se); empanar
tar-ry v. tardar; detenerse
tart n. tarifa
tar-tar n. tártaro
task n. tarea; labor
task-mas-ter n. capataz
tas-sel n. borla
taste n. sabor
tast-y adj. sabroso
tat-ter n. andrajo
tat-tered a. harapiento; andrajoso
tat-too n. tatuaje
taunt v. mofa; sarcasmo; escarnio
taut a. tieso; tirante
tav-ern n. taberna
taw-dry a. charro
taw-ny a. leonado
tax n. impuesto; contribución; carga
tax-i n. taxi
tax-i-cab n. taxi
tea n. té
tea-bag n. sobre de té; muñeca de té
teach v. instruir
teach-er n. maestro; profesora; profesor
tea-cup n. taza para te
tea-ket-tle n. tetera
team n. equipo
team-mate n. compañero de equipo
team-ster n. camionero; camionista
team-work n. cooperación

tea-pot *n.* tetera
tear *n.* lágrima
tear *v.* rasgar(se); romper(se)
tease *v.* tomar el pelo; atormentar
tea-spoon *n.* cucharilla
tea-spoon-ful *n.* cucharadita
tech-ni-cal *adj.* técnico
tech-ni-cian *n.* técnico
tech-nol-o-gy *n.* tecnología
te-di-ous *adj.* tedioso
tel-e-gram *n.* telegrama
tel-e-graph *n.* telégrafo
te-leg-ra-phy *n.* telegrafía
tel-e-phone *n.* teléfono
tel-e-scope *n.* telescopio
tel-e-vi-sion *n.* televisión
tell *v.* mandar; decir
tem-per-a-ment-al *adj.* temperamental
tem-per-a-ture *n.* fiebre
tem-pes-tu-ous *adj.* tempestuoso
tem-ple *n.* templo
tem-po *n.* tiempo
tem-po-ral *adj.* temporal
temp-ta-tion *n.* tentación
ten *adj.*, *n.* diez
tend *v.* tender
ten-den-cy *n.* tendencia
ten-der-ly *adv.* tiernamente
ten-don *n.* tendón
ten-nis *n.* tenis
tense *v.* tensar, *adj.* tenso
ten-sion *n.* tensión
ter-mi-nal *adj.*, *n.* terminal
ter-mi-nate *v.* terminar
ter-mi-nol-o-gy *n.* terminología
ter-rain *n.* terreno
ter-res-tri-al *adj.* terrestre
ter-ri-ble *adj.* terrible
ter-rif-ic *adj.* terrífico
ter-ror *n.* terror
ter-ror-ism *n.* terrorismo
ter-ror-ist *n.* terrorista
test *v.* examinar, *n.* examen
tes-ti-fy *v.* testificar
text *n.* texto
tex-ture *n.* textura
than *conj.* de; que

thanks *n.* gracias
that *adj.* aquella; aquel; esa; ese
the *def. art.* la; le; las; los; lo
the-a-ter *n.* teatro
them *pron.* las; les; los; ellas; ellos
then *adv.* luego; entonces
the-ol-o-gy *n.* teología
the-o-rize *v.* teorizar
the-o-ry *n.* teoría
there *adv.* ahí; allí; allá
ther-mal *adj.* termal
ther-mom-e-ter *n.* termómetro
the-sau-rus *n.* tesauro
these *pron.* estas; estos
they *pron.* ellas; ellos
thick *adj.* denso
thief *n.* ladrón
thigh *n.* muslo
thin *adj.* escaso; delgado
thing *n.* cosa
think *v.* creer; pensar
third *adj.* tercero
thirst *n.* sed
thir-teen *n.*, *adj.* trece
thir-ty *n.*, *adj.* treinta
this *adj.* esta; este, *pron.* esto; esta; este
thorn *n.* espina
thorn-y *adj.* espinoso
thor-ough *adj.* completo
though *adv.* sin embargo, *conj.* aunque
thought-ful *adj.* pensativo
thou-sand *n.*, *adj.* mil
threat-en *v.* amenazar
three *n.*, *adj.* tres
throat *n.* garganta
throne *n.* trono
through *prep.* por
throw *v.* lanzar; echar
thumb *n.* pulgar
Thurs-day *n.* jueves
tib-i-a *n.* tibia
tick-le *v.* cosquillear
tide *n.* marea
ti-gar *n.* tigre
till *prep.* hasta
tim-ber *n.* madero
time *n.* hora; tiempo; vez
tim-Id *adj.* tímido

tim-id-i-ty *n.* timidez
tip *n.* propina
tire *v.* cansar(se)
tired *adj.* cansado
tire-some *a.* molesto
tis-sue *n.* tisu
ti-tan-ic *adj.* titanico
tithe *n.* diezmo
ti-tle *v.* titular, *n.* titulo
tit-ter *v.* reir a medias
tit-u-lar *a.* titular
TNT, T.N.T. *n.* explosivo
to *adv., prep.* hacía, *prep.* hasta; a
toad *n.* sapo
toad-stool *n.* hongo; hongo venenoso
toast *v.* tostar; brindar
to-bac-co *n.* tabaco
to-bog-gan *n.* tobogan
to-day *n., adv.* hoy
toe *n.* dedo del pie
tof-fee, tof-fy *n.* caramelo
to-ga *n.* toga
to-geth-er *adv.* juntos
toil *v.* trabajar asiduamente; afanarse
toi-let *n.* retrete; water; tacado
toi-let-ry *n.* articulo de tocador
to-ken *n.* indicio; prenda; señal
tol-er-a-ble *a.* tolerable; regular
tol-er-ance *n.* tolerancía
tol-er-ant *a.* tolerante
tol-er-ate *v.* permitir; tolerar
toll *n.* peaje
to-ma-to *n.* tomate
tomb *n.* tumba
tomb-stone *n.* lapida sepulcral
to-mor-row *adv., n.* mañana
ton *n.* tonelada
tone *n.* tono; tendencía
tongs *n.* tenazas
tongue *n.* lengua
ton-ic *n.* tonico
to-night *adv.* esta noche
ton-nage *n.* tonelaje
ton-sil *n.* amigdala; tonsila
ton-sil-li-tis *n.* amigdalitis

too *adv.* además; también
tool *n.* herramienta
tooth *n.* diente
tooth-ache *n.* dolor de muelas
tooth-brush *n.* cepillo de dientes
top *n.* tapa
to-paz *n.* topacio
top-coat *n.* sobretodo
top-hat *n.* chistera
top-ic *n.* tema
top-i-cal *adj.* topico
to-pog-ra-phy *n.* topografía
top-ple *v.* venirse abajo
top-sy-tur-vy *adv.* patas arriba
torch *n.* antorcha; hacha
tor-ment *v.* atormentar
tor-na-do *n.* tormento
tor-pe-do *n.* torpedo
tor-rent *n.* torrente
tor-rid *a.* torrido
tor-so *n.* torso
tor-toise *n.* tortuga
tor-tu-ous *a.* tortuoso
tor-ture *v.* torturar
toss *v.* echar
tot *n.* nene; nena
to-tal *n., adj.* total
to-tal-i-tar-i-an *a.* totalitario
to-tal-ly *adv.* totalmente
tote *v. inf.* llevar
to-tem *n.* tótem
tot-ter *v.* bambolearse
touch *v.* tocar(se)
touch-y *a.* irritable
tough *adj.* difícil
tough-en *v.* endurecer(se); hacer(se)
tour *n.* viaje; excursión
tour-ism *n.* turismo
tour-ist *n.* turista
tour-na-ment *n.* torneo
tour-ni-quet *n.* torniquete
tou-sle *v.* despeinar
tow *v.* llevar a remolque
to-ward *prep.* cerca de
tow-el *n.* toalla
tow-er *n.* torre
town *n.* pueblo; ciudad
tox-ic *a.* tóxico
tox-in *n.* toxina

toy n. juguete

trace n. indicio; huella; rastro

tra-che-a n. tráquea

track n. via; pista; senda

tract n. extensión; tratado

trac-tor n. tractor

trade v. comerciar

trade-mark n. marca de fabrica; marca registrado

trade un-ion n. sindicato

tra-di-tion n. tradición

tra-di-tion-al adj. tradicional

tra-duce v. calumniar

traf-fic n. tráfico

trag-e-dy n. tragedia

trag-ic adj. trágico

trail v. arrastrar(se); rastrear

trail-er n. remolque

train n. tren

trait n. caracteristica; rasgo

trai-tor n. traidor

tra-jec-to-ry n. trayectoria

tramp v. andar con pasos pesados

tram-ple v. pisotear

trance n. arrobamiento; estado hipnotico

tran-quil adj. tranquilo

tran-quil-li-ty n. tranquilidad

tran-quil-lize v. tranquilizar

tran-quil-iz-er n. tranquilizante

trans-act v. despachar

trans-ac-tion n. transacción

tran-scend v. sobresalir

tran-scribe v. transcribir

tran-script n. trasunto

tran-scrip-tion n. transcripción

trans-fer v. transferir; trasladar

trans-fer-ence n. transferencia

trans-form v. transformar

trans-for-ma-tion n. transcripción; copia

trans-form-er n. transformador

trans-fu-sion n. transfusión

trans-gress v. traspasar; pecar

trans-gres-sion n. transgresion

tran-sient a. transitorio; pasajero

tran-sis-tor n. transistor

trans-it n. transito

tran-si-tion n. transito

tran-si-tive a. transitivo

tran-si-to-ry adj. transitorio

trans-late v. traducir

trans-la-tion n. traducción

trans-lu-cent a. translucido

trans-mis-sion n. transmisión

trans-mit v. transmitir

trans-mit-ter n. transmisor

tran-som n. travesaño

trans-par-ent a. transparente; claro; obvio

tran-spire v. transpirar; suceder

trans-plant v. trasplantar

trans-port n. transporte, v. transportar

trans-por-ta-tion n. transporte

trans-pose v. transponer

trans-verse a. transversal

trap v. entrampar

tra-peze n. trapecio

trap-e-zoid n. trap-e-zoid

trash n. basura

trau-ma n. trauma

trau-mat-ic adj. traumatico

trav-el v. viajar

trea-son n. traición

treas-ure n. tesoro

treas-ur-er n. tesorero

treas-ur-y n. tesoro

treat v. tratar

trea-tise n. n tratado

treat-ment n. tratamiento

trea-ty n. tratado; pacto

tre-ble a. triple

tree n. arbol

trek v. caminar

trel-lis n. enrejado; espaldera

trem-ble v. temblar

tre-men-dous a. tremendo

trem-or n. temblor

trench n. foso; trinchera

tri-al n. prueba

tri-an-gle n. triángulo

ri-an-gu-lar *adj.* triangular

ri-bu-nal *n.* tribunal

rib-ute *n.* tributo

rick *n.* trucio; trampa; engano

rick-le *v.* gotear

ri-cy-cle *n.* triciclo

ried *adj.* probado

ri-fle *n.* bagatela

ri-fling *a.* sin importancia

rig-ger *n.* gatillo

rig-o-nom-e-try *n.* trigonometria

ril-lion *n.* billon

rim *v.* guarnecer

rin-ket *n.* dije

ri-o *n.* trio

rip *n.* viaje

ri-ple *v.* triplicar(se)

rip-let *n.* trillizo

rip-li-cate *v.* triplicar

ri-pod *n.* tripode

rite *a.* gastado

ri-umph *n.* triunfo

ri-um-phant *a.* triunfante

riv-i-al *a.* trivial; frivolo

riv-i-al-i-ty *n.* trivialidad

rol-ley *n.* tranvia

rom-bone *n.* trombon

roop *n.* tropa; escuadron

roop-er *n.* soldado de caballeria

ro-phy *n.* trofeo

rop-ic *n.* tropico

rop-i-cal *adj.* tropical

rot *v.* ir al trote; hacer trotar

ou-ba-dour *n.* trovador

rou-ble *v.* molestar(se)

rou-ble-some *a.* molesto

rough *n.* abrevadero

roupe *n.* compania

rou-sers *n.* pantalones

rous-seau *n.* ajuar

rout *n.* trucha

row-el *n.* paleta; desplantador

ru-ant *n.* novillero

ruce *n.* tregua

ruck *n.* camion

rue *adj.* verdadero

ru-ly *adv.* verdaderamente; realmente

rump *n.* triunfo

trum-pet *n.* trompeta

trun-cate *v.* truncar

trunk *n.* tronco; baul

trus *v.* empaquetear

trust *v.* esperar, *n.* fideicomiso

trus-tee *n.* fideicomisario

trust-wor-thy *a.* fidedigno; confiable

trust-y *adj.* seguro

truth *n.* verdad

trugh-ful *a.* veraz

try *v.* probar

try-ing *a.* dificil; penoso

tryst *n.* cita

T-shirt *n.* camiseta

tub *n.* bano; tina

tu-ba *n.* tuba

tube *n.* tubo

tu-ber-cu-lo-sis *n.* tuberculosis

tuck *v.* alforzar

Tues-day *n.* martes

tuft *n.* copete

tug *v.* tirar con fuerza; remolcar

tug-boat *n.* remolcador

tu-i-tion *n.* ensenanza

tu-lip *n.* tulipan

tum-ble *v.* caer(se)

tum-bler *n.* volteador; vaso

tu-mor *n.* tumor

tu-mult *n.* tumulto

tu-mul-tu-ous *a.* tumultuoso

tu-na *n.* atun

tun-dra *n.* tundra

tune *n.* aire; afinacion

tu-nic *n.* tunica

tun-nel *n.* tunel

tur-ban *n.* turbante

tur-bid *adj.* turbido

tur-bine *n.* turbina

tur-bu-lence *n.* turbulencia; confusion

tur-bu-lent *adj.* turbulento

tu-reen *n.* sopera

turf *n.* cesped

tur-key *n.* pavo

tur-moil *n.* tumulto

turn *v.* volver(se); girar

turn-coat *n.* traidor

tur-nip *n.* nabo

turn-out *n.* ocncurrencia;

producción

turn-pike n. autopista de peaje

turn-stile n. torniquete

tur-pen-tin n. trementina

tur-quoise n. turquesa

tur-ret n. turrecilla

tur-tle n. tortuga

tusk n. colmillo

tus-sle n. agarrada

tu-te-lage n. tutela

tu-tor n. tutor

tux-e-do n. smoking

TV n. televisión

twang n. tañido; timbre nasal

tweed n. mezcla de lana

tweez-ers n. bruselas

twelfth adj. duodecimo

twelve adj., n. doce

twen-ty adj., n. veinte

twice adv. dos veces

twig n. ramita

twi-light n. crepusculo

twill n. tela cruzada

twin adj., n. gemelo

twine n. guita; bramante

twinge n. dolor agudo

twin-kle v. centellear

twirl v. girar; piruetear

twist v. torcer(se)

twitch v. crisparse

twit-ter v. gorjear

two adj., n. dos

two-faced a. falso; hipoocrita

ty-coon n. magnate

type n. tipo

type-write v. escribir a maquina

type-writ-er n. maquina de escribir

ty-phoid n. fiebre tifoidea

ty-phoon n. tifón

ty-phus n. tifus

typ-i-cal adj. típico

typ-i-fy v. simbolizar

typ-ist n. mecanografo

ty-pog-ra-phy n. tipografía

ty-ran-ni-cal a. tiránico; despotico

tyr-an-nize v. tiranizar

tyr-an-ny n. tiranía

u-biq-ui-tous adj. ubicuo

u-biq-ui-ty n. ubicuidad

ud-der n. ubre

ug-li-ness n. fealdad

ug-ly adj. feo

u-ku-le-le n. ukelele

ul-cer n. úlcera

ul-cer-ate v. ulcerar(se)

ul-cer-ous adj. ulceroso

ul-na n. cúbito

ul-te-ri-or adj. ulterior

ul-ti-mate adj. último

ul-ti-ma-tum n. ultimatum

ul-tra adj. excesivo

ul-tra-mod-ern adj. ultramoderno

ul-tra-son-ic adj. ultrasonico

ul-tra-sound n. ultrasonido

ul-tra-vi-o-let adj. ultravioleta

ul-u-late v. ulular

um-bil-i-cal adj. umbilical

um-bil-i-cus n. ombligo

um-brel-la n. paraguas

um-pire n. arbitro

ump-teen a. muchos

un-a-bashed a. desvergonzado; descarado

un-a-ble adj. incapaz

un-a-bridged adj. no abreviado

un-ac-cent-ed adj. sin acento

un-ac-cept-a-ble adj. inaceptable

un-ac-count-a-ble adj. inexplicable

un-ac-cus-tomed adj. no acostumbrado

un-ac-knowl-edged adj. no econocido

un-a-dorned adj. sin adorno

un-a-dul-ter-at-ed adj. no adulterado

un-af-fect-ed adj. sin afectación

un-a-fraid adj. sin temor

un-aid-ed adj. sin ayuda

un-am-big-u-ous adj. sin ambiguedad

u-nan-i-mous adj. unanime

un-an-swer-a-ble adj. incontestable

un-ap-proach-a-ble adj. in-

accesible
-armed adj. desarmado
-as-sail-a-ble adj. inexpugnable
-as-sist-ed adj. sin ayuda; sencillo
-as-sum-ing a. modesto; sencillo
-at-tached adj. suelto
-at-tend-ed adj. desatendido
n-at-trac-tive adj. inatractivo
n-au-thor-ized adj. sin autorización
n-a-void-a-ble adj. inevitable
n-a-ware adj. ignorante
-a-wares adv. de improviso
n-bal-anced adj. desequilibrado
-beat-a-ble adj. invencible
-beat-en adj. invicto
-be-com-ing a. que sienta mal
-be-lief n. incredulidad
-be-liev-a-ble adj. increíble
-be-liev-er n. descreído
-be-liev-ing adj. incrédulo
n-bend v. desencorvar; aflojar
-bend-ing adj. inflexible
-bi-ased a. imparcial
n-bind v. desatar
n-blem-ished adj. puro
-born a. no nacido
n-bos-om v. revelar
-bound-ed adj. ilimitado
-bowed adj. recto
n-break-a-ble adj. irrompible
-breath-a-ble adj. irrespirable
n-bri-dled adj. desenfrenado
n-bro-ken adj. inviolado; sin romper
-buck-le v. deshebillar
-bur-den v. descargar
n-but-ton v. desabotonar(se)
-caged adj. suelto

un-called-for a. inmerecido
un-can-ny a. extraño; misterioso
un-cap v. destapar
un-ceas-ing adj. incesante
un-cer-e-mo-ni-ous a. informal
un-cer-tain adj. indeciso
un-cer-tain-ty n. incertidumbre
un-change-a-ble adj. inalterable
un-changed adj. inalterado
un-chang-ing adj. invariable
un-chart-ed adj. desconocido
un-civ-il adj. incivil
un-civ-i-lized adj. incivilizado
un-clad adj. desnudo
un-clasp v. separar
un-cle n. tío
un-clean adj. sucio
un-clear adj. confuso
un-clog v. desatascar
un-com-fort-a-ble adj. incómodo
un-com-mon adj. raro
un-com-mu-ni-ca-tive a. poco comunicativo
un-com-pro-mis-ing a. inflexible
un-con-cern n. indiferencia
un-con-nect-ed adj. inconexo
un-con-scious adj. inconsciente
un-con-sid-ered adj. inconsiderado
un-con-trolled adj. desenfrenado
un-cooked adj. crudo
un-count-ed adj. innumerable
un-cross v. descruzar
un-de-cid-ed adj. indeciso
un-der-es-ti-mate v. subestimar
un-der-ground adj. subterráneo
un-der-line v. subrayar
un-der-neath adv. debajo, prep. bajo
un-der-wear n. ropa interior

un-do v. desatar
un-fin-ished adj. incompleto
unn-fold v. extender; abrir
u-ni-form n. uniforme
un-ion n. unión
u-ni-ted adj. unido
u-ni-ver-sal adj. universal
un-luck-y adj. desdichado
un-rest n. inquietud
un-sa-vor-y adj. desagradable
un-seem-ly adj. indecoroso
un-skilled adj. inexperto
un-so-phis-ti-cat-ed adj. candido
un-sta-ble adj. inestable
un-stead-y adj. inseguro
un-til prep. hasta
un-truth-ful adj. mentiroso
un-u-su-al adj. raro
un-wrap v. desenvolver
up prep. subiendo, adj. ascendente, adv. acabado; arriba
up-hill adj. ascendente
up-hol-ster-y n. tapiceria
up-on prep. sobre; encima de
up-per adj. alto
up-per-cut n. gancho
up-roar n. alboroto
up-set n. trastorno; v. volcar
up-stairs adj. arriba
u-ra-ni-um n. uranio
U-ra-nus n. Urano
ur-ban adj. urbano
urge n. impulso, v. incitar
ur-gent adj. urgente
u-rine n. orina
urn n. urna
us pron. nosotras; nosotros; nos
use n. uso, v. utilizar; usar
use-less adj. inútil
u-su-al adj. usual
u-ten-sil n. utensilio
utilitarian n. utilitario
u-til-i-ty n. utilidad
u-til-ize v.t. utilizar
ut-ter-ance n. expresion
u-ter-us n. útero
uxorious a. uxorio; gurromino

va-can-cy n. vacante
va-cant adj. vacío
va-ca-tion n. vacación
vac-ci-nate v. vacunar
vac-ci-na-tion n. vacunación
vac-cine n. vacuna
vac-il-late v. vacilar
vac-il-la-tion n. vacilacon; fluctuación
va-cu-i-ty n. vacuidad
vac-u-um n. vacio
va-gar-y n. capricho
va-grant n. vagabundo
vague adj. incierto; vago
vain adj. vano
vale n. valle
val-e-dic-to-ry n. discurso de despedida
val-en-tine n. novia o novio en el dia de San Valentine
val-id adj. valido
val-i-date v. validar
va-lid-i-ty n. validez
va-lise n. maleta
val-ley n. valle
val-or n. valor; valentia
val-u-a-ble a. valioso; costoso; precioso
val-u-a-tion n. valuación
val-ue v. valuar, n. valor
valve n. valvula
vam-pire n. vampiro
van n. vanguardia; camion de mudanzas
van-dal n. vandalo
van-dal-ism n. vandalismo
vane n. veleta
van-guard n. vanguardia
va-nil-la n. vainilla
van-ish v. desaparecer
van-i-ty n. vanidad
van-quish v. vencer; conquistar
van-tage n. ventaja; provecho
vap-id a. insipido
va-por n. vapor
va-por-ize v. vaporizar(se)
va-por-ous adj. vaporoso
var-i-a-bil-i-ty n. variabilidad
var-i-a-ble n., adj. variable
var-i-a-tion n. variación
var-i-cose a. varicoso

var-ied *adj.* variado
va-ri-e-ty *n.* variedad
var-i-ous *adj.* variado
var-nish *n.* barniz
var-si-ty *n.* equip principal de una universidad
var-y *v.* variar; desviarse; cambiar
vase *n.* jarrón
vast *adj.* vasto
veal *n.* ternera
veg-e-ta-ble *n.* legumbre
veg-e-tar-i-an *n.* vegetariano
veg-e-tate *v.* vegetar
veg-e-ta-tion *n.* vegetacion
ve-hi-cle *n.* vehículo
vein *n.* vena
ve-loc-i-ty *n.* velocidad
ve-nal-i-ty *n.* venalidad
vend *v.* vender
ven-er-a-ble *adj.* venerable
ven-er-a-tion *n.* veneración
ve-ni-al *adj.* venial
ven-om *n.* veneno
ven-om-ous *adj.* venenoso
ven-ti-late *v.* ventilar
ven-tral *adj.* ventral
ven-tri-cle *n.* ventrículo
ven-ture-some *adj.* aventurero
Ve-nus *n.* Venus
ve-ra-cious *adj.* veraz
verb *n.* verbo
ver-bal *adj.* verbal
ver-bose *adj.* verboso
ver-bos-i-ty *n.* verbosidad
ver-dict *n.* veredicto
ver-i-fy *v.* verificar
ver-mouth *n.* vermut
ver-nal *adj.* vernal
ver-sa-til-i-ty *n.* adaptabilidad
verse *n.* versículo
ver-sion *n.* versión
ver-te-bra *n.* vertebra
ver-te-brate *adj.* vertebrado
ver-ti-cal *adj.* vertical
ver-y *adj.* mismo, *adv.* muy
ves-sel *n.* vaso
vest *n.* chaleco
vet-er-an *adj., n.* veterano
vet-er-i-nar-i-an *n.*

veterinario
vet-er-i-nar-y *adj., n.* veterinario
vi-brant *adj.* vibrante
vi-brate *v.* oscilar
vi-bra-tion *n.* vibración
vic-ar *n.* vicario
vi-car-i-ous *a.* substituto
vice *n.* vicio
vice-pres-i-dent *n.* vicepresidente
vice-roy *n.* virrey
vice ver-sa *adv.* viceversa
vi-cin-i-ty *n.* vecindad
vi-cious *a.* depravado; vicioso; cruel
vic-tim *n.* victima
vic-tim-ize *v.* hacer victima
vic-to-ri-ous *adj.* victorioso
vic-to-ry *n.* victoria
view *n.* ver, *n.* escena
vig-i-lance *n.* vigilancia
vig-or *n.* vigor
vig-or-ous *adj.* vigoroso
vil-lage *n.* aldea
vin-di-cate *v.* vindicar
vine *n.* vid
vin-e-gar *n.* vinagre
vi-o-la *n.* viola
vi-o-la-tion *n.* violación
vi-o-lent *adj.* violento
vi-o-let *adj.* violado
vi-o-lin *n.* violín
vir-ile *adj.* viril
vi-ril-i-ty *n.* virilidad
vir-tu-al *adj.* virtual
vir-tu-al-ly *adv.* virtualmente
vir-u-lent *adj.* virulento
vi-rus *n.* virus
vis-cos-i-ty *n.* viscosidad
vis-count *n.* vizconde
vis-count-ess *n.* vizcondesa
vise *n.* tornillo
vis-i-bil-i-ty *n.* visibilidad
vis-i-ble *a.* visible; conspicuo
vi-sion *n.* visión
vi-sion-ar-y *n.* visionario
vis-it *n.* visita, *v.* visitar
vis-it-a-tion *n.* visitación
vi-sor *n.* visera
vis-u-al *adj.* visual
vis-u-al-ize *v.* representarse en la mente

vi-tal *adj.* vital
vi-tal-i-ty *n.* vitalidad
vi-ta-min *n.* vitamina
vit-re-ous *a.* vitreo
vit-ri-ol *n.* vitriolo
vi-tu-per-ate *v.* vituperar
vi-va-cious *a.* vivaz; animado; vivaracho
vi-vac-i-ty *n.* vivacidad; animacion
viv-id *adj.* intenso; vivo
vix-en *n.* arpia; zorra
vo-cab-u-lar-y *n.* vocabulario
vo-cal *adj.* vocal
vo-cal-ist *n.* cantante
vo-ca-tion *n.* vocacion
vod-ka *n.* vodka
vogue *n.* moda; boga
voice *n.* voz
void *a.* nulo; vacio
vol-can-ic *adj.* volcanico
vol-ca-no *n.* volcan
vo-li-tion *n.* voluntad; volicion
vol-ley *n.* descarga; voleo
volt *n.* voltio
volt-age *n.* voltaje
vol-u-ble *a.* hablador
vol-ume *n.* cantidad; volumen
vol-un-tar-y *adj.* voluntario
vol-un-teer *n.* voluntario
vo-lup-tu-ar-y *n.* voluptuoso
vo-lup-tu-ous *a.* voluptuoso
vom-it *n.* vomito, *v.* vomitar
vom-it-ing *n.* vomito
voo-doo *n.* vodu
vo-ra-cious *a.* voraz
voracity *n.* voracidad
vor-tex *n.* vortice
votary *n.* devoto; partidario
vote *v.* votar, *n.* voto
vo-ter *n.* votante
vot-ing *n.* votacion
vo-tive *a.* votivo; exvoto
vouch *v.i.* afirmar
vouch-er *n.* comprobante
vow-el *n.* vocal
voy-age *v.* viajar, *n.* viaje
vul-gar *adj.* vulgar
vul-gar-ize *v.* vulgarizar
vul-ner-a-ble *a.* vulnerable
vul-ture *n.* buitre

wack-y *a.* loco; chiflado
wad *n.* fajo; taco; rollo; bolita
wad-dle *v.* anadear
wade *v.* vadear; pasar con dificultad
wag *v.* menear(se)
wage *n.* salario
wag-er *v.* apostar
wag-on *n.* carro
waif *n.* nino abandonado
wail *v.* lamentarse; sollozar
wain-scot *n.* friso de madera
waist *n.* cintura
waist-coat *n.* chaleco
waist-line *n.* talle
wait *n.* espera, *v.* esperar
wait-er *n.* camarero
wait-ress *n.* camarera
waive *v.* renunciar a; abandonar
waiv-er *n.* renuncia
wake *v.* despertar(se)
wake-ful *a.* vigilante
wak-en *v.* despertar(se)
walk *n.* caminata, *v.* caminar; andar
walk-out *n.* huelga
walk-o-ver *n.* triunfo facil
wall *n.* pared
wall-board *n.* carton de yeso
wal-let *n.* cartera
wal-lop *v.* zurrar
wal-low *v.* revp/carse
wall-pa-per *n.* papel pintado
wal-nut *n.* nogal
wal-rus *n.* morsa
waltz *n.* vals
wan *a.* palido
wan-der *v.* desviarse
wan-der-lust *n.* deseo de viajar
wane *v.* disminuir; menguar
want *v.* querer; requerir; desear
want-ing *a.* deficiente
wan-ton *a.* lascivo; desenfrenado
war *v.* guerrear, *n.* guerra
war-ble *v.* trinar
war-cry *n.* grito de guerra
ward *v.* desviar
war-den *n.* guardian; alsaide
ward-robe *n.* guardarropa;

vestuario
ware *n.* mercancias
ware-house *n.* almacén
war-fare *n.* guerra
war-lock *n.* hechicero
warm *v.* calentar(se), *adj.* caluroso; caliente
warm-heart-ed *a.* afectuoso
war-mong-er *n.* belicista
warmth *n.* calor
warn *v.* advertir
warn-ing *n.* advertencia; aviso
warp *v.* albearse; pervertir
war-rant *n.* autorizacion; garantia
war-ran-ty *n.* garantia
war-ren *n.* conejera
war-ri-or *n.* guerrero
wart *n.* verruga
war-y *a.* cauteloso
was *pret* of be
wash *v.* lavar(se)
wash-cloth *n.* paño para lavarse
wash-er *n.* lavadora
wash-ing *n.* lavado
wash-room *n.* lavabo
wash-stand *n.* lavamanos
wash-tub *n.* tin o cuba de lavar
wasp *n.* avispa
wast-age *n.* desgaste; merma
waste *n.* perdida, *v.* desperdiciar
wast-rel *n.* derrochador
watch *n.* reloj, *v.* mirar; observar
watch-ful *a.* vigilante; desvelado
watch-man *n.* vigilante
watch-word *n.* .santo y sena
wa-ter *n.* agua
wa-ter-col-or *n.* acuarela
wa-ter-course *n.* corriente
wa-ter-fall *n.* cascada
wa-ter-fowl *n.* ave acuantica
wa-ter-front *n.* terreno rebereno
wa-ter lil-y *n.* nenufar
wa-ter-logged *a.* anegado
wa-ter-mark *n.* nivel de

agua; filigrana
wa-ter-mel-on *n.* sandia
wa-ter-proof *a.* impermeable
wa-ter-side *n.* orilla del agua
wa-ter sof-ten-er *n.* ablandador quimico de agua
wa-ter-spout *n.* tromba marina; mangua
wa-ter-tight *a.* estanco; seguro
wa-ter-way *n.* canal
wa-ter-y *adj.* insipido
watt *n.* vatio
wave *v.* ondular, *n.* onda
wa-ver *v.* oscilar; vacilar
wav-y *a.* ondulado
wax *n.* cera
wax-en *a.* de cara; palido
wax-work *n.* figura de cera
way *n.* camino; modo; direccion
way-far-er *n.* viajero
way-lay *v.* asaltar
way-side *n.* borde del camino
way-ward *a.* voluntarioso; travieso
we *pron.* nosotras; nosotros
weak *adj.* debil
weak-en *v.* debilitar(se)
weak-ling *n.* alfenique
weak-ly *a.* achacoso
weak-mind-ed *a.* sin voluntad
weak-ness *n.* debilidad
wealth *n.* riqueza
wealth-y *adj.* rico
wean *v.* destetar
weap-on *n.* arma
weap-on-ry *n.* armas
wear *v.* desgastar(se); llevar
wear-ing *adj.* penoso
wea-ri-some *a.* fastidioso
wea-ry *a.* fatigado; aburrido
wea-sel *n.* comadreja
weath-er *n.* tiempo
weath-er-beat-en *a.* curtido pro la intemperie
weath-er-glass *n.* barometro
weath-er-man *n.* pronosticador de tiempo
weave *v.* tejido
web *n.* tela

web-bing n. cincha
wed v. casar(se)
wed-ding n. boda
wedge n. cuña
wed-lock n. matrimonio
Wednes-day n. miércoles
wee a. paqueñito
weed v. escardar
week n. semana
week-day n. día laborable o de trabajo
week-end n. fin de la semana
week-ly a. semanal
weep v. llorar
wee-vil n. gorgojo
weigh v. pesar
weight n. pesa
weight-y adj. pesado
weird adj. extraño
wel-come adj. agradable
weld v. soldar
wel-fare n. bienestar
well adv. pues, n. fuente
well-be-ing n. bienestar
well-bred a. bien criado
well-dis-posed a. bien dispuesto
well-known adj. famoso
well-off a. adinerado
well-read a. leído
well-thought-of a. bien mirado
well-timed a. oportuno
well-to-do a. acaudalado
welt n. verdugón
wel-ter v. revolcar(se)
wench n. moza
were pret. of be
were-wolf n. hombre que puede transformarse en lobo
west n. oeste
west-ern adj. occidental
wet v. mojar(se)
whack v. golpear
whale n. ballena
whale-bone n. ballena
wharf n. muelle
what pron. qué; lo que; cual
what-ev-er pron. todo lo que
what-not n. estante; juguetero

wheat n. trigo
whee-dle v. engatusar; halagar
wheel n. rueda
wheel-bar-row n. carretilla
wheel-chair n. silla de ruedas
wheeze v. respirar asmáticamente
when conj. cuando
whence adv. de donde; de que
when-ev-er adv. siempre que
where conj., adv. donde, adv. adonde
where-a-bouts n. paradero
where-as conj. visto que
where-up-on adv. con lo cual
wher-ev-er adv. dondequiera
wheth-er conj. si
whey n. suero de la leche
which pron. lo que; cual; la; le
which-ev-er pron. cualquiera
whiff n. olorcillo
while conj. mientras
whim v. lloriquear
whim-per v. lloriquear
whim-si-cal a. caprichoso
whine v. gimotear
whin-ny n. relincho
whip v. batir
whir v. zumbar; batir
whirl v. girar rápidamente
whirl-pool n. remolino
whirl-wind n. torbellino
whisk-ers n. barbas; bigotes
whis-key n. whisky
whis-per n. cuchicheo, v. cuchichear
whis-tle v. silbar
white n., adj. blanco
white-col-lar a. oficinesco
whit-en v. blanquear
white-wash n. jalbeque
whith-er conj. adonde
whit-tle v. cortar poco a poco
whiz v. silbar; rehilar
who pron. la; el; lo; quién;

que
who-ev-er *pron.* quienquiere
  que
whole *n., adj.* todo
whole-heart-ed *a.* sincero;
  incondicional
whole-sale *n.* venta al por
  menor
whole-some *a.* saludable
whol-ly *adv.* completamente
whom *pron.* a quién
whom-ev-er *pron.* a quien-
  quiera
whoop *n.* alarido
whore *n.* puta; prostituta
whose *pron.* cuyo
why *adv.* ¿por qué?
wick *n.* mecha
wick-ed *adj.* malicioso
wick-er *a.* de mimbre
wide *adj.* ancho
wide-a-wake *a.* despabilado
wid-en *v.* ensanchar(se)
wide-spread *a.* extendido;
  difuso
wid-ow *n.* viuda
wid-ow-er *n.* viudo
width *n.* anchura
wield *v.* ejercer; mandar;
  manejar
wife *n.* esposa
wig *n.* peluca
wig-gle *v.* menear(se);
  cimbrearse
wild *adj.* descabellado
wild boar *n.* jabalí
wil-der-ness *n.* yermo;
  desierto
wile *n.* ardid
will *v.* querer
will-ful *a.* voluntarioso; terco;
  premeditado
will-ing *a.* dispuesto; complaciente
wil-low *n.* sauce
wil-low-y *a.* esbelto
wil-ly-nil-ly *adv.* de grado o
  por fuerza
wilt *v.* marchitar(se)
win *n.* victoria, *v.* lograr;
  ganar
wince *v.* estremecerse;
  respingar

winch *n.* torno
wind *n.* viento
wind *v.* arrollar(se)
wind-fall *n.* ganacia in-
  esperada
wind-mill *n.* molino de viento
win-dow *n.* ventana
win-dow-pane *n.* cristal
wind-shield *n.* parabrisas
wind-y *adj.* ventoso
wine *n.* vino
win-er-y *n.* lagar; candiotera
wing *n.* ala
wink *v.* guinar; pestanear
win-ner *n.* ganador
win-ning *n.* ganancias
win-now *v.* aventar
win-some *a.* atractivo; alegre
win-ter *n.* invierno
win-try *adj.* invernal
wipe *v.* enjugar; secar; borrar
wire *n.* alambre
wire-tap *v.* intervenir
wir-ing *n.* instalación de
  alambres
wir-y *a.* nervudo
wis-dom *n.* sabiduria
wise *adj.* acertado; sabio
wise-crack *n.* cuchufleta;
  pulla
wish *n.* deseo, *v.* desear
wish-ful *adj.* deseoso
wit *n.* sal
witch *n.* bruja
witch-craft *n.* brujeria
with *prep.* con
with-draw-al *n.* retirada
with-drawn *a.* ensimismado
with-er *v.* marchitar(se);
  secarse
with-hold *v.* retener
with-in *adv.* dentro
with-out *adv.* por fuera
with-stand *v.* resistir
wit-less *a.* tonto
wit-ness *n.* testigo
wi-ti-cism *n.* dicho gracioso
wit-ty *a.* salado; ingenioso
wiz-ard *n.* hechicero
wob-ble *v.* bambolear; bailar
woe *n.* aflicción; infortunio
wolf *n.* lobo
wom-an *n.* mujer

wom-an-kind *n.* sexo femenino

womb *n.* matriz

wom-en's rights *n.* derechos de la mujer

won-der *v.* asombrarse

won-der-ful *adj.* maravilloso

woo *v.* cortejar

wood *n.* madera

wood-en *a.* de madera; sin expresión

wood-land *n.* monte

wood-peck-er *n.* picamaderos

wood-y *adj.* lenoso

wool *n.* lana

wool-ly *adj.* lanudo

word *n.* palabra

work *v.* trabajar, *n.* obra; trabajo

work-book *n.* cuaderno

work-er *n.* trabajador

work-shop *n.* taller

world *n.* mundo

world-ly *adj.* mundano

world-wide *a.* mundial

worm *n.* gusano

worm-eaten *a.* carcomido

wormwood *n.* ajenjo

worn *adj.* usado

worrier *n.* aprensivo; pesimista

wor-ry *v.* inquietar(se)

wors-en *v.* empeorar

wor-ship *v.* venerar

worth *n.* valor

worth-less *adj.* despreciable

wound *v.* herir

wrap *v.* envolver

wreck *v.* naufragar, *n.* ruina

wrin-kle *v.* arrugar(se), *n.* arruga

wrist *n.* muñeca

write *v.* escribir

writ-er *n.* escritora; escritor

writ-ing *n.* escrito

wrong *adj.* equivocado

wrong-ful *a.* injusto; falso

wrong-head-ed *a.* terco

wrought *a.* forjado; trabajado

wry *a.* torcido; ironico; mueca

x-ray *v.* radiografiar, *n.* radiografia

yank *v.* sacar de un tirón

Yan-kee *n.* yanqui

yard *n.* yarda

yard-goods *n.* tejidos

yard-stick *n.* vara de medir

yarn *n.* hilaza

yar-row *n.* milenrama

yawn *n.* bostezo, *v.* bostezar

ye *pron.* vosotros

yea *adv.* si

year *n.* año

year-ling *n.* primal

year-ly *adv.* anualmente

yearn *v.* suspirar; anhelar

yearn-ing *n.* anhelo

yeast *n.* levadura

yell *n.* grito, *v.* gritar

yel-low *n.*, *adj.* amarillo

yes *adv.* si

yes-ter-day *n.* ayer

yet *adv.* todavía

yew *n.* tejo

yield *v.* rendir(se)

yolk *n.* yema

yon-der *adv.* alli; allá

yore *n.* antaño

you *pron.* vosotras; vosotros; tu

young *adj.* joven

young-ster *n.* jovencito

your *adj.* sus; tus; vuestras; vuestros

yours *pron.* tu; vos; vosotros; vosotras

your-self *pron.* usted mismo; tu mismo

youth *n.* jovenes

youth-ful *adj.* juvenil

zeal *n.* ardor

zeal-ous *adj.* celoso

ze-bra *n.* cebra

ze-nith *n.* cenit

ze-ro *n.* cero

ze-ro hour *n.* hora de ataque

zest *n.* gusto

zone *n.* zona

zoo *n.* jardín zoologico

zo-o-log-i-cal *adj.* zoologico

zuc-chi-ni *n.* cidracayote de verano